SEEING THINGS AS THEY ARE

Also by George Orwell

FICTION
Burmese Days
A Clergyman's Daughter
Keep the Aspidistra Flying
Coming Up for Air
Animal Farm
Nineteen Eighty-Four

NON-FICTION
Down and Out in Paris and London
The Road to Wigan Pier
Homage to Catalonia
A Kind of Compulsion (1903–36)
Facing Unpleasant Facts (1937–39)
A Patriot After All (1940–41)
All Propaganda Is Lies (1941–42)
Keeping Our Little Corner Clean (1942–43)
Two Wasted Years (1943)
I Have Tried to Tell the Truth (1943–44)
I Belong to the Left (1945)
Smothered Under Journalism (1946)
It Is What I Think (1947–48)
Our Job Is to Make Life Worth Living (1949–50)
Critical Essays
Narrative Essays
Diaries
A Life in Letters

GEORGE ORWELL

Seeing Things As They Are

Selected Journalism
and Other Writings

SELECTED AND ANNOTATED

by

Peter Davison

Harvill *Secker*
LONDON

Published by Harvill Secker 2014

2 4 6 8 10 9 7 5 3 1

Copyright © the Estate of the late Sonia Brownell Orwell
Compilation copyright © the Estate of the late Sonia Brownell Orwell 2014
Introduction and notes copyright © Peter Davison 2014

This book is sold subject to the condition that it shall not, by way of trade or otherwise,
be lent, resold, hired out, or otherwise circulated without the publisher's prior consent in
any form of binding or cover other than that in which it is published and without a similar
condition including this condition being imposed on the subsequent purchaser

First published in Great Britain in 2014 by
HARVILL SECKER
Random House
20 Vauxhall Bridge Road
London SW1V 2SA

www.vintage-books.co.uk

Addresses for companies within The Random House Group Limited can be found at:
www.randomhouse.co.uk/offices.htm

The Random House Group Limited Reg. No. 954009

Collected from *The Complete Works of George Orwell*, edited by Peter Davison, OBE,
published in Great Britain in 1998 by Secker & Warburg

The title is a quotation from 'Why I Write', *CW*, XVIII, 318: 'Desire to see things as they are,
to find out true facts and store them up for the use of posterity.'

George Orwell's NUJ membership card is reproduced by kind permission of
UCL Library Services, Special Collections

A CIP catalogue record for this book is available from the British Library

ISBN 9781846558993

The Random House Group Limited supports The Forest Stewardship Council (FSC®),
the leading international forest certification organisation. Our books carrying the
FSC label are printed on FSC® certified paper. FSC is the only forest certification scheme
supported by the leading environmental organisations, including Greenpeace.
Our paper procurement policy can be found at www.randomhouse.co.uk/environment

Typeset in Dante by Palimpsest Book Production Ltd, Falkirk, Stirlingshire

Printed and bound in the UK by Clays Ltd, St Ives PLC

CONTENTS

INTRODUCTION

If one discounts what Orwell wrote in his schooldays and the very few scraps that survive from his time in Burma, he was a published author for twenty-one years, from the time the Paris journal *Monde* published his 'La Censure en Angleterre' (translated from his English text by H.-J. Salemson) on 6 October 1928, to 22 July 1949 when *The Socialist Call* of New York published his refutation that *Nineteen Eighty-Four* was an attack on the British Labour Government (see p. 449). It may be slightly fortuitous but the fact that these two publications appeared not in England but abroad and in two different continents says something of his reach as a journalist. In those twenty-one years, as the twenty volumes of his *Complete Works* and also *The Lost Orwell* demonstrate, he was remarkably prolific and, almost sixty-five years after his death, he is read even more widely and in many more languages. It is remarkable given that much journalism is ephemeral that a signifi-cant amount of Orwell's writing is still relevant and speaks directly to us.

Orwell wrote perceptively in his essay 'Why I Write' of what drove him to write. He famously described his own motivation as sheer egoism, aesthetic enthusiasm (hence perhaps his first and life-long attempts at poetry), historical impulse (that is a 'Desire to see things as they are, to find out true facts and store them up for the use of posterity'), and political purpose – using the word 'political' in the widest possible sense – as the desire to push the world in a certain direc-tion (*Orwell and Politics*, Penguin Books, 2001, p. 460). He wished, he wrote, 'to make political writing into an art', and 'because there is some lie that I want to expose'. Journalism is the perfect medium for this, although some journalism – unlike Orwell's – might not be seen as art. Orwell described all writers – presum-ably including himself – as 'vain, selfish and lazy'. Orwell lazy? Hardly! In 'Why I Write' he says he wrote his first poem when he was about four or five and he was about sixteen when he 'suddenly discovered the joy of mere words'. He never lost his love of poetry nor his desire to write it and scraps of unfinished poems appear in his last literary notebook. Writing poetry was not his *forte*, and he would never have claimed to be 'a poet', but a number of his poems still delight and are included here.

It is clear why Orwell wrote and so is the way he approached writing, but I think we must also ask why he was not merely prolific but seemed so driven as a writer. Time, it must have seemed to him, was not on his side. Indeed, four of his nine books begin with a reference to time, memorably *Nineteen Eighty-Four*:

'It was a bright cold day in April, and the clocks were striking thirteen.'
[This was originally written as: 'It was a cold, blowy day in early April, and a million radios were striking thirteen.']

A fifth has a reference not to early morning but to last thing at night:

'Mr Jones, of the Manor Farm, had locked the hen-houses for the night, but he was too drunk to remember to shut the pop-holes.' *Animal Farm*

Even in his journalism, such as his review of Peter Fleming's *News from Tartary* (15 August 1936 – see pp. 42-3), he can ponder lyrically on passing time:

A journey by train or car or aeroplane is not an event but an interregnum between events, and the swifter the vehicle the more boring the journey becomes. The nomad of the steppe or the desert may have to put up with every kind of discomfort, but at any rate he is living while he is travelling, and not, like the passengers in a luxury liner, merely suffering a temporary death.

With the benefit of hindsight and our knowledge of Orwell's wretched health and early death, is it assuming too much to argue that he was driven by a desperate if unconscious need to write whilst he still had life? The idea of wasting time was anathema to him.

Orwell arrived in Burma on 27 November 1922 to serve in the Indian Imperial Police. On returning to England on leave in August 1927 he decided to resign his commission and in the spring of 1928 he went to live in Paris intending to become a novelist. It is unclear whether he wrote one or two novels (he gives both numbers) but he destroyed what he wrote, much to his later regret. However, he did have some success as a journalist, and, indeed, was paid for the seven articles which were published – six in Paris and one in England. These articles encapsulate what would be his prime topics of interest: social justice, literary criticism, the evils of imperialism, censorship, and a format that he virtually created: popular culture (which appeared in the title of one of his books when published in New York decades before it became fashionable in universities). Two representative articles have been selected for inclusion here – that on popular journalism and one on the evils of Empire. Although Orwell continued to the end of his days to strive for success as a novelist, three of his nine 'books' are the product of his journalism in a form in which he excelled: documentary reportage – *Down and Out in Paris and London*, *The Road to Wigan Pier* and *Homage to Catalonia*.

Daniel George, chief reader for the publisher Jonathan Cape, in the first sustained critique of Orwell as essayist and journalist, broadcast by the BBC on 16 September 1946 (and printed here for the first time, pp. 373-9), stated that Orwell 'writes about what he has experienced rather than what he has read'. Given that Orwell's corpus of journalism includes 379 reviews of some seven hundred books, plays and films, George is presumably arguing that in his writing on the political and social Orwell draws not on theory but his own experience and a close involvement in the world about him. This one can see from the writings reproduced in this selection in such essays as 'Common Lodging Houses' (p. 25); 'Spilling the Spanish Beans' (p. 53); the review of Borkenau's *Spanish Cockpit*' (p. 61); 'Three

Years of Home Guard' (p. 229); 'Democracy in the British Army' (p. 77); and 'Defeatism and German Propaganda' (p. 158). George continues:

> He writes nothing that has not an immediate bearing on life in the present and future. And he is a passionate defender of intellectual liberty. What seems to distress him particularly is not that writers – daily journalists particularly – have often to distort or suppress truth but that they are losing faith in the virtue of personal integrity. 'Political writing in our time', he says, 'consists almost entirely of prefabricated phrases bolted together like pieces of a child's Meccano set . . . To write in plain, vigorous language one has to think fearlessly, and if one thinks fearlessly one cannot be politically orthodox' . . . Orwell himself is not orthodox either in politics or literature. That is why he writes fearlessly, but, as I have tried to indicate, it is not a loud-voiced fearlessness. Insidious persuasion is his method.

Without a private income Orwell increasingly turned to book (and later theatre and film) reviewing and to journalism. Motivated, as he put it, by 'a feeling of partisanship, a sense of injustice', he succeeded in creating an art of political writing and, in particular, the analysis of popular culture. This 'sense of injustice' was not any injustice he might have felt he suffered, but invariably that experienced by others – by George Gissing (pp. 223–5); by P.G. Wodehouse when fiercely unpopular at the war's end (pp. 317–31); by Poles under the threat of deportation to a vengeful Communist government in their homeland (pp. 338–40, 380–81, and 410–11); by the persecution of writers in the USSR (pp. 405–07); and even injustice suffered by someone whose politics he abhorred – Konni Zilliacus (pp. 421–27).

Orwell's National Union of Journalists' Membership Card

Perhaps no topics more directly show Orwell thinking in this vein than 'On Hanging' (p. 381) and the review of Jim Phelan's *Jail Journey* (p. 100). In the latter he considers an aspect of life that was virtually unmentionable at the time he wrote – 1940. 'The central fact about jails and concentration camps' (this, of course, before the horrors of Belsen and Buchenwald were exposed to the world) 'is something unmentionable.' Then, subtly and directly, a dozen lines later he states that although prison reformers will cry out against leg-irons and bread-and-water they are 'shocked by the suggestion that convicts should be allowed a normal sexual life'.

It is a mark of Orwell's genius that so much of his journalism is still relevant, whether he is discussing 'Anti-Semitism' (p. 261), 'Skin Colour and Living Standards' (p. 250) and 'The Colour Bar' (p. 289), or 'Scottish Nationalism' (p. 411) and 'Polish Immigration' (p. 380). Even when an article is firmly rooted in its time such as the 'Sporting Spirit' (prompted by the 1945 soccer match between Moscow Dynamos and Glasgow Rangers, p. 346), it is still strikingly relevant today. And some of his journalism has a timeless quality. 'Woolworth's Roses' (p. 257) roused the ire of some readers of *Tribune* because it was deemed a piece of 'bourgeois nostalgia' and that it had been written as if by Godfrey Winn rather than George Orwell, but as Orwell correctly responded: 'One of the outstanding characteristics of the working class of this country is their love of flowers . . . sometimes even growing roses to the exclusion of vegetables.'

Orwell's urge 'to push the world in a certain direction' depended upon his writing for journals to provide a very modest income whilst giving him time to write books. It is evident that he was sometimes short of money on his return to England from Paris. There is a memorable instance in his Diary for *The Road to Wigan Pier* when, desperately cold and not wanting to spend the night on the winter streets, he first tried to pawn his raincoat – but the shop had too many and wanted no more. Fortunately, he was able instead to pawn his scarf for 1s 11d and was thus able to spend the night in a common lodging house.

In a letter to Jack Common from Marrakech of 12 October 1938, he wrote:

> I don't know what my financial situation will be next year. I don't believe my book on Spain sold at all, and if I have to come back to England and start on yet another book [he was then writing *Coming Up for Air*] with about £50 in the world I would rather have a roof over my head from the start. It's a great thing to have a roof over your head even if it's a leaky one. When Eileen and I were first married, when I was writing *Wigan Pier*, we had so little money that sometimes we hardly knew where the next meal was coming from.
>
> *A Life in Letters*, pp. 130–1

We do not know what income Eileen might have had. She worked in Whitehall at the start of the war for a censorship department (itself somewhat ironic) and later for the Ministry of Food. In a letter to Orwell written just before she died she mentions the possibility of selling 'the Harefield house' (*A Life in Letters*,

p. 248 and fn. 7, p. 255). This was let but it is not known for how much.

It is difficult – indeed, impossible – to give precise figures for Orwell's earnings after he returned to Europe in 1927 and until he joined the BBC in 1941. We do know that when he was in Paris, *Le Progrès civique* paid him 225 francs for each article it published (about £1 16s in 1928). *Adelphi* paid £2 for articles and reviews; *New Statesman* and *Horizon* paid £2 for reviews and *Tribune* £5 for articles and 10 shillings to £2 for reviews. *New English Weekly* seems not to have paid him anything. Advances from Gollancz for books seem to have varied from £33 to £50. Gollancz liked to ensure that further payments would be recouped from sales. Secker & Warburg paid a relatively huge advance of £150 for *Homage to Catalonia* but that seems not to have been earned by sales in Orwell's lifetime. Although too much reliance cannot be placed on the figures, Orwell's income from reviewing, writing articles, book advances and, sometimes, subsequent royalties, and part-time work can be estimated for the period 1922 to 1945 as shown in the tables in appendix II.

From July 1943 to December 1945 we have precise details of what Orwell earned from writing articles and reviews because he kept a very careful record in order that an accurate income tax return might be submitted to the Inland Revenue (*CW*, XVII, 463–78). A by-product of this record is that Orwell also calculated the word counts of what he wrote for this period. The figures are slightly inaccurate – Orwell seems to have been better with words than figures – but corrected they show that in this period he published 244,650 words and received £1,709 1s 0d. However, the word counts do not include fifty-nine 'As I Please' columns which amount to about 80,000 words. A further 5,400 words were excluded for two articles that were not published and for another that he seems to have overlooked, but Orwell did include *Animal Farm* (for which he records an advance of £132 16s 4d). When all this is taken into account it appears he wrote some 330,000 words in this thirty-month period – some 11,000 words a month, month after month, comprising almost 180 articles, reviews and broadcast talks.

The title Orwell used for his article on George Gissing in April 1943 – 'Not Enough Money' – must often have applied to him, but by September 1946, in answering the questionnaire for *Horizon's* 'The Cost of Letters', he could write:

> Personally I am satisfied, i.e. in a financial sense, because I have been lucky, at any rate during the last few years. I had to struggle desperately at the beginning, and if I had listened to what people said to me I would never have been a writer. . . . To a young writer who is conscious of having something in him, the only advice I can give is not to take advice. . . . If one simply wants to make a living by putting words on paper, then the B.B.C., the film companies, and the like are reasonably helpful. But if one wants to be primarily a *writer*, then, in our society, one is an animal that is tolerated but not encouraged – something rather like a house sparrow – and one gets on better if one realizes one's position from the start (p. 372).

For Orwell perhaps a rather large house sparrow! When Orwell died he was owed £670 in sums ranging from £25 to £250 which he had lent to seven friends. Probate on his estate was granted in May 1950 showing it amounted to just under £9,909. It was only after his death that the value of his estate grew markedly, from the proceeds of *Animal Farm* and *Nineteen Eighty-Four*.

Orwell's abomination of time-wasting is particularly apparent of his months at the BBC. He joined the Indian section of the BBC Overseas Service on 18 August 1941, initially as a Talks Assistant. Just over two years later, as he was leaving its service, he complained in a letter to Philip Rahv on 9 December 1943 (*CW*, XVI, p. 22) that he had 'wasted two years' at the BBC. But Orwell had not wasted his time. He had, of course, an enormous amount of administrative work arranging broadcasts and persuading distinguished authors and academics to broadcast for very small fees – the likes of T.S. Eliot, E.M. Forster, Joseph Needham, Ritchie Calder and Gordon Childe. However, he managed to write some 220 commentaries on current events – not news bulletins – for broadcast in English and for translation into several Indian languages: approximately four commentaries a week. Their topics are, naturally, now very dated but the two examples reproduced here – on the Soviet victories at Rostov and Kharkov (p. 209) and his final commentary (broadcast to Indonesia; p. 218) – give an insight into his radio journalism. Though he feared no one heard these commentaries in the Far East, especially in occupied Malaya and Indonesia, there is evidence to show that they did. By chance I bought, in a batch of books, a diary for the year 1943 kept by Albert Gentry, a civilian prisoner of the Japanese held in a fenced-off portion of Bangkok's University of Moral and Political Science. These prisoners were allowed out of the camp and Mr Gentry records hearing broadcasts from London probably at either the Swedish or Swiss consulates. (This diary is now in the Imperial War Museum.) We also know that nuns in Malaya heard Orwell frequently and passed on the news to others (see *A Life in Letters*, p. 195).

Long before the founding of 'distance learning' as practised by the Open University in the UK and the Deutsches Institut für Fernstudien, Tübingen, Germany, Orwell organised thirteen courses in literature, science, medicine, agriculture and psychology for students of Bombay and Calcutta Universities based on their syllabuses; these he then had printed in book form. One example is reproduced here – his broadcast on Jack London in his series 'Landmarks in American Literature' (p. 212). That he was able to attract speakers of an international stature is a mark of the quality of what he was innovating. He also ran practical drama courses and those had a dynamic effect in India, especially on one of the main participants, Balraj Sahni (1913–73), who became a leading film actor.

Orwell also invented a form of broadcast literary magazine programme (see his introduction to the first of these, p. 172) which attracted leading poets and critics. Another of his innovations is shown in his 'Imaginary Interview with Jonathan Swift' (p. 192). He was not afraid, despite the circumstances, to run a series of talks on 'great books', which included *The Koran* and *Das Kapital*, and arranged discussions on such social problems as 'Moslem Minorities in Europe' and 'The Status of Women in Europe'. Despite censorship, he was allowed to organise talks by the Quaker Reg Reynolds on prison literature at a time when leading Indians such as Mahatma Gandhi and Pandit Nehru were imprisoned by the British in India. He adapted famous books and stories, such as *The Emperor's New Clothes* and Ignazio Silone's 'The Fox', for radio. After leaving the BBC he dramatised *Little Red Riding Hood* for the BBC's *Children's Hour*, and wrote a radio play, *The Voyage of the* Beagle. It was, however, a bitter disappointment to him that listening figures in India – partly because of lack of radios there, time shifts, and language problems – were tiny.

Laurence Brander, the BBC's Intelligence Officer for India and one of the first to write a biography of Orwell, wrote that what Orwell did for Indian students 'was the inspiration of that rudimentary (BBC) Third Programme'. That came into being not long before Orwell's death. For many people, of whom I am one, the Third Programme has opened minds and eyes to worlds that might well have passed them by. Indeed, it was hearing Chaucer's *Canterbury Tales* recited in the late 1940s that inspired me to study in my spare time, become an academic, and in due time edit Orwell's work.

The extent of his work for the BBC Overseas Service is apparent from the fact that of the eleven volumes of the *Complete Works* containing his letters and essays, three are chiefly devoted to these 'two wasted years'. For a man who believed that 'every book is a failure' ('Why I Write', p. 463) it is easy to see why he responded in this way to the frustrations of dealing with the bureaucracy of the BBC's Indian Service. This, surely, is typified by his choosing the number 101 for the dreaded room in *Nineteen Eighty-Four*: it was the room in which he had to attend committee meetings at 55 Portland Place, a couple of hundred yards from Broadcasting House. If time is wasted it is in committee rooms.

Orwell's last day at the BBC was Tuesday 23 November 1943. He started writing letters on *Tribune*'s headed paper on Monday 29 November so it is likely that that was the day he started work as its Literary Editor. In addition to organising book reviews for the journal, one of Orwell's principal contributions to *Tribune* as literary editor was a personal column, 'As I Please', a random causerie, some-times deeply serious, often light-hearted. He wrote eighty 'As I Please' columns, sometimes with longish breaks between one and another. The first appeared on 3 December 1943 and the last on 4 April 1947. Raymond Postgate had contributed to a short series under that title in *Controversy* (edited by C.A. Smith) in 1939. Jon Kimche told the editor of this volume that it was he who suggested to Orwell that he use that title for his series. Another earlier use of the title, by a writer whom Orwell noted in a list of those with real or suspected left-wing leanings, was *I Write As I Please*, by Walter Duranty (1935). (Duranty, who died in 1957, was foreign correspondent for the *New York Times*, 1913–39.)

Sir Bernard Crick suggested that Orwell was probably paid 'only £500 a year' as literary editor of *Tribune*, rather less than he was paid at the BBC. Only two payments from *Tribune* to Orwell are noted in Orwell's Payments Book whilst he was literary editor: £5 5s 0d for a special article of 2,000 words on 20 December 1943 and 10s 6d for a poem of thirty-six lines on 17 January 1944. His salary as literary editor, whatever it was, seems therefore to have also covered his writing of 'As I Please'.

Aneurin Bevan (1897–1960), creator of the National Health Service, was a powerful director of *Tribune* whilst Orwell wrote for the journal, and gave Orwell free rein to conduct his 'As I Please' columns precisely as Orwell did please. As a result, 'Protests were frequent, both at the frivolous use he made of his column and at his frequent attacks on the Soviet Communist Party.' Bevan defended Orwell, and without his support Orwell 'might not have lasted – even though the circulation manager coolly reported that those who wrote in regularly threatening to cancel their subscriptions were rarely subscribers' (Crick, 445–6).

Orwell's Head of Department at the BBC, Rushbrook Williams, writing a confidential report on him in August 1943, praised not only his work but 'his moral as well as his intellectual capacity. He is transparently honest, incapable of subterfuge . . . a mind and a spirit of real and distinguished worth' (*A Life in Letters*, pp. 195–6). This, I would argue, is apparent not only from his work for the BBC but in all that he strove to say in essays, personal columns, and reviews. This selection of a few poems, quite a large number of reviews (including one or two of drama and film), some critical essays and broadcasts, extracts from the 'London Letters' addressed to American readers of *Partisan Review*, and many items from his causerie 'As I Please', does, I hope, in its many varieties demonstrate Rushbrook Williams's assessment and also confirms Daniel George's summation of Orwell's approach:

> Orwell strikes no attitude, adopts no pose. He never proudly claims to be a lowbrow. All he appears to claim is common sense. His style is a common sense style, unadorned by tricks and graces. It represents the man himself – a man, one cannot help feeling, who assumed the garb of simplicity after some practice. He now wears it naturally. It is now natural, or at least habitual, for him to see things not so much from the point of view of, as on behalf of, a much lower social class than that to which by birth and education he belongs. The old Etonian speaks for the Islingtonian – oh, but not crudely, not in his language, and not, on the other hand, with too-too exquisite sympathy or with smart paradox. He sees no nobility in poverty and no advantage in lack of education, no point in bad taste, no virtue in humility.

Peter Davison

Poem: 'Awake! Young Men of England'

Henley and South Oxfordshire Standard, 2 OCTOBER 1914

From September 1911 until December 1916 Orwell was a boarder at St Cyprian's, a private preparatory school in Eastbourne, Sussex. This experience motivated him much later to write the long essay, 'Such, Such Were the Joys' (CW, XIX, 353-87). This poem, written just a century ago when Orwell – as Eric Blair – was eleven years old and inspired by the fever of excitement at the outbreak of war and the rush to the colours, was sent, perhaps by his mother, to the Henley and South Oxfordshire Standard, *which printed it on 2 October 1914. St Cyprian's headmaster's wife, Mrs Vaughan Wilkes, with whom Orwell hardly saw eye to eye, felt moved to read it out at school assembly. By the end of the month Eton had already lost sixty-five former pupils, and Wellington thirty-eight, two schools at which Orwell was destined to study (Max Hastings,* Catastrophe, *p. 422).*

Oh! give me the strength of the lion,
The wisdom of Reynard the fox,
And then I'll hurl troops at the Germans,
And give them the hardest of knocks.

Oh! think of the War lord's mailed fist,
That is striking at England to-day;
And think of the lives that our soldiers
Are fearlessly throwing away.

Awake! oh you young men of England,
For if, when your Country's in need
You do not enlist by the thousand,
You truly are cowards indeed.

Poem: 'Our minds are married, but we are too young'

unpublished, CHRISTMAS, 1918

Jacintha Buddicom was a neighbour of the Blairs when they all lived at Shiplake near Henley-on-Thames, Oxfordshire. He famously introduced himself by standing on his head to attract the attention of the Buddicom children whilst they were playing French cricket. He and Jacintha became close friends and shared literary interests. Although as they grew older he attempted to press his affection on her too ardently, so that they fell out permanently, the influence of that friendship proved long lasting on Orwell. For example, when she was ill he read her, twice successively, Beatrix Potter's The Tale of Pigling Bland; *that would be one of a number of influences that can be detected in* Animal Farm *– one has only to look even casually at Beatrix Potter's illustrations to see that. He wrote Jacintha a number of poems but it seems she did not respond to any of his letters written from Burma and they never met on or after his return. For a full account of their association, see her* Eric & Us *(1974) especially in its 2006 edition with an important postscript by Jacintha's cousin, Dione Venables. See also* A Life in Letters, *pp. 8–11. Despite their not meeting again after Orwell had left for Burma, she remained an important influence on his life and writing.*

FOR JACINTHA BUDDICOM

Our minds are married, but we are too young
For wedlock by the customs of this age
When parent homes pen each in separate cage
And only supper-earning songs are sung.

Times past, when medieval woods were green,
Babes were betrothed, and that betrothal brief.
Remember Romeo in love and grief—
Those star-crossed lovers—Juliet was fourteen.

Times past, the caveman by his new-found fire
Rested beside his mate in woodsmoke's scent.
By our own fireside we shall rest content
Fifty years hence keep troth with hearts desire.

We shall remember, when our hair is white,
These clouded days revealed in radiant light.

'John Flory: My Epitaph'

unpublished, 1926–28(?)

Although there is obviously a link between Orwell's novel Burmese Days *and this epitaph, its precise nature is uncertain. Some critics believe it to have been written whilst Orwell was still serving in the Burmese police service, some that it was written on his return. If the latter he must have brought a stock of paper back to England from Burma because the Epitaph is handwritten in ink on Government of Burma paper.*

Goodness knows where they will bury me, – in their own grave yard I suppose, two feet deep in a painted coffin. There will be no mourners, and no rejoicers either, which seems sadder still, for the Burmese celebration of a funeral with music & gambling is nicer than our beastly mummeries. But if there were anyone here whose hand could form the letters, I would [like] him to carve this on the bark of some great peepul tree above my head.

JOHN FLORY

Born 1890

Died of Drink 1927.

'Here lies the bones of poor John Flory;
His story was the old, old story.
Money, women, cards & gin
Were the four things that did him in.

He has spent sweat enough to swim in
Making love to stupid women;
He has known misery past thinking
In the dismal art of drinking.

O stranger, as you voyage here
And read this welcome, shed no tear;
But take the single gift I give,
And learn from me how not to live.'

'A Farthing Newspaper'

G.K.'s Weekly, 29 DECEMBER 1928

This was Orwell first writing to be published professionally in England. 'G.K.' was G.K. Chesterton (1874–1936), remembered now for his comic verse and Father Brown detective stories. The farthing newspaper, L'Ami du Peuple, pursued anti-left policies and was financed by François Coty (1874–1934), best known for his perfumery business. It took its name, ironically, from a French Revolutionary radical newspaper edited by Jean-Paul Marat (1743–93).

The *Ami du Peuple* is a Paris newspaper. It was established about six months ago, and it has achieved something really strange and remarkable in the world where everything is a 'sensation,' by being sold at ten centimes, or rather less than a farthing the copy. It is a healthy, full-size sheet, with news, articles, and cartoons quite up to the usual standard, and with a turn for sport, murders, nationalist sentiment and anti-German propaganda. Nothing is abnormal about it except its price.

Nor is there any need to be surprised at this last phenomenon, because the proprietors of the *Ami du Peuple* have just explained all about it, in a huge manifesto which is pasted on the walls of Paris wherever billsticking is not *defendu*. On reading this manifesto one learns with pleased surprise that the *Ami du Peuple* is not like other newspapers, it was the purest public spirit, uncontaminated by any base thoughts of gain, which brought it to birth. The proprietors, who hide their blushes in anonymity, are emptying their pockets for the mere pleasure of doing good by stealth. Their objects, we learn, are to make war on the great trusts, to fight for a lower cost of living, and above all to combat the powerful newspapers which are strangling free speech in France. In spite of the sinister attempts of these other newspapers to put the *Ami du Peuple* out of action, it will fight on to the last. In short, it is all that its name implies.

One would cheer this last stand for democracy a great deal louder, of course, if one did not happen to know that the proprietor of the *Ami du Peuple* is M. Coty, a great industrial capitalist, and also proprietor of the *Figaro* and the *Gaulois*. One would also regard the *Ami du Peuple* with less suspicion if its politics were not anti-radical and anti-socialist, of the goodwill-in-industry, shake-hands-and-make-it-up species. But all that is beside the point at this moment. The important questions, obviously, are these: Does the *Ami du Peuple* pay its way? And if so, how?

The second question is the one that really matters. Since the march of progress is going in the direction of always bigger and nastier trusts, any departure is worth noticing which brings us nearer to that day when the newspaper will be simply a sheet of advertisement and propaganda, with a little well-censored news to sugar the pill. It is quite possible that the *Ami du Peuple* exists on its advertisements, but it is equally possible that it makes only an indirect profit, by putting across the sort of propaganda wanted by M. Coty and his associates. In the above mentioned manifesto, it was declared that the proprietors might rise to an even dizzier height of philanthropy by giving away the *Ami du Peuple* free of charge. This is not so impossible as it may sound. I have seen a daily paper (in India) which was given away free for some time with apparent profit to its backers, a ring of advertisers who found a free newspaper to be a cheap and satisfactory means of blowing their own trumpet. Their paper was rather above the average Indian level, and it supplied, of course, just such news as they themselves approved, and no other. That obscure Indian paper forecast the logical goal of modern journalism; and the *Ami du Peuple* should be noticed, as a new step in the same direction.

But whether its profits are direct or indirect, the *Ami du Peuple* is certainly prospering. Its circulation is already very large, and though it started out as a mere morning paper it has now produced an afternoon and late evening edition. Its proprietors speak with perfect truth when they declare that some of the other papers have done their best to crush this new champion of free speech. These others (they, too, of course, acting from the highest altruistic motives) have made a gallant attempt to [have] it excluded from the news-agents' shops, and have even succeeded as far as the street-corner kiosks are concerned. In some small shops, too, whose owners are socialists, one will even see the sign 'Ici on ne vend pas *l'Ami du Peuple*' exhibited in the windows. But the *Ami du Peuple* is not worrying. It is sold in the streets and the cafés with great vigour, and it is sold by barbers and tobacconists and all kinds of people who have never done any newsagency before. Sometimes it is simply left out on the boulevard in great piles, together with a tin for the two-sou pieces, and with no attendant whatever. One can see that the proprietors are determined, by hook or by crook, to make it the most widely-read paper in Paris.

And supposing they succeed—what then? Obviously the *Ami du Peuple* is going to crowd out of existence one or more of the less prosperous papers—already several are feeling the pinch. In the end, they will presumably either be destroyed, or they will survive by imitating the tactics of the *Ami du Peuple*. Hence every paper of this kind, whatever its intentions, is the enemy of free speech. At present France is the home of free speech, in the Press if not elsewhere. Paris alone has daily papers by the dozen, nationalist, socialist, and communist, clerical and anti-clerical, militarist and anti-militarist, pro-semitic and anti-semitic. It has the *Action Française*, a Royalist paper and still one of the leading dailies, and it has *Humanité*, the reddest daily paper outside Soviet Russia. It has *La Libertà*, which is written in Italian and yet may not even be sold in Italy, much less published there. Papers are printed in Paris in French, English, Italian, Yiddish, German, Russian, Polish, and languages whose very alphabets are unrecognizable by a western European. The kiosks are stuffed with papers, all different. The Press combine, about which French journalists are already grumbling, does not really exist yet in France. But the *Ami du Peuple*, at least, is doing its gallant best to make it a reality.

And supposing that this kind of thing is found to pay in France, why should it not be tried elsewhere? Why should we not have our farthing, or at least our half-penny newspaper in London? While the journalist exists merely as the publicity agent of big business, a large circulation, got by fair means or foul, is a newspaper's one and only aim. Till recently various of our newspapers achieved the desired level of 'net sales' by the simple method of giving away a few thousand pounds now and again in football competition prizes. Now the football competitions have been stopped by law, and doubtless some of the circulations have come down with an ugly bump. Here, then, is a worthy example for our English Press magnates. Let them imitate the *Ami du Peuple* and sell their papers at a farthing. Even if it does no other good whatever, at any rate the poor devils of the public will at last feel that they are getting the correct value for their money.

'How a Nation Is Exploited: The British Empire in Burma'

Le Progrès civique, 4 MAY 1929

After returning from Burma, Orwell went to live in Paris where he attempted to teach himself the craft of writing. Although he failed to produce a publishable novel (he destroyed, to his later regret, what he had drafted – see Introduction to Down and Out, *n. 1 below), he had some success in having articles published in French journals. These were on censorship, the unemployed, a day in the life of a tramp, London beggars, John Galsworthy, and the article below. These, with 'A Farthing Newspaper', pretty well summarise what would in his later life be his major concerns.[1] Le Progrès* civique *paid him 225 francs for each article they published (about £1.80 in 1928, perhaps equivalent to £50 today).*

Following the recent troubles in India, we have asked our contributor, Mr E.A. Blair, whose investigations on 'The Plight of the British Worker' have already appeared in these pages, to tell us something of the unrest which has been fermenting in the sub-continent for some years, and which is threatening to spread to English Indo-China.

Mr E.A. Blair, who lived in Burma for some years, has written the following interesting article for us, which shows the methods the British Empire uses to milk dry her Asian colonies.

Burma lies between India and China. Ethnologically it belongs to Indo-China.

It is three times the size of England and Wales, with a population of about fourteen million, of whom roughly nine million are Burmese.

The rest is made up of countless Mongol tribes who have emigrated at various periods from the steppes of Central Asia, and Indians who have arrived since the English occupation.

The Burmese are Buddhists; the tribesmen worship various pagan gods.

To be able to talk in their own language to the people of such diverse origins living in Burma, you would need to know a hundred and twenty different languages and dialects.

---

1. Orwell wrote the articles in English and they were translated into French by Raoul Nicole. The original English texts have not survived but the French has been translated into English here by Janet Percival and Ian Willison. Orwell tended to write in long paragraphs so that the short paragraphs in the article here are the work of the French copy-editor. Such short paragraphs will be found in other newspaper articles, such as in Orwell's view of L.A.G. Strong's *Authorship*, pp. 311–13.

This country, the population of which is one-tenth as dense as that of England, is one of the richest in the world. It abounds in natural resources which are only just beginning to be exploited.

Its forests are full of timber trees, an ideal source of first-class building materials.

There are tin, tungsten, jade and rubies, and these are the least of its mineral resources.

At this moment it produces five per cent of the world's petroleum, and its reserves are far from exhausted.

But the greatest source of wealth—and that which feeds between eighty and ninety per cent of the population—is the paddy-fields.

Rice is grown everywhere in the basin of the Irrawaddy, which flows through Burma from north to south.

In the south, in the huge delta where the Irrawaddy brings down tons of alluvial mud every year, the soil is immensely fertile.

The harvests, which are remarkable in both quality and quantity, enable Burma to export rice to India, Europe, even to America.

Moreover, variations in temperature are less frequent and sharp than in India.

Thanks to abundant rainfall, especially in the south, drought is unknown, and the heat is never excessive. The climate as a whole can thus be considered one of the healthiest to be found in the tropics.

If we add that the Burmese countryside is exceptionally beautiful, with broad rivers, high mountains, eternally green forests, brightly coloured flowers, exotic fruits, the phrase 'earthly paradise' naturally springs to mind.

So it is hardly surprising that the English tried for a long time to gain possession of it.

In 1820 they seized a vast expanse of territory. This operation was repeated in 1852, and finally in 1882 the Union Jack flew over almost all the country.

Certain mountainous districts in the north, inhabited by small savage tribes, had until recently escaped the clutches of the British, but it is more and more likely that they will meet the same fate as the rest of the country, thanks to the process euphemistically known as 'peaceful penetration', which means, in plain English, 'peaceful annexation'.

In this article I do not seek to praise or blame this manifestation of British imperialism; let us simply note it is a logical result of any imperialist policy.

It will be much more profitable to examine the good and bad sides of British administration in Burma from an economic and a political standpoint.

Let us turn first to politics.

The government of all the Indian provinces under the control of the British Empire is of necessity despotic, because only the threat of force can subdue a population of several million subjects.

But this despotism is latent. It hides behind a mask of democracy.

The great maxim of the English in governing an oriental race is 'never get something done by a European when an Oriental can do it'. In other words, supreme power remains with the British authorities, but the minor civil servants who have to carry out day-to-day administration and who must come into contact with the people in the course of their duties are recruited locally.

In Burma, for example, the lower grade magistrates, all policemen up to the rank of inspector, members of the postal service, government employees, village elders etc. are Burmese.

Recently, to appease public opinion and put a stop to nationalist agitation which was beginning to cause concern, it was even decided to accept the candidature of educated natives for several important posts.

The system of employing natives as civil servants has three advantages.

First, natives will accept lower salaries than Europeans.

Secondly, they have a better idea of the workings of their fellow countrymen's minds, and this helps them to settle legal disputes more easily.

Thirdly, it is to their own advantage to show their loyalty to a government which provides their livelihood.

And so peace is maintained by ensuring the close collaboration of the educated or semi-educated classes, where discontent might otherwise produce rebel leaders.

Nevertheless the British control the country. Of course, Burma, like each of the Indian provinces, has a parliament—always the show of democracy—but in reality its parliament has very little power.

Nothing of any consequence lies within its jurisdiction. Most of the members are puppets of the government, which is not above using them to nip in the bud any Bill which seems untimely.

In addition, each province has a Governor, appointed by the English, who has at his disposal a veto just as absolute as that of the President of the United States to oppose any proposal which displeases him.

Yet although the British government is, as we have shown, essentially despotic, it is by no means unpopular.

The English are building roads and canals—in their own interest, of course, but the Burmese benefit from them—they set up hospitals, open schools, and see to the maintenance of law and order.

And after all, the Burmese are mere peasants, occupied in cultivating the land. They have not yet reached that stage of intellectual development which makes for nationalists.

Their village is their universe, and as long as they are left in peace to cultivate their fields, they do not care whether their masters are black or white.

A proof of this political apathy on the part of the people of Burma is the fact that the only British military forces in the country are two English infantry battalions and around ten battalions of Indian infantry and mounted police.

Thus twelve thousand armed men, mostly Indians, are enough to subdue a population of fourteen million.

The most dangerous enemies of the government are the young men of the educated classes. If these classes were more numerous and were *really* educated, they could perhaps raise the revolutionary banner. But they are not.

The reason is firstly that, as we have seen, the majority of the Burmese are peasants.

Secondly, the British government is at pains to give the people only summary instruction, which is almost useless, merely sufficient to produce messengers, low-grade civil servants, petty lawyers' clerks and other white-collar workers.

Care is taken to avoid technical and industrial training. This rule, observed throughout India, aims to stop India from becoming an industrial country capable of competing with England.

It is true to say that in general, any really educated Burmese was educated in England, and belongs as a result to the small class of the well-to-do.

So, because there are no educated classes, public opinion, which could press for rebellion against England, is non-existent.

Let us now consider the economic question. Here again we find the Burmese in general too ignorant to have a clear understanding of the way in which they are being treated and, as a result, too ignorant to show the least resentment.

Besides, for the moment they have not suffered much economic damage.

It is true that the British seized the mines and the oil wells. It is true that they control timber production. It is true that all sorts of middlemen, brokers, millers, exporters, have made colossal fortunes from rice without the producer—that is the peasant—getting a thing out of it.

It is also true that the get-rich-quick businessmen who made their pile from fire, petrol etc. are not contributing as they should be to the well-being of the country, and that their money, instead of swelling local revenues in the form of taxes, is sent abroad to be spent in England.

If we are honest, it is true that the British are robbing and pilfering Burma quite shamelessly.

But we must stress that the Burmese hardly notice it *for the moment*. Their country is so rich, their population so scattered, their needs, like those of all Orientals, so slight that they are not conscious of being exploited.

The peasant cultivating his patch of ground lives more or less as his ancestors did in Marco Polo's day. If he wishes, he can buy virgin land for a reasonable price.

He certainly leads an arduous existence, but he is on the whole free from care.

Hunger and unemployment are for him meaningless words. There is work and food for everyone. Why worry needlessly?

But, and this is the important point, the Burmese will begin to suffer when a large part of the richness of their country has declined.

Although Burma has developed to a certain extent since the war, already the peasant there is poorer than he was twenty years ago.

He is beginning to feel the weight of land taxation, for which he is not compensated by the increased yield of his harvests.

The worker's wages have not kept up with the cost of living.

The reason is that the British government has allowed free entry into Burma for veritable hordes of Indians, who, coming from a land where they were literally dying of hunger, work for next to nothing and are, as a result, fearsome rivals for the Burmese.

Add to this a rapid rise in population growth—at the last census the population registered an increase of ten million in ten years—and it is easy to see that sooner or later, as happens in all overpopulated countries, the Burmese will be dispossessed of their lands, reduced to a state of semi-slavery in the service of capitalism, and will have to endure unemployment into the bargain.

They will then discover what they hardly suspect today, that the oil wells, the mines, the milling industry, the sale and cultivation of rice are all controlled by the British.

They will also realise their own industrial incompetence in a world where industry dominates.

British politics in Burma is the same as in India.

Industrially speaking, India was deliberately kept in ignorance.

She only produces basic necessities, made by hand. The Indians would be incapable, for example, of making a motor-car, a rifle, a clock, an electric-light bulb etc. They would be incapable of building or sailing an ocean-going vessel.

At the same time they have learnt in their dealings with Westerners to depend on certain machine-made articles. So the products of English factories find an important outlet in a country incapable of manufacturing them herself.

Foreign competition is prevented by an insuperable barrier of prohibitive customs tariffs. And so the English factory-owners, with nothing to fear, control the markets absolutely and reap exorbitant profits.

We said that the Burmese have not yet suffered too much, but this is because they have remained, on the whole, an agricultural nation.

Yet for them as for all Orientals, contact with Europeans has created the demand, unknown to their fathers, for the products of modern industry. As a result, the British are stealing from Burma in two ways:

In the first place, they pillage her natural resources; secondly, they grant themselves the exclusive right to sell her the manufactured products she now needs.

And the Burmese are thus drawn into the system of industrial capitalism, without any hope of becoming capitalist industrialists themselves.

Moreover the Burmese, like all the other peoples of India, remain under the rule of the British Empire for purely military considerations. For they are in effect incapable of building ships, manufacturing guns or any other arms necessary for modern warfare, and, as things now stand, if the English were to give up India, it would only result in a change of master. The country would simply be invaded and exploited by some other Power.

British domination in India rests essentially on exchanging military protection for a commercial monopoly, but, as we have tried to show, the bargain is to the advantage of the English whose control reaches into every domain.

To sum up, if Burma derives some incidental benefit from the English, she must pay dearly for it.

Up till now the English have refrained from oppressing the native people too much because there has been no need. The Burmese are still at the beginning of a period of transition which will transform them from agricultural peasants to workers in the service of the manufacturing industries.

Their situation could be compared with that of any people of eighteenth-century Europe, apart from the fact that the capital, construction materials, knowledge and power necessary for their commerce and industry belong exclusively to foreigners.

So they are under the protection of a despotism which defends them for its own ends, but which would abandon them without hesitation if they ceased to be of use.

Their relationship with the British Empire is that of slave and master.

Is the master good or bad? That is not the question; let us simply say that his control is despotic and, to put it plainly, self-interested.

Even though the Burmese have not had much cause for complaint up till now, the day will come when the riches of their country will be insufficient for a population which is constantly growing.

Then they will be able to appreciate how capitalism shows its gratitude to those to whom it owes its existence.

Review: J.B. Priestley, *Angel Pavement*

The Adelphi, OCTOBER 1930

Orwell was much encouraged as a writer by the literary journal, The Adelphi, and its owner and nominal editor, John Middleton Murry (1889–1957), even though they had quite sharp differences of opinion. Much of the editorial work fell on Sir Richard Rees (1900–70) and the pacifist, Max Plowman (1883–1941). Both remained close friends of Orwell. Rees was to become Orwell's joint literary executor (with Sonia Orwell), and Ravelston in Keep the Aspidistra Flying *owes something to his generous nature.*

Abandoning provincial life, Mr Priestley has turned his attention to London, in a novel about one Mr Golspie, an able rogue who descends upon a struggling city firm, quietly ruins it, and vanishes. The intention, more or less explicit, is to set forth the romance of London, to make a pattern of beauty from the eventless, dismal lives which interlace in a city office. Abandon, says Mr Priestley in effect, all your sneering about industrial civilisation. Remember that these clerks and typists who look so unpleasantly like ants as they stream over London Bridge at the rush hour, these clerks whom you in your superiority despise—they too are human —they too are romantic. And thus far, who will contradict him? Clerks are men and brothers, and fit material for art—applause, therefore, to the writer who can use them.

But unfortunately, a novelist is not required to have good intentions but to convey beauty. And when one has finished applauding Mr Priestley's effort to make clerks and typists interesting, one must add that the effort does not, even for a single page, come off. It is not that he writes ineptly, or is lumpishly dull, or consciously plays for cheap effects; it is simply that his writing does not touch the level at which memorable fiction begins. One compares these six hundred competent pages (and one must make the comparison, after all that has been said of Mr Priestley) with other novels of London; with Mr Arnold Bennett in *Riceyman Steps*, with Conrad in *The Secret Agent*, with Dickens in *Bleak House*; and one wonders incredulously whether anyone has really mistaken Mr Priestley for a master. His work has no damning faults, but neither has it a single gleam of beauty, nor any profundity of thought, nor even memorable humour; the book is simply a middle article spun out to six hundred pages, with all the middle article's high spirits and conscientious wit, and the same utter lack of anything intensely felt or profitably conveyed.

'Warwick's restaurant . . . might have been French or Italian or even Spanish or Hungarian; there was no telling; but it was determinedly foreign in a de-nationalised fashion, rather as if the League of Nations had invented it.'

'. . . the bus stopped by the dark desolation of Lord's cricket ground, swallowed two women who were all parcels, comic hats, and fuss (a sure sign this that Christmas was near, for you never saw these parcel-and-comic-hat women at any other time) and rolled on . . .'

The point about these two extracts is that they are as good as anything in *Angel Pavement*; there are thousands of sentences like them, seldom worse, never better, never going deeper than this beneath the skin of things. And yet consider what themes Mr Priestley is handling in this shallow and sprightly way! A cunning business swindle, dinner parties in an Earl's Court maisonette, squabbles in a Stoke Newington villa, a hospital deathbed, an attempted murder, a projected suicide! One imagines what these things might have become in other hands. One imagines, for example, Conrad brooding in his own sombre way over Turgis, the pimply and lovesick clerk; or Hardy describing the scene in which Turgis, intending suicide, has not a shilling for the gas meter; or Mr H.G. Wells, in his earlier manner, reporting the conversations of Mr Pelumpton, the boozy second-hand broker; or Mr Bennett upon the women's hostel where incipient old maids starved for adventure. But one does not get what these writers would have given, nor anything resembling it more closely than London draught beer resembles beer made with hops. What one does get is six hundred pages of middle article, quite readable and quite forget-table, with—when the plot calls for intense feeling—something like this:

'He sat there in a dream ecstasy of devotion, in which remembered kisses glittered like stars.'

When a novel lacks the indefinable, unmistakable thing we call beauty, one looks in it for sound delineation of character, or humour of situation, or verbal wit. But one looks in vain in *Angel Pavement*—Mr Priestley can be clever, but he cannot be in any way memorable. All his characters—Mr Dersingham the incompetent business man, Mr Golspie the adventurous rogue, Miss Matfield the bored typist, Mr Smeeth the desiccated accountant —are alike in their unreality, mere attenuated ghosts from the pages of Mr Hugh Walpole and Mr Arnold Bennett. All the dialogue is the same in this, that being neither incredible nor unreadable, it is not funny and has not the compelling semblance of life. All the analysis, the reflections, are alike in the ease with which they are understood, and, having been understood, are forgotten. Even the observation is suspect. Towards the end of the book there is an account of a game of bridge, and the account contains two errors which would never have been made by a careful observer. It is a small point, but it confirms the general impression that Mr Priestley's work is written altogether too easily, is not laboured upon as good fiction must be—not, in the good sense of the phrase, *worked out*.

One would not thus assail a competent and agreeable novel, if Mr Priestley had not been so extravagantly praised. He has been likened, absurdly, to Dickens, and when a novelist is likened to Dickens one must stop and ask the reason. Is it not a safe guess that Mr Priestley owes his popularity to his frank optimism? In *Angel Pavement*, it is true, he deals with gloomy subjects, but by implication—by his manner of writing—he is as cheerful as ever. He is not a professional backslapper, but he can be quoted by such, and to some of them, probably, he appears as a champion against those gloomy and obscene highbrows who are supposed to be forever corrupting English literature. It is for this reason that such a blatantly second-rate novelist has been likened to Dickens, the great master of prose, psychology and wit. Once this absurd praise is discounted, we can salute Mr Priestley for the qualities which he really possesses, and take *Angel Pavement* for what it is, an excellent holiday novel, genuinely gay and pleasant, which supplies a good bulk of reading matter for ten and sixpence.

'Common Lodging Houses'

New Statesman and Nation, 5 SEPTEMBER 1932

The New Statesman *was founded in 1913 by Sidney and Beatrice Webb and was supported by members of the Fabian Society. Thus, from its birth to the present day it has offered a left-wing critique of British politics. In 1931 it merged with* The Nation and Athenaeum, *a journal supporting the Liberal Party. It changed its name to* New Statesman and Nation *but dropped* and Nation *in 1961. With the rise of Fascism it became more vociferous and under Kingsley Martin, its editor from 1930 to 1960, its circulation markedly increased. It was thus a natural 'home' for Orwell's independent left-wing stance. However Martin and Orwell fell out owing to the former's rejection of Orwell's article, 'Eye-Witness in Barcelona', on the grounds, it would seem, that 'it would cause trouble'. As a sop Orwell was asked to review Franz Borkenau's* The Spanish Cockpit *(see page 61) but Martin – not the journal's distinguished literary editor, Raymond Mortimer – also rejected that.*

Common lodging houses, of which there are several hundred in London, are night-shelters specially licensed by the LCC. They are intended for people who cannot afford regular lodgings, and in effect they are extremely cheap hotels. It is hard to estimate the lodging-house population, which varies continually, but it always runs into tens of thousands, and in the winter months probably approaches fifty thousand. Considering that they house so many people and that most of them are in an extraordinarily bad state, common lodging houses do not get the attention they deserve.

To judge the value of the LCC legislation on this subject, one must realise what life in a common lodging house is like. The average lodging house ('doss house', it used to be called) consists of a number of dormitories, and a kitchen, always subterranean, which also serves as a sitting-room. The conditions in these places, especially in southern quarters such as Southwark or Bermondsey, are disgusting. The dormitories are horrible fetid dens, packed with anything up to a hundred men, and furnished with beds a good deal inferior to those in a London casual ward. Normally these beds are about 5 ft 6 in. long by 2 ft 6 in. wide, with a hard convex mattress and a cylindrical pillow like a block of wood; sometimes, in the cheaper houses, not even a pillow. The bed-clothes consist of two raw-umber-coloured sheets, supposed to be changed once a week, but actually, in many cases, left on for a month, and a cotton counterpane;

in winter there may be blankets, but never enough. As often as not the beds are verminous, and the kitchens invariably swarm with cockroaches or black beetles. There are no baths, of course, and no room where any privacy is attainable. These are the normal and accepted conditions in all ordinary lodging houses. The charges paid for this kind of accommodation vary between 7d and 1/1d a night. It should be added that, low as these charges sound, the average common lodging house brings in something like £40 net profit a week to its owner.

Besides the ordinary dirty lodging houses, there are a few score, such as the Rowton Houses and the Salvation Army hostels, that are clean and decent. Unfortunately, all of these places set off their advantages by a discipline so rigid and tiresome that to stay in them is rather like being in jail. In London (curiously enough it is better in some other towns) the common lodging house where one gets both liberty and a decent bed does not exist.

The curious thing about the squalor and discomfort of the ordinary lodging house is that these exist in places subject to constant inspection by the LCC. When one first sees the murky, troglodytic cave of a common lodging-house kitchen, one takes it for a corner of the early nineteenth century which has somehow been missed by the reformers; it is a surprise to find that common lodging houses are governed by a set of minute and (in intention) exceedingly tyrannical rules. According to the LCC regulations, practically everything is against the law in a common lodging house. Gambling, drunkenness, or even the introduction of liquor, swearing, spitting on the floor, keeping tame animals, fighting—in short, the whole social life of these places—are all forbidden. Of course, the law is habitually broken, but some of the rules are enforceable, and they illustrate the dismal uselessness of this kind of legislation. To take an instance: some time ago the LCC became concerned about the closeness together of beds in common lodging houses, and enacted that these must be at least 3 ft apart. This is the kind of law that is enforceable, and the beds were duly moved. Now, to a lodger in an already overcrowded dormitory it hardly matters whether the beds are 3 ft apart or 1 ft; but it does matter to the proprietor, whose income depends upon his floor space. The sole real result of this law, therefore, was a general rise in the price of beds. Please notice that though the space between the beds is strictly regulated, nothing is said about the beds themselves—nothing, for instance, about their being fit to sleep in. The lodging-house keepers can, and do, charge

1/– for a bed less restful than a heap of straw, and there is no law to prevent them.

Another example of LCC regulations. From nearly all common lodging houses women are strictly excluded; there are a few houses specially for women, and a very small number—too small to affect the general question—to which both men and women are admitted. It follows that any homeless man who lives regularly in a lodging house is entirely cut off from female society—indeed, cases even happen of man and wife being separated owing to the impossibility of getting accommodation in the same house. Again, some of the cheaper lodging houses are habitually raided by slumming parties, who march into the kitchen uninvited and hold lengthy religious services. The lodgers dislike these slumming parties intensely, but they have no power to eject them. Can anyone imagine such things being tolerated in a hotel? And yet a common lodging house is only a hotel at which one pays 8d a night instead of 10/6d. This kind of petty tyranny can, in fact, only be defended on the theory that a man poor enough to live in a common lodging house thereby forfeits some of his rights as a citizen.

One cannot help feeling that this theory lies behind the LCC rules for common lodging houses. All these rules are in the nature of interference-legislation—that is, they interfere, but not for the benefit of the lodgers. Their emphasis is on hygiene and morals, and the question of comfort is left to the lodging-house proprietor, who, of course, either shirks it or solves it in the spirit of organised charity. It is worth pointing out the improvements that could actually be made in common lodging houses by legislation. As to cleanliness, no law will ever enforce that, and in any case it is a minor point. But the sleeping accommodation, which is the important thing, could easily be brought up to a decent standard. Common lodging houses are places in which one pays to sleep, and most of them fail in their essential purpose, for no one can sleep well in a rackety dormitory on a bed as hard as bricks. The LCC would be doing an immense service if they compelled lodging-house keepers to divide their dormitories into cubicles and, above all, to provide comfortable beds; for instance, beds as good as those in the London casual wards. And there seems no sense in the principle of licensing all houses for 'men only' or 'women only', as though men and women were sodium and water and must be kept apart for fear of an explosion; the houses should be licensed for both sexes alike, as they are in some provincial towns. And the lodgers should be protected by law against various swindles which the proprietors and managers are now able to practise on them. Given these conditions, common lodging houses would serve their purpose, which is an important one, far better than they do now. After all, tens of thousands of unemployed and partially employed men have literally no other place in which they can live. It is absurd that they should be compelled to choose, as they are at present, between an easy-going pigsty and a hygienic prison.

Poem: 'Sometimes in the middle autumn days'

The Adelphi, MARCH 1933

Sometimes in the middle autumn days,
The windless days when the swallows have flown,
And the sere elms brood in the mist,
Each tree a being, rapt, alone,

I know, not as in barren thought,
But wordlessly, as the bones know,
What quenching of my brain, what numbness,
Wait in the dark grave where I go.

And I see the people thronging the street,
The death-marked people, they and I
Goalless, rootless, like leaves drifting,
Blind to the earth and to the sky;

Nothing believing, nothing loving,
Not in joy nor in pain, not heeding the stream
Of precious life that flows within us,
But fighting, toiling as in a dream.

O you who pass, halt and remember
What tyrant holds your life in bond;
Remember the fixed, reprieveless hour,
The crushing stroke, the dark beyond.

And let us now, as men condemned,
In peace and thrift of time stand still
To learn our world while yet we may,
And shape our souls, however ill;

And we will live, hand, eye and brain,
Piously, outwardly, ever-aware,
Till all our hours burn clear and brave
Like candle flames in windless air;

So shall we in the rout of life
Some thought, some faith, some meaning save,
And speak it once before we go
In silence to the silent grave.

Poem: 'Summer-like for an instant'

The Adelphi, MAY 1933

Summer-like for an instant the autumn sun bursts out,
And the light through the turning elms is green and clear;
It slants down the path and the ragged marigolds glow
Fiery again, last flames of the dying year.

A blue-tit darts with a flash of wings, to feed
Where the coconut hangs on the pear tree over the well;
He digs at the meat like a tiny pickaxe tapping
With his needle-sharp beak as he clings to the swinging shell.

Then he runs up the trunk, sure-footed and sleek like a mouse,
And perches to sun himself; all his body and brain
Exult in the sudden sunlight, gladly believing
That the cold is over and summer is here again.

But I see the umber clouds that drive for the sun,
And a sorrow no argument ever can make away
Goes through my heart as I think of the nearing winter,
And the transient light that gleams like the ghost of May;

And the bird unaware, blessing the summer eternal,
Joyfully labouring, proud in his strength, gay-plumed,
Unaware of the hawk and the snow and the frost-bound nights,
And of his death foredoomed.

Review: G.K. Chesterton, *Criticisms and Opinions of the Works of Charles Dickens*

The Adelphi, DECEMBER 1933

There is one great advantage about Mr. Chesterton's manner of approaching Dickens, and that is that it is not too purely literary. Most modern literary criticism is literary and nothing else—that is, it concentrates on an author's style and thinks it rather vulgar to notice his subject matter. Undoubtedly the influence of this type of criticism has been healthy (it has saved us from Shakespeare the Great Moral Teacher and all that, and from the windy platitudes of the Bernard Shaw era, when duds like Brieux were foisted upon us for the sake of their sermons), but it misses part of the point with such a writer as Dickens. Dickens was essentially a moralist, and he cannot be treated as though he were, say, Flaubert.

Being a moralist, Dickens did not invent his characters merely *as* characters, but rather as embodiments of the human qualities that he liked and disliked. And it is probably the secret of their vitality, that Dickens's likes and dislikes are such as any decent man would share. He was always, when he understood the issue, on the side of the weak against the strong. As Mr. Chesterton says, Dickens 'saw that under many forms there was one fact, the tyranny of man over man; and he struck at it when he saw it, whether it was old or new.' This is perfectly true. Dickens's view of life was sometimes one-eyed and he was not free from a rather disagreeable petty-bourgeois class-feeling, but on the whole his instincts were sound. It was only when he outraged them he went astray, artistically as well as morally.

The best instance is in *David Copperfield*. As Mr. Chesterton points out, the artistic collapse of *David Copperfield* has an ethical cause. It is perfectly clear that *David Copperfield* is autobiography (imaginative autobiography, of course), and it is equally clear if one looks closely that towards the end Dickens begins telling lies. He wrenches the book out of its natural channel and gives it a conventional happy ending, which is not only unconvincing but also abominably priggish. Dora is made to die of nothing in particular, the improvident and lovable characters are hustled off to Australia, and David marries the insufferable Agnes—a marriage which has, like so many marriages in Victorian fiction, a nasty suggestion of incest. The result is disaster, culminating in the rather horrible saturnalia at the end, in which everything is turned upside down and Dickens temporarily loses not only his comic genius but even his sense of decency. The prison scene in the last chapter is really disgusting. It is worthy of Edgar Wallace. Dickens had some ugly moods upon which Mr. Chesterton evidently does not care to dwell. The essay on *David Copperfield* is, however, an excellent piece of writing, and by a great deal the most interesting thing in the book.

Of course, Mr. Chesterton would not be himself if he did not make Dickens a mouthpiece for various of his own fads. Where Dickens's opinion happens to coincide with Mr. Chesterton's, as for instance upon the subject of the English Poor Law, well and good, that is Dickens's opinion; where it happens not to coincide, as for instance on the subject of the Middle Ages, or the French Revolution, or the Roman Catholic Church, Mr. Chesterton explains that Dickens did not really think that, he only thought he thought it. Dickens is used as a stick to beat all modern novelists and most nineteenth-century ones, including Thackeray. (Why are Dickens and Thackeray always compared? They are completely unlike. The novelist among Dickens's contemporaries who most resembled him was Surtees.) Again, some of Dickens's faults—his morbid love of corpses, for instance—are exalted into virtues because Mr. Chesterton either shares them or feels that he ought to share them. There is an attempt, though it is not as pronounced as it might be, to affiliate Dickens with the Middle Ages—the mythical Middle Ages beloved of Roman Catholics, when peasants were boozy but monogamous, and there was no serfdom and no Holy Inquisition. However, there is one thing which Mr. Chesterton has not said, and which he must be honoured for not saying. He has not said that if Dickens had had a little more brains he would have turned Roman Catholic. Not many of our Catholic apologists would have refrained from saying that. It would be absurd to pretend that Mr. Chesterton is not a Catholic apologist, but at least he has never joined in the great game of pretending that no book by a Protestant author can be readable.

Mr. Chesterton is at his best when he writes about Dickens. He has this in common with Dickens, too, that however much one may disagree with him, and even when one considers him a definitely bad and cheap writer, one cannot help liking him. It would be interesting to see his special method of criticism applied to some of our other major novelists —in particular, to Fielding.

Poem: 'On a Ruined Farm Near the His Majesty's Voice Gramophone Factory'

The Adelphi, APRIL 1934

As I stand at the lichened gate
With warring worlds on either hand—
To left the black and budless trees,
The empty sties, the barns that stand

Like tumbling skeletons—and to right
The factory-towers, white and clear
Like distant, glittering cities seen
From a ship's rail—as I stand here,

I feel, and with a sharper pang,
My mortal sickness; how I give
My heart to weak and stuffless ghosts,
And with the living cannot live.

The acid smoke has soured the fields,
And browned the few and windworn flowers;
But there, where steel and concrete soar
In dizzy, geometric towers—

There, where the tapering cranes sweep round
And great wheels turn, and trains roar by
Like strong, low-headed brutes of steel—
There is my world, my home; yet why

So alien still? For I can neither
Dwell in that world, nor turn again
To scythe and spade, but only loiter
Among the trees the smoke has slain.

Yet when the trees were young, men still
Could choose their path—the wingèd soul,
Not cursed with double doubts, could fly,
Arrow-like to a foreseen goal;

And they who planned those soaring towers,
They too have set their spirit free;
To them their glittering world can bring
Faith, and accepted destiny;

But none to me as I stand here
Between two countries, both-ways torn,
And moveless still, like Buridan's donkey[1]
Between the water and the corn.

1. Buridan's ass (rather than donkey) died of starvation because, standing midpoint between two kinds of food, it could not decide which was the more attractive and so stood stockstill. This problem is attributed to Jean Buridan, French scholastic philosopher of the fourteenth century.

Introduction to the French Edition[1] of *Down and Out in Paris and London*

15 OCTOBER 1934

My kind translator[2] has asked me to write a short preface for the French edition of this book. As probably many of my French readers will wonder what chain of events brought me to Paris at the time when the incidents described in this book took place, I think it would be best to begin by giving them a few biographical details.

I was born in 1903. In 1922 I went to Burma where I joined the Indian Imperial Police. It was a job for which I was totally unsuited: so, at the beginning of 1928, while on leave in England, I gave in my resignation in the hopes of being able to earn my living by writing. I did just about as well at it as do most young people who take up a literary career—that is to say, not at all. My literary efforts in the first year barely brought me in twenty pounds.

In the spring of 1928 I set off for Paris so as to live cheaply while writing two novels[3]—which I regret to say were never published—and also to learn French. One of my Parisian friends found me a room in a cheap hotel in a working-class district which I have described briefly in the first chapter of this book, and which any sharp-witted Parisian will doubtless recognise. During the summer of 1929 I had written my two novels, which the publishers left on my hands, to find myself almost penniless and in urgent need of work. At that time it was not illegal—or at any rate not seriously illegal—for foreigners living in France to take jobs and it seemed more natural to me to stay in the city I was in, rather than return to

---

1. The English translation given here was by Shirley Jones and Sonia Orwell.
2. Orwell's English text of *Down and Out in Paris and London* was translated into French by René-Noël Raimbault (1882–1962) as *La Vache Enragée* (1935). Raimbault not only taught French Literature, Greek and Latin at the Lycée de Mans but had a distinguished earlier career as a wood engraver. He and Orwell exchanged twenty letters and post-cards – and little gifts. Orwell often wrote his letters in French. The letters were edited by Céline Place and Madeleine Renouard and published in a bi-lingual edition in Paris, 2006, the translations in English being the responsibility of Peter Davison who included the correspondence in French and English in *The Lost Orwell*. A selection of the letters is also included in *Orwell: A Life in Letters*.
3. The manuscript of neither novel survives. Writing to Michael Meyer on 12 March 1949 Orwell said, 'I simply destroyed my first novel after unsuccessfully submitting it to one publisher, for which I'm rather sorry now.'

England where, at the time, there were about two and a half million unemployed. So I stayed on in Paris and the events which I describe in this book took place towards the end of the autumn of 1929.

As for the truth of my story, I think I can say that I have exaggerated nothing except in so far as all writers exaggerate by selecting. I did not feel I had to describe events in the exact order in which they happened, but everything I have described did take place at one time or another. At the same time I have refrained, as far as possible, from drawing individual portraits of particular people. All the characters I have described in both parts of the book are intended more as representative types of the Parisian or Londoner of the class to which they belong than as individuals.

I should also add that this book makes no claims to giving a complete picture of life in Paris or London but only to portray one particular aspect. As almost without exception all the scenes and incidents in which I was involved have something repugnant about them it might seem that, without wishing to do so, I have given the impression that I think Paris and London are unpleasant cities. This was never my intention and if, at first sight, the reader should get this impression this is simply because the subject-matter of my book is essentially unattractive: my theme is poverty. When you haven't a penny in your pocket you are forced to see any city or country in its least favourable light and all human beings, or nearly all, appear to you either as fellow sufferers or as enemies. I want to emphasise this point particularly for my French readers because I would be distressed if they thought I have the least animosity towards a city of which I have very happy memories.

At the beginning of this preface I promised to give the reader some biographical details. So, for those it might interest, I will just add that after leaving Paris towards the end of 1929 I earned my living largely by teaching and in a small way by writing. Since the publication in England of *Down and Out in Paris and London*—the book here translated—I have written two novels, the second of which I have, indeed, just completed.[4] The first of these is due to be published in a day or two by a New York publishing house.[5]

4. *A Clergyman's Daughter.*
5. *Burmese Days*, published by Harper & Brothers, 25 October 1934.

Review: Kenneth Saunders, *The Ideals of East and West*

The Adelphi, DECEMBER 1934

This book consists of a series of lectures on the leading religious systems of the world, delivered to the Pacific School of Religion in Berkeley, California, and it is mainly wind. The most interesting parts of it are various analects from Chinese, Indian, Japanese, and other writings, including a number of popular proverbs. But even here there is a good deal that was not worth reproducing ('A youth, when at home, should be filial, and abroad, respectful to his elders'—Confucius), and I can think of at least three Oriental proverbs that have more meat in them than the great majority of those quoted. The book ends with an imaginary conversation between the representatives of five religions, who vie with one another in sentiments of dreary uplift.

Mr. Saunders's manner of writing is at times so like a parody of the familiar American Wisdom of the East stuff as to arouse the suspicion that he is doing it on purpose. Presumably he is not, but when one encounters, in the poem with which the book opens, a couplet like this:—

> That Love that transmutes pagan attitudes
> To something nearer the Beatitudes,

the suspicion is very hard to escape. This is the kind of book that brings both Asia and America into undeserved discredit.[1]

---

1. This was Orwell's last review to be published by *The Adelphi* as by Eric Blair. Hereafter all his contributions were signed 'George Orwell'. Orwell used pseudonyms when tramping and had considered publishing *Down and Out in Paris and London* anonymously. In an undated letter to his literary agent, Leonard Moore, probably of about 19 November 1932 (see *A Life in Letters*, pp. 22–3) he suggested three pseudonyms: Kenneth Miles, George Orwell, and H. Lewis Allways. He remarked, 'I rather favour George Orwell'. He thought George a very English name and the Orwell is a river near where his family lived at Southwold in Suffolk. The change was made for *Down and Out* but only intermittently for reviews and articles. In a radio broadcast of 6 July 1958, his friend and Literary Executor Sir Richard Rees (1900–70) said that Orwell once told him seeing his real name in print 'gave him an unpleasant feeling . . . because how can you be sure your enemy won't cut it out and work some kind of black magic on it?' – just whimsy according to Sir Richard: but 'you could not always be quite certain if he was serious or not'.

Review: Henry Miller, *Tropic of Cancer*

New English Weekly, 14 NOVEMBER 1935

New English Weekly *was founded in 1932 by A.R. Orage (1873–1934). It advertised itself as being concerned with public affairs, literature and the arts. Politically it supported the Social Credit Movement. That, according to C.H. Douglas (1879–1952), was motivated by the belief that 'systems were made for men, and not men for systems'.*

Modern man is rather like a bisected wasp which goes on sucking jam and pretends that the loss of its abdomen does not matter. It is some perception of this fact which brings books like *Tropic of Cancer* (for there will probably be more and more of them as time goes on) into being.

Tropic of Cancer is a novel, or perhaps rather a chunk of autobiography, about Americans in Paris—not the monied dilettante type, but the out-at-elbow, good-for-nothing type. There is much in it that is remarkable, but its most immediately noticeable and perhaps essential feature is its descriptions of sexual encounters. These are interesting not because of any pornographic appeal (quite the contrary), but because they make a definite attempt to get at real facts. They describe sexual life from the point of view of the man in the street—but, it must be admitted, rather a debased version of the man in the street. Nearly all the characters in the book are habitués of the brothel. They act and describe their action with a callous coarseness which is unparalleled in fiction, though common enough in real life. Taken as a whole, the book might even be called a vilification of human nature. As it may justly be asked what good is done by vilifying human nature, I must amplify the remark I made above.

One result of the breakdown of religious belief has been a sloppy idealization of the physical side of life. In a way this is natural enough. For if there is no life beyond the grave, it is obviously harder to face the fact that birth, copulation, etc., are in certain aspects disgusting. In the Christian centuries, of course, a pessimistic view of life was taken more or less for granted. 'Man that is born of woman hath but a short time to live and is full of misery,' says the Prayer Book, with the air of stating something obvious. But it is a different matter to admit that life is full of misery when you believe that the grave really finishes you. It is easier to comfort yourself with some kind of optimistic lie. Hence the tee-heeing brightness of *Punch*, hence Barrie and his bluebells, hence H. G. Wells

and his Utopiæ infested by nude school-marms. Hence, above all, the
monstrous soppification of the sexual theme in most of the fiction of the
past hundred years. A book like *Tropic of Cancer*, which deals with sex by
brutally insisting on the facts, swings the pendulum too far, no doubt,
but it does swing it in the right direction. Man is not a Yahoo, but he is
rather like a Yahoo and needs to be reminded of it from time to time.
All one asks of a book of this kind is that is shall do its job competently
and without snivelling—conditions that are satisfied in this case, I think.

Probably, although he chooses to describe ugly things, Mr. Miller would
not answer to the name of pessimist. He even has passages of rather
Whitmanesque enthusiasm for the process of life. What he seems to be
saying is that if one stiffens oneself by the contemplation of ugliness, one
ends by finding life not less but more worth living. From a literary point
of view his book is competent, though not dazzlingly so. It is firmly done,
with very few lapses into the typical modern slipshoddy. If it attracts
critical attention it will no doubt be coupled with *Ulysses*, quite wrongly.
Ulysses is not only a vastly better book, but also quite different in intention. Joyce is primarily an artist; Mr. Miller is a discerning though hard-
boiled person giving his opinions about life. I find his prose difficult to
quote because of the unprintable words which are scattered all over it,
but here is one sample:—

'When the tide is on the ebb and only a few syphilitic mermaids are
left stranded in the muck the Dome looks like a shooting gallery that's
been struck by a cyclone. Everything is slowly dribbling back to the sewer.
For about an hour there is a death-like calm during which the vomit is
mopped up. Suddenly the trees begin to screech. From one end of the
boulevard to the other a demented song rises up. It is the signal that
announces the close of the exchange. What hopes there were are swept
up. The moment has come to void the last bagful of urine. The day is
sneaking in like a leper. . . .'

There is a fine rhythm to that. The American language is less flexible
and refined than the English, but it has more life in it, perhaps. I do not
imagine that in *Tropic of Cancer* I have discovered the great novel of the
century, but I do think it a remarkable book, and I strongly advise anyone
who can get hold of a copy to have a look at it.

'Rudyard Kipling'

New English Weekly, 23 JANUARY 1936

On 31 January 1936 Orwell set out to travel to Wigan chiefly by bus but also walking many miles in order to examine conditions in the Depressed Areas. It was bitterly cold but after hearing that Rudyard Kipling had died on 18 January he made a long diversion, walking via Rudyard Lake (after which Kipling was named), and composed this tribute to him. He would later write a much more detailed assessment of Kipling which was published in Horizon *in February 1942.*

Rudyard Kipling was the only popular English writer of this century who was not at the same time a thoroughly bad writer. His popularity was, of course, essentially middle-class. In the average middle-class family before the War, especially in Anglo-Indian families, he had a prestige that is not even approached by any writer of to-day. He was a sort of household god with whom one grew up and whom one took for granted whether one liked him or whether one did not. For my own part I worshipped Kipling at thirteen, loathed him at seventeen, enjoyed him at twenty, despised him at twenty-five and now again rather admire him. The one thing that was never possible, if one had read him at all, was to forget him. Certain of his stories, for instance *The Strange Ride, Drums of the Fore and Aft* and *The Mark of the Beast*, are about as good as it is possible for that kind of story to be. They are, moreover, exceedingly well told. For the vulgarity of his prose style is only a surface fault; in the less obvious qualities of construction and economy he is supreme. It is, after all (see the 'Times Literary Supplement'), much easier to write inoffensive prose than to tell a good story. And his verse, though it is almost a by-word for badness, has the same peculiarly memorable quality.

'I've lost Britain, I've lost Gaul, 'I've lost Rome, and, worst of all, 'I've lost Lalage!'[1]

may be only a jingle, and *The Road to Mandalay* may be something worse

---

1. The Roman poet Horace professed his love for Lalage but more relevant here is that Lalage features prominently in Kipling's poem, 'Rimini – Marching Song of a Roman Legion of the Later Empire'.

than a jingle, but they do 'stay by one.' They remind one that it needs a streak of genius even to become a by-word.

What is much more distasteful in Kipling than sentimental plots or vulgar tricks of style, is the imperialism to which he chose to lend his genius. The most one can say is that when he made it the choice was more forgivable than it would be now. The imperialism of the 'eighties and 'nineties was sentimental, ignorant and dangerous, but it was not entirely despicable. The picture then called up by the word 'empire' was a picture of overworked officials and frontier skirmishes, not of Lord Beaverbrook and Australian butter. It was still possible to be an imperialist and a gentleman, and of Kipling's *personal* decency there can be no doubt. It is worth remembering that he was the most widely popular English writer of our time, and yet that no one, perhaps, so consistently refrained from making a vulgar show of his personality.

If he had never come under imperialist influences, and if he had developed, as he might well have done, into a writer of music-hall songs, he would have been a better and more lovable writer. In the rôle he actually chose, one was bound to think of him, after one had grown up, as a kind of enemy, a man of alien and perverted genius. But now that he is dead, I for one cannot help wishing that I could offer some kind of tribute—a salute of guns, if such a thing were available—to the story-teller who was so important to my childhood.

Review: Peter Fleming, *News from Tartary*

Time and Tide, 15 AUGUST 1936

According to Gordon Bowker in his George Orwell *(2003), Orwell was introduced to* Time and Tide *by Geoffrey Gorer (1905–85). He quotes from an unpublished letter to Brenda Salkeld of 2 May 1936 that the journal was his* bête noire *and added, 'You see [to] what depths one has to sink in the literary life' (p. 186).* Time and Tide *ran from 1920 to 1979. It was edited from 1926 by Margaret, Lady Rhondda, who, because it was loss-making, appears to have subsidised it. It began on the left but moved to the political right.*

A journey by train or car or aeroplane is not an event but an interregnum between events, and the swifter the vehicle the more boring the journey becomes. The nomad of the steppe or the desert may have to put up with every kind of discomfort, but at any rate he is living while he is travelling, and not, like the passengers in a luxury liner, merely suffering a temporary death. Mr. Peter Fleming, who set out from Pekin and travelled on horseback across Sinkiang and down into India via the Pamirs (a distance of well over two thousand miles) knows how to make this clear. His account of the frightful discomforts of the journey—the icy winds, the constant hunger, the impossibility of washing and the struggles with galled camels and exhausted ponies—so far from making one shudder and thank God for *confort moderne*, simply fill one with acute pangs of envy.

'We travelled for seventeen days with the Prince of Dzun. . . . There is something very reassuring about a big caravan. . . . There it wound, stately, methodical, through the bleak and empty land, 250 camels pacing in single file. At the head of it, leading the first string, usually rode an old woman on a white pony, a gnarled and withered crone whose conical fur-brimmed hat enhanced her resemblance to a witch. Scattered along the flanks, outriders to the main column, went forty or fifty horsemen. . . . The little ponies were dwarfed by the bulging sheepskins which encased their masters. Everyone carried, slung across his back, an ancient musket or a matchlock with a forked rest, and a few of the Chinese had repeating carbines, mostly from the arsenal at Taiyuanfu and all of an extremely unreliable appearance. Some people wore broadswords as well.'

The journey needed not only toughness but also supreme tact and cunning, for it was made through more or less forbidden territory and neither Mr. Fleming nor his companion (a girl) had a proper passport. There was also the language difficulty and the difficulties caused by some curious gaps in the equipment of the expedition. They had, for example, two portable type-writers (a frightful thing to have to drag across Central Asia) but only one frying pan. For food they had to depend largely on what they could shoot, and their only effective weapon was a .22 rook rifle. Mr. Fleming took the rifle in preference to a shotgun because it made less noise and the ammunition was less bulky; but it was a bold thing to do, for a rifle is not much use unless your game will obligingly sit still to be shot at. By the way, Mr. Fleming describes himself as killing an antelope with the .22 rifle at 400 yards. He says he paced the distance out; I can't help thinking (I only whisper this) that he may have taken rather short paces.

Mr. Fleming seems to have set out on the journey mainly for fun but partly to find out what was happening in Sinkiang. His conclusion is that the U.S.S.R. already controls part of the province and has designs on the rest, less from its own sake than as a strategic jumping-off place against Japanese expansion. It is noticeable that he seems to disapprove rather strongly of the U.S.S.R.'s new imperialistic ambitions. It is a queer tribute to the moral prestige of Communism that we are always rather shocked when we find that the Communists are no better than anybody else.

I prophesy without misgivings that this book will be a best-seller. Parts of it are very badly written—why do writers of travel-books spend so much time in trying to be funny?—but the fascinating material would outweigh far worse faults. The real achievement was not to write the book but to make the journey. And the photographs, mostly taken by Mr. Fleming himself, are so good and so numerous as to make twelve and sixpence a very low price for the book[1].

1. Peter Fleming was the elder brother of Ian Fleming, creator of James Bond.

'In Defence of the Novel'

New English Weekly, 12 and 19 NOVEMBER 1936

It hardly needs pointing out that at this moment the prestige of the novel is extremely low, so low that the words 'I never read novels,' which even a dozen years ago were generally uttered with a hint of apology are now *always* uttered in a tone of conscious pride. It is true that there are still a few contemporary or roughly contemporary novelists whom the intelligentsia consider it permissible to read; but the point is that the ordinary good-bad novel is habitually ignored while the ordinary good-bad book of verse or criticism is still taken seriously. This means that if you write novels you automatically command a less intelligent public than you would command if you had chosen some other form. There are two quite obvious reasons why this must presently make it impossible for good novels to be written. Even now the novel is visibly deteriorating, and it would deteriorate much faster if most novelists had any idea who reads their books. It is, of course, easy to argue (*vide* for instance Belloc's queerly rancorous essay[1]) that the novel is a contemptible form of art and that its fate does not matter. I doubt whether that opinion is even worth disputing. At any rate, I am taking it for granted that the novel is worth salvaging and that in order to salvage it you have got to persuade intelligent people to take it seriously. It is therefore worthwhile to analyse one of the main causes—in my opinion, *the* main cause—of the novel's lapse in prestige.

The trouble is that the novel is being shouted out of existence. Question any thinking person as to why he 'never reads novels,' and you will usually find that, at bottom, it is because of the disgusting tripe that is written by the blurb-reviewers. There is no need to multiply examples. Here is just one specimen, from last week's *Sunday Times*: 'If you can read this book and not shriek with delight, your soul is dead.' That or something like it is now being written about *every* novel published, as you can see by studying the quotes on the blurbs. For anyone who takes the *Sunday Times* seriously, life must be one long struggle to catch up. Novels are

---

1. Hilaire Belloc (1870–1953) wrote regularly for a number of journals; some of his essays were collected in a series of books. This reference may be to 'On People in Books', reprinted in *On Anything* (1920), essays originally in the *Morning Post* and *Morning Leader*. Here and elsewhere, Belloc shows a preference for historical writing over the novel.

being shot at you at the rate of fifteen a day, and every one of them an unforgettable masterpiece which you imperil your soul by missing. It must make it so difficult to choose a book at the library, and you must feel so guilty when you fail to shriek with delight. Actually, however, no one who matters is deceived by this kind of thing, and the contempt into which novel-reviewing has fallen is extended to novels themselves. When *all* novels are thrust upon you as works of genius, it is quite natural to assume that all of them are tripe. Within the literary intelligentsia this assumption is now taken for granted. To admit that you like novels is nowadays almost equivalent to admitting that you have a hankering after coconut ice or prefer Rupert Brooke to Gerard Manley Hopkins.

All this is obvious. What I think is rather less obvious is the way in which the present situation has arisen. On the face of it, the book-ramp is a quite simple and cynical swindle. Z writes a book which is published by Y and reviewed by X in the 'Weekly W.' If the review is a bad one Y will remove his advertisement, so X has to hand out 'unforgettable master-piece' or get the sack. Essentially that *is* the position, and novel-reviewing has sunk to its present death largely because every reviewer has some publisher or publishers twisting his tail by proxy. But the thing is not so crude as it looks. The various parties to the swindle are not consciously acting together, and they have been forced into their present position partly against their will.

To begin with, one ought not to assume, as is so often done (see for instance Beachcomber's column, *passim*), that the novelist enjoys and is even in some way responsible for the reviews he gets. Nobody *likes* being told that he has written a palpitating tale of passion which will last as long as the English language; though, of course, it is disappointing not to be told that, because all novelists are being told the same, and to be left out presumably means that your books won't sell. The hack-review is in fact a sort of commercial necessity, like the blurb on the dust-jacket, of which it is merely an extension. But even the wretched hack-reviewer is not to be blamed for the drivel he writes. In his special circumstances he could write nothing else. For even if there were no question of bribery, direct or indirect, there can be no such thing as good novel-criticism so long as it is assumed that *every novel is worth reviewing*.

A periodical gets its weekly wad of books and sends off a dozen of them to X, the hack-reviewer, who has a wife and family and has got to earn his guinea, not to mention the half-crown per vol. which he gets by selling his review copies. There are two reasons why it is totally impossible for X to tell the truth about the books he gets. To begin with, the chances are that eleven out of the twelve books will fail to rouse in him the faintest spark of interest. They are not more than ordinarily bad, they are merely neutral, lifeless and pointless. If he were not paid to do so he would never read a line of any of them, and in nearly every case the only truthful review he could write would be: 'This book inspires in me no thoughts whatever.' But will anyone pay you to write that kind of thing? Obviously not. As a start, therefore, X is in the false position of having to manufacture, say, three hundred words about a book which means nothing to him whatever. Usually he does it by giving a brief resumé of the plot (incidentally betraying to the author the fact that he hasn't read the book) and handing out a few compliments which for all their fulsomeness are about as valuable as the smile of a prostitute.

But there is a far worse evil than this. X is expected not only to say what a book is about but to give his opinion as to whether it is good or bad. Since X can hold a pen he is probably not a fool, at any rate not such a fool as to imagine that *The Constant Nymph* is the most terrific tragedy ever written. Very likely his own favourite novelist, if he cares for novels at all, is Stendhal, or Dickens, or Jane Austen, or D. H. Lawrence, or Dostoievski—or at any rate, someone immeasurably better than the ordinary run of contemporary novelists. He has got to start, therefore, by immensely lowering his standards. As I have pointed out elsewhere, to apply a decent standard to the ordinary run of novels is like weighing a flea on a spring-balance intended for elephants. On such a balance as that a flea would simply fail to register; you would have to start by constructing another balance which revealed the fact that there are big fleas and little fleas. And this approximately is what X does. It is no use monotonously saying, of book after book, 'This book is tripe,' because, once again, no one will pay you for writing that kind of thing. X has got to discover something which is *not* tripe, and pretty frequently, or get the sack. This means sinking his standards to a depth at which, say, Ethel M. Dell's *Way of an Eagle* is a fairly good book. But on a scale of values which makes *The Way of an Eagle* a good book, *The Constant Nymph* is a superb book, and *The Man of Property* is—what? A palpitating tale of passion, a terrific, soul-shattering masterpiece, an unforgettable epic which will last as long as the English language, and so on and so forth. (As for any *really* good book, it would burst the thermometer.) Having started with the assumption that all novels are good, the reviewer is driven ever upwards

on a topless ladder of adjectives. And *sic itur ad* Gould.[2] You can see
reviewer after reviewer going the same road. Within two years of starting
out with at any rate moderately honest intentions, he is proclaiming with
maniacal screams that Miss Barbara Bedworthy's[3] *Crimson Night* is the
most terrific, trenchant, poignant, unforgettable, of the earth earthy and
so forth masterpiece which has ever, etc., etc., etc. There is no way out
of it when you have once committed the initial sin of pretending that a
bad book is a good one. But you cannot review novels for a living without
committing that sin. And meanwhile every intelligent reader turns away,
disgusted, and to despise novels becomes a kind of snobbish duty. Hence
the queer fact that it is possible for a novel of real merit to escape notice,
merely because it has been praised in the same terms as tripe.

Various people have suggested that it would be all to the good if no
novels were reviewed at all. So it would, but the suggestion is useless,
because nothing of the kind is going to happen. No paper which depends
on publishers' advertisements can afford to throw them away, and though
the more intelligent publishers probably realise that they would be no
worse off if the blurb-review were abolished, they cannot put an end to
it for the same reason as the nations cannot disarm—because nobody
wants to be the first to start. For a long time yet the blurb-reviews are
going to continue, and they are going to grow worse and worse; the only
remedy is to contrive in some way that they shall be disregarded. But this
can only happen if somewhere or other there is decent novel-reviewing
which will act as a standard of comparison. That is to say, there is need
of just *one* periodical (one would be enough for a start) which makes a
speciality of novel-reviewing but refuses to take any notice of tripe, and
in which the reviewers *are* reviewers and not ventriloquists' dummies
clapping their jaws when the publisher pulls the string.

It may be answered that there are such periodicals already. There are
quite a number of highbrow magazines, for instance, in which the novel-
reviewing, what there is of it, is intelligent and not suborned. Yes, but
the point is that periodicals of that kind do not make a speciality of
novel-reviewing, and certainly make no attempt to keep abreast of the
current output of fiction. They belong to the highbrow world, the world

2. Gerald Gould (1885–1936) reviewed for *The Observer*.
3. Miss Bedworthy appears in *Keep the Aspidistra Flying, CW*, IV, 18. In a letter to Brenda
   Salkeld, 15 January 1935, Orwell says that because many women writers choose male
   pen-names he might choose a woman's name – such as Miss Barbara Bedworthy.

in which it is already assumed that novels, as such, are despicable. But the novel is a popular form of art, and it is no use to approach it with the *Criterion-Scrutiny* assumption that literature is a game of back-scratching (claws in or claws out according to circumstances) between tiny cliques of highbrows. The novelist is primarily a story-teller, and a man may be a very good story-teller (*vide* for instance Trollope, Charles Reade,[4] Mr. Somerset Maugham) without being in the narrow sense an 'intellectual.' Five thousand novels are published every year, and Ralph Straus[5] implores you to read all of them, or would if he had all of them to review. The *Criterion* probably deigns to notice a dozen. But between the dozen and the five thousand there may be a hundred or two hundred or even five hundred which at different levels have genuine merit, and it is on these that any critic who cares for the novel ought to concentrate.

But the first necessity is some method of *grading*. Great numbers of novels never ought to be mentioned at all (imagine for instance the awful effects on criticism if every serial in *Peg's Paper* had to be solemnly reviewed!), but even the ones that are worth mentioning belong to quite different categories. *Raffles* is a good book, and so is *The Island of Dr. Moreau*, and so is *La Chartreuse de Parme*, and so is *Macbeth*; but they are 'good' at very different levels: Similarly, *If Winter Comes* and *The Well-Beloved* and *An Unsocial Socialist* and *Sir Launcelot Greaves* are all bad books, but at different levels of 'badness.' This is the fact that the hack-reviewer has made it his special business to obscure. It ought to be possible to devise a system, perhaps quite a rigid one, of grading novels into classes A, B, C and so forth, so that whether a reviewer praised or damned a book, you would at least know how seriously he meant it to be taken. As for the reviewers, they would have to be people who really cared for the art of the novel (and that means, probably, neither highbrows nor lowbrows nor midbrows, but elastic-brows), people interested in technique and still more interested in discovering what a book is *about*. There are plenty of such people in existence; some of the very worst of the hack-reviewers, though now past praying for, started like that, as you can see

4. Charles Reade (1814–84) was a dramatist and reforming novelist much admired by Orwell. He was concerned with, for example, contemporary abuses in the prison and asylum systems. Orwell described *A Jack of All Trades* (1858) and *The Autobiography of a Thief* (also 1858) as 'brilliant long-short stories'. Reade is probably still best known for his novel *The Cloister and the Hearth* (1861).
5. Ralph Straus (1882–1950) was chief fiction reviewer for the *Sunday Times* from 1928 until his death.

by glancing at their earlier work. Incidentally, it would be a good thing if more novel-reviewing were done by amateurs. A man who is not a practised writer but has just read a book which has deeply impressed him is more likely to tell you what it is *about* than a competent but bored professional. That is why American reviews, for all their stupidity, are better than English ones; they are more amateurish, that is to say, more serious.

I believe that in some such way as I have indicated the prestige of the novel could be restored. The essential need is a paper that would keep abreast of current fiction and yet refuse to sink its standards. It would have to be an obscure paper, for the publishers would not advertise in it; on the other hand, once they had discovered that somewhere there was praise that was real praise, they would be ready enough to quote it on their blurbs. Even if it were a very obscure paper it would probably cause the general level of novel-reviewing to rise, for the drivel in the Sunday papers only continues because there is nothing with which to contrast it. But even if the blurb-reviewers continued exactly as before, it would not matter so long as there also existed decent reviewing to remind a few people that serious brains can still occupy themselves with the novel. For just as the Lord promised that he would not destroy Sodom if ten right-eous men could be found there, so the novel will not be utterly despised while it is known that somewhere or other there is even a handful of novel-reviewers with no straws in their hair.

At present, if you care about novels and still more if you write them, the outlook is depressing in the extreme. The word 'novel' calls up the words 'blurb,' 'genius' and 'Ralph Straus' as automatically as 'chicken' calls up 'bread sauce.' Intelligent people avoid novels almost instinctively; as a result, established novelists go to pieces and beginners who 'have something to say' turn in preference to almost any other form. The degeneration that must follow is obvious. Look for instance at the fourpenny novelettes that you see piled up on any cheap stationer's counter. These things are the decadent off-spring of the novel, bearing the same relation to *Manon Lescaut* and *David Copperfield* as the lap-dog bears to the wolf. It is quite likely that before long the average novel will be not much different from the fourpenny novelette, though doubtless it will still appear in a seven and sixpenny binding and amid a flourish of publishers' trumpets. Various people have prophesied that the novel is doomed to disappear in the near future. I do not believe that it will disap-pear, for reasons which would take too long to set forth but which are fairly obvious. It is much likelier, if the best literary brains cannot be induced to return to it, to survive in some perfunctory, despised and hopelessly degenerate form, like modern tomb-stones, or the Punch and Judy show.

Poem: 'A happy vicar I might have been'

The Adelphi, DECEMBER 1936

A happy vicar I might have been
Two hundred years ago,
To preach upon eternal doom
And watch my walnuts grow;

But born, alas, in an evil time,
I missed that pleasant haven,
For the hair has grown on my upper lip
And the clergy are all clean-shaven.

And later still the times were good,
We were so easy to please,
We rocked our troubled thoughts to sleep
On the bosoms of the trees.

All ignorant we dared to own
The joys we now dissemble;
The greenfinch on the apple bough
Could make my enemies tremble.

But girls' bellies and apricots,
Roach in a shaded stream,
Horses, ducks in flight at dawn,
All these are a dream.

It is forbidden to dream again;
We maim our joys or hide them;
Horses are made of chromium steel
And little fat men shall ride them.

I am the worm who never turned,[1]
The eunuch without a harem;
Between the priest and the commissar
I walk like Eugene Aram;[2]

And the commissar is telling my fortune
While the radio plays,
But the priest has promised an Austin Seven,[3]
For Duggie always pays.[4]

I dreamed I dwelt in marble halls,
And woke to find it true;
I wasn't born for an age like this;
Was Smith? Was Jones? Were you?

1. 'The smallest worm will turn, being trodden on', 3 Henry VI, 2. 2. 17.
2. Eugene Aram was a schoolmaster of some learning and good repute in Knaresborough, Yorkshire. In 1745 he murdered a man named Clark, but the murder was not discovered until 1758. Aram was arrested while teaching a class, tried, and executed in 1759. Thomas Hood (a favourite of Orwell's) wrote a poem, 'The Dream of Eugene Aram', in 1829. Three years later Edward Bulwer-Lytton based a novel on the incident.
3. The Austin Seven was the first successful small family car produced in Britain. The seven refers to the horsepower of its engine.
4. This is a corruption of an advertising slogan for the bookmaker Douglas Stuart: 'Duggie never owes.'

'Spilling the Spanish Beans'

New English Weekly, 29 JULY **and** 2 SEPTEMBER 1937

On 15 December 1935 Orwell sent his literary agent, Leonard Moore (?–1959), the typescript of The Road to Wigan Pier. *Four days later, his publisher, Victor Gollancz (1893–1967) sent him a telegram asking him to call at his offices on 21 December to discuss the book's publication. Orwell tried to enlist the help of Harry Pollitt (1890–1960), Secretary-General of the Communist Party, in getting to Spain to fight on behalf of those opposing the forces commanded by General Francisco Franco (1892–1975). Pollitt deemed Orwell 'unreliable' and refused his help but did advise him to obtain a safe conduct from the Spanish Embassy. Orwell arrived in Barcelona about 26 December and joined the Independent Labour Party contingent fighting with the POUM (the Partido Obrero de Unificación Marxista – the Revolutionary (Anti-Stalinist) Communist Party). His experiences in Spain, his being wounded in the throat, sought by the Communists, and his escape to France in June 1937 are the subject matter of* Homage to Catalonia. *He wrote prolifically about this experience, and about its implications for society generally, starting with this essay, 'Spilling the Spanish Beans'. The Spanish Civil War, together with the experiences described in* The Road to Wigan Pier, *had the most profound influence on him, his politics, and his writing. For a fuller account see* Orwell in Spain, *ed. Peter Davison, Penguin Books, 2001.*

I

The Spanish war has probably produced a richer crop of lies than any event since the Great War of 1914–18, but I honestly doubt, in spite of all those hecatombs of nuns who have been raped and crucified before the eyes of *Daily Mail* reporters, whether it is the pro-Fascist newspapers that have done the most harm. It is the left-wing papers, the *News Chronicle* and the *Daily Worker*, with their far subtler methods of distortion, that have prevented the British public from grasping the real nature of the struggle.

The fact which these papers have so carefully obscured is that the Spanish Government (including the semi-autonomous Catalan Government) is far more afraid of the revolution than of the Fascists. It is now almost certain that the war will end with some kind of compromise, and there is even reason to doubt whether the Government, which let Bilbao fall without raising a finger, wishes to be too victorious; but there is no doubt whatever about the thoroughness with which it is crushing its own revolutionaries. For some time past a reign of terror—forcible suppression of political parties, a stifling censorship of the Press, ceaseless espionage and mass-imprisonment without trial—has been in progress. When I left Barcelona in late June the jails were bulging; indeed, the regular jails had long since overflowed and the prisoners were being huddled into empty shops and any other temporary dump that could be found for them. But the point to notice is that the people who are in prison now are not Fascists but revolutionaries; they are there not because their opinions are too much to the Right, but because they are too much to the Left. And the people responsible for putting them there are those dreadful revolutionaries at whose very name Garvin[1] quakes in his goloshes —the Communists.

Meanwhile the war against Franco continues, but, except for the poor devils in the front-line trenches, nobody in Government Spain thinks of it as the real war. The real struggle is between revolution and counter-revolution; between the workers who are vainly trying to hold on to a little of what they won in 1936, and the Liberal-Communist bloc who are so successfully taking it away from them. It is unfortunate that so few people in England have yet caught up with the fact that Communism is now a counter-revolutionary force; that Communists everywhere are in alliance with bourgeois reformism and using the whole of their powerful machinery to crush or discredit any party that shows signs of revolutionary tendencies. Hence the grotesque spectacle of Communists assailed as wicked 'Reds' by right-wing intellectuals who are in essential agreement with them. Mr. Wyndham Lewis,[2] for instance, ought to love the Communists, at least temporarily. In Spain the Communist-Liberal alliance has been almost completely victorious. Of all that the Spanish workers won for themselves in 1936 nothing solid remains, except for a few collective farms and a certain amount of land seized by the peasants last year; and presumably even the peasants will be sacrificed later, when there is no longer any need to placate them. To see how the present situation arose, one has got to look back to the origins of the civil war.

Franco's bid for power differed from those of Hitler and Mussolini in

---

1. J.L. Garvin (1868–1947) was the right-wing editor of *The Observer*, 1908–42.
2. Percy Wyndham Lewis (1882–1957) was a painter, author, satirist, and critic. His review, *Blast* (1914 and 1915), espoused Vorticism. He supported Franco and flirted with Nazism, recanting in 1939; see *Time and Tide*, 17 January and 14 February 1939, and *The Hitler Cult, and How it will End* (1939). In Orwell's words, 'Lewis attacked everyone in turn; indeed, his reputation as a writer rests largely on these attacks.'

that it was a military insurrection, comparable to a foreign invasion, and therefore had not much mass backing, though Franco has since been trying to acquire one. Its chief supporters, apart from certain sections of Big Business, were the land-owning aristocracy and the huge, parasitic Church. Obviously a rising of this kind will array against it various forces which are not in agreement on any other point. The peasant and the worker hate feudalism and clericalism; but so does the 'liberal' bourgeois, who is not in the least opposed to a more modern version of Fascism, at least so long as it isn't called Fascism. The 'liberal' bourgeois is genuinely liberal up to the point where his own interests stop. He stands for the degree of progress implied in the phrase 'la carrière ouverte aux talents.' For clearly he has no chance to develop in a feudal society where the worker and the peasant are too poor to buy goods, where industry is burdened with huge taxes to pay for bishops vestments, and where every lucrative job is given as a matter of course to the friend of the catamite of the duke's illegitimate son. Hence, in the face of such a blatant reactionary as Franco, you get for a while a situation in which the worker and the bourgeois, in reality deadly enemies, are fighting side by side. This uneasy alliance is known as the Popular Front (or, in the Communist Press, to give it a spuriously democratic appeal, People's Front). It is a combination with about as much vitality, and about as much right to exist, as a pig with two heads or some other Barnum and Bailey monstrosity.

In any serious emergency the contradiction implied in the Popular Front is bound to make itself felt. For even when the worker and the bourgeois are both fighting against Fascism, they are not fighting for the same things; the bourgeois is fighting for bourgeois democracy, *i.e.*, capitalism, the worker, in so far as he understands the issue, for Socialism. And in the early days of the revolution the Spanish workers understood the issue very well. In the areas where Fascism was defeated they did not content themselves with driving the rebellious troops out of the towns; they also took the opportunity of seizing land and factories and setting up the rough beginnings of a workers' government by means of local committees, workers' militias, police forces, and so forth. They made the mistake, however (possibly because most of the active revolutionaries were Anarchists with a mistrust of all parliaments), of leaving the Republican Government in nominal control. And, in spite of various changes in personnel, every subsequent Government had been of approximately the same bourgeois-reformist character. At the beginning this seemed not to matter, because the Government, especially in Catalonia, was almost powerless and the bourgeoisie had to lie low or even (this was still happening when I reached Spain in December) to disguise themselves as workers. Later, as power slipped from the hands of the Anarchists into the hands of the Communists and right-wing Socialists, the Government was able to reassert itself, the bourgeoisie came out of hiding and the old division of society into rich and poor reappeared, not much modified. Henceforward every move, except a few dictated by military emergency, was directed towards undoing the work of the first few months of revolution. Out of the many illustrations I could choose, I will cite only one, the breaking-up of the old workers' militias, which were organised on a genuinely democratic system, with officers and men receiving the same pay and mingling on terms of complete equality, and the substitution of the Popular Army (once again, in Communist jargon, 'People's Army'), modelled as far as possible on an ordinary bourgeois army, with a privileged officer-caste, immense differences of pay, etc., etc. Needless to say, this is given out as a military necessity, and almost certainly it does make for military efficiency, at least for a short period. But the undoubted purpose of the change was to strike a blow at equalitarianism. In every department the same policy has been followed, with the result that only a year after the outbreak of war and revolution you get what is in effect an ordinary bourgeois State, with, in addition, a reign of terror to preserve the status quo.

This process would probably have gone less far if the struggle could have taken place without foreign interference. But the military weakness of the Government made this impossible. In the face of Franco's foreign mercenaries they were obliged to turn to Russia for help, and though the quantity of arms supplied by Russia has been greatly exaggerated (in my first three months in Spain I saw only one Russian weapon, a solitary machine-gun), the mere fact of their arrival brought the Communists into power. To begin with, the Russian aeroplanes and guns, and the good military qualities of the International Brigades (not necessarily Communist but under Communist control), immensely raised the Communist prestige. But, more important, since Russia and Mexico were the only countries openly supplying arms, the Russians were able not only to get money for their weapons, but to extort terms as well. Put in their crudest form, the terms were: 'Crush the revolution or you get no more arms.' The reason usually given for the Russian attitude is that if Russia appeared to be abetting the revolution, the Franco-Soviet pact (and the hoped-for alliance with Great Britain) would be imperilled; it may be, also, that the spectacle of a genuine revolution in Spain would rouse unwanted echoes in Russia. The Communists, of course, deny that any direct pressure has been exerted by the Russian Government. But this, even if true, is hardly relevant, for the Communist Parties of all countries can be taken as carrying out Russian policy; and it is certain that the Spanish Communist Party, plus the right-wing Socialists whom they control, plus the Communist Press of the whole world, have used all their immense and ever-increasing influence upon the side of counter-revolution.

II

In the first half of this article I suggested that the real struggle in Spain, on the Government side, has been between revolution and counter-revolution; that the Government, though anxious enough to avoid being beaten by Franco, has been even more anxious to undo the revolutionary changes with which the outbreak of war was accompanied.

Any Communist would reject this suggestion as mistaken or wilfully dishonest. He would tell you that it is nonsense to talk of the Spanish Government crushing the revolution, because the revolution never happened; and that our job at present is to defeat Fascism and defend democracy. And in this connection it is most important to see just how the Communist anti-revolutionary propaganda works. It is a mistake to think that this has no relevance in England, where the Communist Party is small and comparatively weak. We shall see its relevance quickly enough if England enters into an alliance with the U.S.S.R.; or perhaps even earlier, for the influence of the Communist Party is bound to increase—visibly is increasing—as more and more of the capitalist class realise that latter-day Communism is playing their game.

Broadly speaking, Communist propaganda depends upon terrifying people with the (quite real) horrors of Fascism. It also involves pretending —not in so many words, but by implication—that Fascism has nothing to do with capitalism. Fascism is just a kind of meaningless wickedness, an aberration, 'mass sadism,' the sort of thing that would happen if you suddenly let loose an asylum full of homicidal maniacs. Present Fascism in this form, and you can mobilise public opinion against it, at any rate for a while, without provoking any revolutionary movement. You can oppose Fascism by bourgeois 'democracy,' meaning capitalism. But meanwhile you have got to get rid of the troublesome person who points out that Fascism and bourgeois 'democracy' are Tweedledum and Tweedledee.

You do it at the beginning by calling him an impracticable visionary. You tell him that he is confusing the issue, that he is splitting the anti-Fascist forces, that this is not the moment for revolutionary phrase-mongering, that for the moment we have got to fight against Fascism without enquiring too closely what we are fighting *for*. Later, if he still refuses to shut up, you change your tune and call him a traitor. More exactly, you call him a Trotskyist.

And what is a Trotskyist? This terrible word—in Spain at this moment you can be thrown into jail and kept there indefinitely, without trial, on the mere rumour that you are a Trotskyist—is only beginning to be bandied to and fro in England. We shall be hearing more of it later. The word 'Trotskyist' (or 'Trotsky-Fascist;') is generally used to mean a disguised Fascist who poses as an ultra-revolutionary in order to split the Left-wing forces. But it derives its peculiar power from the fact that it means three separate things. It can mean one who, like Trotsky, wishes for world-revolution; or a member of the actual organization of which Trotsky is head (the only legitimate use of the word); or the disguised Fascist already mentioned. The three meanings can be telescoped one into the other at will. Meaning No. 1 may or may not carry with it meaning No. 2, and meaning No. 2 almost invariably carries with it meaning No. 3. Thus: 'XY. has been heard to speak favourably of world-revolution; therefore he is a Trotskyist; therefore he is a Fascist.' In Spain, to some extent even in England, *anyone* professing revolutionary Socialism (*i.e.*, professing the things the Communist Party professed until a few years ago) is under suspicion of being a Trotskyist in the pay of Franco or Hitler.

The accusation is a very subtle one, because in any given case, unless one happened to know the contrary, it might be true. A Fascist spy prob-ably *would* disguise himself as a revolutionary. In Spain, everyone whose opinions are to the Left of those of the Communist Party is sooner or later discovered to be a Trotskyist, or at least, a traitor. At the beginning of the war the P.O.U.M., an Opposition Communist party roughly corre-sponding to the English I.L.P., was an accepted party and supplied a minister to the Catalan Government; later it was expelled from the Government; then it was denounced as Trotskyist; then it was suppressed, every member that the police could lay their hands on being flung into jail.

Until a few months ago the Anarcho-Syndicalists were described as 'working loyally' beside the Communists. Then the Anarcho-Syndicalists were levered out of the Government; then it appeared that they were not working so loyally; now they are in the process of becoming traitors. After that will come the turn of the Left-wing Socialists. Caballero, the Left-wing Socialist ex-premier, until May, 1937, the idol of the Communist Press, is already in outer darkness, a Trotskyist and 'enemy of the people.' And so the game continues. The logical end is a régime in which every opposition party and newspaper is suppressed and every dissentient of any importance is in jail. Of course, such a régime will be Fascism. It will not be the same as the Fascism Franco would impose, it will even be better than Franco's Fascism to the extent of being worth fighting for, but it will be Fascism. Only, being operated by Communists and Liberals, it will be called something different.

Meanwhile, can the war be won? The Communist influence has been against revolutionary chaos and has therefore, apart from the Russian aid, tended to produce greater military efficiency. If the Anarchists saved the Government from August to October, 1936, the Communists have saved it from October onwards. But in organizing the defence they have succeeded in killing enthusiasm (inside Spain, not outside). They made a militarized conscript army possible, but they also made it necessary. It is significant that as early as January of this year voluntary recruiting had practically ceased. A revolutionary army can sometimes win by enthusiasm, but a conscript army has got to win with weapons, and it is unlikely that the Government will ever have a large preponderance of arms unless France intervenes or unless Germany and Italy decide to make off with the Spanish colonies and leave Franco in the lurch. On the whole, a deadlock seems the likeliest thing.

And does the Government seriously intend to win? It does not intend to lose, that is certain. On the other hand, an outright victory, with Franco in flight and the Germans and Italians driven into the sea, would raise difficult problems, some of them too obvious to need mentioning. There is no real evidence and one can only judge by the event, but I suspect that what the Government is playing for is a compromise that would leave the war-situation essentially in being. All prophecies are wrong, therefore this one will be wrong, but I will take a chance and say that though the war may end quite soon or may drag on for years, it will end with Spain divided up, either by actual frontiers or into economic zones. Of course, such a compromise might be claimed as a victory by either side, or by both.

All that I have said in this article would seem entirely commonplace in Spain, or even in France. Yet in England, in spite of the intense interest the Spanish war has aroused, there are very few people who have even heard of the enormous struggle that is going on behind the Government lines. Of course, this is no accident. There has been a quite deliberate conspiracy (I could give detailed instances) to prevent the Spanish situation from being understood. People who ought to know better have lent themselves to the deception on the ground that if you tell the truth about Spain it will be used as Fascist propaganda.

It is easy to see where such cowardice leads. If the British public had been given a truthful account of the Spanish war they would have had an opportunity of learning what Fascism is and how it can be combatted. As it is, the *News Chronicle* version of Fascism as a kind of homicidal mania peculiar to Colonel Blimps bombinating in the economic void has been established more firmly than ever. And thus we are one step nearer to the great war 'against Fascism' (cf. 1914, 'against militarism') which will allow Fascism, British variety, to be slipped over our necks during the first week.

Review: Franz Borkenau, *The Spanish Cockpit*

Time and Tide, 31 JULY 1937

Dr. Borkenau has performed a feat which is very difficult at this moment for anyone who knows what is going on in Spain; he has written a book about the Spanish war without losing his temper. Perhaps I am rash in saying that it is the best book yet written on the subject, but I believe that anyone who has recently come from Spain will agree with me. After that horrible atmosphere of espionage and political hatred it is a relief to come upon a book which sums the situation up as calmly and lucidly as this.

Dr. Borkenau is a sociologist and not connected with any political party. He went to Spain with the purpose of doing some 'field work' upon a country in revolution, and he made two trips, the first in August, the second in January. In the difference between those two periods, especially the difference in the social atmosphere, the essential history of the Spanish revolution is contained. In August the Government was almost powerless, local soviets were functioning everywhere and the Anarchists were the main revolutionary force; as a result everything was in terrible chaos, the churches were still smouldering and suspected Fascists were being shot in large numbers, but there was everywhere a belief in the revolution, a feeling that the bondage of centuries had been broken. By January power had passed, though not so completely as later, from the Anarchists to the Communists, and the Communists were using every possible method, fair and foul, to stamp out what was left of the revolution. The pre-revolutionary police-forces had been restored, political espionage was growing keener and keener, and it was not long before Dr. Borkenau found himself in jail. Like the majority of political prisoners in Spain, he was never even told what he was accused of; but he was luckier than most in being released after a few days, and even (very few people have managed this lately) saving his documents from the hands of the police. His book ends with a series of essays upon various aspects of the war and the revolution. Anyone who wants to understand the Spanish situation should read the really brilliant final chapter, entitled 'Conclusions.'

The most important fact that has emerged from the whole business is that the Communist Party is now (presumably for the sake of Russian foreign policy) an anti-revolutionary force. So far from pushing the Spanish Government further towards the Left, the Communist influence has pulled it violently towards the Right. Dr. Borkenau, who is not a revolutionary himself, does not particularly regret this fact; what he does object to is that it is being deliberately concealed. The result is that public opinion throughout Europe still regards the Communists as wicked Reds or heroic revolutionaries as the case may be, while in Spain itself—

> It is at present impossible . . . to discuss openly even the basic facts of the political situation. The fight between the revolutionary and non-revolutionary principle, as embodied in Anarchists and Communists respectively, is inevitable, because fire and water cannot mix. . . . But as the Press is not even allowed to mention it, nobody is fully aware of the position, and the political antagonism breaks through, not in open fight to win over public opinion, but in backstairs intrigues, assassinations by Anarchist bravos, legal assassinations by Communist police, subdued allusions, rumours. . . . The concealment of the main political facts from the public and the maintenance of this deception by means of censorship and terrorism carries with it far-reaching detrimental effects, which will be felt in the future even more than at present.

If that was true in February, how much truer it is now! When I left Spain in late June the atmosphere in Barcelona, what with the ceaseless arrests, the censored newspapers and the prowling hordes of armed police, was like a nightmare.

Response to 'Authors Take Sides on the Spanish War'

unpublished, 3–6 AUGUST 1937

In June 1937 Left Review *solicited responses from authors, seeking that they take sides on the Spanish Civil War. A left-wing publisher issued the responses in a leaflet in December 1937. Orwell responded vitriolically but his attitude was in part – possibly a large part – a result of news he had had from his friend and commandant, George Kopp (1902–51), regarding the terrible conditions prisoners held by the Communists were undergoing. Orwell's response may appear tactless but it accurately reflects the bitterness and despair he felt about what his colleagues were suffering at the hands of their alleged allies, the Communists.*

Will you please stop sending me this bloody rubbish. This is the second or third time I have had it. I am not one of your fashionable pansies like Auden and Spender, I was six months in Spain, most of the time fighting, I have a bullet-hole in me at present and I am not going to write blah about defending democracy or gallant little anybody. Moreover, I know what is happening and has been happening on the Government side for months past, i.e. that Fascism is being rivetted on the Spanish workers under the pretext of resisting Fascism; also that since May a reign of terror has been proceeding and all the jails and any place that will serve as a jail are crammed with prisoners who are not only imprisoned without trial but are half-starved, beaten and insulted. I dare say you know it too, though God knows anyone who could write the stuff overleaf would be fool enough to believe anything, even the war-news in the *Daily Worker*. But the chances are that you—whoever you are who keep sending me this thing—have money and are well-informed; so no doubt you know something about the inner history of the war and have deliberately joined in the defence of 'democracy' (i.e. capitalism) racket in order to aid in crushing the Spanish working class and thus indirectly defend your dirty little dividends.

This is more than 6 lines, but if I did compress what I know and think about the Spanish war into 6 lines you wouldn't print it. You wouldn't have the guts.

By the way, tell your pansy friend Spender that I am preserving specimens of his war-heroics and that when the time comes when he squirms for shame at having written it, as the people who wrote the war-propaganda in the Great War are squirming now, I shall rub it in good and hard.

'The Lure of Profundity'

New English Weekly, 30 DECEMBER 1937

There is one way of avoiding thoughts, and that is to think too deeply. Take any reasonably true generalization—that women have no beards, for instance—twist it about, stress the exceptions, raise side-issues, and you can presently disprove it, or at any rate shake it, just as, by pulling a table-cloth into its separate threads, you can plausibly deny that it is a table-cloth. There are many writers who constantly do this, in one way or another. Keyserling is an obvious example. Who has not read a few pages by Keyserling? And who has read a whole book by Keyserling? He is constantly saying illuminating things—producing paragraphs which, taken separately, make you exclaim that this is a very remarkable mind —and yet he gets you no forrarder. His mind is moving in too many directions, starting too many hares at once. It is rather the same with Señor Ortega y Gasset, whose book of essays, *Invertebrate Spain*, has just been translated and reprinted.

Take, for instance, this passage which I select almost at random:—

'Each race carries within its own primitive soul an ideal of landscape which it tries to realize within its own borders. Castile is terribly arid because the Castilian is arid. Our race has accepted the dryness about it because it was akin to the inner wastes of its own soul.'

It is an interesting idea, and there is something similar on every page. Moreover, one is conscious all through the book of a sort of detachment, an intellectual decency, which is much rarer nowadays than mere cleverness. And yet, after all, what is it *about*? It is a series of essays, mostly written about 1920, on various aspects of the Spanish character. The blurb on the dust-jacket claims that it will make clear to us 'what lies behind the Spanish civil war.' It does not make it any clearer to me. Indeed, I cannot find any general conclusion in the book whatever.

What is Señor Ortega y Gasset's explanation of his country's troubles? The Spanish soul, tradition, Roman history, the blood of the degenerate Visigoths, the influence of geography on man and (as above) of man on geography, the lack of intellectually eminent Spaniards—and so forth. I am always a little suspicious of writers who explain everything in terms of blood, religion, the solar plexus, national souls and what not, because it is obvious that they are avoiding something. The thing that they are avoiding is the dreary Marxian 'economic' interpretation of history. Marx is a difficult author to read, but a crude version of his doctrine is believed in by millions and is in the consciousness of all of us. Socialists of every school can churn it out like a barrel-organ. It is so simple! If you hold such-and-such opinions it is because you have such-and-such an amount of money in your pocket. It is also blatantly untrue in detail, and many writers of distinction have wasted time in attacking it. Señor Ortega y Gasset has a page or two on Marx and makes at least one criticism that starts an interesting train of thought.

But if the 'economic' theory of history is merely untrue, as the flat-earth theory is untrue, why do they bother to attack it? Because it is *not* altogether untrue, in fact, is quite true enough to make every thinking person uncomfortable. Hence the temptation to set up rival theories which often involve ignoring obvious facts. The central trouble in Spain is, and must have been for decades past, plain enough: the frightful contrast of wealth and poverty. The blurb on the dust-jacket of 'Invertebrate Spain' declares that the Spanish war is 'not a class struggle,' when it is perfectly obvious that it is very largely that. With a starving peasantry, absentee landlords owning estates the size of English counties, a rising discontented bourgeoisie and a labour movement that had been driven underground by persecution, you had material for all the civil wars you wanted. But that sounds too like the records on the Socialist gramophone! Don't let's talk about the Andalusian peasants starving on two pesetas a day and the children with sore heads begging round the food-shops. If there is something wrong with Spain, let's blame it on the Visigoths.

The result—I should really say the *method*—of such an evasion is excess of intellectuality. The over-subtle mind raises too many side-issues. Thought becomes fluid, runs in all directions, forms memorable lakes and puddles, but gets nowhere. I can recommend this book to anybody, just as a book to read. It is undoubtedly the product of a distinguished mind. But it is no use hoping that it will explain the Spanish civil war. You would get a better explanation from the dullest doctrinaire Socialist, Communist, Anarchist, Fascist or Catholic.

Review: Eugene Lyons, *Assignment in Utopia*

New English Weekly, 9 JUNE 1938

To get the full sense of our ignorance as to what is really happening in the U.S.S.R., it is worth trying to translate the most sensational Russian event of the past two years, the Trotskyist trials, into English terms. Make the necessary adjustments, let Left be Right and Right be Left, and you get something like this:

Mr. Winston Churchill, now in exile in Portugal, is plotting to overthrow the British Empire and establish Communism in England. By the use of unlimited Russian money he has succeeded in building up a huge Churchillite organisation which includes members of Parliament, factory managers, Roman Catholic bishops and practically the whole of the Primrose League. Almost every day some dastardly act of sabotage is laid bare—sometimes a plot to blow up the House of Lords, sometimes an outbreak of foot and mouth disease in the Royal racing-stables. Eighty per cent. of the Beefeaters at the Tower are discovered to be agents of the Comintern. A high official of the Post Office admits brazenly to having embezzled postal orders to the tune of £5,000,000, and also to having committed *lèse majesté* by drawing moustaches on postage stamps. Lord Nuffield, after a 7-hour interrogation by Mr. Norman Birkett, confesses that ever since 1920 he has been fomenting strikes in his own factories. Casual half-inch paras in every issue of the newspapers announce that fifty more Churchillite sheep-stealers have been shot in Westmorland or that the proprietress of a village shop in the Cotswolds has been transported to Australia for sucking the bullseyes and putting them back in the bottle. And meanwhile the Churchillites (or Churchillite-Harmsworthites as they are called after Lord Rothermere's execution) never cease from proclaiming that it is *they* who are the real defenders of Capitalism and that Chamberlain and the rest of his gang are no more than a set of Bolsheviks in disguise.

Anyone who has followed the Russian trials knows that this is scarcely a parody. The question arises, could anything like this happen in England? Obviously it could not. From our point of view the whole thing is not merely incredible as a genuine conspiracy, it is next door to incredible as a frame-up. It is simply a dark mystery, of which the only seizable fact —sinister enough in its way—is that Communists over here regard it as a good advertisement for Communism.

Meanwhile the truth about Stalin's régime, if we could only get hold of it, is of the first importance. Is it Socialism, or is it a peculiarly vicious form of state-capitalism? All the political controversies that have made life hideous for two years past really circle round this question, though for several reasons it is seldom brought into the foreground. It is difficult to go [to] Russia, once there it is impossible to make adequate investigations, and all one's ideas on the subject have to be drawn from books which are so fulsomely 'for' or so venomously 'against' that the prejudice stinks a mile away. Mr. Lyons's book is definitely in the 'against' class, but he gives the impression of being much more reliable than most. It is obvious from his manner of writing that he is not a vulgar propagandist, and he was in Russia a long time (1928–34) as correspondent for the United Press Agency, having been sent there on Communist recommendation. Like many others who have gone to Russia full of hope he was gradually disillusioned, and unlike some others he finally decided to tell the truth about it. It is an unfortunate fact that any hostile criticism of the present Russian regime is liable to be taken as propaganda *against Socialism*; all Socialists are aware of this, and it does not make for honest discussion.

The years that Mr. Lyons spent in Russia were years of appalling hardship, culminating in the Ukraine famine of 1933, in which a number estimated at not less than three million people starved to death. Now, no doubt, after the success of the Second Five Year Plan,[1] the physical conditions have improved, but there seems no reason for thinking that the social atmosphere is greatly different. The system that Mr. Lyons describes does not seem to be very different from Fascism. All real power is concentrated in the hands of two or three million people, the town proletariat, theoretically the heirs of the revolution, having been robbed even of the elementary right to strike; more recently, by the introduction of the internal passport system, they have been reduced to a status

---

1. Lyons's account of the 'Five Year Plan in Four Years' and his recording of the formula used to express that, 2 + 2 = 5, directly influenced Orwell's writing of *Nineteen Eighty-Four* (although this formula is to be found at least as early as the mid-eighteenth century, in Sterne's *Tristram Shandy*, a copy of which Orwell had in his possession, and in Dostoevski's *Notes from Underground*, 1864).

resembling serfdom.[2] The G. P. U. are everywhere, everyone lives in constant terror of denunciation, freedom of speech and of the press are obliterated to an extent we can hardly imagine. There are periodical waves of terror, sometimes the 'liquidation' of kulaks or Nepmen, sometimes some monstrous state trial at which people who have been in prison for months or years are suddenly dragged forth to make incredible confessions, while their children publish articles in the newspapers saying 'I repudiate my father as a Trotskyist serpent.' Meanwhile the invisible Stalin is worshipped in terms that would have made Nero blush. This —at great length and in much detail—is the picture Mr. Lyons presents, and I do not believe he has misrepresented the facts. He does, however, show signs of being embittered by his experiences, and I think he probably exaggerates the amount of discontent prevailing among the Russians themselves.

He once succeeded in interviewing Stalin, and found him human, simple and likeable. It is worth noticing that H. G. Wells said the same thing,[3] and it is a fact that Stalin, at any rate on the cinematograph, has a likeable face. Is it not also recorded that Al Capone was the best of husbands and fathers, and that Joseph Smith (of Brides in the Bath fame) was sincerely loved by the first of his seven wives and always returned to her between murders?

2. Under the tsars, serfs needed internal passports to leave their villages to take up seasonal work elsewhere.
3. See *Stalin-Wells Talk: The Verbatim Record, and a Discussion* by G. Bernard Shaw, H.G. Wells, J.M. Keynes, Ernst Toller, and others (1934).

'Why I Join the I.L.P.'

The New Leader, 24 JUNE 1938

Although the New Leader *had its roots in the miners' trade union at the end of the nineteenth century, it became, as* The New Leader, *the organ of the Independent Labour Party in the 1930s. Its editor from 1931 to 1946 was Fenner Brockway (1888–1988) who served as the ILP's representative in Spain during the Civil War. The journal earned Orwell's displeasure when it published 'Night Attack on the Aragon Front' (30 April 1937). This was elaborated from the experiences of members of the ILP, including Orwell, who complained that 'they blew it up into a sort of 1914–18 battle'.*

Perhaps it will be frankest to approach it first of all from the personal angle.

I am a writer. The impulse of every writer is to 'keep out of politics.' What he wants is to be left alone so that he can go on writing books in peace. But unfortunately it is becoming obvious that this ideal is no more practicable than that of the petty shopkeeper who hopes to preserve his independence in the teeth of the chain-stores.

To begin with, the era of free speech is closing down. The freedom of the Press in Britain was always something of a fake, because in the last resort, money controls opinion; still, so long as the legal right to say what you like exists, there are always loopholes for an unorthodox writer. For some years past I have managed to make the Capitalist class pay me several pounds a week for writing books against Capitalism. But I do not delude myself that this state of affairs is going to last for ever. We have seen what has happened to the freedom of the Press in Italy and Germany, and it will happen here sooner or later. The time is coming—not next year, perhaps not for ten or twenty years, but it is coming—when every writer will have the choice of being silenced altogether or of producing the dope that a privileged minority demands.

I have got to struggle against that, just as I have got to struggle against castor oil, rubber truncheons and concentration-camps. And the only regime which, in the long run, will dare to permit freedom of speech is a Socialist regime. If Fascism triumphs I am finished as a writer—that is to say, finished in my only effective capacity. That of itself would be a sufficient reason for joining a Socialist party.

I have put the personal aspect first, but obviously it is not the only one.

It is not possible for any thinking person to live in such a society as our own without wanting to change it. For perhaps ten years past I have had some grasp of the real nature of Capitalist society. I have seen British Imperialism at work in Burma, and I have seen something of the effects of poverty and unemployment in Britain. In so far as I have struggled against the system, it has been mainly of writing books which I hoped would influence the reading public. I shall continue to do that, of course, but at a moment like the present writing books is not enough. The tempo of events is quickening; the dangers which once seemed a generation distant are staring us in the face. One has got to be actively a Socialist, not merely sympathetic to Socialism, or one plays into the hands of our always-active enemies.

Why the I.L.P. more than another?

Because the I.L.P. is the only British party—at any rate the only one large enough to be worth considering—which aims at anything I should regard as Socialism.

I do not mean that I have lost all faith in the Labour Party. My most earnest hope is that the Labour Party will win a clear majority in the next General Election. But we know what the history of the Labour Party has been, and we know the terrible temptation of the present moment—the temptation to fling every principle overboard in order to prepare for an Imperialist war. It is vitally necessary that there should be in existence some body of people who can be depended on, even in face of persecution, not to compromise their Socialist principles.

I believe that the I.L.P. is the only party which, as a party, is likely to take the right line either against Imperialist war or against Fascism when this appears in its British form. And meanwhile the I.L.P. is not backed by any monied interest, and is systematically libelled from several quarters. Obviously it needs all the help it can get, including any help I can give it myself.

Finally, I was with the I.L.P. contingent in Spain. I never pretended, then or since, to agree in every detail with the policy the P.O.U.M. put forward and the I.L.P. supported, but the general course of events has borne it out. The things I saw in Spain brought home to me the fatal danger of mere negative 'anti-Fascism.' Once I had grasped the essentials of the situation in Spain I realised that the I.L.P. was the only British party I felt like joining – and also the only party I could join with at least the certainty that I would never be led up the garden path in the name of Capitalist democracy.[1]

1. Orwell's membership card for the Independent Labour Party was issued on 13 June 1938.

Extract from 'Looking Back on the Spanish War'

1942(?)

Two memories, the first not proving anything in particular, the second, I think, giving one a certain insight into the atmosphere of a revolutionary period.

Early one morning another man and I had gone out to snipe at the Fascists in the trenches outside Huesca. Their line and ours here lay three hundred yards apart, at which range our aged rifles would not shoot accurately, but by sneaking out to a spot about a hundred yards from the Fascist trench you might, if you were lucky, get a shot at someone through a gap in the parapet. Unfortunately the ground between was a flat beet-field with no cover except a few ditches, and it was necessary to go out while it was still dark and return soon after dawn, before the light became too good. This time no Fascists appeared, and we stayed too long and were caught by the dawn. We were in a ditch, but behind us were two hundred yards of flat ground with hardly enough cover for a rabbit. We were still trying to nerve ourselves to make a dash for it when there was an uproar and a blowing of whistles in the Fascist trench. Some of our aeroplanes were coming over. At this moment a man, presumably carrying a message to an officer, jumped out of the trench and ran along the top of the parapet in full view. He was half-dressed and was holding up his trousers with both hands as he ran. I refrained from shooting at him. It is true that I am a poor shot and unlikely to hit a running man at a hundred yards, and also that I was thinking chiefly about getting back to our trench while the Fascists had their attention fixed on the aeroplanes. Still, I did not shoot partly because of that detail about the trousers. I had come here to shoot at 'Fascists'; but a man who is holding up his trousers isn't a 'Fascist', he is visibly a fellow creature, similar to yourself, and you don't feel like shooting at him.

What does this incident demonstrate? Nothing very much, because it is the kind of thing that happens all the time in all wars. The other is different. I don't suppose that in telling it I can make it moving to you who read it, but I ask you to believe that it is moving to me, as an incident characteristic of the moral atmosphere of a particular moment in time.

One of the recruits who joined us while I was at the barracks was a wild-looking boy from the back streets of Barcelona. He was ragged and barefooted. He was also extremely dark (Arab blood, I dare say), and made gestures you do not usually see a European make; one in particular —the arm outstretched, the palm vertical—was a gesture characteristic of Indians. One day a bundle of cigars, which you could still buy dirt cheap at that time, was stolen out of my bunk. Rather foolishly I reported this to the officer, and one of the scallywags I have already mentioned promptly came forward and said quite untruly that twenty-five pesetas had been stolen from his bunk. For some reason the officer instantly decided that the brown-faced boy must be the thief. They were very hard on stealing in the militia, and in theory people could be shot for it. The wretched boy allowed himself to be led off to the guardroom to be searched. What most struck me was that he barely attempted to protest his innocence. In the fatalism of his attitude you could see the desperate poverty in which he had been bred. The officer ordered him to take his clothes off. With a humility that was horrible to me he stripped himself naked, and his clothes were searched. Of course neither the cigars nor the money were there; in fact he had not stolen them. What was most painful of all was that he seemed no less ashamed after his innocence had been established. That night I took him to the pictures and gave him brandy and chocolate. But that too was horrible—I mean the attempt to wipe out an injury with money. For a few minutes I had half believed him to be a thief, and that could not be wiped out.

Poem: 'The Italian soldier shook my hand' from 'Looking Back on the Spanish War'

The Italian soldier shook my hand
Beside the guard-room table;
The strong hand and the subtle hand
Whose palms are only able

To meet within the sound of guns,
But oh! what peace I knew then
In gazing on his battered face
Purer than any woman's!

For the fly-blown words that make me spew
Still in his ears were holy,
And he was born knowing what I had learned
Out of books and slowly.

The treacherous guns had told their tale
And we both had bought it,
But my gold brick was made of gold—
Oh! whoever would have thought it?

Good luck go with you, Italian soldier!
But luck is not for the brave;
What would the world give back to you?
Always less than you gave.

Between the shadow and the ghost,
Between the white and the red,
Between the bullet and the lie,
Where would you hide your head?

For where is Manuel Gonzalez,
And where is Pedro Aguilar,
And where is Ramon Fenellosa?
The earthworms know where they are.

Your name and your deeds were forgotten
Before your bones were dry,
And the lie that slew you is buried
Under a deeper lie;

But the thing that I saw in your face
No power can disinherit:
No bomb that ever burst
Shatters the crystal spirit.

Review: Bertrand Russell, *Power: A New Social Analysis*

The Adelphi, JANUARY 1939

If there are certain pages of Mr. Bertrand Russell's book, *Power*, which seem rather empty, that is merely to say that we have now sunk to a depth at which the restatement of the obvious is the first duty of intelligent men. It is not merely that at present the rule of naked force obtains almost everywhere. Probably that has always been the case. Where this age differs from those immediately preceding it is that a liberal intelligentsia is lacking. Bully-worship, under various disguises, has become a universal religion, and such truisms as that a machine-gun is still a machine-gun even when a 'good' man is squeezing the trigger—and that in effect is what Mr. Russell is saying—have turned into heresies which it is actually becoming dangerous to utter.

The most interesting part of Mr. Russell's book is the earlier chapters in which he analyses the various types of power—priestly, oligarchical, dictatorial and so forth. In dealing with the contemporary situation he is less satisfactory, because like all liberals he is better at pointing out what is desirable than at explaining how to achieve it. He sees clearly enough that the essential problem of to-day is 'the taming of power' and that no system except democracy can be trusted to save us from unspeakable horrors. Also that democracy has very little meaning without approximate economic equality and an educational system tending to promote tolerance and toughmindedness. But unfortunately he does not tell us how we are to set about getting these things; he merely utters what amounts to a pious hope that the present state of things will not endure. He is inclined to point to the past; all tyrannies have collapsed sooner or later, and 'there is no reason to suppose (Hitler) more permanent than his predecessors.'

Underlying this is the idea that common sense always wins in the end. And yet the peculiar horror of the present moment is that we cannot be sure that this is so. It is quite possible that we are descending into an age in which two and two will make five when the Leader says so. Mr. Russell points out that the huge system of organised lying upon which the dictators depend keeps their followers out of contact with reality and therefore tends to put them at a disadvantage as against those who know the facts. This is true so far as it goes, but it does not prove that the slave-society at which the dictators are aiming will be unstable. It is quite easy to imagine a state in which the ruling caste deceive their followers without deceiving themselves. Dare anyone be sure that something of the kind is not coming into existence already? One has only to think of the sinister possibilities of the radio, State-controlled education and so forth, to realise that 'the truth is great and will prevail'[1] is a prayer rather than an axiom.

Mr. Russell is one of the most readable of living writers, and it is very reassuring to know that he exists. So long as he and a few others like him are alive and out of jail, we know that the world is still sane in parts. He has rather an eclectic mind, he is capable of saying shallow things and profoundly interesting things in alternate sentences, and sometimes, even in this book, he is less serious than his subject deserves. But he has an essentially *decent* intellect, a kind of intellectual chivalry which is far rarer than mere cleverness. Few people during the past thirty years have been so consistently impervious to the fashionable bunk of the moment. In a time of universal panic and lying he is a good person to make contact with. For that reason this book, though it is not so good as *Freedom and Organisation*, is very well worth reading.

---

1. From Coventry Patmore, 'The Unknown Eros'.

'Democracy in the British Army'

Left Forum, SEPTEMBER 1939

Left Forum *began life as* Controversy *in 1932 when the Independent Labour Party dis-affiliated from the Labour Party. At first it functioned as the Party's internal bulletin but changed character in 1936 to reflect without rancour the diverse views of working-class people. It changed its name to* Left Forum *in 1939 and then became simply* Left. *It ceased publication in May 1950. Much of its success was due to its editor, Dr C.A. Smith, a London headmaster and later a University of London lecturer.*

When the Duke of Wellington described the British army as 'the scum of the earth, enlisted for drink,' he was probably speaking no more than the truth. But what is significant is that his opinion would have been echoed by any non-military Englishman for nearly a hundred years subsequently.

The French Revolution and the new conception of 'national' war changed the character of most Continental armies, but England was in the exceptional position of being immune from invasion and of being governed during most of the nineteenth century by non-military bourgeoisie. Consequently its army remained, as before, a small professional force more or less cut off from the rest of the nation. The war-scare of the sixties produced the Volunteers, later to develop into the Territorials, but it was not till a few years before the Great War that there was serious talk of universal service. Until the late nineteenth century the total number of white troops, even in war-time, never reached a quarter of a million men, and it is probable that every great British land battle between Blenheim and Loos was fought mainly by foreign soldiers.

In the nineteenth century the British common soldier was usually a farm labourer or slum proletarian who had been driven into the army by brute starvation. He enlisted for a period of at least seven years—sometimes as much as twenty-one years—and he was inured to a barrack life of endless drilling, rigid and stupid discipline, and degrading physical punishments. It was virtually impossible for him to marry, and even after the extension of the franchise he lacked the right to vote. In Indian garrison towns he could kick the 'niggers' with impunity, but at home he was hated or looked down upon by the ordinary population, except in wartime, when for brief periods he was discovered to be a hero. Obviously such a man had severed his links with his own class. He was essentially a merce-nary, and his self-respect depended on his conception of himself not as a worker or a citizen but simply as a fighting animal.

Since the war the conditions of army life have improved and the conception of discipline has grown more intelligent, but the British army has retained its special characteristics—small size, voluntary enlistment, long service and emphasis on regimental loyalty. Every regiment has its own name (not merely a number, as in most armies), its history and relics, its special customs, traditions, etc., etc., thanks to which the whole army is honeycombed with snobberies which are almost unbelievable unless one has seen them at close quarters. Between the officers of a 'smart' regiment and those of an ordinary infantry regiment, or still more a regi-ment of the Indian Army, there is a degree of jealousy almost amounting to a class difference. And there is no question that the long-term private soldier often identifies with his own regiment almost as closely as the officer does. The effect is to make the narrow 'non-political' outlook of the mercenary come more easily to him. In addition, the fact that the British Army is rather heavily officered probably diminishes class friction and thus makes the lower ranks less accessible to 'subversive' ideas.

But the thing which above all else forces a reactionary viewpoint on the common soldier is his service in overseas garrisons. An infantry regi-ment is usually quartered abroad for eighteen years consecutively, moving from place to place every four or five years, so that many soldiers serve their entire term in India, Africa, China, etc. They are only there to hold down a hostile population and the fact is brought home to them in unmistakable ways. Relations with the 'natives' are almost invariably bad, and the soldiers—not so much the officers as the men—are the obvious targets for anti-British feeling. Naturally they retaliate, and as a rule they develop an attitude towards the 'niggers' which is far more brutal than that of the officials or business men. In Burma I was constantly struck by the fact that the common soldiers were the best-hated section of the white community, and, judged simply by their behaviour, they certainly deserved to be. Even as near home as Gibraltar they walk the streets with a swaggering air which is directed at the Spanish 'natives.' And in practice some such attitude is absolutely necessary; you could not hold down a subject empire with troops infected by notions of class-solidarity. Most of the dirty work of the French empire, for instance, is done not by French conscripts but by illiterate negroes and by the Foreign Legion, a corps of pure mercenaries.

To sum up: in spite of the technical advances which do not allow the professional officer to be quite such an idiot as he used to be, and in spite of the fact that the common soldier is now treated a little more like a human being, the British army remains essentially the same machine as it was fifty years ago. A little while back any Socialists would have admitted this without argument. But we happen to be at a moment when the rise of Hitler has scared the official leaders of the Left into an attitude not far removed from jingoism. Large numbers of Left-wing publicists are almost openly agitating for war. Without discussing this subject at length, it can be pointed out that a Left-wing party which, within a capitalist society, becomes a war party, has already thrown up the sponge, because it is demanding a policy which can only be carried out by its opponents. The Labour leaders are intermittently aware of this—witness their shufflings on the subject of conscription. Hence, in among the cries of 'Firm front!' 'British prestige!' etc., there mingles a quite contradictory line of talk. It is to the effect that 'this time' things are going to be 'different.' Militarisation is not going to mean militarisation. Colonel Blimp is no longer Colonel Blimp. And in the more soft-boiled Left-wing papers a phrase is bandied to and fro—'democratising the army.' It is worth considering what it implies.

'Democratising' an army, if it means anything, means doing away with the predominance of a single class and introducing a less mechanical form of discipline. In the British army this would mean an entire reconstruction which would rob the army of efficiency for five or ten years. Such a process is only doubtfully possible while the British Empire exists, and quite unthinkable while the simultaneous aim is to 'stop Hitler.' What will actually happen during the next couple of years, war or no war, is that the armed forces will be greatly expanded, but the new units will take their colour from the existing professional army. As in the Great War, it will be the same army, only bigger. Poorer sections of the middle-class will be drawn on for the supply of officers, but the professional military caste will retain its grip. As for the new Militias, it is probably quite a mistake to imagine that they are the nucleus of a 'democratic army' in which all classes will start from scratch. It is fairly safe to prophesy that even if there is no class-favouritism (as there will be, presumably), Militiamen of bourgeois origin will tend to be promoted first. Hore-Belisha and others have already hinted as much in a number of speeches. A fact not always appreciated by Socialists is that in England the whole of the bourgeoisie is to some extent militarised. Nearly every boy who has been to a public school has passed through the O.T.C. (theoretically voluntary but in practice compulsory), and though this training is done between the ages of 13 and 18, it ought not to be despised. In effect the Militiaman with an O.T.C. training behind him will start with several months' advantage of the others. In any case the Military Training Act is only an experiment, aimed partly at impressing opinion abroad and partly at accustoming the English people to the idea of conscription. Once the novelty has worn off some method will be devised of keeping proletarians out of positions of command.

It is probable that the nature of modern war has made 'democratic army' a contradiction in terms. The French army, for instance, based on universal service, is hardly more democratic than the British. It is just as much dominated by the professional officer and the long-service N.C.O., and the French officer is probably rather more 'Prussian' in outlook than his British equivalent. The Spanish Government militias during the first six months of war—the first year, in Catalonia—were a genuinely democratic army, but they were also a very primitive type of army, capable only of defensive actions. In that particular case a defensive strategy, coupled with propaganda, would probably have had a better chance of victory than the methods casually adopted. But if you want military efficiency in the ordinary sense, there is no escaping from the professional soldier, and so long as the professional soldier is in control he will see to it that the army is not democratised. And what is true within the armed forces is true of the nation as a whole; every increase in the strength of the military machine means more power for the forces of reaction. It is possible that some of our Left-wing jingoes are acting with their eyes open. If they are, they must be aware that the *News Chronicle* version of 'defence of democracy' leads directly *away* from democracy, even in the narrow nineteenth-century sense of political liberty, independence of the trade unions and freedom of speech and the press.

Review: Tom Harrisson and Charles Madge, *War Begins at Home*

Time and Tide, 2 MARCH 1940

War Begins at Home is the Mass Observers'[1] first report on civilian morale in England. After four months of war (the book was completed in December) they find the bulk of the people bored, bewildered and a little irritated, but at the same time buoyed up by a completely false idea that winning the war is going to be an easy business. As the Mass Observers see it, the main weakness of the home front is the class-structure and out-of-date mentality of the present Government. Practically every inquiry they have made, whether it is into food prices, air-raid panics, the evacuation or the effect of the war on football and jazz, leads back to the fact that our present rulers simply do not understand the viewpoint of ordinary people, and are not even capable of grasping that it matters. Their civil defence schemes, and their propaganda (the best example is the very uninspiring red posters, about which the Mass Observers have a lot to say), are always based on the half-conscious assumption that the whole of the population lives above the £5 a week level. In so far as they deign to notice public opinion at all, they draw their ideas of it from the daily press, which is bound up with private trading interests and is often actively misleading. Meanwhile the critical period of the war approaches, and before long sacrifices are going to be demanded for which the people have in no way been psychologically prepared. On the whole it is a depressing picture.

I do, however, believe that it is a slightly misleading one. The volume of discontent, apathy, bewilderment and, in general, war-weariness in England is probably far smaller than the Mass Observers seem to imply. The fact is that any inquiry of this type is bound to be coloured to some extent by preconceived opinions. A couple of years ago the Mass Observers

---

1. Mass Observation was described by one of its founders, Tom Harrisson (1911–76), as 'the science of ourselves'. The movement, initiated in 1937, endeavoured to organise detailed observation of the masses, using large numbers of amateur 'observers' in order to publish accurate accounts of the state of contemporary Britain. Its first and most famous report (republished in 1987) was *May the Twelfth* (1937), the day George VI was crowned king. It was prepared by more than two hundred observers and edited by Humphrey Jennings (1907–50), later a distinguished film-maker, and Charles Madge (1912–96), poet and later professor of sociology. Observers did not hesitate to disguise themselves or pretend to be drunk in order to make their observations go unnoticed. Mass Observation diaries were still being completed as late as 1981.

published a long report on the coronation of George VI. It brought many interesting facts to light, but what it did not contain, or barely contained, was any indication that royalist sentiment is still a reality in England. And yet one knows well enough that it *is* a reality, otherwise a thing like the coronation (somewhat less interesting, merely as a spectacle, than a travelling circus) would be simply ignored instead of being attended by enormous crowds. It is rather the same with *War Begins at Home*. The one thing that the compilers do not seem to have encountered is the sentiment of patriotism. If one may make a guess at the reason, it is that people capable even of imagining a thing like Mass Observation are necessarily exceptional people—exceptional enough not to share the rather unthinking patriotism of the ordinary man. Consequently there is a certain temptation to overrate the importance of mere grumbling. People grumble about the black-out, about the evacuation, about transport difficulties, etc., etc. Yes, but isn't it just possible that the same people were grumbling about something else before the war started? The majority of human beings, always and everywhere, are vaguely discontented with their lot, and in countries where free speech is permitted it is the rarest thing in the world to hear a friendly comment on the Government in power at the moment. But for practical purposes how much does it all amount to?

War Begins at Home contains an introduction in which the Mass Observers explain their methods of going to work. It leaves me with the feeling that the subjective factor (the observer's own reaction) is not excluded so completely as it ought to be and probably could be. But that is not to say that the work they are doing is not useful. Now even more than at other times it is of the most vital importance that something of the kind should be attempted and brought to as many people's notice as possible. In war it is civilian morale, especially working-class morale, that is decisive in the long run, and there is little or no sign that the Government recognizes this. According to Messrs. Harrisson and Madge:

'When our organization was told to make a big investigation on the Government red posters for the Ministry of Information, we found, as we briefly describe in this book, that these posters were extremely unsuccessful in attaining their alleged aims. The rumour runs around Whitehall that when the results of this report were seen by one key Cabinet Minister, he remarked: "Very good work. But if we're going to find out things as unpleasant as that, we'd better not find out anything at all".'

I do not know whether this anecdote is apocryphal; I sincerely hope it is. For if it happens to be true, God help us!

Review: Adolf Hitler, *Mein Kampf*

New English Weekly, 21 MARCH 1940

It is a sign of the speed at which events are moving that Hurst and Blackett's unexpurgated edition of *Mein Kampf,* published only a year ago, is edited from a pro-Hitler angle. The obvious intention of the translator's preface and notes is to tone down the book's ferocity and present Hitler in as kindly a light as possible. For at that date Hitler was still respectable. He had crushed the German labour movement, and for that the property-owning classes were willing to forgive him almost anything. Both Left and Right concurred in the very shallow notion that National Socialism was merely a version of Conservatism.

Then suddenly it turned out that Hitler was not respectable after all. As one result of this, Hurst and Blackett's edition was reissued in a new jacket explaining that all profits would be devoted to the Red Cross. Nevertheless, simply on the internal evidence of *Mein Kampf,* it is difficult to believe that any real change has taken place in Hitler's aims and opinions. When one compares his utterances of a year or so ago with those made fifteen years earlier, a thing that strikes one is the rigidity of his mind, the way in which his world-view *doesn't* develop. It is the fixed vision of a monomaniac, and not likely to be much affected by the temporary manœuvres of power politics. Probably, in Hitler's own mind, the Russo–German pact represents no more than an alteration of time-table. The plan laid down in *Mein Kampf* was to smash Russia first, with the implied intention of smashing England afterwards. Now, as it has turned out, England has got to be dealt with first, because Russia was the more easily bribed of the two. But Russia's turn will come when England is out of the picture—that, no doubt, is how Hitler sees it. Whether it will turn out that way is of course a different question.

Suppose that Hitler's programme could be put into effect. What he envisages, a hundred years hence, is a continuous state of 250 million Germans with plenty of 'living room' (i.e., stretching to Afghanistan or thereabouts), a horrible brainless empire in which, essentially, nothing ever happens except the training of young men for war and the endless breeding of fresh cannon-fodder. How was it that he was able to put this monstrous vision across? It is easy to say that at one stage of his career he was financed by the heavy industrialists, who saw in him the man who would smash the Socialists and Communists. They would not have backed him, however, if he had not talked a great movement into existence already. Again, the situation in Germany, with its seven million unemployed, was obviously favourable for demagogues. But Hitler could not have succeeded against his many rivals if it had not been for the attraction of his own personality, which one can feel even in the clumsy writing of *Mein Kampf*, and which is no doubt overwhelming when one hears his speeches. I should like to put it on record that I have never been able to dislike Hitler. Ever since he came to power—till then, like nearly everyone, I had been deceived into thinking that he did not matter—I have reflected that I would certainly kill him if I could get within reach of him, but that I could feel no personal animosity. The fact is that there is something deeply appealing about him. One feels it again when one sees his photographs—and I recommend especially the photograph at the beginning of Hurst and Blackett's edition, which shows Hitler in his early Brownshirt days. It is a pathetic, doglike face, the face of a man suffering under intolerable wrongs. In a rather more manly way it reproduces the expression of innumerable pictures of Christ crucified, and there is little doubt that that is how Hitler sees himself. The initial, personal cause of his grievance against the universe can only be guessed at; but at any rate the grievance is there. He is the martyr, the victim, Prometheus chained to the rock, the self-sacrificing hero who fights single-handed against impossible odds. If he were killing a mouse he would know how to make it seem like a dragon. One feels, as with Napoleon, that he is fighting against destiny, that he *can't* win, and yet that he somehow deserves to. The attraction of such a pose is of course enormous; half the films that one sees turn upon some such theme.

Also he has grasped the falsity of the hedonistic attitude to life. Nearly all Western thought since the last war, certainly all 'progressive' thought, has assumed tacitly that human beings desire nothing beyond ease, security and avoidance of pain. In such a view of life there is no room, for instance, for patriotism and the military virtues. The Socialist who finds his children playing with soldiers is usually upset, but he is never able to think of a substitute for the tin soldiers; tin pacifists somehow won't do. Hitler, because in his own joyless mind he feels it with exceptional strength, knows that human beings *don't* only want comfort, safety, short working-hours, hygiene, birth-control and, in general, common sense; they also, at least intermittently, want struggle and self-sacrifice, not to mention drums, flags and loyalty-parades. However they may be as economic theories, Fascism and Nazism are psychologically far sounder than any hedonistic conception of life. The same is probably true of Stalin's militarised version of Socialism. All three of the great dictators have enhanced their power by imposing intolerable burdens on their peoples. Whereas Socialism, and even capitalism in a more grudging way, have said to people 'I offer you a good time,' Hitler has said to them 'I offer you struggle, danger and death,' and as a result a whole nation flings itself at his feet.[1] Perhaps later on they will get sick of it and change their minds, as at the end of the last war. After a few years of slaughter and starvation 'Greatest happiness of the greatest number'[2] is a good slogan, but at this moment 'Better an end with horror than a horror without end' is a winner. Now that we are fighting against the man who coined it, we ought not to underrate its emotional appeal.

1. Compare Winston Churchill in the House of Commons two months after this review: 'I have nothing to offer but blood, toil, tears and sweat' (13 May 1940).
2. Francis Hutcheson, *Concerning Moral Good and Evil* (1720).

'New Words'

unpublished, FEBRUARY–APRIL 1940(?)

Why and when Orwell wrote this essay is a mystery. He writes of what Joyce 'is now doing', referring presumably to the language of Finnegans Wake. *That was published on 4 May 1939 but extracts had been published between 1928 and 1937 so that reference is of little help in dating the essay. It has been suggested that Orwell may have intended it for the journal* Persuasion *which paid him £15 15s for 'Propaganda and Demotic Speech' in the summer of 1944. As he says in the essay's last paragraph, 'I have written all this down hastily', and it may be that when he had studied* Finnegans Wake *more carefully he realised that this essay needed not merely expansion but recasting. The text is taken from Orwell's typescript.*

At present the formation of new words is a slow process (I have read somewhere that English gains about six and loses about four words a year) and no new words are deliberately coined except as names for material objects. Abstract words are never coined at all, though old words (eg. 'condition', 'reflex' etc.) are sometimes twisted into new meanings for scientific purposes. What I am going to suggest here is that it would be quite feasible to invent a vocabulary, perhaps amounting to several thousands of words, which would deal with parts of our experience now practically unamenable to language. There are several obvious objections to the idea, and I will deal with these as they arise. The first step is to indicate the kind of purpose for which new words are needed.

Everyone who thinks at all has noticed that our language is practically useless for describing anything that goes on inside the brain. This is so generally recognized that writers of high skill (eg. Trollope and Mark Twain) will start their autobiographies by saying that they do not intend to describe their inner life, because it is of its nature indescribable. So [as] soon as we are dealing with anything that is not concrete or visible (and even there to a great extent—look at the difficulty of describing anyone's appearance) we find that words are no liker to the reality than chessmen to living beings. To take an obvious case which will not raise side-issues, consider a dream. How do you describe a dream? Clearly you *never* describe it, because no words that convey the atmosphere of dreams exist in our language. Of course, you can give a crude approximation of some of the major facts in a dream. You can say, 'I dreamed that I was walking down

Regent Street with a porcupine wearing a bowler hat' etc. but this is no real description of the dream. And even if a psychologist interprets your dream in terms of 'symbols', he is still going largely by guesswork; for the *real* quality of the dream, the quality that gave the porcupine its sole significance, is outside the world of words. In fact, describing a dream is like translating a poem into the language of one of Bohn's cribs; it is a paraphrase which is meaningless unless one knows the original.

I chose dreams as an instance that would not be disputed, but if it were only dreams that were indescribable, the matter might not be worth bothering about. But, as has been pointed out over and over again, the waking mind is not so different from the dreaming mind as it appears—or as we like to pretend that it appears. It is true that most of our waking thoughts are 'reasonable'—that is, there exists in our minds a kind of chessboard upon which thoughts move logically and verbally; we use this part of our minds for any straightforward intellectual problem, and we get into the habit of thinking (ie. thinking in our chessboard moments) that it is the whole of the mind. But obviously it is not the whole. The disordered, un-verbal world belonging to dreams is never quite absent from our minds, and if any calculation were possible I dare say it would be found that quite half the volume of our waking thoughts were of this order. Certainly the dream-thoughts take a hand even when we are trying to think verbally, they influence the verbal thoughts, and it is largely they that make our inner life valuable. Examine your thoughts at any casual moment. The main movement in it will be a stream of nameless things —so nameless that one hardly knows whether to call them thoughts, images or feelings. In the first place there are the objects you see and the sounds you hear, which are in themselves describable in words, but which as soon as they enter your mind become something quite different and totally indescribable.[1] And besides this there is the dream-life which your mind unceasingly creates for itself—and though most of this is trivial and soon forgotten, it contains things which are beautiful, funny etc. beyond anything that ever gets into words. In a way this un-verbal part of your mind is even the most important part, for it is the source of nearly all *motives*. All likes and dislikes, all aesthetic feelings, all notions

1. 'The mind, that Ocean where each kind
   Doth straight its own resemblance find;
   Yet it creates, transcending these,
   Far other worlds, and other seas' etc.
   [Orwell's footnote. From Andrew Marvell, 'The Garden', lines 43–46.]

of right and wrong (aesthetic and moral considerations are in any case inextricable) spring from feelings which are generally admitted to be subtler than words. When you are asked 'Why do you do, or not do, so and so' you are invariably aware that your *real* reason will not go into words, even when you have no wish to conceal it; consequently you rationalise your conduct, more or less dishonestly. I don't know whether everyone would admit this, and it is a fact that some people seem unaware of being influenced by their inner life, or even of having any inner life. I notice that many people never laugh when they are alone, and I suppose that if a man does not laugh when he is alone his inner life must be relatively barren. Still, every individual man has an inner life, and is aware of the practical impossibility of understanding others or being understood —in general, of the star-like isolation in which human beings live. Nearly all literature is an attempt to escape from this isolation by roundabout means, the direct means (words in their primary meanings) being almost useless.

'Imaginative' writing is as it were a flank-attack upon positions that are impregnable from the front. A writer attempting anything that is not coldly 'intellectual' can do very little with words in their primary meanings. He gets his effect if at all by using words in a tricky roundabout way, relying on their cadences and so forth, as in speech he would rely upon tone and gesture. In the case of poetry this is too well-known to be worth arguing about. No one with the smallest understanding of poetry supposes that

> The mortal moon hath her eclipse endured,
> And the sad augurs mock their own presage[2]

really *means* what the words 'mean' in their dictionary-sense. (The couplet is said to refer to Queen Elizabeth having got over her grand climacteric safely.) The dictionary-meaning has, as nearly always, *something* to do with the real meaning, but not more than the 'anecdote' of a picture has to do with its design. And it is the same with prose, mutatis mutandis. Consider a novel, even a novel which has ostensibly nothing to do with the inner life—what is called a 'straight story'. Consider *Manon Lescaut*. Why does the author invent this long rigmarole about an unfaithful girl and a runaway abbé? Because he has a certain feeling, vision, whatever you like to call it, and knows, possibly after experiment, that it is no use trying to convey

2. Shakespeare, Sonnet 107.

this vision by describing it as one would describe a crayfish for a book of zoology. But by *not* describing it, by inventing something else (in this case a picaresque novel: in another age he would choose another form) he can convey it, or part of it. The art of writing is in fact largely the perversion of words, and I would even say that the less obvious this perversion is, the more thoroughly it has been done. For a writer who *seems* to twist words out of their meanings (eg. Gerard Manley Hopkins) is really, if one looks closely, making a desperate attempt to use them straightforwardly. Whereas a writer who seems to have no tricks whatever, for instance the old ballad-writers, is making an especially subtle flank-attack, though, in the case of the ballad-writers, this is no doubt unconscious. Of course one hears a lot of cant to the effect that all good art is 'objective' and every true artist keeps his inner life to himself. But the people who say this do not mean it. All they mean is that they want the inner life to be expressed by an exceptionally roundabout method, as in the ballad or the 'straight story.'

The weakness of the roundabout method, apart from its difficulty, is that it usually fails. For anyone who is not a considerable artist (possibly for them too) the lumpishness of words results in constant falsification. Is there anyone who has ever written so much as a love letter in which he felt that he had said exactly what he intended? A writer falsifies himself both intentionally and unintentionally. Intentionally, because the accidental qualities of words constantly tempt and frighten him away from his true meaning. He gets an idea, begins trying to express it, and then, in the frightful mess of words that generally results, a pattern begins to form itself more or less accidentally. It is not by any means the pattern he wants, but it is at any rate not vulgar or disagreeable; it is 'good art'. He takes it, because 'good art' is a more or less mysterious gift from heaven, and it seems a pity to waste it when it presents itself. Is not anyone with any degree of mental honesty conscious of telling lies all day long, both in talking and writing, simply because lies will fall into artistic shape when truth will not? Yet if words represented meanings as fully and accurately as height multiplied by base represents the area of a parallelogram, at least the *necessity* for lying would never exist. And in the mind of reader or hearer there are further falsifications, because, words not being a direct channel of thought, he constantly sees meanings which are not there. A good illustration of this is our supposed appreciation of foreign poetry. We know, from the *Vie Amoureuse du Watson Docteur* stuff of foreign critics, that true understanding of foreign literature is almost impossible; yet quite ignorant people profess to get, do get, vast pleasure out of poetry in foreign and even dead languages. Clearly the pleasure they derive may come from something the writer never intended, possibly from something that would make him squirm in his grave if he knew it was attributed to him. I say to myself 'Vixi puellis nuper idoneus',[3] and I repeat this over and over for five minutes for the beauty of the word 'Idoneus'. Yet, considering the gulf of time and culture, and my ignorance of Latin, and the fact that no one even knows how Latin was pronounced, is it possible that the effect I am enjoying is the effect Horace was trying for? It is as though I were in ecstasies over the beauty of a picture, and all because of some splashes of paint which had accidentally got on to the canvas 200 years after it was painted. Notice, I am not saying that *art* would necessarily improve if words conveyed meaning more reliably. For all I know art thrives on the crudeness and vagueness of language. I am only criticising *words* in their supposed function as vehicles of thought. And it seems to me that from the point of view of exactitude and expressiveness our language has remained in the Stone Age.

The solution I suggest is to invent new words as deliberately as we would invent new parts for a motor-car engine. Suppose that a vocabulary existed which would accurately express the life of the mind, or a great part of it. Suppose that there need be no stultifying feeling that life is inexpressible, no jiggery-pokery with artistic tricks; expressing one's meaning simply a matter of taking the right words and putting them in place, like working out an equation in algebra. I think the advantages of this would be obvious. It is less obvious, though, that to sit down and deliberately coin words is a commonsense proceeding. Before indicating a way in which satisfactory words might be coined, I had better deal with the objections which are bound to arise.

If you say to any thinking person 'Let us form a society for the invention of new and subtler words', he will first of all object that it is the idea of a crank, and then probably say that our present words, properly handled, will meet all difficulties. (This last, of course, is only a theoretical objection. In practice everyone recognizes the inadequacy of language—consider such expressions as 'Words fail', 'It wasn't what he said, it was the way he said it' etc.) But finally he will give you an answer something like this: 'Things cannot be done in that pedantic way. Languages can only grow slowly, like flowers; you can't patch them up like pieces of machinery. Any *made-up* language must be characterless and lifeless—look at Esperanto etc. The

3. 'I have lived till recently meet for young women's love,' Horace, *Odes*, III, 26.1.

whole meaning of a word is in its slowly-acquired associations' etc.

In the first place, this argument, like most of the arguments produced when one suggests changing anything, is a longwinded way of saying that what is must be. Hitherto we have never set ourselves to the deliberate creation of words, and all living languages have grown slowly and haphazardly; *therefore* language cannot grow otherwise. At present, when we want to say anything above the level of a geometrical definition, we are obliged to do conjuring tricks with sounds, associations etc; *therefore* this necessity is inherent in the nature of words. The non sequitur is obvious. And notice that when I suggest coining abstract words I am only suggesting an extension of our present practice. For we do now coin concrete words. Aeroplanes and bicycles are invented, and we invent names for them, which is the natural thing to do. It is only a step to coining names for the now unnamed things that exist in the mind. You say to me, 'Why do you dislike Mr Smith?' and I say 'Because he is a liar, coward etc.' and I am almost certainly giving the wrong reason. In my own mind the answer runs 'Because he is a —— kind of man', —— standing for something which I understand, and you would understand if I could tell it you. Why not find a name for ——? The only difficulty is to agree about *what* we are naming. But long before this difficulty arises, the reading, thinking type of man will have recoiled from such an idea as the invention of words. He will produce arguments like the one I indicated above, or others of a more or less sneering, question-begging kind. In reality all these arguments are humbug. The recoil comes from a deep unreasoned instinct, superstitious in origin. It is the feeling that any direct rational approach to one's difficulties, any attempt to solve the problems of life as one would solve an equation, can lead nowhere—more, is definitely *unsafe*. One can see this idea expressed everywhere in a roundabout way. All the bosh that is talked about our national genius for 'muddling through', and all the squashy god-less mysticism that is urged against any hardness and soundness of intellect, mean au fond that it is *safer not to think*. This feeling starts, I am certain, in the common belief of children that the air is full of avenging demons waiting to punish presumption.[4] In adults the belief

4. The idea is that the demons will come down on you for being too self-confident. Thus children believe that if you hook a fish and say 'Got him' before he is landed, he will escape. That if you put your pads on before it is your turn to bat you will be out first ball etc. Such beliefs often survive in adults. Adults are only less superstitious than children in proportion as they have more power over their environment. In predicaments where everyone is powerless (eg. war, gambling) everyone is superstitious [Orwell's footnote. The first sentence is written in the margin].

survives as a fear of too-rational thinking. I the Lord thy God am a jealous God, pride comes before a fall etc.—and the most dangerous pride is the false pride of the intellect. David was punished because he numbered the people—ie. because he used his intellect scientifically. Thus such an idea as, for instance, ectogenesis, apart from its possible effects upon the health of the race, family life etc. is felt to be *in itself* blasphemous. Similarly any attack on such a fundamental thing as language, an attack as it were on the very structure of our own minds, is blasphemy and therefore dangerous. To reform language is practically an interference with the work of God—though I don't say that anyone would put it quite in these words. This objection is important, because it would prevent most people from even considering such an idea as the reform of language. And of course the idea is useless unless undertaken by large numbers. For one man, or a clique, to try and make up a language, as I believe James Joyce is now doing, is as absurd as one man trying to play football alone. What is wanted is several thousands of gifted but normal people who would give themselves to word-invention as seriously as people now give themselves to Shakespearean research. Given these, I believe we could work wonders with language.

Now as to the means. One sees an instance of the successful invention of words, though crude and on a small scale, among the members of large families. All large families have two or three words peculiar to themselves—words which they have made up and which convey subtilised, non-dictionary meanings. They say 'Mr Smith is a —— kind of man', using some home-made word, and the others understand perfectly; here then, within the limits of the family, exists an adjective filling one of the many gaps left by the dictionary. What makes it possible for the family to invent these words is the basis of their common experience. Without common experience, of course, no word can mean anything. If you say to me 'What does bergamot smell like?' I say 'Something like verbena', and so long as you know the smell of verbena you are somewhere near understanding me. The method in inventing words, therefore, is the method of analogy based on unmistakeable common knowledge; one must have standards that can be referred to without any chance of misunderstanding, as one can refer to a physical thing like the smell of verbena. In effect it must come down to giving words a physical (probably visible) existence. Merely *talking* about definitions is futile; one can see this whenever it is attempted to define one of the words used by literary critics. (eg.

'Sentimental',[5] 'vulgar', 'morbid' etc. All meaningless—or rather, having a different meaning for everyone who uses them.) What is needed is to *show* a meaning in some unmistakeable form, and then, when various people have identified it in their own minds and recognized it as worth naming, to give it a name. The question is simply of finding a way in which one can give thought an objective existence.

The thing that suggests itself immediately is the cinematograph. Everyone must have noticed the extraordinary powers that are latent in the film—the powers of distortion, of fantasy, in general of escaping the restrictions of the physical world. I suppose it is only from commercial necessity that the film has been used chiefly for silly imitations of stage-plays, instead of concentrating as it ought on things that are beyond the stage. Properly used, the film is the one possible medium for conveying mental processes. A dream, for instance, as I said above, is totally inde-scribable in words, but it can quite well be represented on the screen. Years ago I saw a film of Douglas Fairbanks', part of which was a repre-sentation of a dream. Most of it, of course, was silly joking about the dream where you have no clothes on in public, but for a few minutes it really was like a dream, in a manner that would have been impossible in words, or even in a picture, or, I imagine, in music. I have seen the same kind of thing by flashes in other films. For instance in 'Dr Caligari'[6]—a film, however, which was for the most part merely silly, the fantastic element being exploited for its own sake and not to convey any definite meaning. If one thinks of it, there is very little in the mind that could not *somehow* be represented by the strange distorting powers of the film. A millionaire with a private cinematograph, all the necessary props and a troupe of intelligent actors could, if he wished, make practically all of his inner life known. He could explain the real reasons of his actions instead of telling rationalised lies, point out the things that seemed to him beautiful, pathetic, funny etc.—things that an ordinary man has to keep locked up because there are no words to express them. In general, he could make other people understand him. Of course, it is not desirable

5. I once began making a list of writers whom the critics called 'sentimental'. In the end it included nearly every English writer. The word is in fact a meaningless symbol of hatred, like the bronze tripods in Homer which were given to guests as a symbol of friendship [Orwell's footnote].

6. *The Cabinet of Dr. Caligari* was a 1919 German expressionist film directed by Robert Wiene (1873–1938).

that any one man, short of a genius, should make a show of his inner life. What is wanted is to discover the now nameless feelings that men have *in common*. All the powerful motives which will not go into words and which are a cause of constant lying and misunderstanding, could be tracked down, given visible form, agreed upon, and named. I am sure that the film, with its almost limitless powers of representation, could accomplish this in the hands of the right investigators; though putting thoughts into visible shape would not always be easy—in fact, at first it might be as difficult as any other art.

A note on the actual form new words ought to take. Suppose that several thousands of people with the necessary time, talents and money undertook to make additions to language; suppose that they managed to agree upon a number of new and necessary words; they would still have to guard against producing a mere Volapuk[7] which would drop out of use as soon as it was invented. It seems to me probable that a word, even a not yet existing word, has as it were a natural form—or rather, various natural forms in various languages. If language were truly expressive there would be no need to play upon the sounds of words as we do now, but I suppose there must always be *some* correlation between the sound of a word and its meaning. An accepted (I believe) and plausible theory of the origin of language is this. Primitive man, before he had words, would naturally rely upon gesture, and like any other animal he would cry out at the moment of gesticulating, in order to attract attention. Now one instinctively makes the gesture that is appropriate to one's meaning, and all parts of the body follow suit, including the tongue. Hence certain tongue-movements—ie. certain sounds—would come to be associated with certain meanings. In poetry one can point to words which, apart from their direct meanings, regularly convey certain ideas by their sound. Thus: 'Deeper than did ever *plummet* sound' (Shakespeare—more than once I think.) 'Past the *plunge* of *plummet*' (A. E. Housman). 'The un*plumbed*, salt, estranging sea' (Matthew Arnold.) etc.[8] Clearly, apart from direct meanings, the sound plum- or plun- has something to do with bottomless oceans. Therefore in forming new words one would have to pay attention to appropriateness of sound as well as exactitude of meaning.

7. Volapük, 'world-speech', was an international language created about 1879 by Johann Schleyer.
8. Orwell is correct: Shakespeare uses this expression, slightly varied, twice in *The Tempest*, 5.1.56 (as here) and 3.3.101. The line from Housman is from *A Shropshire Lad*, XIV, line 5, and that from Matthew Arnold is from 'Isolation, or To Marguerite.'

It would not do, as at present, to clip a new word of any real novelty by making it out of old ones, but it also would not do to make it out of a mere arbitrary collection of letters. One would have to determine the natural form of the word. Like agreeing upon the actual meanings of the words, this would need the cooperation of a large number of people.

I have written all this down hastily, and when I read through it I see that there are weak patches in my argument and much of it is commonplace. To most people in any case the whole idea of reforming language would seem either dilettant-ish or crankish. Yet it is worth considering what utter incomprehension exists between human beings—at least, between those who are not deeply intimate. At present, as Samuel Butler said, the best art (ie. the most perfect thought-transference) must be 'lived' from one person to another. It need not be so if our language were more adequate. It is curious that when our knowledge, the complication of our lives and therefore (I think it must follow) our minds, develop so fast, language, the chief means of communication, should scarcely stir. For this reason I think that the idea of the deliberate invention of words is at least worth thinking over.[9]

9. On the back of the last page of the typescript there is a drawing illustrating the theorem of Pythagoras that in a right-angled triangle the square on the hypotenuse is equal to the sum of the squares on the other two sides.

Review: Malcolm Muggeridge, *The Thirties*

New English Weekly, 25 APRIL 1940

Mr. Malcolm Muggeridge's 'message'—for it is a message, though a negative one—has not altered since he wrote 'Winter in Moscow.'[1] It boils
down to a simple disbelief in the power of human beings to construct a
perfect or even a tolerable society here on earth. In essence, it is the *Book
of Ecclesiastes* with the pious interpolations left out.

No doubt everyone is familiar with this line of thought. Vanity of
vanities, all is vanity. The Kingdom of Earth is forever unattainable. Every
attempt to establish liberty leads directly to tyranny. One tyrant takes over
from another, the captain of industry from the robber baron, the Nazi
gauleiter from the captain of industry, the sword gives way to the chequebook and the chequebook to the machine-gun, the Tower of Babel perpet-
ually rises and falls. It is the Christian pessimism, but with this important
difference, that in the Christian scheme of things the Kingdom of Heaven
is there to restore the balance:

> Jerusalem, my happy home,
> Would God I were in thee!
> Would God my woes were at an end,
> Thy joys that I might see![2]

And after all, even your earthly 'woes' don't matter so very greatly,
provided that you really 'believe.' Life is short and even Purgatory does
not last for ever, so you are bound to be in Jerusalem before long. Mr.
Muggeridge, needless to say, refuses this consolation. He gives no more
evidence of believing in God than of trusting in Man. Nothing is open
to him, therefore, except an indiscriminate walloping of all human activities whatever. But as a social historian this does not altogether invalidate
him, because the age we live in invites something of the kind. It is an

1. *Winter in Moscow* was published in 1933.
2. Orwell misquotes, doubtless relying on memory. The verse should read:
> Jerusalem, my happy home,
> When shall I come to thee?
> When shall my labours have an end?
> Thy joys when shall I see?
The author of this sixteenth- or seventeenth-century hymn is known only as F. B. P.

age in which every *positive* attitude has turned out a failure. Creeds, parties, programmes of every description have simply flopped, one after another. The only 'ism' that has justified itself is pessimism. Therefore at this moment good books can be written from the angle of Thersites, though probably not very many.

I don't think Mr. Muggeridge's history of the 'thirties is strictly truthful, but I think it is nearer to essential truth than any 'constructive' outlook could have made it. He is looking only on the black side, but it is doubtful whether there is any bright side to look on. What a decade! A riot of appalling folly that suddenly becomes a nightmare, a scenic railway ending in a torture-chamber. It starts off in the hangover of the 'enlightened' post-war age, with Ramsay Macdonald soft-soaping into the microphone and the League of Nations flapping vague wings in the background, and it ends up with twenty thousand bombing planes darkening the sky and Himmler's masked executioner whacking women's heads off on a block borrowed from the Nuremberg museum. In between are the politics of the umbrella and the hand-grenade. The National Government coming in to 'save the pound,' Macdonald fading out like the Cheshire Cat, Baldwin winning an election on the disarmament ticket in order to rearm (and then failing to rearm), the June purge, the Russian purges, the glutinous humbug of the abdication, the ideological mix-up of the Spanish war, Communists waving Union Jacks, Conservative MPs cheering the news that British ships have been bombed, the Pope blessing Franco, Anglican dignitaries beaming at the wrecked churches of Barcelona, Chamberlain stepping out of his Munich aeroplane with a misquotation from Shakespeare, Lord Rothermere acclaiming Hitler as 'a great gentleman,' the London air-raid syrens blowing a false alarm as the first bombs drop on Warsaw. Mr. Muggeridge, who is not loved in 'left' circles, is often labelled 'reactionary' or even 'Fascist,' but I don't know of any leftwing writer who has flayed Macdonald, Baldwin and Chamberlain with equal ferocity. Mixed up with the buzz of conferences and the crash of guns are the day-to-day imbecilities of the gutter press. Astrology, trunk murders, the Oxford Groupers with their 'sharing' and their praying-batteries, the Rector of Stiffkey (a great favourite with Mr. Muggeridge: he makes several appearances) photographed with naked female acquaintances, starving in a barrel and finally devoured by lions, James Douglas and his dog Bunch, Godfrey Winn with his yet more emetic dog and his political reflections ('God and Mr. Chamberlain—for I see no blasphemy in coupling these names'), spiritualism, the Modern Girl, nudism, dog racing, Shirley Temple, B.O., halitosis, night starvation, should a doctor tell?

The book ends on a note of extreme defeatism. The peace that is not a peace slumps into a war that is not a war. The epic events that everyone had expected somehow don't happen, the all-pervading lethargy continues just as before. 'Shape without form, shade without colour, paralysed force, gesture without motion.' What Mr. Muggeridge appears to be saying is that the English are powerless against their new adversaries because there is no longer anything that they believe in with sufficient firmness to make them willing for sacrifice. It is the struggle of people who have no faith against people who have faith in false gods. Is he right, I wonder? The truth is that it is impossible to discover what the English people are really feeling and thinking, about the war or about anything else. It has been impossible all through the critical years. I don't myself believe that he is right. But one cannot be sure until something of a quite unmistakeable nature—some great disaster, probably—has brought home to the mass of the people what kind of world they are living in.

The final chapters are, to me, deeply moving, all the more because the despair and defeatism that they express is not altogether sincere. Beneath Mr. Muggeridge's seeming acceptance of disaster there lies the unconfessed fact that he does after all believe in something—in England. He does not want to see England conquered by Germany, though if one judges merely by the earlier chapters one might well ask what difference it would make. I am told that some months back he left the Ministry of Information to join the army,[3] a thing which none of the ex-warmongers of the Left has done, I believe. And I know very well what underlies these closing chapters. It is the emotion of the middle-class man, brought up in the military tradition, who finds in the moment of crisis that he is a patriot after all. It is all very well to be 'advanced' and 'enlightened,' to snigger at Colonel Blimp and proclaim your emancipation from all traditional loyalties, but a time comes when the sand of the desert is sodden red and what have I done for thee, England, my England? As I was brought up in this tradition myself I can recognize it under strange disguises, and also sympathise with it, for even at its stupidest and most sentimental it is a comelier thing than the shallow self-righteousness of the leftwing intelligentsia.

3. Muggeridge served in East and North Africa, Italy, and France, 1939–45. The French government awarded him La Légion d'Honneur and La Croix de Guerre avec Palme.

Theatre Review: *Garrison Theatre*, Palladium

Time and Tide, 25 MAY 1940

Translated from the radio to the stage, this variety show goes with a swing and has not many tedious moments. Acrobats fling themselves into the air, troops of beautiful girls kick their hats with military precision, Joe Davis, world's snooker champion, plays billiard-strokes which seem incredible even when one sees them; Moore Marriott, Graham Moffatt and Harry Tate (junior)[1] make ineffectual attempts to start their motor car, and in the intervals while the scenes are being changed Jack Warner exchanges gloriously vulgar badinage with his 'little gel', Joan Winters. Perhaps the best turn of all is the Three Aberdonians, who enliven a good acrobatic display with mild obscenities. There are two definitely patriotic items, the second of which, a scene on a minesweeper, with the Fifty Singing Marines, is a clever piece of staging and makes good use of the picturesque background. The only black spot is the bi-national anthem which ends the performance. May I suggest that to tack the first four bars of the 'Marseillaise' on to the last four bars of 'God Save the King' is *not* the way to make a good tune? England and France have pooled their economic resources, and surely that should be enough.

1. This act, created by Harry Tate Senior, dated from before World War I. Harry Tate Senior was killed in an air-raid on 14 February 1940.

Review: Jim Phelan, *Jail Journey*

Horizon, JUNE 1940

Writing to Geoffrey Gorer on 10 January 1940 Orwell asked, 'Have you seen the new monthly magazine, Horizon, *that Cyril Connolly & Stephen Spender are running? They are trying to get away from the bloody political squirrel-cage, & about time too' (see* A Life in Letters, *p. 174).* Horizon *was undoubtedly a literary and journalistic success and Orwell was delighted to write for it. Connolly (1903–74) was with Orwell at St Cyprian's Preparatory School and Eton. They met again after Connolly had reviewed* Burmese Days *and remained friends. Sir Stephen Spender (1909–95) was a prolific poet, novelist and critic. He was later co-editor of* Encounter, *1953–65, only leaving that journal when it was discovered it was partially financed by the US Central Intelligence Agency. Initially Orwell included Spender amongst those he castigated as 'parlour Bolsheviks'. They were reconciled in mid April 1938 (see Orwell's letter to Spender,* A Life in Letters, *pp. 104–5).*

In a book that is always lively and readable, the thing that stands out as truly important is Mr. Phelan's straightforward discussion of the sex life of prisons. The existing penal system simply ignores the fact that man is a sexual animal. In Mr. Phelan's book, and especially in Chapters XIV–XVI, you can study the results of this, and they make horrible reading, but genuinely horrible, and not just pornography in disguise.

The essential fact about a prison is that it is a place where you are cut off from the opposite sex. As Mr. Phelan points out, it is not enough to say that this is part of the punishment; it *is* the punishment. And sex-deprivation does not simply mean the cutting-off of a luxury, like tobacco, but the starvation of a powerful instinct which will take its revenge in one way or another. It is perfectly well known to anyone with even a third-hand acquaintance with prisons that nearly all prisoners are chronic masturbators. In addition there is homosexuality, which is almost general in long-term jails. If Macartney's *Walls Have Mouths* is to be believed, some prisons are such hotbeds of vice that even the warders are infected. Mr. Phelan's revelations are less lurid, but they are certainly bad enough. Over sixty unnatural forms of the sexual act, he says, are now practised in Dartmoor and Parkhurst. The thing is taken for granted and joked about by prisoners, warders and everyone else connected with a prison, at the same time as it cannot even be hinted at in any public discussion of the subject. All modern civilized societies rest ultimately on the jail and the concentration camp, and the central fact about jails and concentration camps is something unmentionable. The question Mr. Phelan asks is whether 'they', the respectable people, the clergymen, scoutmasters and maiden ladies who believe that prison is 'good for you', know just what imprisonment means. He concludes that they do know, and when he was serving his own sentence he was even tempted to believe that they rather enjoy the knowledge. He records (very interesting if true) that the majority of women go in for some or other form of exhibitionism when they pass a file of convicts on the road. Even prison-reformers are almost always shocked by the suggestion that convicts should be allowed a normal sexual life. (The formula is: 'Oh, but that's impossible!') They cry out against leg-irons and bread-and-water, but they are willing to tolerate sodomy. And in fact it has got to be tolerated so long as prisons exist.

Mr. Phelan was 'in' for killing somebody (he served thirteen years of a life-sentence and was then released), and even a wilful murderer is not in the ordinary sense a criminal. This no doubt accounts for the detached, good-tempered attitude that Mr. Phelan is able to take. The whining note which is so common in prison literature is completely absent from his book. On the whole he is recording rather than commenting, and though the record is more damning than any diatribe, he makes few positive suggestions. He seems content to point out that our present methods of dealing with criminals are worse than useless, and to leave it at that. In prison he kept up a ceaseless, conscious struggle to keep his mind intact, to avoid slipping back into the neuroses and the downright lunacy which he saw all round him. He spent years planning escape (a most ingenious escape, which, however, finally had to be abandoned), studied chess and foreign languages, made himself into a skilled blacksmith and a first-rate gardener, and wrote enormously on pilfered sheets of paper. (He doesn't say how he smuggled his writings out of jail. That could be 'telling', of course, but the tip might come in useful one of these days.) The information that he gives about prison slang and about the various rackets and unofficial recreations is most interesting. This is the book of an individualist, with a streak of rather childish vanity; but a more modest man would never have remained sane enough to write it.

Review: E.L. Grant Wilson, *Priest Island*

Tribune, 21 JUNE 1940

Tribune was founded in 1937 by two Labour Party MPs, Sir Stafford Cripps (1889–1952) and George Strauss (1901–93). It is nominally independent but in the main supports the Labour Party from a left-wing perspective. It was edited by Raymond Postgate (1896–1971) from 1940–42. He was best known at this time for the book he wrote with G.D.H Cole, The Common People, 1746–1938 *(1938). Postgate was removed as editor in 1941 by the Welsh Labour MP, Aneurin Bevan (1897–1960; now chiefly remembered for his work in the setting up of the National Health Service). Much of the day-to-day work was done by Jon Kimche (1909–94) who had worked with Orwell at Booklovers' Corner, 1934–35. Orwell was appointed literary editor in 1943 and worked as such until 1945 though he continued to contribute until 1947. Sir Bernard Crick believed he was paid less than when at the BBC, perhaps about £500 a year. However, he was also paid from 10 shillings to £2 for reviews and articles. It would be fair to say that Orwell's contributions have become a touchstone for the best in political journalism without rancour.*

More emphatically 'escape literature' is *Priest Island*,[1] which is that evergreen favourite, a desert-island story. All desert-island stories are good, but some are better than others, and I am afraid that *Priest Island* must be put rather low in the list, because it concentrates too much on the psychological side of the story and not enough on the all-absorbing physical side. For that is the real interest of a desert-island story—the concrete details of the struggle to keep alive. One doesn't particularly want to know what the hero *felt*; what one wants to know is whether he possessed a pen-knife or any fish-hooks and how he managed about lighting a fire.

Priest Island rather fails in these respects, because the hero has things made too easy for him. He is a young Scotsman exiled for sheep-stealing (the date is not given, but it is presumably about a hundred years ago) to a small island in the Hebrides. Later a woman who has heard of his fate voluntarily comes and joins him, bringing goats, hens, and other stock for a small farm. But long before her arrival the hero has made himself a lot more comfortable than would in practice have been possible. Arriving

---

1. 'More emphatically' than Mikhail Yurevich Lermontov's *A Hero of Our Times*, also reviewed in this contribution to *Tribune*.

late in the season, with only a spade with which to tackle rocky virgin ground, he has been able to grow enough potatoes to feed him through the winter. I flatly refuse to believe this.

I also refuse to believe that the following year he would have been able to break in enough ground to grow a crop of oats, using a home-made wooden plough which he draws himself, his wife guiding the handles. Mr. Wilson also speaks glibly of 'trapping' wild ducks, without explaining how this difficult feat was done. Such criticism seems rather petty, perhaps, but the whole interest of a desert-island story is on the physical side, and the details ought to be accurate. But as a love-story, with a certain 'dark earth' element, the book is rather good, and the ghost who haunts the island (whence its name) is more credible than most.

Letter to *Time and Tide*: 'On preparation for imminent invasion'

22 JUNE 1940

Sir: It is almost certain that England will be invaded within the next few days or weeks, and a large-scale invasion by sea-borne troops is quite likely. At such a time our slogan should be ARM THE PEOPLE. I am not competent to deal with the wider questions of repelling the invasion, but I submit that the campaign in France and the recent civil war in Spain have made two facts clear. One is that when the civil population is unarmed, parachutists, motor cyclists and stray tanks can not only work fearful havoc but draw off large bodies of regular troops who should be opposing the main enemy. The other fact (demonstrated by the Spanish war) is that the advantages of arming the population outweigh the danger of putting weapons into the wrong hands. By-elections since the war started have shown that only a tiny minority among the common people of England are disaffected, and most of these are already marked down.

ARM THE PEOPLE is in itself a vague phrase, and I do not, of course, know what weapons are available for immediate distribution. But there are at any rate several things that can and should be done *now*, i.e. within the next three days:

1. Hand grenades. These are the only modern weapon of war that can be rapidly and easily manufactured, and they are one of the most useful. Hundreds of thousands of men in England are accustomed to using hand grenades and would be only too ready to instruct others. They are said to be useful against tanks and will be absolutely necessary if enemy parachutists with machine-guns manage to establish themselves in our big towns. I had a front-seat view of the street fighting in Barcelona in May, 1937, and it convinced me that a few hundred men with machine-guns can paralyse the life of a large city, because of the fact that a bullet will not penetrate an ordinary brick wall. They can be blasted out with artillery, but it is not always possible to bring a gun to bear. On the other hand, the early street fighting in Spain showed that armed men can be driven out of stone buildings with grenades or even sticks of dynamite if the right tactics are used.

2. Shotguns. There is talk of arming some of the Local Defence Volunteer contingents with shotguns. This may be necessary if all

the rifles and Bren guns are needed for the regular troops. But in that case the distribution should be made *now* and all weapons should be immediately requisitioned from the gunsmiths' shops. There was talk of doing this weeks ago, but in fact many gunsmiths' windows show rows of guns which are not only useless where they are, but actually a danger, as these shops could easily be raided. The powers and limitations of the shotgun (with buckshot, lethal up to about sixty yards) should be explained to the public over the radio.

3.   Blocking fields against aircraft landings. There has been much talk of this, but it has only been done sporadically. The reason is that it has been left to voluntary effort, i.e. to people who have insufficient time and no power of requisitioning materials. In a small thickly-populated country like England we could within a very days make it impossible for an aeroplane to land anywhere except at an aerodrome. All that is needed is the labour. Local authorities should therefore have powers to conscript labour and requisition such materials as they require.

4.   Painting out place-names. This has been well done as regards signposts, but there are everywhere shopfronts, tradesmen's vans, etc., bearing the name of their locality. Local authorities should have the power to enforce the painting-out of these immediately. This should include the brewers' names on public houses. Most of these are confined to a fairly small area, and the Germans are probably methodical enough to know this.

5.   Radio sets. Every Local Defence Volunteer headquarters should be in possession of a radio receiving set, so that if necessary it can receive its orders over the air. It is fatal to rely on the telephone in a moment of emergency. As with weapons, the Government should not hesitate to requisition what it needs.

All of these are things that could be done within the space of a very few days. Meanwhile, let us go on repeating ARM THE PEOPLE, in the hope that more and more voices will take it up. For the first time in decades we have a Government with imagination, and there is at least a chance that they will listen.

Review: A.J. Jenkinson, *What Do Boys and Girls Read?*

Life and Letters,[1] July 1940

This book, compiled mostly from questionnaires directed to teachers and pupils at Secondary and Elementary Schools, is a useful sociological fragment, a sort of detailed footnote to the researches of the Mass Observers.

Mr. Jenkinson's main object was to decide whether the teaching of English literature, as now practised, is of any value and has any real relationship to the development of the child. He concludes that to drive a child of fourteen through Addison's Essays is useless if not positively harmful, and that the less literature is taught as an examinable 'subject' the better. But incidentally his researches have brought out a number of interesting points. One is the sharp difference between children in the Secondary Schools and those of the same age in the 'Senior' Schools (higher forms of Elementary Schools). The former have been picked out by the scholarship system and belong to a more intellectual and more slowly-maturing type. The Secondary schoolgirl of fourteen is still a child, but a child with fairly good literary taste. The Elementary schoolgirl of the same age is for most purposes an under-developed adult; she is already reading sensational erotic novelettes side by side with 'comics' of the most infantile kind. Another point is the phase of philistinism that most children seem to go through between the ages of twelve and fourteen. And another is the importance of the 'blood' (or 'penny dreadful') in the development of the child. It seems that nearly all English-teachers now recognize this. Attempts to suppress the reading of 'bloods' have ceased, and some teachers even state that they make use of them in their English lessons.

But the most striking point of all is the improvement in literacy and intelligence that is unquestionably taking place. Mr. Jenkinson, starting out with very high standards, seems rather to underrate this. He gives detailed lists of the books taken out of school libraries, and though, of course, there is an immense consumption of trash, the fact remains that the children of both sexes do voluntarily read great numbers of 'good' books in their spare time. Dickens (especially *David Copperfield*), Defoe, and Stevenson are steady favourites, and Wells, Kipling, Blackmore, Tom

1. *Life and Letters* ran from June 1928 to June 1950 (as *Life and Letters Today*, September 1935 to June 1945). Cyril Connolly made significant contributions to it and he possibly prompted Orwell's contributions.

Hughes, Conan Doyle, and G. K. Chesterton all appear in the lists. Poetry is less well-represented, the favourite poems usually being patriotic battle-pieces, but Shakespeare seems to be fairly extensively read. Considering that the children under examination are aged 12–15 and belong to the poorest class in the community, these results are extremely encouraging. It also appears that nearly all children now read the newspapers, and read the news as well as the comic columns, etc. It is unfortunate that the favourite paper should in most cases be the *Daily Mail*, but a child's choice of papers is governed by that of its parents. Except for the *Herald*, no left-wing paper appears to have any footing among school-children.

Students of social change should lay by this book. It casts a lot of light on the direction in which society is moving, and, were they capable of using it, could give valuable hints to the left-wing propagandists who at present totally fail to reach the mass of the population.

Reviews: Jack London, *The Iron Heel*; H.G. Wells, *When the Sleeper Awakes;*[1] Aldous Huxley, *Brave New World*; Ernest Bramah, *The Secret of the League*

Tribune, 12 JULY 1940

The reprinting of Jack London's *The Iron Heel* (Werner Laurie 5/–) brings within general reach a book which has been much sought after during the years of Fascist aggression. Like others of Jack London's books it has been widely read in Germany, and it has had the reputation of being an accurate forecast of the Coming of Hitler. In reality it is not that. It is merely a tale of capitalist oppression, and it was written at a time when various things that have made Fascism possible—for instance, the tremendous revival of nationalism—were not easy to foresee.

Where London did show special insight, however, was in realising that the transition to Socialism was not going to be automatic or even easy. The capitalist class was not going to 'perish of its own contradictions' like a flower dying at the end of the season. The capitalist class was quite clever enough to see what was happening, to sink its own differences and counter-attack against the workers; and the resulting struggle would be the most bloody and unscrupulous the world had ever seen.

It is worth comparing *The Iron Heel* with another imaginative novel of the future which was written somewhat earlier and to which it owes something, H. G. Wells' *The Sleeper Wakes* (Collins, 2/6). By doing so one can see both London's limitations and also the advantage he enjoyed in not being, like Wells, a fully civilized man. As a book, *The Iron Heel* is hugely inferior. It is clumsily written, it shows no grasp of scientific possibilities, and the hero is the kind of human gramophone who is now disappearing even from Socialist tracts. But because of his own streak of savagery London could grasp something that Wells apparently could not, and that is that hedonistic societies do not endure.

Everyone who has ever read *The Sleeper Wakes* remembers it. It is a vision of a glittering, sinister world in which society had hardened into a caste-system and the workers are permanently enslaved. It is also a world without purpose, in which the upper castes for whom the workers toil are completely soft, cynical and faithless. There is no consciousness of

1. The full title is *When the Sleeper Wakes: A Story of the Years to Come* (1899).

any object in life, nothing corresponding to the fervour of the revolutionary or the religious martyr.

In Aldous Huxley's *Brave New World* (Chatto & Windus, 4/-), a sort of post-war parody of the Wellsian Utopia, these tendencies are immensely exaggerated. Here the hedonistic principle is pushed to its utmost, the whole world has turned into a Riviera hotel. But though *Brave New World* was a brilliant caricature of the present (the present of 1930), it probably casts no light on the future. No society of that kind would last more than a couple of generations, because a ruling class which thought principally in terms of a 'good time' would soon lose its vitality. A ruling class has got to have a strict morality, a quasi-religious belief in itself, a *mystique*. London was aware of this, and though he describes the caste of plutocrats who rule the world for seven centuries as inhuman monsters, he does not describe them as idlers or sensualists. They can only maintain their position while they honestly believe that civilization depends on themselves alone, and therefore in a different way they are just as brave, able and devoted as the revolutionaries who oppose them.

In an intellectual way London accepted the conclusions of Marxism, and he imagined that the 'contradictions' of capitalism, the unconsumable surplus and so forth, would persist even after the capitalist class had organised themselves into a single corporate body. But temperamentally he was very different from the majority of Marxists. With his love of violence and physical strength, his belief in 'natural aristocracy,' his animal-worship and exaltation of the primitive, he had in him what one might fairly call a Fascist strain. This probably helped him to understand just how the possessing class would behave when once they were seriously menaced.

It is just here that Marxian Socialists have usually fallen short. Their interpretation of history has been so mechanistic that they have failed to foresee dangers that were obvious to people who had never heard the name of Marx. It is sometimes urged against Marx that he failed to predict the rise of Fascism. I do not know whether he predicted it or not—at that date he could only have done so in very general terms—but it is at any rate certain that his followers failed to see any danger in Fascism until they themselves were at the gates of the concentration camp. A year or more *after* Hitler had risen to power official Marxism was still proclaiming that Hitler was of no importance and 'social-fascism' (*i.e.*, democracy) was the real enemy. London would probably not have made this mistake. His instincts would have warned him that Hitler was dangerous. He knew that economic laws do not operate in the same way as the law of gravity, that they can be held up for long periods by people who, like Hitler, believe in their own destiny.

The Iron Heel and *The Sleeper Wakes* are both written from the popular standpoint. *Brave New World*, though primarily an attack on hedonism, is also by implication an attack on totalitarianism and caste rule. It is interesting to compare them with a less well-known Utopia which treats the class struggle from the upper or rather the middle-class point of view, Ernest Bramah's *The Secret of the League*.

The Secret of the League was written in 1907, when the growth of the labour movement was beginning to terrify the middle class, who wrongly imagined that they were menaced from below and not from above. As a political forecast it is trivial, but it is of great interest for the light it casts on the mentality of the struggling middle class.

The author imagines a Labour Government coming into office with so huge a majority that it is impossible to dislodge them. They do not, however, introduce a full Socialist economy. They merely continue to operate capitalism for their own benefit by constantly raising wages, creating a huge army of bureaucrats and taxing the upper classes out of existence. The country is therefore 'going to the dogs' in the familiar manner; moreover in their foreign politics the Labour Government behave rather like the National Government between 1931 and 1939. Against this there arises a secret conspiracy of the middle and upper classes. The manner of their revolt is very ingenious, provided that one looks upon capitalism as something internal. It is the method of the consumers' strike. Over a period of two years the upper-class conspirators secretly hoard fuel-oil and convert coal-burning plant to oil-burning; then they suddenly boycott the principal British industry, the coal industry. The miners are faced with a situation in which they will be able to sell no coal for two years. There is vast unemployment and distress, ending in civil war, in which (thirty years before General Franco!) the upper classes receive foreign aid. After their victory they abolish the trade unions and institute a 'strong' non-parliamentary *régime*—in other words a *régime* that we should now describe as Fascist. The tone of the book is good-natured, as it could afford to be at that date, but the trend of thought is unmistakeable.

Why should a decent and kindly writer like Ernest Bramah find the crushing of the proletariat a pleasant vision? It is simply the reaction of a struggling class which felt itself menaced not so much in its economic position as in its code of conduct and way of life. One can see the same purely social antagonism to the working class in an earlier writer of much greater calibre, George Gissing.[2] Time and Hitler have taught the middle classes a great deal, and perhaps they will not again side with their oppressors against their natural allies. But whether they do so or not depends partly on how they are handled, and the stupidity of Socialist propaganda, with its constant baiting of the 'petty bourgeois,' has a lot to answer for.

2. George Gissing (1857–1903) was much admired by Orwell who wrote two articles about him: 'Not Enough Money', see page 223, and 'George Gissing' (CW, XIX, 347–52). Gissing wrote twenty-three novels of which New Grub Street (1891), The Odd Woman (1893) and In the Year of the Jubilee (1894) are particularly remembered.

Theatre Review: George Bernard Shaw, *The Devil's Disciple*, Piccadilly Theatre

Time and Tide, AUGUST 1940

The Devil's Disciple, which is perhaps the best play Shaw ever wrote, is not acted as often as it deserves, probably because of the largeness of the cast. It was a brave gesture to put it on at this moment, but evidently it is going to be justified. On the second night, which is always a critical moment, the house was packed to the walls and wildly enthusiastic—a little too enthusiastic, in fact, for there was much clapping during the scenes, a habit that Mr Shaw himself rightly protested against in his critical days fifty years ago.

The play is essentially a melodrama, and a melodrama of the kind that depends upon somebody being 'shown up in his true colours'. Two men, opposites in character and reputation, suddenly tear off their masks at a critical moment and reveal that each is in reality the other. Dick Dudgeon, eldest son of a New England family, has grown up in the horrible atmosphere of hypocritical puritanism and reacted against it by proclaiming himself a worshipper of the Devil. The God of the Calvinists is in fact so evil in every way that one can make a tolerable sort of God by simply reversing His attributes. Over against the sinful Dick is Mr Anderson, the local Presbyterian minister, who has every appearance of being a saint— except that he is a man of powerful physique who has married a pretty wife in middle age. The period of the play is the American War of Independence. Suddenly the English soldiers arrive at the minister's house —they have had orders to hang one rebel, *in terrorem*, and a hanged clergyman is expected to have a particularly strong moral effect—and by a well-contrived mistake they arrest Dick Dudgeon instead of Mr Anderson. Just here the professional bad man finds that he is not a bad man after all, but something more like a martyr. It is psychologically impossible for him to take his neck out of the noose and put another man's into it. So he lets the soldiers lead him away, without revealing his identity. But the clergyman, it turns out, has equally mistaken his own character. He is not a saint but a man of action. When he finds out what has happened he does not meekly give himself up to be hanged in Dick's place. Instead he flings himself on to a horse, rides to the nearest rebel lines (the familiar melodramatic ride against time—if it were on the films we should see the same old white horse going over the same bit of ground) and procures for himself a safe-conduct which he knows is to be given to an emissary from the rebels to General Burgoyne. Then, just as Dick is mounting the gallows, he arrives, announces his identity, and presents the safe-conduct. He explains that he is leaving the Church and starting life anew as a captain in the Springfield Militia. Dick, we are left to under-stand, will probably become a clergyman.

Watching this witty and well-made play, one cannot help feeling how much it owes to the time in which it was written. In the late 'eighties or early 'nineties there was still an accepted code to fight against, and it was possible to make a good book or play out of mere naughtiness and debunking. Nowadays there is nothing left to debunk, except the new orthodoxies of which Mr Shaw is such a warm admirer. For by a strange irony Mr Shaw himself was to go through a psychological 'showing up' very similar to that of the two main characters in *The Devil's Disciple*. The seeming rebel was actually an apostle of the authoritarian State. Naturally —for it would have seemed natural at that date—he is on the side of the American colonists against the British. All of Mr Shaw's best work belongs to the period 1890–1914, when he was dealing with something he had grown up in and understood, the humbug of a puritanical monied society. It was something solid to kick against, and he kicked memorably.

Mr Robert Donat, as Dick Dudgeon, understood his part well and looked it even better, but in my opinion he acted a shade too boisterously. Mr Roger Livesey, as Anthony Anderson, was extremely good. The dramatic moment in which he drops his saintly air and shouts for his horse and pistols—a difficult thing to bring off successfully—was entirely convincing. The women were less satisfactory, but they have rather poor parts, and that of Mrs Anderson (Miss Rosamund John) is complicated by an abortive love-affair which is not really necessary to the plot. Mr Milton Rosmer was excellent as General Burgoyne. This character, an able commander who sees his battles being lost for him by wire-pullers in London, has all the best lines in the second act. His remark, 'The British soldier can stand up to anything except the British War Office' was much appreciated by an audience well sprinkled with uniforms.

Review: Sacheverell Sitwell, *Poltergeists*

Horizon, SEPTEMBER 1940

To judge from the newspapers, poltergeists appear fairly frequently but seldom get a thorough investigation, because they will not, as a rule, 'perform' in the presence of strangers. But there are quite enough authenticated cases—Mr. Sitwell gives detailed accounts of four of the best-known, but there is a number of others—to suggest that the poltergeist is not imaginary in the ordinary sense of the word.

These cases are almost always very much alike. They consist of a series of evil-minded and frightening practical jokes, often with an undercurrent of obscenity. Crockery is smashed, objects fly through the air in an inexplicable manner, there are rapping noises and sometimes tremendous explosions and the violent ringing of bells. Sometimes, also, there are mysterious voices and apparitions of animals. In nearly, though not quite all, cases, there is in the house some young person, usually a girl about the age of puberty, who can be identified as the medium. As a rule she is ultimately caught and admits that she has been playing tricks, after which the phenomena cease. But the thing is not so simple as this makes it appear. To begin with, there are cases in which no conscious fraud appears to exist, and others in which the medium only seems to have resorted to deliberate trickery after his or her 'genuine' powers had begun to wane. But the most striking fact of all is that even when the mediums are consciously cheating they seem to acquire powers that they would not normally have. At the least they become accomplished conjurors. The mysterious voices, for instance, are obviously due to ventriloquism, which is not much easier to learn than walking the tightrope. In a few cases the disturbances have continued for years on end without any human agent being caught in the act.

As with spiritualistic phenomena, three explanations are possible. One is 'spirits', one is hypnotism and hallucination, and another is vulgar fraud. Few sensible people would accept the first, and there is a good deal of evidence for the third. Houdini, for instance, was fond of demonstrating that all spiritualist 'manifestations' can be faked; some of the details are given in his biography. Mr. Sitwell takes it for granted that all poltergeist phenomena are due to human trickery, conscious and unconscious, but, as he points out, it is just there that the interest begins. Ghosts are completely uninteresting, but the aberrations of the human mind are not.

In the case of the poltergeist you have an aberration by which one member of a family is impelled to play terrifying tricks on the others, and to show diabolical secretiveness and cunning in doing so. Why they do it, what pleasure they get out of it, is completely unknown. There is possibly a clue in the fact that the same phenomena recur in cases that are centuries apart. If one takes the view that the poltergeist disturbances never actually happen, that the whole thing is simply a pack of lies, then one is faced by an even stranger psychological puzzle—that of whole households suffering collective hallucination or conspiring together to tell stories that are bound to get them laughed at.

Mr. Sitwell links the subject up with sexual hysteria on the one hand, and on the other with witchcraft, in which hallucination was mixed up with the remains of a pre-Christian fertility-worship. The famous Sabbaths at which the witches had sexual intercourse with the Devil were presumably dreams induced by auto-suggestion and drugs. According to Mr. Sitwell, the ointment with which they rubbed themselves before mounting their broomsticks is now known to have contained drugs which would give a sleeping person the sensation of flying. It was only recently that witchcraft could be seriously studied, because it was only recently that the 'supernatural' explanation of it could be finally rejected. So also with the poltergeist, so long accepted as a real ghost or laughed at as an old wives' story. It is probably neither, but a rare and interesting form of insanity. When it has been further studied it will probably, like spiritualism, teach us a little more about hallucination and group-psychology.[1]

1. See also Orwell's letter to Sitwell, 6 July 1940, *A Life in Letters*, pp. 181–2.

Theatre Review: *Applesauce*, Holborn Empire

Time and Tide, 7 SEPTEMBER 1940

Anyone wanting to see something really vulgar should visit the Holborn Empire, where you can get quite a good matinée seat for three shillings. Max Miller[1] of course, is the main attraction, but there is a good supporting programme with some brilliant sketches. The best of these is a skit on the Home Guard which incidentally does some good propaganda for that neglected body. Doris Hare does a skit on a strip-tease act, and there are some good acrobatics by the Dolinoffs and Raya Sisters. One of their acts is a sort of music-hall version of *La Boutique Fantasque*, the other an optical illusion which probably casts some light on the 'manifestations' at spiritualistic séances.

Max Miller, who looks more like a Middlesex Street hawker than ever when he is wearing a tail coat and a shiny top hat, is one of a long line of English comedians who have specialized in the Sancho Panza side of life, in real *lowness*. To do this probably needs more talent than to express nobility. Little Tich[2] was a master at it. There was a music-hall farce which Little Tich used to act in, in which he was supposed to be factotum to a crook solicitor. The solicitor is giving, him his instructions:—

Now, our client who's coming this morning is a widow with a good figure. Are you following me?
Little Tich: I'm ahead of you.

As it happens, I have seen this farce acted several times with other people in the same part, but I have never seen anyone who could approach the utter baseness that Little Tich could get into these simple words. There is a touch of the same quality in Max Miller. Quite apart from the laughs

1. Max Miller (1895–1963), known as 'the Cheekie Chappie', was the last outstanding music-hall low comedian and carried the tradition on into the 1950s – until the buildings in which he performed had been, in the main, pulled down or converted to other uses. He underlies Archie Rice in John Osborne's play *The Entertainer* (1956).
2. Little Tich (Harry Relph) (1867–1928), named in mockery of the Tichborne claimant, whom he was said to look like, was very small and, in addition to having a turn of wit that descended from that of the clowns of Shakespeare's day, was remarkably dextrous physically. He was as skilful in French as in English, and in 1910 was made an officer of the Académie Française.

they give one, it is important that such comedians should exist. They express something which is valuable in our civilization and which might drop out of it in certain circumstances. To begin with, their genius is entirely masculine. A woman cannot be low without being disgusting, whereas a good male comedian can give the impression of something irredeemable and yet innocent, like a sparrow. Again, they are intensely national. They remind one how closely-knit the civilization of England is, and how much it resembles a family, in spite of its out-of-date class distinctions. The startling obscenities which occur in *Applesauce* are only possible because they are expressed in *doubles entendres* which imply a common background in the audience. Anyone who had not been brought up on the *Pink 'Un* would miss the point of them. So long as comedians like Max Miller are on the stage and the comic coloured postcards which express approximately the same view of life are in the stationers' windows, one knows that the popular culture of England is surviving. Meanwhile, *Applesauce* is a first-rate variety show, with only the minimum of 'glamorous' songs between the comic acts.[3]

3. The singer of the 'glamorous' songs was Vera Lynn (1917–; DBE), the 'Forces' Sweetheart.' In her *We'll Meet Again: A Personal and Social Memory of World War Two* (1989), she records that the show was closed for a time because the Holborn Empire had sustained a direct hit. It reopened at the Palladium in March 1941. One of the glamorous songs was certain to have been 'We'll Meet Again'.

Review: T.C. Worsley, *Barbarians and Philistines: Democracy and the Public Schools*

Time and Tide, 14 SEPTEMBER 1940

The title of this book is not intended as a denunciation. It refers to the distinction drawn by Matthew Arnold between the 'barbarian' spirit of the old landed aristocracy and the 'Philistine' spirit of the monied bourgeoisie who progressively overwhelmed them from 1830 onwards.[1] The majority of our public schools were founded in the mid-nineteenth century, and the ones that already existed were altered out of recognition at about the same date. The new class who were coming into power naturally wanted a more civilized type of school than the Rugby described by Tom Hughes, and through the efforts of Dr Arnold and other reformers they got it. But the aristocracy had by no means disappeared, they intermarried with the bourgeoisie and deeply influenced their view of life, and the new schools were modified in consequence. The 'barbarous' element persisted in the hatred of intellectuality and the worship of games, which Arnold had certainly not foreseen or intended. And the fact that the British Empire needed administrators, less adventurous and more reliable than the men who had conquered it, set the public schools to turning out the brave, stupid, fairly decent mediocrities who are still their typical products today. Indeed the system has not altered markedly since the 'eighties of the last century.

Mr Worsley, writing from the angle of a Left Wing intellectual, is naturally hostile to the public schools, but it is doubtful whether his criticisms are altogether relevant. Broadly speaking, his charge is that the public schools are 'not democratic'. This is unquestionably true. The atmosphere of nearly all these schools is deeply reactionary. Ninety-nine public-school boys out of a hundred, if they had votes, would vote Tory. But that is not the same as saying—and this is what Mr Worsley suggests —that the public schools produce types favourable to Fascism. On the contrary, one of the striking things about the British ruling class has been their complete failure to understand Fascism, either to combat it or to imitate it, and the old-fashioned Toryism that is absorbed in the public schools is partly responsible for this. Again, when he says that the public

---

1. See his *Culture and Anarchy* (1869); e.g.: 'Thus we have got three distinct terms, Barbarians, Philistines, Populace, to denote roughly the three great classes into which our society is divided.'

schools breed an undemocratic mentality, he appears to mean that they do not turn out boys who can accommodate themselves to a world of equal suffrage, free speech, intellectual tolerance and international co-operation. This would be a valid criticism if any such world lay ahead of us. But unfortunately that version of democracy is even more a lost cause than feudalism. What is ahead of us is not an age of reason but an age of bombing planes, and the sort of 'democrat' that Mr Worsley seems to postulate would be even worse off in it than the average public-school boy, who has at any rate not been brought up as a pacifist or a believer in the League of Nations. The brutal side of public-school life, which intellectuals always deprecate, is not a bad training for the real world. The trouble is that in every other way these schools have remained in the nineteenth century, breeding-grounds of a privileged class which could not bring itself up to date without losing its self-confidence in the process.

Merely to make fun of the public schools, *more* Beachcomber,[2] would hardly be worthwhile. It is too easy, and besides, it is flogging a dead horse, or a dying one, for all but three or four schools will be killed financially by the present war. Mr Worsley has some fun with Newbolt's celebrated *Vitäi Lampada*[3] but he makes constructive suggestions as well. Much in the public-school system, he thinks, is well suited to boys of sixteen or under. Up to that age boys profit by an atmosphere of gang-loyalty, games-worship and homosexuality, and it is in the last two years of school that the harm is done to them. What he advocates is a system of junior universities at which the type of boy, who is still teachable at sixteen can continue his education in a comparatively adult atmosphere. This war, however it ends, will leave us with big educational problems, and when the public schools have finally vanished we shall see virtues in them that are now hidden from us. But it is too early to say so, and Mr Worsley's attack on an obsolete system, if not always quite fair, will do more good than harm.

2. 'Beachcomber' was the pseudonym for a rather jokey column in the *Daily Express*. It was started by D.B. Wyndham Lewis (1891–1969) and run from 1924 by J.B. Morton (1893–1979), a fellow Roman Catholic. It was, for Orwell, a *bête noire*.

3. Sir Henry John Newbolt (1862–1938) was a writer of much patriotic verse ('Admirals All', 'Drake's Drum') that schoolboys often had to learn by heart in the first half of the twentieth century. His 'Vitäi Lampada' (given incorrectly in this review as 'Lampada Vitai') includes the famous stanza beginning 'There's a breathless hush in the Close tonight' and concludes with a schoolboy rallying the troops with the cricket captain's adjuration, 'Play up! play up! and play the game!' (inscribed on a plaque outside Lord's Cricket Ground). Orwell compares this poem and John Cornford's 'Before the Storming of Huesca' in 'My Country Right or Left'.

Review: Hadley Cantril with Hazel Gaudet and Herta Herzog, *The Invasion from Mars*

New Statesman and Nation, 26 OCTOBER 1940

Nearly two years ago Mr. Orson Welles[1] produced on the Columbia Broadcasting System in New York a radio play based on H. G. Wells's fantasia *The War of the Worlds*. The broadcast was not intended as a hoax, but it had an astonishing and unforeseen result. Thousands mistook it for a news broadcast and actually believed for a few hours that the Martians had invaded America and were marching across the countryside on steel legs a hundred feet high, massacring all and sundry with their heat rays. Some of the listeners were so panic-stricken that they leapt into their cars and fled. Exact figures are, of course, unobtainable, but the compilers of this survey (it was made by one of the research departments of Princeton) have reason to think that about six million people heard the broadcast and that well over a million were in some degree affected by the panic.

At the time this affair caused amusement all over the world, and the credulity of 'those Americans' was much commented on. However, most of the accounts that appeared abroad were somewhat misleading. The text of the Orson Welles production is given in full, and it appears that apart from the opening announcement and a piece of dialogue towards the end the whole play is done in the form of news bulletins, ostensibly real bulletins with names of stations attached to them. This is a natural enough method of producing a play of that type, but it was also natural that many people who happened to turn on the radio after the play had started should imagine that they were listening to a news broadcast. There were therefore two separate acts of belief involved: (i) that the play was a news bulletin, and (ii) that a news bulletin can be taken as truthful. And it is just here that the interest of the investigation lies.

---

1. Orson Welles (1915–1985) was at this time starting his highly innovative film career, highlighted by *Citizen Kane* (1941) and *The Magnificent Ambersons* (1942). In 1936 he had directed an all-black cast in the Negro People's Theatre *Macbeth*; in 1937 he formed the Mercury Theatre. The Mercury players provided the cast for this broadcast. The script was written by Howard Koch (1902–1994). It was clearly stated at the outset that this 'radio play' was suggested by H.G. Wells's *The War of the Worlds*. Koch published 'the whole story' in *The Panic Broadcast* (1970). He won an Oscar for the script of *Casablanca* (1942) and wrote the script for *Mission to Moscow*. As a Communist he was subpoenaed before the House Un-American Activities Committee and blacklisted by Hollywood for many years.

In the U.S.A. the wireless is the principal vehicle of news. There is a great number of broadcasting stations, and virtually every family owns a radio. The authors even make the surprising statement that it is more usual to possess a radio than to take in a newspaper. Therefore, to transfer this incident to England, one has perhaps to imagine the news of the Martian invasion appearing on the front page of one of the evening papers. Undoubtedly such a thing would cause a great stir. It is known that the newspapers are habitually untruthful, but it is also known that they cannot tell lies of more than a certain magnitude and anyone seeing huge head-lines in their paper announcing the arrival of a cylinder from Mars would probably believe what he read, at any rate for the few minutes that would be needed to make some verification.

The truly astonishing thing, however, was that so few of the listeners attempted any kind of check. The compilers of the survey give details of 250 persons who mistook the broadcast for a news bulletin. It appears that over a third of them attempted no kind of verification; as soon as they heard that the end of the world was coming, they accepted it uncriti-cally. A few imagined that it was really a German or Japanese invasion, but the majority believed in the Martians, and this included people who had only heard of the 'invasion' from neighbours, and even a few who had started off with the knowledge that they were listening to a play. Here are excerpts from one or two of their statements:

'I was visiting the pastor's wife when a boy came and said, "Some star just fell." We turned the radio on—we all felt the world was coming to an end. . . . I rushed to the neighbours to tell them the world was coming to an end.'

'I called in to my husband: "Dan, why don't you get dressed? You don't want to die in your working clothes."'

'My husband took Mary into the kitchen and told her that God had put us on this earth for His honour and glory and that it was for Him to say when it was our time to go. Dad kept calling "O God, do what you can to save us."'

'I looked in the icebox and saw some chicken left from Sunday dinner. . . . I said to my nephew, "We may as well eat this chicken —we won't be here in the morning."'

'I was looking forward with some pleasure to the destruction of the entire human race. . . . If we have Fascist domination of the world, there is no purpose in living anyway.'

The survey does not reveal any single all-embracing explanation of the panic. All it establishes is that the people most likely to be affected were the poor, the ill-educated and, above all, people who were economically insecure or had unhappy private lives. The evident connection between personal unhappiness and readiness to believe the incredible is its most interesting discovery. Remarks like 'Everything is so upset in the world that anything might happen,' or 'So long as everybody was going to die, it was all right,' are surprisingly common in the answers to the question-naire. People who have been out of work or on the verge of bankruptcy for ten years may be actually relieved to hear of the approaching end of civilisation. It is a similar frame of mind that has induced whole nations to fling themselves into the arms of a Saviour. This book is a footnote to the history of the world depression, and in spite of being written in the horrible dialect of the American psychologist, it makes very entertaining reading.

'Our Opportunity'

Left News, JANUARY 1941

The Left News *was the organ of The Left Book Club and was edited by Victor Gollancz. This is the first of three articles contributed by Orwell, the other two being 'Fascism and Democracy', February 1941, and 'Will Freedom Die with Capitalism', April 1941. The first two were printed, slightly amended, in Gollancz's* The Betrayal of the Left.

The fact that there has been no general election or other major political event in England during the past twelve months ought not to hide from us the swing of opinion that is taking place beneath the surface. England is on the road to revolution, a process that started, in my opinion, about the end of 1938. But *what kind* of revolution depends partly on our recognizing in time the real forces at work and not using phrases out of nineteenth-century textbooks as a substitute for thought.

England spent the first eight months of war in almost the same state of twilight sleep as it had spent the eight preceding years. There was widespread vague discontent, but no active defeatism, as the votes at the by-elections showed. In so far as it thought about the war the nation comforted itself with two completely false strategic theories, one of them official, the other peculiar to the Left. The first was that Hitler would be driven by the British blockade to smash himself to pieces against the Maginot Line; the other was that by agreeing to partition Poland Stalin had in some mysterious manner 'stopped' Hitler, who would thereafter be unable to perpetrate further conquests. Both have been utterly falsified by events. Hitler simply walked round the Maginot Line and entered Rumania via Hungary, as could have been foreseen from the start by anyone able to read a map. But the acceptance of these geographical absurdities was a reflection of the general apathy. So long as France stood, the nation did not feel itself in danger of conquest, and on the other hand the easy victory which was supposedly to be brought about by 'economic' means, leaving Chamberlain in power and everything just as it had been before, did not inspire much enthusiasm. No doubt most of us would have preferred a victory for the British businessmen to a victory for Hitler, but it was not a thing to grow lyrical about. The notion that *England could only win the war by passing through revolution* had barely been mooted.

Then came the startling disasters of May and June.[1] Although there was no political upheaval to mark it, no one who used his ears and eyes at the time could mistake the leftward swing of public opinion. The British people had had the jolt that they had been needing for years past. There had been demonstrated to them in a way that could not be mistaken the decay of their ruling class, the inefficiency of private capitalism, the urgent need for economic reorganisation and the destruction of privilege. Had any real leadership existed on the Left, there is little doubt that the return of the troops from Dunkirk could have been the beginning of the end of British capitalism. It was a moment at which the willingness for sacrifice and drastic changes extended not only to the working class but to nearly the whole of the middle class, whose patriotism, when it comes to the pinch, is stronger than their sense of self-interest. There was apparent, sometimes in the most unexpected people, a feeling of being on the edge of a new society in which much of the greed, apathy, injustice and corruption of the past would have disappeared. But no adequate leadership existed, the strategic moment passed, the pendulum swung back. The expected invasion failed to take place, and terrible though the air-raids have been, they were nothing to what had been feared. Since about October confidence has come back, and with confidence, apathy. The forces of reaction promptly counter-attacked and began to consolidate their position, which had been badly shaken in the summer days when it looked as though they would have to turn to the common people for help. The fact that, against all expectation, England had not been conquered had vindicated the ruling classes to some extent, and the matter was clinched by Wavell's victory in Egypt. Following promptly on Sidi Barrani[2] came Margesson's entry into the Cabinet[3]—an open, unmistakable slap in the face for all shades of progressive opinion. It was not

1. Evacuation of 338,000 British and Allied servicemen from Dunkirk, 26 May–4 June 1940; and the fall of France, the German armistice terms being accepted on 22 June.
2. Sidi Barrani, Egypt, some 250 miles west of Alexandria, was taken by the 4th Indian Division, the 4th Armoured Brigade, and the 7th Armoured Division on 10 December 1940 in General Wavell's advance to Benghazi, Libya, which fell in early February. Instead of being allowed to continue to Tripoli, on 12 February Wavell was instructed by the War Cabinet to leave only a small holding force in Libya and to send as many troops as possible to Greece.
3. David R. Margesson (1890–1965; Viscount 1942), Conservative MP for Rugby, 1924–42; Chief Whip, 1931–40; proved loyal to each Prime Minister he served. Continued as a Joint Chief Whip when Churchill became Prime Minister and after six months was appointed Secretary of State for War.

possible to bring Chamberlain out of his grave, but Margesson's appointment was the nearest approach to it.

However, the defeats of the summer had brought out something more important than the tendency, normal to nearly all régimes, to swing to the left in moments of disaster and to the right in moments of security. What it had brought out was the integrity of British national feeling. After all, and in spite of all, the common people were patriotic. It is of the profoundest importance to face this fact and not try to dispose of it with easy formulæ. It may possibly be true that 'the proletarian has no country.' What concerns us, however, is the fact that the proletarian, at any rate in England, *feels* that he has a country and will act accordingly. The conventional Marxist notion that 'the workers' don't care twopence whether or not their country is conquered is as false as the *Daily Telegraph* notion that every Englishman chokes with emotion on hearing 'Rule Britannia.' It is quite true that the working class, unlike the middle class, have no imperialist feeling and dislike patriotic bombast. Almost any working man sees promptly the equivocal meaning of 'YOUR Courage, YOUR Cheerfulness, YOUR Resolution will bring US Victory.' But let it appear that England is about to be conquered by a foreign power, and the case is altered. There was a moment in the summer when our allies had deserted us, our army had been heavily defeated and had barely escaped with the loss of all its equipment, and England, internally, was all but defenceless. Then, if ever, was the moment for a stop-the-war movement to arise, to the tune of 'The enemy is in your own country,' etc., etc. Well, that was exactly the moment at which the British working class flung itself into a huge effort to increase armaments-production and prevent invasion. Eden's appeal for Local Defence Volunteers got a quarter of a million recruits in the first day and another million in the next few weeks; I have reason to believe that a larger number could have been obtained. Let it be remembered that at that moment the invasion was expected to happen immediately and that the men who enrolled themselves believed that they would have to fight the German army with shotguns and bottles of petrol. It is perhaps more significant that in the six months since that date the Home Guard—a spare-time, practically unpaid organisation—has barely fallen off in numbers, except through the calling-up of the younger members. And now let anyone compare the membership figures of the Home Guard with those of the political parties which assume that the common man is not patriotic. The Communist Party, the I.L.P., Mosley's organisation and the P.P.U. may perhaps have between them an unstable membership of 150,000. In by-elections held since the war, only one stop-the-war candidate has even saved his election deposit. Is not the conclusion obvious, except to those who are unable to face facts?

But the revelation of working-class patriotism coincided with the swing of opinion that I have spoken of earlier, the sudden perception that the existing social order was rotten. People dimly grasped—and not always so dimly, to judge from certain conversations I listened to in pubs at the time—that it was our duty both to defend England and to turn it into a genuine democracy. England is in some ways politically backward, extremist slogans are not bandied to and fro as they are in continental countries, but the feeling of all true patriots and all true Socialists is at bottom reducible to the 'Trotskyist' slogan: 'The war and the revolution are inseparable.' We cannot beat Hitler without passing through revolution, nor consolidate our revolution without beating Hitler. Useless to pretend, with the Communists, that you can somehow get rid of Hitler by surrendering to him. Useless to imagine, with the *Daily Telegraph*, that you can defeat Hitler without disturbing the *status quo*. A capitalist Britain cannot defeat Hitler; its potential resources and its potential allies cannot be mobilised. Hitler can only be defeated by an England which can bring to its aid the progressive forces of the world—an England, therefore, which is fighting against the sins of its own past. The Communists and others profess to believe that the defeat of Hitler means no more than a renewed stabilisation of British capitalism. This is merely a lie designed to spread disaffection in the Nazi interest.[4] Actually, as the Communists themselves would have pointed out a year ago, the opposite is the truth: British capitalism can only survive by coming to terms with Fascism. Either we turn England into a Socialist democracy or by one route or another we become part of the Nazi empire; there is no third alternative.

But part of the process of turning England into a Socialist democracy is to avoid conquest from without. We cannot, as some people appear to imagine, call off the war by arrangement and then proceed to have a private revolution with no outside interference. Something rather of this kind happened in the Russian Revolution, partly because Russia is a difficult country to invade, partly because the chief European powers were

---

4. *The Betrayal of the Left* has here this footnote: 'I feel bound to dissociate myself from the words "in the Nazi interest", unless the word "objectively" is understood, as no doubt the author intends.—Victor Gollancz.'

at the time engaged in fighting one another. For England, 'revolutionary defeatism' would only be a thinkable policy if the chief centres of population and industry in the British Empire were in, say, Australia. Any attempt to overthrow our ruling class *without* defending our shores would simply lead to the prompt occupation of Britain by the Nazis, and the setting-up of a reactionary puppet government, as in France.[5] In the social revolution that we have got to carry through there can be no such gap in our defences as existed, potentially, in the Russia of 1917–18. A country within gunshot of the Continent and dependent on imports for its food is not in a position to make a Brest-Litovsk peace.[6] Our revolution can only be a revolution behind the British fleet. But that is another way of saying that we must do the thing that British extremist parties have always failed to do, the thing they have alternately declared to be unnecessary and impossible —to win over the middle classes.

Economically there are in England two main dividing lines. One is—at the present standard of living—at £5 a week, the other at £2,000 a year. The class that lies between, though not numerous compared with the working class, holds a key position, because in it is included practically the whole of the technocracy (engineers, chemists, doctors, airmen, etc., etc.) without which a modern industrial country could not exist for a week. It is a fact that these people benefit very little from the existing order of society and that their way of life would not be very profoundly altered by the change-over to a Socialist economy. It is also a fact that they have always tended to side with the capitalist class and against their natural allies, the manual workers, partly because of an educational system designed to have just that effect, partly because of the out-of-dateness of Socialist propaganda. Nearly all Socialists who even *sounded* as though they meant business have always talked in terms of the old-fashioned 'proletarian revolution,' a conception which was formed before the modern technical middle class came into being. To the middle-class man, 'revolution' has been presented as a process by which he and his kind are killed off or exiled, and the entire control of

---

5. The Vichy government (1940–44) led by Marshal Pétain (1856–1951). Pétain had successfully led the defence of Verdun in 1916 and was regarded as a national hero. He was tried after the war for collaboration with the Nazis and sentenced to death but President de Gaulle commuted his sentence to solitary confinement for life.
6. The Treaty of Brest-Litovsk was concluded separately by Russia and the Central Powers in 1918, bringing to an end the war on the Eastern Front. Amongst its provisions, Russia recognised Poland, Estonia, Latvia, and Lithuania. The treaty was declared void by the general peace agreement that concluded World War I.

the state is handed over to manual workers, who, he is well aware, would be unable to run a modern industrial country unaided. The concept of revolution as a more or less voluntary act of the majority of the people —the only kind of revolution that is conceivable under modern Western conditions—has always been regarded as heretical.

But how, when you aim at any fundamental change, can you get the majority of the people on your side? The position is that a few people are actively for you, a few actively against you, and the great mass are capable of being pushed one way or the other. The capitalist class, as a whole, *must* be against you. No hope that these people will see the error of their ways, or abdicate gracefully. Our job is not to try to win them over, but to isolate them, expose them, make the mass of the people see their reactionary and semi-treacherous nature. But how about the indispensable middle class that I have spoken of above? Can you really bring them over to your side? Is there any chance of turning an airman, a naval officer, a railway engineer or what-not into a convinced Socialist? The answer is that a revolution which waited for the full conversion of the entire population would never happen. The question is not so much whether the men in key positions are fully on your side as whether they are sufficiently against you to sabotage. It is no use hoping that the airmen, destroyer-commanders, etc. on whom our very existence depends will all turn into orthodox Marxists; but we can hope, if we approach them rightly, that they will continue to do their jobs when they see behind their backs a Labour government putting through Socialist legislation. The approach to these people is through their patriotism. 'Sophisticated' Socialists may laugh at the patriotism of the middle classes, but let no one imagine that it is a sham. Nothing that makes men willing to die in battle—and relative to numbers more of the middle class than of the working class are killed in war—is a sham. These people will be with us if they can be made to see that a victory over Hitler demands the destruction of capitalism; they will be against us if we let it appear that we are indifferent to England's independence. We have got to make far clearer than it has been made hitherto the fact that at this moment of time a revolutionary has to be a patriot, and a patriot has to be a revolutionary. 'Do you want to defeat Hitler? Then you must be ready to sacrifice your social prestige. Do you want to establish Socialism? Then you must be ready to defend your country.' That is a crude way of putting it, but it is along those lines that our propaganda must move. That is the thing that we missed the chance to say in the summer months, when the rottenness of private capitalism was already partly clear to people who a year earlier would have described themselves as Conservatives, and when people who all their lives had laughed at the very notion of patriotism discovered that they did not want to be ruled by foreigners after all.

At the moment we are in a period of backwash, when the forces of reaction, reassured by a partial victory, are regaining the ground they lost earlier. Priestley is shoved off the air.[7] Margesson goes into the Cabinet, the army is bidden to polish its buttons, the Home Guard is brought more and more under the control of Blimps, there is talk of suppressing this newspaper and that, the Government bargains with Pétain and Franco —big and small, these things are indications of the general trend. But presently, in the spring perhaps, or even earlier, there will come another moment of crisis. And that, quite possibly, will be our final chance. At that moment it may be decided once and for all whether the issues of this war are to be made clear and who is to control the great middling mass of people, working class and middle class, who are capable of being pushed in either one direction or the other.

Much of the failure of the English Left is traceable to the tendency of Socialists to criticise current movements from the outside instead of trying to influence them from within. When the Home Guard was formed, it was impossible not to be struck by the lack of political instinct which led Socialists of nearly all shades to stand aloof from the whole business, not seeing in this sudden spontaneous movement any opportunity for themselves. Here were a million men springing, as it were, out of the ground, asking for arms to defend their country against a possible invader, and organising themselves into a military body almost without direction from above. Would one not have expected those Socialists who had talked for years about 'democratising the army,' etc., etc. to do their utmost to guide this new force along the right political lines? Instead of which the vast majority of Socialists paid no attention, or, in the case of the doctrinaires, said weakly, 'This is Fascism.' It apparently did not occur to them that the political colour of such a force, compelled by the circumstances of the time to organise itself independently, would be determined by the people who were in it. Only a handful of Spanish war veterans like Tom Wintringham and Hugh Slater[8] saw the danger and the opportunity and

7. 'Priestley is shoved off the air' is omitted from The Betrayal of the Left.
8. Both organised a training centre for the Home Guard. See page 138, n. 6 for Wintringham.

have since done their best, in the face of discouragement from several quarters, to form the Home Guard into a real People's Army. At the moment the Home Guard stands at the cross-roads. It is patriotic, the bulk of its members are definitely anti-Fascist, but it is politically undirected. A year hence, if it still exists, it may be a democratic army capable of having a strong political influence on the regular forces, or it may be a sort of S.A.[9] officered by the worst sections of the middle class. A few thousand Socialists within its ranks, energetic and knowing what they want, could prevent the second development. But they can only do so *from within*. And what I have said of the Home Guard applies to the whole war effort and the steady tendency of Socialists to hand executive power to their enemies. In pre-war days, when the appeasement policy still ruled, it was an ironical thing to read through a membership list of the House of Commons. It was Labour and Communist members who clamoured for a 'firm stand against Germany,' but it was Conservative members who were members of the R.N.V.R. or R.A.F.V.R.

It is only if we associate ourselves with the war effort, by acts as well as words, that we have any chance of influencing national policy; it is only if we have some sort of control over national policy that the war can be won. If we simply stand aside, make no effort to permeate the armed forces with our ideas or to influence those who are patriotic but politically neutral, if we allow the pro-Nazi utterances of the Communists to be taken as representative of 'left' opinion, events will pass us by. We shall have failed to use the lever which the patriotism of the common man has put into our hands. The 'politically unreliable' will be elbowed out of positions of power, the Blimps will settle themselves tighter in the saddle, the governing classes will continue the war in their own way. And their way can only lead to ultimate defeat. To believe that, it is not necessary to believe that the British governing class are consciously pro-Nazi. But so long as they are in control the British war-effort is running on one cylinder. Since they will not—*cannot*, without destroying themselves—put through the necessary social and economic changes, they cannot alter the balance of forces, which is at present heavily against us. While our social system is what it is, how can they set free the enormous energies of the English people? How can they turn the coloured peoples from exploited coolies into willing allies? How (even if they wanted to) can they mobilise the revolutionary forces of Europe? Does anyone suppose that the

9. S.A. stands for *Sturmabteilung* – German Storm Troopers.

conquered populations are going to rebel on behalf of the British dividend-drawers? Either we turn this war into a revolutionary war or we lose it. And we can only turn it into a revolutionary war if we can bring into being a revolutionary movement capable of appealing to a majority of the people; a movement, therefore, not sectarian, not defeatist, not 'anti-British,' not resembling in any way the petty fractions[10] of the extreme left, with their heresy-hunting and their Græco-Latin jargon. The alternative is to leave the conduct of the war to the British ruling class and to go gradually down through exhaustion into defeat—called, no doubt, not 'defeat' but 'negotiated peace'—leaving Hitler in secure control of Europe. And does anyone in his senses feel much doubt as to what that will mean? Does anyone except a handful of Blackshirts and pacifists pay any attention to Hitler's claims to be 'the friend of the poor man,' the 'enemy of plutocracy,' etc.? Are such claims credible, after the past seven years? Do not his deeds speak louder than his words?

At George V's Silver Jubilee there occurred a popular demonstration which was 'spontaneous' in a different sense from the organised loyalty-parades of totalitarian countries. In the south of England, at any rate, the response was big enough to surprise the authorities and lead them to prolong the celebrations for an extra week. In certain very poor London streets, which the people had decorated of their own accord, I saw chalked across the asphalt two slogans: 'Poor, but loyal' and 'Landlords, keep away' (or 'No landlords wanted'). It is most improbable that these slogans had been suggested by any political party. Most doctrinaire Socialists were furious at the time, and not wrongly. Certainly it is appalling that people living in the London slums should describe themselves as 'poor, but loyal.' But there would have been far more reason for despair if the other slogan had been 'Three cheers for the landlord' (or words to that effect). For was there not something significant, something we might have noticed at the time, in that instinctive antithesis between the King and the landlord? Up to the death of George V the King probably stood for a majority of English people as the symbol of national unity. These people believed—quite mistakenly, of course—in the King as someone who was on their side against the monied class. They were patriotic, but they were not Conservative. And did they not show a sounder instinct than those who tell us that patriotism is something disgraceful and national liberty a

10. 'Fractions' also in *The Betrayal of the Left*; 'factions' might have been intended but Orwell does use 'fractions' elsewhere.

matter of indifference? Although the circumstances were far more dramatic, was it not the same impulse that moved the Paris workers in 1793, the Communards in 1871, the Madrid trade unionists in 1936[11]—the impulse to defend one's country, and to make it a place worth living in?

11. '1793': the revolutionary government established in the second half of that year, an important element of which was the Committee of Public Safety (under Robespierre from 27 July 1793); one outcome was the Reign of Terror, which began in October 1793. 'Communards in 1871': a popular revolutionary government proclaimed on 18 March 1871 in Paris in opposition to the National Assembly; it was crushed with heavy loss of life, 21–28 May 1871. The rising in Madrid, 19–20 July 1936, was organised by the CNT (Anarcho-Syndicalist Trades Union) and the UGT (Socialist Trade Union); see Hugh Thomas, *The Spanish Civil War*, pp. 243–47.

'London Letter', 3 January 1941: The Political Situation; The Intellectual Life of England; Air raids

Partisan Review,[1] MARCH–APRIL 1941

On 9 December, Clement Greenberg, on behalf of the editors of Partisan Review, *wrote to Orwell: 'The editors of* Partisan Review *would like very much to have you do an English letter for them. There are things the news reports do not tell us. For instance, what's happening under the surface in the way of politics? Among the labor groups? What is the general mood, if there is such a thing, among writers, artists and intellectuals? What transmutations have their lives and their preoccupations suffered? You can be as gossipy as you please and refer to as many personalities as you like. The more the better. You can use your own judgment as to length.'*

Payment was to be at the rate of $2.00 per printed page – $11.00 per letter (approximately £2.75 at the rate of exchange then). This invitation had been prompted by Desmond Hawkins, with whom Orwell was later to be associated at the BBC. Hawkins contributed a regular 'London Letter' until, as he puts it in When I Was *(1989), 'wartime conditions reduced my essential contacts and I suggested that George Orwell should replace me'. Orwell contributed 'London Letters' until the summer of 1946 and continued to write for* Partisan Review *until a few months before he died. 'Such, Such Were the Joys' was published posthumously by the review in its September–October 1952 issue. In the main only extracts (often lengthy) are drawn from these Letters in this volume.*

Dear Editors:

As I am writing this letter in answer to a privately-addressed one of your own, perhaps I had better start by quoting what you said, so as to make clear what questions I am trying to answer:

1. *Partisan Review*, the most influential of U.S. left-wing literary journals, was first published by the Communist John Reed Club of New York in 1934, edited by William Phillips (1906–2002) and Philip Rahv (Ilya Greenberg; 1908–1973) for four decades. It was suspended for most of 1937 and, when it was resurrected at the end of that year, it was more literary and anti-Stalinist politically. Among its contributors were Edmund Wilson, Samuel Beckett, Norman Mailer, Allen Tate, Saul Bellow, Delmore Schwartz, Gore Vidal, and Mary McCarthy, who was also on staff. See, especially for the period when Orwell was contributing, *The Partisan Reader: Ten Years of Partisan Review, 1934–1944: An Anthology*, edited by William Phillips and Philip Rahv (1946), with a helpful introduction, 'The Function of the Little Magazine', by Lionel Trilling; and William Phillips, *A Partisan View: Five Decades of the Literary Life* (1984).

'There are things the news reports do not tell us. For instance, what's happening under the surface in the way of politics? Among the labor groups? What is the general mood, if there is such a thing, among writers, artists and intellectuals? What transmutations have their lives and their preoccupations suffered?'

The Political Situation

Well, as to the political situation, I think it is true to say that at the moment we are in the middle of a backwash which is not going to make very much ultimate difference. The reactionaries, which means roughly the people who read the *Times*, had a bad scare in the summer, but they saved themselves by the skin of their teeth, and they are now consolidating their position against the new crisis which is likely to arise in the spring. In the summer what amounted to a revolutionary situation existed in England, though there was no one to take advantage of it. After twenty years of being fed on sugar and water the nation had suddenly realised what its rulers were like, and there was a widespread readiness for sweeping economic and social changes, combined with absolute determination to prevent invasion. At that moment, I believe, the opportunity existed to isolate the monied class and swing the mass of the nation behind a policy in which resistance to Hitler and destruction of class-privilege were combined. Clement Greenberg's remark in his article in *Horizon*[2] that the working class is the only class in England that seriously means to defeat Hitler, seems to me quite untrue. The bulk of the middle class are just as anti-Hitler as the working class, and their morale is probably more reliable. The fact which Socialists, especially when they are looking at the English scene from the outside, seldom seem to me to grasp, is that the patriotism of the middle classes is a thing to be made use of. The people who stand to attention during 'God Save the King' would readily transfer their loyalty to a Socialist regime, if they were handled with the minimum of tact. However, in the summer months no one saw the opportunity, the Labour leaders (with the possible exception of Bevin) allowed themselves to be made the tame cats of the Government, and when the invasion failed to come off and the air raids were less terrible than everyone had expected,

2. Clement Greenberg (1909–1994), associate editor of *Partisan Review*, had written 'An American View' of the progress of the war for *Horizon*, September 1940. An editorial comment in that issue, though almost certainly written by Cyril Connolly, shows Orwell's influence. From 1945 to 1947, Greenberg edited *Contemporary Jewish Record* (afterwards, *Commentary*), to which Orwell contributed three articles.

the quasi-revolutionary mood ebbed away. At present the Right are counter-attacking. Margesson's entry into the Cabinet—the nearest equivalent possible to bringing Chamberlain out of his grave—was a swift cash-in on Wavell's victory in Egypt. The campaign in the Mediterranean is not finished, but events there have justified the Conservatives as against the Left and they can be expected to take advantage of it. It is not impossible that one or two leftish newspapers will be suppressed before long. Suppression of the *Daily Worker* is said to have been mooted already in the Cabinet. But this swing of the pendulum is not vitally important unless one believes, as I do not—and I doubt whether many people under fifty believe it either—that England can win the war without passing through revolution and go straight back to pre-1939 'normality,' with 3 million unemployed, etc., etc.

But at present there does not effectively exist any policy between being patriotic in the 'King and Country' style and being pro-Hitler. If another wave of anti-capitalist feeling arrived it could at the moment only be canalised into defeatism. At the same time there is little sign of this in England, though the morale is probably worse in the industrial towns than elsewhere. In London, after four months of almost ceaseless bombing, morale is far better than a year ago when the war was stagnant. The only people who are overtly defeatist are Mosley's followers,[3] the Communists and the pacifists. The Communists still possess a footing in the factories and may some time stage a come-back by fomenting grievances about working-hours, etc. But they have difficulty in getting their working-class followers to accept a definitely pro-Hitler policy, and they had to pipe down during the desperate days in the summer. With the general public their influence is nil, as one can see by the votes in the by-elections, and the powerful hold they had on the press in the years 1935–9 has been completely broken. Mosley's Blackshirts have ceased to exist as a legal organisation, but they probably deserve to be taken more seriously than the Communists, if only because the tone of their propaganda is more acceptable to soldiers, sailors and airmen. No left-wing organisation in England has ever been able to gain a footing in the armed forces. The Fascists have, of course, tried to put the blame for both the war and the discomfort caused by the air-raids onto the Jews, and during the worst of the East End bombings they did succeed in raising a mutter of anti-Semitism, though only a faint one. The most interesting development on the anti-war front has been

3. British Union of Fascists.

the interpenetration of the pacifist movement by Fascist ideas, especially anti-Semitism. After Dick Sheppard's death[4] British pacifism seems to have suffered a moral collapse; it has not produced any significant gesture nor even many martyrs, and only about 15 per cent of the membership of the Peace Pledge Union now appear to be active. But many of the surviving pacifists now spin a line of talk indistinguishable from that of the Blackshirts ('Stop this Jewish war' etc.), and the actual membership of the P.P.U. and the British Union overlap to some extent. Put all together, the various pro-Hitler organisations can hardly number 150,000 members, and they are not likely to achieve much by their own efforts, but they might play an important part at a time when a government of the Pétain type was contemplating surrender. There is some reason to think that Hitler does not want Mosley's organisation to grow too strong. Lord Haw-Haw, the most effective of the English-language German broadcasters, has been identified with fair certainty as Joyce, a member of the split-off Fascist party and a very bitter personal enemy of Mosley.[5]

The Intellectual Life of England
You ask also about the intellectual life of England, the various currents of thought in the literary world, etc. I think the dominating factors are these:

(a) The complete destruction, owing to the Russo–German pact, of the left-wing 'anti-fascist' orthodoxy of the past five years.
(b) The fact that physically fit people under 35 are mostly in the army, or expect soon to be so.
(c) The increase in book-consumption owing to the boredom of war, together with the unwillingness of publishers to risk money on unknown writers.
(d) The bombing (of which more presently—but I should say here that it is less terrifying and more of a nuisance than you perhaps imagine).

4. The Reverend Hugh Richard Lowrie ('Dick') Sheppard (1880–1937) was a prominent pacifist and instrumental in founding the Peace Pledge Union. A man of great integrity and charisma, he served as a chaplain in France in 1914 and then as Vicar of St Martin-in-the-Fields, 1914–27, and Dean of Canterbury, 1929–31
5. William Joyce (1908–46), referred to in Britain as Lord Haw-Haw, endeavoured to spread fear by forecasting which cities would be bombed, but his frequent inaccuracies (notably the reported sinking of HMS *Ark Royal*) led to his being treated as a joke, especially by music-hall comedians.

The Russo–German pact not only brought the Stalinists and near-Stalinists into the pro-Hitler position, but it also put an end to the game of 'I told you so' which the left-wing writers had been so profitably playing for five years past. 'Anti-Fascism' as interpreted by the *News Chronicle*, the *New Statesman* and the Left Book Club depended on the belief—I think it was also half-consciously a hope—that no British government would ever stand up to Hitler. When the Chamberlain government finally went to war it took the wind out of the left-wingers' sails by putting into effect the policy which they themselves had been demanding. In the few days before war was declared it was extremely amusing to watch the behaviour of orthodox Popular Fronters, who were exclaiming dolefully 'It's going to be another Munich,' although in fact it had been obvious for months past that war was inevitable. These people were in reality *hoping* for another Munich, which would allow them to continue with their Cassandra role without having to face the facts of modern war. I was recently in very severe trouble for saying in print that those who were most 'anti-Fascist' during the period 1935–9 were most defeatist now. Nevertheless I believe that this is broadly true, and not only of the Stalinists. It is a fact that as soon as war began all the fire went out of orthodox 'anti-Fascism.' All the stuff about Fascist atrocities, denunciations of Chamberlain, etc., which it had been completely impossible to get away from in any high-brow magazine in peace-time, suddenly came to an end, and far more fuss has been made among the left-wing intelligentsia about the internment of German refugees than about anything done by the enemy. During the Spanish civil war the left-wing intellectuals felt that this was 'their' war and that they were influencing events in it to some extent. In so far as they expected the war against Germany to happen they imagined that it would be a sort of enlarged version of the war in Spain, a left-wing war in which poets and novelists could be important figures. Of course, it is nothing of the kind. It is an all-in modern war fought mainly by technical experts (airmen etc.) and conducted by people who are patriotic according to their lights but entirely reactionary in outlook. At present there is no function in it for intellectuals. From the start the Government have more or less frankly gone on the principle of 'keeping the Reds out of it,' and it was not till after the disaster in France that they began to allow men known to have fought in Spain to join the army. Consequently the chief activity among left-wing writers is a rather pettifogging criticism which turns into a kind of dismay when England wins a victory, because this always falsifies their predictions. In the summer the left-wing intelligentsia were completely defeatist, far more so than they allowed to appear in print. At the moment when England seemed likely to be invaded one well-known left-wing writer actually wanted to discourage the idea of mass resistance, on the ground that the Germans would behave more leniently if not opposed. There was also a move on foot, with an eye to the coming Nazi occupation, to get the Scotland Yard Special Branch to destroy the political dossiers which, no doubt, most of us possess. All this was in marked contrast to the attitude of the common people, who either had not woken up to the fact that England was in danger, or were determined to resist to the last ditch. But certain left-wing writers and lecturers who had fought in Spain, notably Tom Wintringham, did a lot to stem the tide of defeatism.[6]

Personally I consider it all to the good that the confident war-mongering mood of the Popular Front period, with its lying propaganda and its horrible atmosphere of orthodoxy, has been destroyed. But it has left a sort of hole. Nobody knows what to think, nothing is being started. It is very difficult to imagine any new 'school' of literature arising at a moment when the youngish writers have had their universe punctured and the very young are either in the army or kept out of print by lack of paper. Moreover the economic foundations of literature are shifting, for the highbrow literary magazine, depending ultimately on leisured people who have been brought up in a minority culture, is becoming less and less possible. *Horizon* is a sort of modern democratised version of this (compare its general tone with that of the *Criterion* of ten years ago), and even *Horizon* keeps going only with difficulty. On the other hand the reading public is increasing and the intel-. lectual level of the popular press has taken a tremendous bound upwards since the outbreak of war. But hardly any good *books* are appearing. Novels are still being published in great numbers, but they are of a trashiness that passes belief. Only the mentally dead are capable of sitting down and writing novels while this nightmare is going on. The conditions that made it possible for Joyce and Lawrence to do their best work during the war of 1914–18 (i.e.,

6. Henry Tom Wintringham (1898–1949) served in the Royal Flying Corps in World War I, edited *Left Review*, 1934–36, and went to Spain as a war correspondent and commanded the British Battalion of the International Brigade near Madrid in 1937. He was a founder member of the British Communist Party. His ideas were given space in Edward Hulton's *Picture Post* and in a weekly column in the *Daily Mirror*. Hulton had financed the Home Guard school founded by Wintringham and others. Though there was much resistance from the War Office, which attempted to close the school, Wintringham's ideas and energy were such that, after Dunkirk, the War Office was forced to take it over, with Wintringham still in charge.

the consciousness that presently the world would be sane again) no longer exist. There is such a doubt about the continuity of civilization as can hardly have existed for hundreds of years, and meanwhile there are the air-raids, which make continuous intellectual life very difficult. I don't mean because of physical danger. It is true that by this time everyone in London has had at least one 'providential escape'—these so common that it is now considered bad form to talk about them—but the actual casualties are very few and even the damage, though enormous, is mostly localised to the City of London and the East End slums. But the disorganisation of transport, communications, etc., causes endless inconvenience. One seems to spend half one's time trying to buy a sack of coal because the electricity has failed, or trying to put through telephone calls on a wire that has gone dead, or wandering about looking for a bus—and this is a miserably cold, slushy winter. The night life of London has almost ceased, not because of the bombs but because of the shrapnel, which is often plentiful enough to make it dangerous to go out after dusk. The movies close early and theatres have stopped altogether, except for a few matinees. Only the pubs are much as usual, in spite of the now enormous price of beer. On nights when the raids are bad the deafening racket of the guns makes it difficult to work. It is a time in which it is hard to settle down to anything and even the writing of a silly newspaper article takes twice as long as usual.

Air raids

I wonder whether, even in what I have said, I exaggerate the seriousness of the air raids? It is worth remembering that at the worst period of the blitz it was calculated that only 15 per cent of London's population were sleeping in shelters. The number is added to by those whose homes are destroyed by bombs, but also constantly decreased by those who grow gradually callous. When all is said and done one's main impression is the immense stolidity of ordinary people, the widespread vague consciousness that things can never be the same again, and yet, together with that, the tendency of life to slip back into the familiar pattern. On the day in September when the Germans broke through and set the docks on fire, I think few people can have watched those enormous fires without feeling that this was the end of an epoch. One seemed to feel that the immense changes through which our society has got to pass were going to happen there and then. But to an astonishing extent things have slipped back to normal. I will end with a few extracts from my diary, to try and give you some idea of the atmosphere:

'The aeroplanes come back and back, every few minutes. It is just like in an eastern country, when you keep thinking you have killed the last mosquito inside your net, and every time, as soon as you have turned the light out, another starts droning. . . . The commotion made by the mere passage of a bomb through the air is astonishing. The whole house shakes, enough to rattle objects on the table. Why it is that the electric lights dip when a bomb passes close by, nobody seems to know. . . . Oxford Street yesterday, from Oxford Circus up to the Marble Arch, completely empty of traffic, and only a few pedestrians, with the late afternoon sun shining straight down the empty roadway and glittering on innumerable fragments of broken glass. Outside John Lewis's, a pile of plaster dress models, very pink and realistic, looking so like a pile of corpses that one could have mistaken them for that at a little distance. Just the same sight in Barcelona, only there it was plaster saints from desecrated churches. . . . Regular features of the time: neatly swept-up piles of glass, litter of stone and splinters of flint, smell of escaping gas, knots of sightseers waiting at the cordons where there are unexploded bombs. . . . Nondescript people wandering about, having been evacuated from their houses because of delayed-action bombs. Yesterday two girls stopping me in the street, very elegant in appearance except that their faces were filthily dirty: 'Please, sir, can you tell us where we are?' . . . Withal, huge areas of London almost normal, and everyone quite happy in the daytime, never seeming to think about the coming night, like animals which are unable to foresee the future so long as they have a bit of food and a place in the sun.'

Cyril Connolly and Stephen Spender send all the best. Good luck to America.

Yours sincerely, George Orwell

Documentary Film Reviews: *Eyes of the Navy; The Heart of Britain*[1]; *Unholy War*

Time and Tide, 15 FEBRUARY 1941

The supporting programme is made up of three short propaganda films, one American and two British. Although above I have pointed out one of the faults of the American film, one sees in this short piece (*Eyes of the Navy*—it deals with the U.S.A. naval air arm) the immense technical superiority of the Americans, their understanding of what is and is not impressive, their intolerance of amateurishness generally. The British films (*The Heart of Britain*,[2] produced by the G.P.O.,[3] and *Unholy War*, produced by the Ministry of Information[4]) are terrible. What is the use, in the

---

1. Orwell's review of *The Heart of Britain*, 1941, made by England's most distinguished documentary director, Humphrey Jennings, shows it clearly failed to impress him. Orwell had only a slight grasp of documentary film in the 1930s; he makes no mention of, for example, the famous documentary films *Housing Problems*, 1935, and *Enough to Eat?*, 1936, which, one would have thought, would have greatly interested him. His link with the innovative filmmaker, Len Lye (1903–80), is far from clear and very curious. Among Orwell's papers is a letter addressed 'dear Eric' on GPO Film Unit stationery and identified by Jack Common as from Len Lye, partly confirmed by an attractive design typical of Lye at the end of the letter. Lye is remarkable, especially in the thirties, for creating short films by painting on film stock. Among these are *Trade Tattoo*, *Rainbow Dance*, and *Swinging the Lambeth Walk*. In 1936 he made a puppet film for Shell-Mex, *The Birth of the Robot*, with music by Gustav Holst. This and other examples of his work can be seen on the internet.

    It is impossible to date the year of this letter with certainty. Lye said he had been asked to conjure up another film for Shell and was seeking Orwell's co-operation. He wrote to say that 'Shell are beginning to get cold on the stuff as I've had a month to supply them with an idea so if you can let's have something to work on soon O.K.' He hopes Orwell has not been ill, since everyone he knows has had flu or similar ailments. That could point to any winter, but might be especially applicable to 1937–38, when there was a severe flu epidemic in London. Much later, in June 1949, Lye wrote to Orwell suggesting that *Animal Farm* would make 'an excellent basis for a film about individualism' (David Ford, *Len Lye: A Biography*, p. 242).

2. *The Heart of Britain*, directed by Humphrey Jennings, edited by Stewart McAllister, was the first of a group of films described by Elizabeth Sussex, in her less-than-sycophantic study *The Rise and Fall of British Documentary* (1975), as bringing 'a new inspiration to British documentary'.

3. General Post Office, but here standing for the GPO Film Unit, developed from the Empire Film Marketing Board under John Grierson, 'father' of British documentary films. The unit, later the Crown Film Unit, was closed down by Churchill in January 1952.

4. The Ministry of Information, housed in the Senate House of the University of London, became the setting for Minitrue in *Nineteen Eighty-Four*.

middle of a desperate war, in which propaganda is a major weapon, of wasting time and money on producing this kind of stuff? *Unholy War* takes as its theme the 'anti-Christian' nature of Nazism, and illustrates this with a series of photographs of wrecked churches, with much blah about the architectural glories that have perished. Hitler wants to destroy the Christian religion, and therefore his airmen drop bombs on churches —that is the argument. Cannot our leaders realize (a) that to ninety-nine people out of a hundred the destruction of a church seems much less important than the destruction of a dwelling house, (b) that even very ignorant people know that a bomb does not necessarily hit the object that it is aimed at, and (c) that anyone who understands the anti-Christian nature of Nazism knows that the Christian religion, or any other, does not stand or fall with the stones of its churches? If we have got to rouse resentment against the enemy, which is an inevitable part of war, surely we can find something more effective to say than that the Germans have a spite against Gothic architecture? And, since films of this kind need a spoken commentary, why cannot the M.O.I. choose someone who speaks the English language as it is spoken in the street? Some day perhaps it will be realized that that dreadful B.B.C. voice,[5] with its blurred vowels, antagonizes the whole English-speaking world except for a small area in southern England, and is more valuable to Hitler than a dozen new submarines. In a war in which words are at least as important as guns, these two films are a wretched achievement to set beside Wavell's victories.

---

5. A letter signed 'Southerner' was published by *Time and Tide* on 1 March 1941 which wondered whom Orwell would choose as an exponent of English speaking – the King, the Prime Minister (Mr Churchill) or John Gielgud. And would that differ from how the current BBC announcers spoke? It seemed to the writer that Orwell was guilty of inverted snobbery. And see Orwell's own defence of the BBC's 'Kensingtonian' accent, 'As I Please', 8, on page 256.

Extract from *The Lion and the Unicorn*: 'Proposed War Aims'

19 FEBRUARY 1941

The Lion and the Unicorn *was the first of the Searchlight Book series. They were planned in the summer of 1940 by Fredric Warburg, Tosco Fyvel, and Orwell at Scarlett's Farm, where Warburg lived, near Twyford, Berkshire. At the time, as Warburg recalled, bombs were beginning to fall on London and British fighter planes zoomed overhead. Orwell wrote at speed and delivered the typescript in November 1940. Warburg published it as a 64-page 'pamphlet' on 19 February 1941 at two shillings. Initially 5,000 copies were planned but they sold quickly and the run was extended to 7,500. A second impression was ordered in March 1941. However, when Plymouth was bombed (where it was being printed) the type, and that of* Homage to Catalonia, *was destroyed.*

It is time for *the people* to define their war-aims. What is wanted is a simple, concrete programme of action, which can be given all possible publicity, and round which public opinion can group itself.

I suggest that the following six-point programme is the kind of thing we need. The first three points deal with England's internal policy, the other three with the Empire and the world:—

I. Nationalization of land, mines, railways, banks and major industries.

II. Limitation of incomes, on such a scale that the highest tax-free income in Britain does not exceed the lowest by more than ten to one.

III. Reform of the educational system along democratic lines.

IV. Immediate Dominion status for India, with power to secede when the war is over.

V. Formation of an Imperial General Council, in which the coloured peoples are to be represented.

VI. Declaration of formal alliance with China, Abyssinia and all other victims of the Fascist powers.

The general tendency of this programme is unmistakable. It aims quite frankly at turning this war into a revolutionary war and England into a Socialist democracy. I have deliberately included in it nothing that the simplest person could not understand and see the reason for. In the form in which I have put it, it could be printed on the front page of the *Daily Mirror*. But for the purposes of this book a certain amount of amplification is needed.

Broadcast: *Frontiers of Art and Propaganda*: 'Literary Criticism'

The Listener, BBC, 30 APRIL 1941

On 16 September 1940 C.V. Salmon, a BBC producer, wrote to Orwell to tell him that the BBC Home Service was planning a series of talks in the autumn on writers and writing and inviting him to participate. As a result he took part in a discussion on 6 December 1940 entitled 'The Proletarian Writer' in the series The Writer in the Witness-Box *(CW, XII, 294–99) with the novelist and literary critic, Desmond Hawkins (1908–99). In the spring of 1941 he was invited by the head of the Indian section of the BBC, Zulfaqar Ali Bokhari, to give four talks on literary criticism. The series, under the general title* Frontiers of Art and Propaganda, *was published in a slightly shortened form in the BBC's journal,* The Listener. *The first, 'Literary Criticism' (reproduced below) was followed by 'Tolstoy and Shakespeare' and 'The Meaning of a Poem – Felix Randal' (by Gerard Manley Hopkins). The last talk, 'Literature and Totalitarianism', follows on page 148.*

I am speaking on literary criticism, and in the world in which we are actually living that is almost as unpromising as speaking about peace. This is not a peaceful age, and it is not a critical age. In the Europe of the last ten years literary criticism of the older kind—criticism that is really judicious, scrupulous, fair-minded, treating a work of art as a thing of value in itself—has been next door to impossible.

If we look back at the English literature of the last ten years, not so much at the literature as at the prevailing literary attitude, the thing that strikes us is that it has almost ceased to be aesthetic. Literature has been swamped by propaganda. I do not mean that all the books written during that period have been bad. But the characteristic writers of the time, people like Auden and Spender and MacNeice, have been didactic, political writers, aesthetically conscious, of course, but more interested in subject-matter than in technique. And the most lively criticism has nearly all of it been the work of Marxist writers, people like Christopher Caudwell and Philip Henderson and Edward Upward, who look on every book virtually as a political pamphlet and are far more interested in digging out its political and social implications than in its literary qualities in the narrow sense.

This is all the more striking because it makes a very sharp and sudden contrast with the period immediately before it. The characteristic writers of the nineteen-twenties—T. S. Eliot, for instance, Ezra Pound, Virginia

Woolf—were writers who put the main emphasis on technique. They had their beliefs and prejudices, of course, but they were far more interested in technical innovations than in any moral or meaning or political implication that their work might contain. The best of them all, James Joyce, was a technician and very little else, about as near to being a 'pure' artist as a writer can be. Even D. H. Lawrence, though he was more of a 'writer with a purpose' than most of the others of his time, had not much of what we should now call social consciousness. And though I have narrowed this down to the nineteen-twenties, it had really been the same from about 1890 onwards. Throughout the whole of that period, the notion that form is more important than subject-matter, the notion of 'art for art's sake', had been taken for granted. There were writers who disagreed, of course—Bernard Shaw was one—but that was the prevailing outlook. The most important critic of the period, George Saintsbury, was a very old man in the nineteen-twenties, but he had a powerful influence up to about 1930, and Saintsbury had always firmly upheld the technical attitude to art. He claimed that he himself could and did judge any book solely on its execution, its *manner*, and was very nearly indifferent to the author's opinions.

Now, how is one to account for this very sudden change of outlook? About the end of the nineteen-twenties you get a book like Edith Sitwell's book on Pope, with a completely frivolous emphasis on technique, treating literature as a sort of embroidery, almost as though words did not have meanings; and only a few years later you get a Marxist critic like Edward Upward asserting that books can be 'good' only when they are Marxist in tendency. In a sense both Edith Sitwell and Edward Upward were representative of their period. The question is, why should their outlook be so different?

I think one has got to look for the reason in external circumstances. Both the aesthetic and the political attitude to literature were produced, or at any rate conditioned, by the social atmosphere of a certain period. And now that another period has ended—for Hitler's attack on Poland in 1939 ended one epoch as surely as the great slump of 1931 ended another—one can look back and see more clearly than was possible a few years ago the way in which literary attitudes are affected by external events. A thing that strikes anyone who looks back over the last hundred years is that literary criticism worth bothering about, and the critical attitude towards literature, barely existed in England between roughly 1830 and 1890. It is not that good books were not produced in that period. Several of the writers of that time, Dickens, Thackeray, Trollope and others, will probably be remembered longer than any that have come after them. But there are no literary figures in Victorian England corresponding to Flaubert, Baudelaire, Gautier and a host of others. What now appears to us as aesthetic scrupulousness hardly existed. To a mid-Victorian English writer, a book was partly something that brought him money and partly a vehicle for preaching sermons. England was changing very rapidly, a new moneyed class had come up on the ruins of the old aristocracy, contact with Europe had been severed, and a long artistic tradition had been broken. The mid-nineteenth-century English writers were barbarians, even when they happened to be gifted artists, like Dickens.

But in the later part of the century contact with Europe was re-established through Matthew Arnold, Pater, Oscar Wilde and various others, and the respect for form and technique in literature came back. It is from then that the notion of 'art for art's sake'—a phrase very much out of fashion, but still, I think, the best available—really dates. And the reason why it could flourish so long, and be so much taken for granted, was that the whole period between 1890 and 1930 was one of exceptional comfort and security. It was what we might call the golden afternoon of the capitalist age. Even the Great War did not really disturb it. The Great War killed ten million men, but it did not shake the world as this War will shake it and has shaken it already. Almost every European between 1890 and 1930 lived in the tacit belief that civilisation would last for ever. You might be individually fortunate or unfortunate, but you had inside you the feeling that nothing would ever fundamentally change. And in that kind of atmosphere intellectual detachment, and also dilettantism, are possible. It is that feeling of continuity, of security, that could make it possible for a critic like Saintsbury, a real old crusted Tory and High Churchman, to be scrupulously fair to books written by men whose political and moral outlook he detested.

But since 1930 that sense of security has never existed. Hitler and the slump shattered it as the Great War and even the Russian Revolution had failed to shatter it. The writers who have come up since 1930 have been living in a world in which not only one's life but one's whole scheme of values is constantly menaced. In such circumstances detachment is not possible. You cannot take a purely aesthetic interest in a disease you are dying from; you cannot feel dispassionately about a man who is about to cut your throat. In a world in which Fascism and Socialism were fighting one another, any thinking person had to take sides, and his feelings had to find their way not only into his writing but into his judgements on literature. Literature had to become political, because anything else would have entailed mental dishonesty. One's attachments and hatreds were too near the surface of consciousness to be ignored. What books were *about* seemed so urgently important that the way they were written seemed almost insignificant.

And this period of ten years or so in which literature, even poetry, was mixed up with pamphleteering, did a great service to literary criticism, because it destroyed the illusion of pure aestheticism. It reminded us that propaganda in some form or other lurks in every book, that every work of art has a meaning and a purpose—a political, social and religious purpose—and that our aesthetic judgments are always coloured by our prejudices and beliefs. It debunked art for art's sake. But it also led for the time being into a blind alley, because it caused countless young writers to try to tie their minds to a political discipline which, if they had stuck to it, would have made mental honesty impossible. The only system of thought open to them at that time was official Marxism, which demanded a nationalistic loyalty towards Russia and forced the writer who called himself a Marxist to be mixed up in the dishonesties of power politics. And even if that was desirable, the assumptions that these writers built upon were suddenly shattered by the Russo–German pact. Just as many writers about 1930 had discovered that you cannot really be detached from contemporary events, so many writers about 1939 were discovering that you cannot really sacrifice your intellectual integrity for the sake of a political creed—or at least you cannot do so and remain a writer. Aesthetic scrupulousness is not enough, but political rectitude is not enough either. The events of the last ten years have left us rather in the air, they have left England for the time being without any discoverable literary trend, but they have helped us to define, better than was possible before, the frontiers of art and propaganda.

Broadcast: 'Literature and Totalitarianism'[1]

BBC, 21 MAY 1941

In these weekly talks I have been speaking on criticism, which, when all is said and done, is not part of the main stream of literature. A vigorous literature can exist almost without criticism and the critical spirit, as it did in nineteenth-century England. But there is a reason why, at this particular moment, the problems involved in any serious criticism cannot be ignored. I said at the beginning of my first talk that this is not a critical age. It is an age of partisanship and not of detachment, an age in which it is especially difficult to see literary merit in a book whose conclusions you disagree with. Politics—politics in the most general sense—have invaded literature to an extent that doesn't normally happen, and this has brought to the surface of our consciousness the struggle that always goes on between the individual and the community. It is when one considers the difficulty of writing honest, unbiased criticism in a time like ours that one begins to grasp the nature of the threat that hangs over the whole of literature in the coming age.

We live in an age in which the autonomous individual is ceasing to exist—or perhaps one ought to say, in which the individual is ceasing to have the illusion of being autonomous. Now, in all that we say about literature, and above all in all that we say about criticism, we instinctively take the autonomous individual for granted. The whole of modern European literature—I am speaking of the literature of the past four hundred years—is built on the concept of intellectual honesty, or, if you like to put it that way, on Shakespeare's maxim, 'To thine own self be true'. The first thing that we ask of a writer is that he shan't tell lies, that he shall say what he really thinks, what he really feels. The worst thing we can say about a work of art is that it is insincere. And this is even truer of criticism than of creative literature, in which a certain amount of posing and mannerism and even a certain amount of down-right humbug, doesn't matter so long as the writer has a certain funda-mental sincerity. Modern literature is essentially an individual thing. It

1. This, the fourth of Orwell's broadcasts in the series *Frontiers of Art and Propaganda*, was, like the first three, published in a shortened form in *The Listener*. However, the late W.J. West discovered the original typescript, which is some 20 per cent longer than the version in *The Listener*, and kindly passed it to the editor. That version is reproduced here.

is either the truthful expression of what one man thinks and feels, or it is nothing.

As I say, we take this notion for granted, and yet as soon as one puts it into words one realises how literature is menaced. For this is the age of the totalitarian state, which does not and probably cannot allow the individual any freedom whatever. When one mentions totalitarianism one thinks immediately of Germany, Russia, Italy, but I think one must face the risk that this phenomenon is going to be worldwide. It is obvious that the period of free capitalism is coming to an end and that one country after another is adopting a centralised economy that one can call Socialism or State Capitalism according as one prefers. With that the economic liberty of the individual, and to a great extent his liberty to do what he likes, to choose his own work, to move to and fro across the surface of the earth, comes to end. Now, till recently the implications of this weren't foreseen. It was never fully realised that the disappearance of economic liberty would have any effect on intellectual liberty. Socialism was usually thought of as a sort of moralised Liberalism. The state would take charge of your economic life and set you free from the fear of poverty, unemployment and so forth, but it would have no need to interfere with your private intellectual life. Art could flourish just as it had done in the liberal-capitalist age, only a little more so, because the artist would not any longer be under economic compulsions.

Now, on the existing evidence, one must admit that these ideas have been falsified. Totalitarianism has abolished freedom of thought to an extent unheard of in any previous age. And it is important to realise that its control of thought is not only negative, but positive. It not only forbids you to express—even to *think*—certain thoughts but it dictates what you *shall* think, it creates an ideology for you, it tries to govern your emotional life as well as setting up a code of conduct. And as far as possible it isolates you from the outside world, it shuts you up in an artificial universe in which you have no standards of comparison. The totalitarian state tries, at any rate, to control the thoughts and emotions of its subjects at least as completely as it controls their actions.

The question that is important for us is, can literature survive in such an atmosphere? I think one must answer shortly that it cannot. If totalitarianism becomes worldwide and permanent, what we have known as literature must come to an end. And it won't do—as may appear plausible at first—to say that what will come to an end is merely the literature of post-Renaissance Europe. I believe that literature of every kind, from the epic poem to the critical essay, is menaced by the attempt of the modern state to control the emotional life of the individual. The people who deny this usually put forward two arguments. They say, first of all, that the so-called liberty which has existed during the last few hundred years was merely a reflection of economic anarchy, and in any case largely an illusion. And they also point out that good literature, better than anything that we can produce now, was produced in past ages, when thought was hardly freer than it is in Germany or Russia at this moment. Now this is true so far as it goes. It's true, for instance, that literature could exist in medieval Europe, when thought was under rigid control—chiefly the control of the Church—and you were liable to be burnt alive for uttering a very small heresy. The dogmatic control of the Church didn't prevent, for instance, Chaucer's *Canterbury Tales* from being written. It's also true that medieval literature, and medieval art generally, was less an individual and more a communal thing than it is now. The English ballads, for example, probably can't be attributed to any individual at all. They were probably composed communally, as I have seen ballads being composed in Eastern countries quite recently. Evidently the anarchic liberty which has characterised the Europe of the last few hundred years, the sort of atmosphere in which there are no fixed standards whatever, isn't necessary, perhaps isn't even an advantage, to literature. Good literature can be created within a fixed framework of thought.

But there are several vital differences between totalitarianism and all the orthodoxies of the past, either in Europe or in the East. The most important is that the orthodoxies of the past *didn't change* or at least didn't change rapidly. In medieval Europe the Church dictated what you should believe, but at least it allowed you to retain the same beliefs from birth to death. It didn't tell you to believe one thing on Monday and another on Tuesday. And the same is more or less true of any orthodox Christian, Hindu, Buddhist or Moslem today. In a sense his thoughts are circumscribed, but he passes his whole life within the same framework of thought. His emotions aren't tampered with. Now, with totalitarianism exactly the opposite is true. The peculiarity of the totalitarian state is that though it controls thought, it doesn't fix it. It sets up unquestionable dogmas, and it alters them from day to day. It needs the dogmas, because it needs absolute obedience from its subjects, but it can't avoid the changes, which are dictated by the needs of power politics. It declares itself infallible, and at the same time it attacks the very concept of objective truth. To take a crude, obvious example, every German up to September 1939 had to regard Russian Bolshevism with horror and aversion, and since September 1939 he has had to regard it with admiration and affection. If Russia and Germany go to war, as they may well do within the next few years, another equally violent change will have to take place. The German's emotional life, his loves and hatreds, are expected, when necessary, to reverse themselves overnight. I hardly need to point out the effect of this kind of thing upon literature. For writing is largely a matter of *feeling* which can't always be controlled from outside. It is easy to pay lip-service to the orthodoxy of the moment, but writing of any consequence can only be produced when a man *feels* the truth of what he is saying; without that, the creative impulse is lacking. All the evidence we have suggests that the sudden emotional changes which totalitarianism demands of its followers are psychologically impossible. And that is the chief reason why I suggest that if totalitarianism triumphs throughout the world, literature as we have known it is at an end. And in fact, totalitarianism does seem to have had that effect so far. In Italy literature has been crippled, and in Germany it seems almost to have ceased. The most characteristic activity of the Nazis is burning books. And even in Russia the literary renaissance we once expected hasn't happened, and the most promising Russian writers show a marked tendency to commit suicide or disappear into prison.

I said earlier that liberal capitalism is obviously coming to an end, and therefore I may have seemed to suggest that freedom of thought is also inevitably doomed. But I don't believe this to be so, and I will simply say in conclusion that I believe the hope of literature's survival lies in those countries in which liberalism has struck its deepest roots, the non-military countries, Western Europe and the Americas, India and China. I believe —it may be no more than a pious hope—that though a collectivised economy is bound to come, those countries will know how to evolve a form of Socialism which is not totalitarian, in which freedom of thought can survive the disappearance of economic individualism. That, at any rate, is the only hope to which anyone who cares for literature can cling. Whoever feels the value of literature, whoever sees the central part it plays in the development of human history, must also see the life and death necessity of resisting totalitarianism, whether it is imposed on us from without or from within.

Film Review: *Kipps* (H.G. Wells)

Time and Tide, 17 MAY 1941

It is a pleasure to be able to report, for once, that a novel has been filmed and remained recognizable. This version sticks very closely to the original Wells, even to the point of making a stage play rather than a film out of it. But that is forgivable in what is naturally a good story with a strong period-interest.

It was an exceptionally good piece of casting to give the name-part to Michael Redgrave,[1] who is not only an actor out of the common but looks the part. So does Miss Diana Wynyard as Helen Walsingham, the ambitious and cultured young woman to whom Kipps, when he has come into money and is attempting to 'improve' himself, is briefly and unhappily engaged. It was a bold gesture, but I think justified, to give the Folkestone episodes, with their picture of a society now as remote as that of the Fiji Islands, the same prominence as they had in the novel. Wells-fans will remember how Kipps, a young man working in a drapery, suddenly inherited twenty-six thousand pounds and endeavoured, until the effort became too great for him, to make himself into a gentleman according to the standards of the time. The comedy of the situation depended on class-differences which no longer effectively exist, and on intellectual fashions which are almost completely forgotten. When Kipps painfully crashed his way into 'good' society he was taken up not by the County, but by the intelligentsia of Folkestone, who were then (1908) still in the pre-Raphaelite stage. It was still the era of the *Yellow Book*, of the Burne-Jones maidens with their unhinged necks and russet-coloured hair, of *Omar Khayyam* in limp leather covers, and also of 'the new inmorality' and 'splendid sins'. Helen Walsingham, it will be remembered, eloped with a married novelist, after her brother, a disciple of Nietzsche, had embezzled Kipps's money. As usual, the producers have mistrusted their audience's intelligence and not guyed the Coote-Walsingham intelligentsia quite as amusingly as they might have done, but the other period touches are good and the clothes exceptionally good. Only one mistake did I

---

1. Michael Redgrave, CBE (1908–85), was a very distinguished stage and screen actor and director. He came from an acting family, married an actress, Rachel Kempson, and his children and grandchildren have followed in their steps. He became an actor in 1934, after a spell as a teacher. He joined the Royal Navy in 1941, serving on the lower deck of HMS *Illustrious* but was invalided out after sixteen months.

detect. In one place there is a reference to bustles. That is wrong. An early memory of my own, in 1907 or 1908, is finding a bustle in a cupboard and asking various grown-ups what it was for. Even at that date it seemed an antique.

It is questionable how much of the special atmosphere of an early Wells novel can be got into so different a medium as the film. Curiously enough Mr Wells, the apostle of progress and the future, has been able more than almost any other writer to make the sleepy years at the end of the last century and the beginning of this one seem a good time to live in. There is a certain flavour in *Kipps*, *Mr Polly* and *The Wheels of Chance* which probably could not survive even the most skilful filming. But this is a valiant attempt, and almost certainly as good a screen version of *Kipps* as we shall get. It is a pleasure to see so many films appearing with an Edwardian setting. It is time we stopped laughing at that period and realized that it had its points, as we did with the mid-Victorian age some twenty years ago. I recommend this film both to those who have read the book, and to those who haven't. Besides Mr Redgrave and Miss Wynyard, Mr Arthur Riscoe, Mr Edward Rigby, Mr Max Adrian and Miss Phyllis Calvert all give excellent performances.

'London Letter', 1 January 1942: Whom Are We Fighting Against?; Our Allies; Defeatism and German Propaganda; The Literary Front; The Food Situation

Partisan Review, MARCH–APRIL 1942

At this moment nothing is happening politically in England, and since we probably have ahead of us a long exhausting war in which morale will be all-important, I want to use most of this letter in discussing certain currents of thought which are moving to and fro just under the surface. Some of the tendencies I mention may seem to matter very little at present, but they do I think tell one something about possible future developments.

1. *Whom Are We Fighting Against?*[1]

This question, which obviously had to be answered sooner or later, began to agitate the big public some time in 1941, following on Vansittart's pamphlets and the starting of a German daily paper for the refugees (*Die Zeitung*, mildly Left, circulation about 60,000). Vansittart's thesis is that the Germans are *all* wicked, and not merely the Nazis. I don't need to tell you how gleefully the blimps have seized upon this as a way of escaping from the notion that we are fighting against Fascism. But of late the 'only good German is a dead one' line has taken the rather sinister form of a fresh drive against the refugees. The Austrian monarchists have fallen foul of the German leftwingers, whom they accuse of being pan-Germans in disguise, and this delights the blimps, who are always trying to manœuvre their two enemies, Germany and Socialism, into the same place. The point has now been reached where anyone who describes himself as 'anti-Fascist' is suspected of being pro-German. But the question is much complicated by the fact that the blimps have a certain amount of right on their side. Vansittart, badly though he writes, is an able man with more background than most of his opponents, and he has insisted on two facts which the pinks have done their best to obscure. One is that much of the Nazi philosophy is not new but is merely a continuation of pan-Germanism, and the other is that Britain cannot have a European policy without having an army. The pinks cannot admit that the German

---

1. Subtitles 1, 2 and 3 are included in the original text. They may not be Orwell's but those of a *Partisan Review* sub-editor. Subtitle 4 has been supplied by the editor.

masses are behind Hitler any more than the blimps can admit that their class must be levered out of control if we are to win the war. The controversy has raged for four months or more in the correspondence columns of several papers, and one paper in particular is obviously keeping it going as a way of baiting the refugees and the 'reds' generally. No one, however, airs any racial theories about Germany, which is a great advance on the war propaganda of 1914–18.

Ordinary working people do not seem either to hate the Germans or to distinguish between Germans and Nazis. Here and there there was violent anti-German feeling at the time of the bad air-raids, but it has worn off. The term 'Hun' has not caught on with the working classes this time. They call the Germans Jerries, which may have a mildly obscene meaning but is not unfriendly. All the blame for everything is placed on Hitler, even more than on the Kaiser during the last war. After an air raid one often used to hear people say 'He was over again last night'— 'he' being Hitler. The Italians are generally called Eyeties, which is less offensive than Wops, and there is no popular feeling against them whatever, nor against the Japanese as yet. To judge from photos in the newspapers, the land girls are quite ready to get off with Italian prisoners working on the farms. As to the smaller nations who are supposed to be at war with us, no one remembers which is which. The women who a year ago were busy knitting stockings for the Finns are now busy knitting them for the Russians, but there is no ill feeling. The chief impression one derives from all this chaos of opinions is how little the lack of a positive war aim, or even of any definite mental picture of the enemy, matters to people who are at any rate at one in not wanting to be governed by foreigners.

2.   *Our Allies*

Whatever may be happening among the higher-ups, the effect of the Russian alliance has been a tremendous net increase of pro-Russian sentiment. It is impossible to discuss the war with ordinary working-class and middle-class people without being struck by this. But the enthusiasm that ordinary people feel for Russia is not coupled with the faintest interest in the Russian political system. All that has happened is that Russia has become respectable. An enormous hammer and sickle flag flies daily over Selfridge's, the biggest shop in London. The Communists have not caused so much friction as I expected. They have been tactful in their posters and public pronouncements, and have gone to unheard-of lengths in supporting Churchill. But though they may have gained in numbers as a result of the Russian alliance, they do not seem to have gained in political influence. To a surprising extent ordinary people fail to grasp that there is any connection between Moscow and the Communist party, or even that Communist policy has changed as a result of Russia's entry into the war. Everyone is delighted that the Germans have failed to take Moscow, but no one sees in this any reason for paying any attention to what Palme Dutt[2] and Co. may say. In practice this attitude is sensible, but at the bottom of it there lies a profound lack of interest in doctrinaire politics. The ban has not been taken off the *Daily Worker*. Immediately after it was suppressed it reappeared as a factory sheet which was illegally printed, but was winked at. Now, under the title of 'the *British Worker*,' it is sold on the streets without interference. But it has ceased to be a daily and has lost most of its circulation. In the more important parts of the press the Communist influence has not been regained.

There is no corresponding increase in pro-American sentiment—the contrary, if anything. It is true that the entry of Japan and America into the war was expected by everyone, whereas the German invasion of Russia came as a surprise. But our new alliance has simply brought out the immense amount of anti-American feeling that exists in the ordinary low-brow middle class. English cultural feelings towards America are complicated but can be defined fairly accurately. In the middle class, the people who are *not* anti-American are the declassed technician type (people like radio engineers) and the younger intelligentsia. Up till about 1930 nearly all 'cultivated' people loathed the U.S.A., which was regarded as the vulgariser of England and Europe. The disappearance of this attitude was probably connected with the fall of Latin and Greek from their dominant position as school subjects. The younger intellectuals have no objection to the American language and tend to have a masochistic attitude towards the U.S.A., which they believe to be richer and more powerful than Britain. Of course it is exactly this that excites the jealousy of the ordinary patriotic middle class. I know people who automatically switch off the radio as soon as any American news comes on, and the most banal English film will always get middle-class support because 'it's such a relief to get away from those American voices.'

2. Rajani Palme Dutt (1896–1974), author and journalist, was an executive member of the Communist Party from 1922. He edited the London *Daily Worker*, 1936–38, and wrote a number of political books from the Communist Party standpoint.

Americans are supposed to be boastful, bad-mannered and worshippers of money, and are also suspected of plotting to inherit the British Empire. There is also business jealousy, which is very strong in the trades which have been hit by the Lease-Lend agreement.[3] The working-class attitude is quite different. English working-class people nearly always dislike Americans when in actual contact with them, but they have no preconceived cultural hostility. In the big towns they are being more and more Americanised in speech through the medium of the cinema.

It is uncertain whether English xenophobia is being broken down by the presence in England of large numbers of foreigners. I think it is, but plenty of people disagree with me. There is no doubt that in the summer of 1940 working-class suspicion of foreigners helped to make possible the internment of the refugees. At the time I talked with countless people, and except for Left intellectuals I could find no one who saw anything wrong in it. The blimps were after the refugees because they were largely Socialists, and the working-class line was 'what did they want to come here for?' Underlying this, a hangover from an earlier period, was a resentment against these foreigners who were supposedly taking Englishmen's jobs. In the years before the war it was largely Trade Union opposition that prevented a big influx of German Jewish refugees. Of late feelings have grown more friendly, partly because there is no longer a scramble for jobs, but partly also, I think, owing to personal contacts. The foreign troops who are quartered here in large numbers seem to get on unexpectedly well with the population, the Poles in particular being a great success with the girls. On the other hand there is a certain amount of antisemitism. One is constantly coming on pockets of it, not violent but pronounced enough to be disquieting. The Jews are supposed to dodge military service, to be the worst offenders on the Black Market, etc., etc. I have heard this kind of talk even from country people who had probably never seen a Jew in their lives. But no one wants actually to *do* anything to the Jews, and the idea that the Jews are responsible for the war never seems to have caught on with the big public, in spite of the efforts of the German radio.

3. Lease-Lend, properly Lend-Lease, was an agreement passed by the U.S. Congress, and signed by President Roosevelt 11 March 1941, whereby arms and supplies on a vast scale were given to the Allies – about two-thirds to the British and, under a separate act, nearly a quarter to the U.S.S.R. – to forward the prosecution of the war. Of the $50.6 billion advanced, $7.8 billion was returned in cash and kind (often services for U.S. troops in host countries).

3. *Defeatism and German Propaganda*

Appeasement of the Chamberlain type is not 'dead,' as the newspapers are constantly assuring us, but is lying very low. But there exists another school of right wing defeatism which can be conveniently studied in the weekly paper *Truth*. *Truth* has had a curious history and is a distinctly influential paper. At one time it was a non-political factual paper specialising in a genteel form of muckraking (exposure of patent medicine frauds, etc.), and was taken in as a matter of course in every club and regimental mess throughout the Empire. So far as I know it still has the same circulation, but latterly it has taken a definite political and economic line and become a stronghold of the worst kind of right wing Toryism. Sir Ernest Benn,[4] for instance, writes in it every week. It is not only anti-Labour, but in a discreet way anti-Churchill, anti-Russian and, more markedly, anti-American. It opposed the exchange of naval bases for American destroyers, the only other opposers being the Blackshirts and Communists. The strategy it advocates is to avoid entangling alliances, keep out of Europe and concentrate on self-defence on sea and in the air. The obvious logic of this is to make a compromise peace at the earliest possible moment. The quantity of advertisements for banks and insurance companies which *Truth* contains shows how well it is thought of in those quarters, and recently questions in Parliament brought out the fact that it is partly owned by the Conservative Party machine.

Left-wing defeatism is quite different and much more interesting. One or two of the minor political parties (for instance the British Anarchists, who followed up the German invasion of Russia with a terrific and very able anti-Soviet pamphlet, *The Truth about Russia*) follow a line which by implication is 'revolutionary defeatist.' The I.L.P. is preaching what amounts to a watered version of the 'Ten Propositions' set forth in the *Partisan Review*, but in very indefinite terms, never clearly stating whether or not it 'supports' the war. But the really interesting development is the increasing overlap between Fascism and pacifism, both of which overlap to some extent with 'left' extremism. The attitude of the very young is more significant than that of the *New Statesman* pinks who war-mongered between

---

4. Sir Ernest Benn (1875–1954) was founder of Benn's Sixpenny Library and Sixpenny Poets, and publisher of the Blue Guides (travel books). Among his own publications were *Confessions of a Capitalist* (1925), which espoused an 'austere Victorian *laisser-faire*' philosophy (DNB) and *Governed to Death* (a pamphlet, 1948).

1935 and 1939 and then sulked when the war started. So far as I know, the greater part of the very young intelligentsia are anti-war—this doesn't stop them from serving in the armed forces, of course—don't believe in any 'defence of democracy,' are inclined to prefer Germany to Britain, and don't feel the horror of Fascism that we who are somewhat older feel. The entry of Russia into the war didn't alter this, though most of these people pay lip-service to Russia. With the out-and-out, turn-the-other-cheek pacifists you come upon the much stranger phenomenon of people who have started by renouncing violence ending by championing Hitler. The antisemitic motif is very strong, though usually soft-pedalled in print. But not many English pacifists have the intellectual courage to think their thoughts down to the roots, and since there is no real answer to the charge that pacifism is objectively pro-Fascist, nearly all pacifist literature is forensic—i.e., specialises in avoiding awkward questions. To take one example, during the earlier period of the war the pacifist monthly the *Adelphi*, edited by Middleton Murry, accepted at its face value the German claim to be a 'socialist' state fighting against 'plutocratic' Britain, and more or less equated Germany with Russia. Hitler's invasion of Russia made nonsense of this line of thought, and in the five or six issues that have followed the *Adelphi* has performed the surprising feat of not mentioning the Russo–German war. The *Adelphi* has once or twice engaged in Jew-baiting of a mild kind. *Peace News*, now also edited by Middleton Murry, follows its old tradition of opposing war for different and incompatible reasons, at one moment because violence is wicked, at another because peace will 'preserve the British Empire,' etc.

For some years past there has been a tendency for Fascists and currency reformers to write in the same papers,[5] and it is only recently that they have been joined by the pacifists. I have in front of me a copy of the little anti-war paper *Now* which contains contributions from, among others,

5. In the September–October issue of *Partisan Review* (445–46), Gorham Munson (1896–1969) took issue with Orwell for seemingly linking Social Creditors and Fascists. Orwell should know, 'through his association with the *New English Weekly* . . . that Social Creditors do not include themselves in the currency reform category; they are revolutionary, not reformist, in their social objective.' Orwell's response was printed immediately after Munson's letter: 'I am sorry if I gave the impression that Social Creditors, as such, are pro-Fascist. Certainly Hargrave and the group now running the *New English Weekly* aren't. I am very glad to hear that they have dropped the Duke of Bedford, and apologise for not having known this, which I ought to have done.'

the Duke of Bedford, Alexander Comfort, Julian Symons and Hugh Ross Williamson.[6] Alexander Comfort is a 'pure' pacifist of the other-cheek school. The Duke of Bedford has for years been one of the main props of the Douglas Credit movement, and is also a devout Anglican, a pacifist or near-pacifist, and a landowner upon an enormous scale. In the early months of the war (then Marquess of Tavistock[7]) he went to Dublin on his own initiative and obtained or tried to obtain a draft of peace terms from the German Embassy. Recently he has published pamphlets urging the impossibility of winning the war and describing Hitler as a misunderstood man whose good faith has never really been tested.[8] Julian Symons writes in a vaguely Fascist strain but is also given to quoting Lenin. Hugh Ross Williamson has been mixed up in the Fascist movement for some time, but in the split-off section of it to which William Joyce ('Lord Haw Haw') also belongs. Just before the war he and others formed a fresh Fascist party calling itself the People's Party, of which the Duke of Bedford was a member. The People's Party apparently came to nothing, and in the first period of the war Williamson devoted himself to trying to bring about a get-together between the Communists and Mosley's followers. You see here an example of what I mean by the overlap between Fascism and pacifism.

What is interesting is that every section of anti-war opinion has one section of German radio propaganda, as it were, assigned to it. Since the outbreak of war the Germans have done hardly any direct propaganda in England otherwise than by wireless. The best known of their broadcasts, indeed the only ones that can be said to have been listened to to any appreciable extent, are those of William Joyce. No doubt these are often extravagantly untruthful, but they are a more or less responsible type of

6. See 'Pacifism and the War: A Controversy', September–October 1942, CW, XIII, 392–400 for responses by George Woodcock, Alex Comfort, and others, with particular reference to the persons named here. For the Duke of Bedford, see ns. 7 and 8 below. Alexander Comfort (1920–2000), poet, novelist, and medical biologist, was the author of No Such Liberty (1941), France and Other Poems (1941), The Almond Tree (1942), and a miracle play, Into Egypt (1942). His The Joy of Sex (1972) has sold over ten million copies. He edited Poetry Folios 1–10 with Peter Wells, 1942–46. Julian Symons (1912–1994), poet, novelist, and critic, compiled, for Penguin Books, An Anthology of War Poetry (1942). Many of his novels are detective stories. Hugh Ross Williamson (1901–1978) was a dramatist and critic. In 1946 Orwell contributed to Now.

7. The title Marquess of Tavistock is given to the heirs to the Dukes of Bedford. This duke, the twelfth (1888–1953), succeeded to the title in 1940.

8. The Marquess of Tavistock had published in 1940 the account of his negotiations with the German Legation in Dublin, The Fate of a Peace Effort.

broadcast, well delivered and giving news rather than straight propaganda. But in addition the Germans maintain four spurious 'freedom' stations, actually operating on the continent but pretending to be operating illegally in England. The best known of these is the New British Broadcasting Station, which earlier in the war the Blackshirts used to advertise by means of stickybacks. The general line of these broadcasts is 'uncensored news,' or 'what the Government is hiding from you.' They affect a pessimistic, well-informed manner, as of someone who is on the inside of the inside, and go in for enormous figures of shipping losses, etc. They urge the dismissal of Churchill, talk apprehensively about 'the Communist danger,' and are anti-American. The anti-American strain is even stronger in Joyce's broadcasts. The Americans are swindling us over the Lease-Lend agreement, are gradually absorbing the Empire, etc., etc. More interesting than the New British is the Workers' Challenge Station. This goes in for a line of red-hot revolutionary talks under such titles as 'Kick Churchill Out,' delivered by an authentic British working man who uses plenty of unprintable words. We are to overthrow the corrupt capitalist government which is selling us to the enemy, and set up a real socialist government which will come to the rescue of our heroic comrades of the Red Army and give us victory over Fascism. (This German station does not hesitate to talk about 'the menace of Nazism,' 'the horrors of the Gestapo,' etc.) The Workers' Challenge is not overtly defeatist. The line is always that it is probably too late, the Red Army is done for, but that we *may* be able to save ourselves if only we can 'overthrow capitalism,' which is to be done by means of strikes, mutinies, sabotage in the armament factories, and so forth. The other two 'freedom' stations are the Christian Peace Movement (pacifism) and Radio Caledonia (Scottish nationalism).

You can see how each strain of German propaganda corresponds to one existing, or at any rate potential, defeatist faction. Lord Haw Haw and the New British are aimed at the anti-American middle class, roughly speaking the people who read *Truth*, and the business interests that have suffered from the war. The Workers' Challenge is aimed at the Communists and the Left extremists generally. The Christian Peace Movement is aimed at the P.P.U. I don't want to give the impression, however, that German propaganda has much effect at this moment. There is little doubt that it has been an almost complete flop, especially during the last eighteen months. Various things that have happened have suggested that since the outbreak of war the Germans have not been well informed about internal conditions in England, and much of their propaganda, even if listened to, would fail because of simple psychological errors on which anyone with a real knowledge of England could put them right. But the various strains of defeatist feeling are there, and at some time they may grow. In some of what I have said above I may have seemed to mention people and factions too insignificant to be worth noticing, but in this bloodstained harlequinade in which we are living one never knows what obscure individual or half-lunatic theory may not become important. I do seem to notice a tendency in intellectuals, especially the younger ones, to come to terms with Fascism, and it is a thing to keep one's eye on. The quisling intellectual is a phenomenon of the last two years. Previously we all used to assume that Fascism was so self-evidently horrible that no thinking person would have anything to do with it, and also that the Fascists always wiped out the intelligentsia when they had the opportunity. Neither assumption was true, as we can see from what happened in France. Both Vichy and the Germans have found it quite easy to keep a facade of 'French culture' in existence. Plenty of intellectuals were ready to go over, and the Germans were quite ready to make use of them, even when they were 'decadent.' At this moment Drieu la Rochelle[9] is editing the *Nouvelle Revue Française*, Pound is bellowing against the Jews on the Rome radio, and Céline is a valued exhibit in Paris, or at least his books are. All of these would come under the heading of *kulturbolschewismus*, but they are also useful cards to play against the intelligentsia in Britain and the U.S.A. If the Germans got to England, similar things would happen, and I think I could make out at least a preliminary list of the people who would go over.

4.   *The Literary Front; The Food Situation*
Not much news here. All is very quiet on the literary front. The paper shortage seems to be favouring the appearance of very short books, which may be all to the good and may possibly bring back the 'long-short story,' a form which has never had a fair deal in England. I wrongly told you in an earlier letter that Dylan Thomas was in the army. He is physically unfit

---

9.   Pierre-Eugène Drieu la Rochelle (1893–1945), novelist, short-story writer, journalist, and essayist, oscillated between extreme positions artistically and politically. In his writing he pilloried what he saw as the decline of France, especially its bourgeoisie. In the 1930s he joined the French Nazi Party, the Parti Populaire Français. As editor during the Occupation, he turned *Nouvelle Revue Française* into a pro-Nazi journal. He committed suicide at the end of the war. He features in Allan Massie's novel, *A Question of Loyalties*.

and is doing jobs for the B.B.C. and the M.O.I. So is nearly everybody that used to be a writer, and most of us rapidly going native.

The food situation is much as before. We had our puddings on Christmas day, but they were a little paler than usual. The tobacco situation has righted itself, but matches are very short. They are watering the beer again, the third time since re-armament. The blackout is gradually relaxing in the absence of air-raids. There are still people sleeping in the Tube stations, but only a handful at each station. The basements of demolished houses have been bricked up and turned into water tanks for use in case of fire. They look just like Roman baths and give the ruins an even more Pompeian look than they had before. The stopping of the air raids has had some queer results. During the worst of the blitz they set in hand huge schemes for levelling waste pieces of ground to make playgrounds, using bomb debris as a subsoil. All these have had to stop in the middle, no more bomb debris being available.

All the best. Yours ever, George Orwell

Extracts from 'London Letter', 8 May 1942: The British Crisis; Churchill's Position; Sir Stafford Cripps; Attitudes to the USSR

Partisan Review, JULY–AUGUST 1942

The British Crisis

When I last wrote to you things had begun to go wrong in the Far East but nothing was happening politically. Now, I am fairly certain, we are on the edge of the political crisis which I have been expecting for the better part of two years. The situation is very complicated and I dare say that even before this reaches you much will have happened to falsify my predictions, but I will make the best analysis I can.

The basic fact is that people are now as fed up and as ready for a radical policy as they were at the time of Dunkirk, with the difference that they now have, or are inclined to think they have, a potential leader in Stafford Cripps. I don't mean that people in significant numbers are crying out for the introduction of Socialism, merely that the mass of the nation wants certain things that aren't obtainable under a capitalist economy and is willing to pay almost any price to get them. Few people, for instance, seem to me to feel urgently the need for nationalisation of industry, but all except the interested minority would accept nationalisation without a blink if they were told authoritatively that you can't have efficient war-production otherwise. The fact is that 'Socialism,' called by that name, isn't by itself an effective rallying cry. To the mass of the people 'Socialism' just means the discredited Parliamentary Labour Party, and one feature of the time is the widespread disgust with all the old political parties. But what then do people want? I should say that what they articulately want is more social equality, a complete clean-out of the political leadership, an aggressive war strategy and a tighter alliance with the USSR. But one has to consider the background of these desires before trying to predict what political development is now possible.

The war has brought the class nature of their society very sharply home to English people, in two ways. First of all there is the unmistakable fact that all real power depends on class privilege. You can only get certain jobs if you have been to one of the right schools, and if you fail and have to be sacked, then somebody else from one of the right schools takes over, and so it continues. This may go unnoticed when things are prospering, but becomes obvious in moments of disaster. Secondly there are the hardships of war, which are, to put it mildly, tempered for anyone with over £2000 a year. I don't want to bore you with a detailed account of the way in which the food rationing is evaded, but you can take it that whereas ordinary people have to live on an uninteresting diet and do without many luxuries they are accustomed to, the rich go short of absolutely nothing except, perhaps, wines, fruit and sugar. You can be almost unaffected by food rationing without even breaking the law, though there is also a lively Black Market. Then there is bootleg petrol and, quite obviously, widespread evasion of Income Tax. This does not go unnoticed, but nothing happens because the will to crack down on it is not there while money and political power more or less coincide. To give just one example. At long last, and against much opposition in high places, the Ministry of Food is about to cut down 'luxury feeding' by limiting the sum of money that can be spent on a meal in a hotel or restaurant. Already, before the law is even passed, ways of evading it have been thought out, and these are discussed almost undisguisedly in the newspapers.

There are other tensions which the war has brought out but which are somewhat less obvious than the jealousy caused by the Black Market or the discontent of soldiers blancoing their gasmasks under the orders of twerps of officers. One is the growing resentment felt by the underpaid armed forces (at any rate the Army) against the high wages of the munition workers. If this were dealt with by raising the soldier's pay to the munition-worker's level the result would be either inflation or the diversion of labour from war-production to consumption goods. The only real remedy is to cut down the civilian worker's wages as well, which could only be made acceptable by the most drastic income cuts all round— briefly, 'war communism.' And apart from the class struggle in its ordinary sense there are deeper jealousies within the bourgeoisie than foreigners sometimes realise. If you talk with a BBC accent you can get jobs that a proletarian couldn't get, but it is almost impossible to get beyond a certain point unless you belong socially to the Upper Crust. Everywhere able men feel themselves bottled down by incompetent idiots from the county families. Bound up with this is the crushing feeling we have all had in England these last twenty years that if you have brains 'they' (the Upper Crust) will see to it that you are kept out of any really important job. During the years of investment capital we produced like a belt of fat the huge blimpocracy which monopolises official and military power and has an instinctive hatred of intelligence. This is probably a more important factor in England than in a 'new' country like the USA. It means that our military weakness goes beyond the inherent weakness of a capitalist state.

When in England you find a gifted man in a really commanding position it is usually because he happens to have been born into an aristocratic family (examples are Churchill, Cripps, Mountbatten[1]), and even so he only gets there in moments of disaster when others don't want to take responsibility. Aristocrats apart, those who are branded as 'clever' can't get their hands on the real levers of power, and they know it. Of course 'clever' individuals do occur in the upper strata, but basically it is a class issue, middle class against upper class.

Churchill's Position

The statement in the March–April PR that 'the reins of power are still firmly in the hands of Churchill' is an error. Churchill's position is very shaky. Up to the fall of Singapore it would have been true to say that the mass of the people liked Churchill while disliking the rest of his government, but in recent months his popularity has slumped heavily. In addition he has the right-wing Tories against him (the Tories on the whole have always hated Churchill, though they had to pipe down for a long period), and Beaverbrook is up to some game which I do not fully understand but which must have the object of bringing himself into power. I wouldn't give Churchill many more months of power, but whether he will be replaced by Cripps, Beaverbrook or somebody like Sir John Anderson is still uncertain.

The reason why nearly everyone who was anti-Nazi supported Churchill from the collapse of France onwards was that there was nobody else—i.e., nobody who was already well enough known to be able to step into power and who at the same time could be trusted not to surrender. It is idle to say that in 1940 we ought to have set up a Socialist government; the mass basis for such a thing probably existed, but not the leadership. The Labour party had no guts, the pinks were defeatist, the Communists effectively pro-Nazi, and in any case there did not exist on the Left one single man of really nation-wide reputation. In the months that followed what was wanted was chiefly obstinacy, of which Churchill had plenty. Now, however, the situation has altered.

1. Lord Louis Mountbatten (1900–79) achieved fame in command of HMS *Kelly*, in 1939, and later of the aircraft carrier *Illustrious*. He was Commodore and then Chief of Combined Operations, 1941–43; Supreme Allied Commander, Southeast Asia, 1943–46; and the last Viceroy of India, becoming Governor-General of India after partition. He and members of his family were murdered by the Irish Republican Army in August 1979.

The strategic situation is probably far better than it was in 1940, but the mass of the people don't think so, they are disgusted by defeats some of which they realise were unnecessary, and they have been gradually disillusioned by perceiving that in spite of Churchill's speeches the old gang stays in power and nothing really alters. For the first time since Churchill came to power the government has begun losing by-elections. Of the five most recent it has lost three, and in the two which it didn't lose one opposition candidate was anti-war (I.L.P.[2]) and the other was regarded as a defeatist. In all these elections the polls were extremely low, in one case reaching the depth-record of 24 per cent of the electorate. (Most wartime polls have been low, but one has to write off something for the considerable shift of population.) There is a most obvious loss of the faith in the old parties, and there is a new factor in the presence of Cripps, who enjoys at any rate for the moment a considerable personal reputation. Just at the moment when things were going very badly he came back from Russia in a blaze of undeserved glory. People had by this time forgotten the circumstances in which the Russo–German war broke out and credited Cripps with having 'got Russia in on our side.' He was, however, cashing in on his earlier political history and on having never sold out his political opinions. There is good reason to think that at that moment, with no party machine under his control, he did not realise how commanding his personal position was. Had he appealed directly to the public, through the channels open to him, he could probably then and there have forced a more radical policy on the government, particularly in the direction of a generous settlement with India. Instead he made the mistake of entering the government and the almost equally bad one of going to India with an offer which was certain to be turned down. I can't put in print the little I know about the inner history of the Cripps-Nehru negotiations, and in any case the story is too complex to be written about in a letter of this length. The important thing is to what extent this failure has discredited Cripps. The people most interested in ditching the negotiations were the pro-Japanese faction in the Indian Congress party, and the British right-wing Tories. Halifax's speech made in New York at the time was interpreted here as an effort to tread on as many Indian toes as possible and thus make a get-together between Cripps and Nehru more difficult. Similar efforts are being made

2. Independent Labour Party, of which Orwell had been a member from June 1938 until he resigned shortly after the outbreak of war.

from the opposite end at this moment. The upshot is that Cripps's reputation is damaged in India but not in this country—or, if damaged, then
by his entry into the government rather than by the failure in Delhi.

Sir Stafford Cripps

I can't yet give you a worthwhile opinion as to whether Cripps is the man
the big public think him, or are half-inclined to think him. He is an enig-
matic man who has been politically unstable, and those who know him
only agree upon the fact that he is personally honest. His position rests
purely upon the popular belief in him, for he has the Labour party machine
more or less against him, and the Tories are only temporarily supporting
him because they want to use him against Churchill and Beaverbrook and
imagine that they can make him into another tame cat like Attlee. Some
of the factory workers are inclined to be suspicious of him (one comment
reported to me was 'Too like Mosley'—meaning too much the man of
family who 'goes to the people') and the Communists hate him because
he is suspected of being anti-Stalin. Beaverbrook already appears to be
instituting an attack on Cripps and his newspapers are making use of
anti-Stalinist remarks dropped by Cripps in the past. I note that the
Germans, to judge from their wireless, would be willing to see Cripps in
power if at that price they could get rid of Churchill. They probably
calculate that since Cripps has no party machine to rely on he would soon
be levered out by the right-wing Tories and make way for Sir John
Anderson, Lord Londonderry or someone of that kind. I can't yet say
with certainty that Cripps is not merely a second rate figure to whom
the public have tied their hopes, a sort of bubble blown by popular
discontent. But at any rate, the way people talked about him when he
came back from Moscow was symptomatically important.

There is endless talk about a second front, those who are for and
those who are against being divided roughly along political lines. Much
that is said is extremely ignorant, but even people with little military
knowledge are able to see that in the last few months we have lost by
useless defensive actions a force which, if grouped in one place and used
offensively, might have achieved something. Public opinion often seems
to be ahead of the so-called experts in matters of grand strategy, sometimes even tactics and weapons. I don't myself know whether the opening
of a second front is feasible, because I don't know the real facts about
the shipping situation; the only clue I have to the latter is that the food
situation hasn't altered during the past year. Official policy seems to be

to discountenance the idea of a second front, but just possibly that is only military deception. The right-wing papers make much play with our bombing raids on Germany and suggest that we can tie down a million troops along the coast of Europe by continuous commando raids. The latter is nonsense as the commandos can't do much when the nights get short, and after our own experiences few people here believe that bombing can settle anything. In general the big public is offensive-minded and is always pleased when the government shows by violating international law (eg. Oran, Syria, Madagascar) that it is taking the war seriously. Nevertheless the idea of attacking Spain or Spanish Morocco (much the most hopeful area for a second front in my opinion) is seldom raised. It is agreed by all observers that the Army, ie. rank and file and a lot of the junior officers, is exceedingly browned off, but this does not seem to be the case with the Navy and RAF, and it is easy to get recruits for the dangerous corps such as the commandos and parachute troops. An anonymous pamphlet attacking the blimpocracy, button-polishing, etc., recently sold enormously, and this line is also run by the *Daily Mirror*, the soldiers' favourite paper, which was nearly suppressed a few weeks back for its criticisms of the higher command. On the other hand the pamphlets which used to appear earlier in the war, complaining about the hardships of army life, seem to have faded out. Perhaps symptomatically important is the story now widely circulated, that the real reason why the higher-ups have stuck out against adopting dive bombers is that these are cheap to manufacture and don't represent much profit. I know nothing as to the truth of this story, but I record the fact that many people believe it. Churchill's speech a few days back in which he referred to possible use of poison gas by the Germans was interpreted as a warning that gas warfare will begin soon. Usual comment: 'I hope we start using it first.' People seem to me to have got tougher in their attitude, in spite of general discontent and the lack of positive war aims. It is hard to assess how much the man in the street cared about the Singapore disaster. Working-class people seemed to me to be more impressed by the escape of the German warships from Brest.[3] The opinion seems general that

---

3. The battle-cruisers *Scharnhorst* and *Gneisenau*, with the heavy cruiser *Prinz Eugen*, sailed from Brest on 11 February 1942, passed through the Channel, and reached Wilhelmshaven two days later. Despite being warned in advance of their departure by the French Resistance, and notwithstanding individually courageous attempts, the navy and RAF failed to sink them, though *Gneisenau* was damaged. The RAF lost 42 aircraft; the navy, 6 slow Swordfish torpedo-planes. The effect on the public was dismay and anger.

Germany is the real enemy, and newspaper efforts to work up a hate over Japanese atrocities failed. My impression is that people will go on fighting indefinitely so long as Germany is in the field, but that if Germany should be knocked out they would not continue the war against Japan unless a real and intelligible war aim were produced.

Attitudes to the USSR

I have referred in earlier letters to the great growth of pro-Russian feeling. It is difficult, however, to be sure how deep this goes. A Trotskyist said to me recently that he thought that by their successful resistance the Russians had won back all the credit they lost by the Hitler-Stalin pact and the Finnish war. I don't believe this is so. What has happened is that the USSR has gained a lot of admirers it did not previously have, but many who used to be its uncritical adherents have grown cannier. One notices here a gulf between what is said publicly and privately. In public nobody says a word against the USSR, but in private, apart from the 'disillusioned' Stalinists that one is always meeting, I notice a more sceptical attitude among thinking people. One sees this especially in conversations about the second front. The official attitude of the pinks is that if we open up a second front the Russians will be so grateful that they will be our comrades to the last. In reality, to open a second front without a clear agreement beforehand would simply give the Russians the opportunity to make a separate peace; for if we succeeded in drawing the Germans away from their territories, what reason would they have for going on fighting? Another theory favoured in left-wing papers is that the more fighting we do the more say we shall have in the post-war settlement. This again is an illusion; those who dictate the peace treaties are those who have remained strongest, which usually means those who have managed to avoid fighting (eg. the USA in the last war). Considerations of this kind seldom find their way into print but are admitted readily enough in private. I think people have not altogether forgotten the Russo–German pact and that fear of another doublecross partly explains their desire for a closer alliance. But there is also much sentimental boosting of Russia, based on ignorance and played up by all kinds of crooks who are utterly anti-Socialist but see that the Red Army is a popular line. I must take back some of the favourable references I made in earlier letters to the Beaverbrook press. After giving his journalists a free hand for a year or more, during which some of them did good work in enlightening the big public, Beaverbrook has again cracked the whip and is setting his team at work to attack Churchill and, more directly, Cripps. He is simul-taneously yapping against fuel-rationing, petrol-rationing and other restric-tions on private capitalism, and posing as more Stalinist than the Stalinists. Most of the right-wing press adopts the more cautious line of praising 'the great Russian people' (historic parallels with Napoleon, etc.) while keeping silent about the nature of the Russian regime. The 'Internationale' is at last being played on the wireless. Molotov's speech on the German atrocities was issued as a White Paper, but in deference to somebody's feelings (I don't know whether Stalin's or the King's) the royal arms were omitted from the cover. People in general want to think well of Russia, though still vaguely hostile to Communism. They would welcome a joint declaration of war aims and a close co-ordination of strategy. I think many people realise that a firm alliance with Russia is difficult while the Munich crew are still more or less in power, but much fewer grasp that the comparative political backwardness of the USA presents another difficulty.

Well, that is the set-up as I see it. It seems to me that we are back to the 'revolutionary situation' which existed but was not utilised after Dunkirk. From that time until quite recently one's thoughts necessarily moved in some such progression as this:

We can't win the war with our present social and economic structure.

The structure won't change unless there is a rapid growth in popular consciousness.

The only thing that promotes this growth is military disasters.

One more disaster and we shall lose the war. . . . .

Broadcast: 'A Magazine Programme'

Voice, BBC, 11 AUGUST 1942

One of Orwell's innovations – the kind that would be the inspiration for the BBC's Third Programme (see 'The Cost of Radio Programmes', 1 February, 1946, n. 2 on page 354) – was a 'spoken poetry magazine' complete with spoken editorial by Orwell. In all, six were produced. The later 'issues' were devoted to 'War Poetry', 'Childhood', 'American Literature', 'Oriental Influences on English Literature', and 'Christmas'. One script is missing (that for Oriental Influences), and though they were intended as recitals and free discussions in order to satisfy censorship requirements the entire broadcasts were carefully scripted. Orwell managed to encourage distinguished writers to participate including Herbert Read, William Empson, Mulk Raj Anand, Edmund Blunden, Stephen Spender, Una Marson, Venu Chitale, Narayana Menon, and T.S. Eliot (reading 'What the Thunder Said' from The Waste Land).

This is the worst possible moment to be starting a magazine. While we sit here talking in a more or less highbrow manner—talking about art and literature and whatnot—tens of thousands of tanks are racing across the steppes of the Don and battleships upside down are searching for one another in the wastes of the Pacific. I suppose during every second that we sit here at least one human being will be dying a violent death. It may seem a little dilettante to be starting a magazine concerned primarily with poetry at a moment when, quite literally, the fate of the world is being decided by bombs and bullets. However our magazine—'Voice' we are calling it—isn't quite an ordinary magazine. To begin with it doesn't use up any paper or the labour of any printers or booksellers. All it needs is a little electrical power and half a dozen voices. It doesn't have to be delivered at your door, and you don't have to pay for it. It can't be described as a wasteful form of entertainment. Moreover there are some of us who feel that it is exactly at times like the present that literature ought not to be forgotten. As a matter of fact this business of pumping words into the ether, its potentialities and the actual uses it is put to, has its solemn side. According to some authorities wireless waves, or some wireless waves, don't merely circle our planet, but travel on endlessly through space at the speed of light, in which case what we are saying this afternoon should be audible in the great nebula in Orion nearly a million years hence. If there are intelligent beings there, as there well may be, though Sir James

Jeans[1] doesn't think it likely, it won't hurt them to pick up a few specimens of twentieth century verse along with the swing music and the latest wad of lies from Berlin. But I'm not apologising for our magazine, merely introducing it. I ask you to note therefore that it will appear once monthly on a Tuesday, that it will contain prose but will make a speciality of contemporary poetry, and that it will make particular efforts to publish the work of the younger poets who have been handicapped by the paper shortage and whose work isn't so well known as it ought to be.

'Voice' has now been in existence nearly three minutes. I hope it already has a few readers, or I should say listeners. I hope as you sit there you are imagining the magazine in front of you. It's only a small volume, about twenty pages. One advantage of a magazine of this kind is that you can choose your own cover design. I should favour something in light blue or a nice light grey, but you can take your choice. Now turn to the first page. It's good quality paper, you notice, pre-war paper—you don't see paper like that in other magazines nowadays—and nice wide margins. Fortunately we have no advertisements, so on page one is the Table of Contents. . . . .

---

1. Sir James H. Jeans (1877–1946), physicist and mathematician, wrote a number of books aimed at the general reader including *The Universe Around Us* (1929) and *Through Space and Time* (1934), as well as scholarly studies. Orwell may have had in mind his proposition that matter is in a continuous process of creation.

Broadcast: 'Review on Third Anniversary of Outbreak of the War'

News Review 38, BBC, 5 SEPTEMBER 1942

September 3rd was the third anniversary of the outbreak of war. Before giving our usual resumé of the week's news, it may be worthwhile to look back over the past three years and thus see the present phase of the struggle in its true perspective.

If one looks thus at the whole picture and not merely at one corner of it, the fact which stands out is that after three years of desperate war, Britain is far stronger than she was when the war started. Whereas in the autumn of 1939 the entire British Commonwealth was barely able to mobilise a million trained men, and had only a very small air force and depleted navy, to-day there are several million trained men in Britain alone, putting aside the great armies in the Middle East, in India, and in other places. The R.A.F. has grown till it is more than the equal of the German Air Force, and the Navy, in spite of heavy losses in the unending and difficult work of convoying war materials to Britain, is much more powerful than at the outbreak of war.

When the German commanders survey the situation the fact that their main enemy, Britain, is merely stronger and not weaker after all their attacks—must be the first to strike them. And behind this is the other immense fact that America now stands behind Britain and is re-arming upon an enormous scale and at lightning speed in places where neither the German army nor the German air force can affect the process. The other fact which the German commanders have to take into consideration is the continued resistance of Soviet Russia, the complete failure of the Red Army to disintegrate as it was supposed to do in the Autumn of 1941, and the frightful drain on German manpower which the Russian campaign represents, especially with another winter in the snow looming two or three months ahead.

Looking back we see that there have been really three turning points in the war and at each of them a Fascist victory receded further into the distance. The first was the Battle of Britain, in the late summer of 1940. The Germans, confident of a quick victory, hurled their air force against Britain and not only suffered heavy losses to no purpose, but were brought to realise that they could not win the war quickly, but had got in front of them a long and exhausting struggle in which almost inevitably the rest of the world would end by turning against them. The next turning point was in the winter of 1941, when the German advance on Russia petered out and the Russians drove the Germans back from Rostov. The German attack on Russia had been a direct result of the successful British resistance and the British sea blockade. Unable to break out and establish communications with Asia and America, the Germans had planned to conquer Russia at one blow, after which they would have at their disposal an enormous area which could be plundered of almost all the raw materials they needed, while at the same time they would no longer have the Red Army as a perpetual menace to their rear, so that they could devote their whole forces to a renewed attack on Britain. This also failed, and the Germans, in spite of great gains of territory, found themselves in for an exhausting struggle in which they were fighting against tremendous manpower and impossible climatic conditions, while their air force was so heavily engaged that they could not prevent the R.A.F. from pounding the cities of Western Germany. The third turning point was when Germany succeeded in pushing Japan into the war. The Japanese were mainly concerned with the conquest of East Asia, but the plan from the German point of view was to divert the attention of the Americans and prevent them from sending further aid to Britain. Once again the great gamble failed, for though the Japanese won easy victories at the beginning, they too soon found themselves in for a protracted struggle against a superior enemy, and the Americans, while fighting the Japanese in the Pacific, were not diverted for a moment from sending men and supplies to Europe. In spite of successes which look brilliant on a short term view, each of the three great gambles of the Fascist powers has failed, and they are able to see gradually forming against them a vast coalition of nearly four-fifths of humanity with overwhelming resources and unalterable determination to make an end of Fascist aggression once and for all. In 1940, Britain was alone, poorly armed and not by any means certain of being joined by further Allies. In 1942, Britain has beside her the Red Army, the enormous American war industries and the four hundred million human beings of China. However long the struggle may yet be, its end cannot be in much doubt. That is the picture of the war which we see if we look at it in its broad lines and do not allow yesterday's newspaper to occupy the whole of our attention.

We have occupied most of our time in giving this general review of the war, and we shall therefore give only a short summary of this week's events. . . . .

'Thomas Hardy Looks at War'

Tribune, 18 SEPTEMBER 1942

Thomas Hardy's great poetic drama, *The Dynasts*, is of formidable size, and is generally bound in the sort of depressing gritty cover that one associates with school text books,[1] with the result that it has become one of those books which people can't read and therefore feel obliged to praise. It is nevertheless well worth reading, if only because the war it deals with has a ghostly similarity with this one.

The Dynasts is a sort of versified chronicle of the Napoleonic war, which in atmosphere and even in strategy was much liker to the present war than was the war of 1914–18. It is true that the events are happening in a different order, but even so their similarity is startling. The Russo–German pact is Tilsit, the Battle of France is Jena, the Battle of Britain is Trafalgar, the German invasion of Russia is the Moscow campaign, and so on. (Dunkirk is probably not Corunna, but the disastrous campaign in the Low Countries in 1792.) Moreover, the ideological mix-up, the quisling motif, the treacherous nobles and the patriotic common people, the endless line-ups and double-crossings, even such details as the invasion scare and the hasty formation of a Home Guard in Britain, are all paralleled.

However, the main interest of *The Dynasts* is not in its appositeness to our own times, nor in its historical side at all, for Hardy does not show much grasp of what we should now regard as the underlying issues of the Napoleonic war. The book's theme is sufficiently indicated in its title; Hardy sees the war as simply a clash of power-hungry monarchs, with the common people being slaughtered without any benefit, or even any possibility of benefit, to themselves. Of course, the idea of huge and meaningless suffering appeals deeply to him, and in the form chosen for *The Dynasts* his strange mystical pessimism gets a freer rein than it could get in a novel, where a certain amount of probability is needed.

Hardy set free his genius by writing a drama which was definitely not

1. Orwell probably refers to the green of the Complete Edition, published in 1910. The first part of the play had appeared in 1903; seven years later it was published in full, comprising the nineteen acts to which Orwell refers. Judging by his reference to *The Dynasts* in his War-time Diary for 7.9.42, Orwell may have written this essay shortly before its publication. It marks his return to *Tribune*; his last contribution had been on 20 December 1940.

meant to be acted, and quite unknowingly—for *The Dynasts* was written round about 1900—produced something that would do as it stands for the script of a talkie. Though it is mostly in blank-verse dialogue, it contains a great deal of visual description, and its effect is really got by the constant switching of perspective from one end of Europe to the other, and from the earth to the middle air in a way that could only be reproduced on the screen. Apart from the human characters, certain beings described as spirits are introduced as a sort of chorus to comment on what is happening. But even the spirits, though they can foresee the future, are unable either to alter or to understand it. According to Hardy's vision of life, all events are predetermined, human beings are automata, but they are automata with the illusion of free will and the power of suffering. Everything happens at the behest of something called the Immanent Will—it tells one a great deal about Thomas Hardy that he believes in God and his God is always referred to as It—whose purposes we do not understand and never can understand. At certain key points in *The Dynasts* the Will manifests itself and the landscape turns into a sort of enormous brain in which the struggling human beings are seen to be entirely helpless cells or fibres. For example, at the most desperate moment of the battle of Waterloo:

> SPIRIT OF THE YEARS
> *Know'st not at this stale time*
> *That shaken and unshaken are alike*
> *But demonstrations from the Back of Things?*
> *Must I again reveal It as It hauls*
> *The halyards of the world?*

'A transparency as in earlier scenes again pervades the spectacle. . . .'[2] The web connecting all the apparently separate shapes includes Wellington in its tissue with the rest, and shows him, like them, as acting while discovering his intention to act. By the lurid light the faces of every row, square, group and column of men, French and English, wear the expression of people in a dream.'

That is effective enough even as it stands. In its context, as a climax to the long and hopeless struggle of Napoleon, it is profoundly moving, and

---

2. The ellipsis marks the omission of the original's 'and the ubiquitous urging of the Immanent Will becomes visualized' (Part III, VII. vii; 1910 edition 505).

leaves one with the feeling that *The Dynasts* is one of the very few genuine tragedies that have been written in our time.

One might wonder how any truly tragic effect can be produced by Hardy's morbid and almost superstitious view of life. One might also ask how it is that *The Dynasts* gives an impression of grandeur while Hardy's vision of history is, in fact, extremely limited. He shows hardly any awareness that the Napoleonic war was partly a war of ideas—no hint that the fate of both the French Revolution and the Industrial Revolution were involved—and he deals chiefly with the picturesque high-lights of the war, even at moments showing signs of jingo patriotism. All centres round the personality of Napoleon, whom Hardy represents as a mere vulgar adventurer, which he was.

Why, then, is Napoleon's story moving? Because personal ambition is tragic against a background of fatalism, and the more megalomaniac it is, the more tragic it becomes. If one believes that the future is predetermined, no figure is so pitiful as the 'great' man, the man who a little more than others has the illusion of controlling his destiny.

In places the verse of *The Dynasts* is remarkable. In the huge formless drama (nineteen acts!) Hardy's clumsy genius had elbow-room, and there are wonderful passages here and there. For example:

> *Ay; where is Nelson? Faith, by this late time*
> *He may be sodden; churned in Biscay swirls;*
> *Or blown to polar bears by boreal gales;*
> *Or sleeping amorously in some calm cave*
> *On the Canaries' or Atlantis' shore*
> *Upon the bosom of his Dido dear,*
> *For all that we know!*[3]

This passage is of great technical interest because of its onomatopœic effects. Whereas the third line, for instance, gives an impression of icy cold by means of its long vowel sounds, the easy rhythm of the next three lines seems to call up a vision of a cosy lamp-lit room, with Lady Hamilton waiting beside the fireplace, Nelson's slippers keeping warm in the fender and a dish of crumpets on the hob.

But the main appeal of *The Dynasts* is not in the verse, but in the grandiose and rather evil vision of armies marching and counter-marching

---

3. From the Earl of Malmesbury's last speech (Part I, IV. vi; 1910 edition 80).

through the mists, and men dying by hundreds of thousands in the Russian snows, and all for absolutely nothing. Hardy's pessimism was absurd as well as demoralising, but he could make poetry out of it because he believed in it; thus showing, like Poe, Baudelaire and various others, that even a half-lunatic view of life will do as a basis for literature provided it is sincerely held.

'T.S. Eliot'

Poetry (London), OCTOBER–NOVEMBER 1942

There is very little in Eliot's later work that makes any deep impression on me. That is a confession of something lacking in myself, but it is not, as it may appear at first sight, a reason for simply shutting up and saying no more, since the change in my own reaction probably points to some external change which is worth investigating.

I know a respectable quantity of Eliot's earlier work by heart. I did not sit down and learn it, it simply stuck in my mind as any passage of verse is liable to do when it has really rung the bell. Sometimes after only one reading it is possible to remember the whole of a poem of, say, twenty or thirty lines, the act of memory being partly an act of reconstruction. But as for these three latest poems, I suppose I have read each of them two or three times since they were published, and how much do I verbally remember? 'Time and the bell have buried the day,' 'At the still point of the turning world,' 'The vast waters of the petrel and the porpoise,' and bits of the passage beginning 'O dark dark dark. They all go into the dark.' (I don't count 'In my end is my beginning,' which is a quotation). That is about all that sticks in my head of its own accord. Now one cannot take this as proving that *Burnt Norton* and the rest are worse than the more memorable early poems, and one might even take it as proving the contrary, since it is arguable that that which lodges itself most easily in the mind is the obvious and even the vulgar. But it is clear that something has departed, some kind of current has been switched off, the later verse does not *contain* the earlier, even if it is claimed as an improvement upon it. I think one is justified in explaining this by a deterioration in Mr. Eliot's subject-matter. Before going any further, here are a couple of extracts, just near enough to one another in meaning to be comparable. The first is the concluding passage of *The Dry Salvages*:

> And right action is freedom
> From past and future also.
> For most of us, this is the aim
> Never here to be realised;
> Who are only undefeated
> Because we have gone on trying;

We, content at the last
If our temporal reversion nourish
(Not too far from the yew-tree)
The life of significant soil.

Here is an extract from a much earlier poem:

Daffodil bulbs instead of balls
Stared from the sockets of the eyes!
He knew that thought clings round dead limbs
Tightening its lusts and luxuries.

. . .

He knew the anguish of the marrow
The ague of the skeleton;
No contact possible to flesh
Allayed the fever of the bone.[1]

The two passages will bear comparison since they both deal with the same subject, namely death. The first of them follows upon a longer passage in which it is explained, first of all, that scientific research is all nonsense, a childish superstition on the same level as fortune-telling, and then that the only people ever likely to reach an understanding of the universe are saints, the rest of us being reduced to 'hints and guesses.' The keynote of the closing passage is, 'resignation.' There is a 'meaning' in life and also in death; unfortunately we don't know what it is, but the fact that it exists should be a comfort to us as we push up the crocuses, or whatever it is that grows under the yew trees in country churchyards. But now look at the other two stanzas I have quoted. Though fathered on to somebody else, they probably express what Mr. Eliot himself felt about death at that time, at least in certain moods. They are not voicing resignation. On the contrary, they are voicing the pagan attitude towards death, the belief in the next world as a shadowy place full of thin, squeaking ghosts, envious of the living, the belief that however bad life may be, death is worse. This conception of death seems to have been

1. The quotation from 'The Dry Salvages', *Poetry (London)* omitted the comma after 'us' in line 3. In the second and fourth stanzas from 'Whispers of Immortality' (written about 1918), 'his eyes' was printed for 'the eyes'; 'how thought' for 'that thought'; a semi-colon appeared for a full-stop after 'luxuries', and a colon for a semi-colon after 'skeleton'.

general in antiquity, and in a sense it is general now. 'The anguish of the marrow, the ague of the skeleton,' Horace's famous ode *Eheu fugaces*,[2] and Bloom's unuttered thoughts during Paddy Dignam's funeral, are all very much of a muchness. So long as man regards himself as an individual, his attitude towards death must be one of simple resentment. And however unsatisfactory this may be, if it is intensely felt it is more likely to produce good literature than a religious faith which is not really *felt* at all, but merely accepted against the emotional grain. So far as they can be compared, the two passages I have quoted seem to me to bear this out. I do not think it is questionable that the second of them is superior as verse, and also more intense in feeling, in spite of a tinge of burlesque.

What are these three poems, *Burnt Norton* and the rest, 'about'? It is not so easy to say what they are about, but what they appear on the surface to be about is certain localities in England and America with which Mr. Eliot has ancestral connections. Mixed up with this is a rather gloomy musing upon the nature and purpose of life, with the rather indefinite conclusion I have mentioned above. Life has a 'meaning,' but it is not a meaning one feels inclined to grow lyrical about; there is faith, but not much hope, and certainly no enthusiasm. Now the subject-matter of Mr. Eliot's early poems was very different from this. They were not hopeful, but neither were they depressed or depressing. If one wants to deal in antitheses, one might say that the later poems express a melancholy faith and the earlier ones a glowing despair. They were based on the dilemma of modern man, who despairs of life and does not want to be dead, and on top of this they expressed the horror of an over-civilised intellectual confronted with the ugliness and spiritual emptiness of the machine age. Instead of 'not too far from the yew-tree' the keynote was 'weeping, weeping multitudes', or perhaps 'the broken fingernails of dirty hands.' Naturally these poems were denounced as 'decadent' when they first appeared, the attacks only being called off when it was perceived that Eliot's political and social tendencies were reactionary. There was, however, a sense in which the charge of 'decadence' could be justified. Clearly these poems were an end-product, the last gasp of a cultural tradition, poems which spoke only for the cultivated third-generation rentier, for people able to feel and criticise but no longer able to act. E. M. Forster praised *Prufrock* on its first appearance because 'it sang of people who were

2. *Eheu fugaces, Postume* . . . Ah, Postumus, the fleeting years are slipping by, Horace, *Odes*, II, *xiv*, 1.

ineffectual and weak' and because it was 'innocent of public spirit' (this was during the other war, when public spirit was a good deal more rampant than it is now). The qualities by which any society which is to last longer than a generation actually has to be sustained—industry, courage, patriotism, frugality, philoprogenitiveness—obviously could not find any place in Eliot's early poems. There was only room for *rentier* values, the values of people too civilised to work, fight or even reproduce themselves. But that was the price that had to be paid, at any rate at that time, for writing a poem worth reading. The mood of lassitude, irony, disbelief, disgust, and not the sort of beefy enthusiasm demanded by the Squires[3] and Herberts,[4] was what sensitive people actually felt. It is fashionable to say that in verse only the words count and the 'meaning' is irrelevant, but in fact every poem contains a prose-meaning, and when the poem is any good it is a meaning which the poet urgently wishes to express. All art is to some extent propaganda. *Prufrock* is an expression of futility, but it is also a poem of wonderful vitality and power, culminating in a sort of rocket-burst in the closing stanzas:

> I have seen them riding seaward on the waves
> Combing the white hair of the waves blown back
> When the wind blows the water white and black.
>
> We have lingered in the chambers of the sea
> By sea-girls wreathed with seaweed red and brown
> Till human voices wake us, and we drown.[5]

3. Sir J.C. Squire (1884–1958), poet and essayist, was, according to Martin Seymour-Smith, 'critically obtuse, being all for "straightforwardness" and over-prejudiced against poetry he could not understand. . . . In his parodies (*Collected Parodies*, 1921), however, he was often brilliantly funny. . . . He was a kind and generous man, and a better poet than many who now enjoy temporary reputations and have not heard of him' (*Guide to Modern World Literature*, 3rd ed., 1985, 232–33). His *Collected Poems* (1959) has a preface by John Betjeman.
4. Alan Patrick Herbert (1890–1971; Kt., CH), humourist, novelist, dramatist, and author of much light poetry. From 1935 until university constituencies were abolished in 1950, he represented Oxford University as an Independent MP. Though he wrote frequently for *Punch*, he had a serious side; his play *Holy Deadlock* (1934) dramatised anomalies in the divorce laws, and as an MP he introduced the Matrimonial Causes Bill (enacted in 1937), which made significant changes to the divorce laws. He served in the Royal Naval Division, 1914–17.
5. *Poetry (London)* did not hyphenate 'sea-girls'; it added a comma after 'brown'.

There is nothing like that in the later poems, although the rentier despair on which these lines are founded has been consciously dropped.

But the trouble is that conscious futility is something only for the young. One cannot go on 'despairing of life' into a ripe old age. One cannot go on and on being 'decadent,' since decadence means falling and one can only be said to be falling if one is going to reach the bottom reasonably soon. Sooner or later one is obliged to adopt a positive attitude towards life and society. It would be putting it too crudely to say that every poet in our time must either die young, enter the Catholic Church, or join the Communist Party, but in fact the escape from the consciousness of futility is along those general lines. There are other deaths besides physical deaths, and there are other sects and creeds besides the Catholic Church and the Communist Party, but it remains true that after a certain age one must either stop writing or dedicate oneself to some purpose not wholly aesthetic. Such a dedication necessarily means a break with the past:

>   . . . every attempt
> Is a wholly new start, and a different kind of failure
> Because one has only learnt to get the better of words
> For the thing one no longer has to say, or the way in which
> One is no longer disposed to say it. And so each venture
> Is a new beginning, a raid on the inarticulate
> With shabby equipment always deteriorating
> In the general mess of imprecision of feeling,
> Undisciplined squads of emotion.

Eliot's escape from individualism was into the Church, the Anglican Church as it happened. One ought not to assume that the gloomy Pétainism to which he now appears to have given himself over was the unavoidable result of his conversion. The Anglo-Catholic movement does not impose any political 'line' on its followers, and a reactionary or austro-fascist tendency had always been apparent in his work, especially his prose writings. In theory it is still possible to be an orthodox religious believer without being intellectually crippled in the process; but it is far from easy, and in practice books by orthodox believers usually show the same cramped, blinkered outlook as books by orthodox Stalinists or others who are mentally unfree. The reason is that the Christian churches still demand assent to doctrines which no one seriously believes in. The most obvious case is the immortality of the soul. The various 'proofs' of personal immortality which can be advanced by Christian apologists are psychologically of no importance; what matters, psychologically, is that hardly anyone nowadays *feels* himself to be immortal. The next world may be in some sense 'believed in' but it has not anywhere near the same actuality in people's minds as it had a few centuries ago. Compare for instance the gloomy mumblings of these three poems with *Jerusalem my happy home*; the comparison is not altogether pointless. In the second case you have a man to whom the next world is as real as this one. It is true that his vision of it is incredibly vulgar—a choir practice in a jeweller's shop—but he believes in what he is saying and his belief gives vitality to his words. In the other case you have a man who does not really *feel* his faith, but merely assents to it for complex reasons. It does not in itself give him any fresh literary impulse. At a certain stage he feels the need for a 'purpose,' and he wants a 'purpose' which is reactionary and not progressive; the immediately available refuge is the Church, which demands intellectual absurdities of its members; so his work becomes a continuous nibbling round those absurdities, an attempt to make them acceptable to himself. The Church has not now any living imagery, any new vocabulary to offer:

> The rest
> Is prayer, observance, discipline, thought and action.

Perhaps what we need is prayer, observance, etc., but you do not make a line of poetry by stringing those words together. Mr. Eliot speaks also of

> the intolerable wrestle
> With words and meanings. The poetry does not matter.

I do not know, but I should imagine that the struggle with meanings would have loomed smaller, and the poetry would have seemed to matter more, if he could have found his way to some creed which did not start off by forcing one to believe the incredible.

There is no saying whether Mr. Eliot's development could have been much other than it has been. All writers who are any good develop throughout life, and the general direction of their development is determined. It is absurd to attack Eliot, as some left-wing critics have done, for being a 'reactionary' and to imagine that he might have used his gifts in the cause of democracy and Socialism. Obviously a scepticism about democracy and a disbelief in 'progress' are an integral part of him; without them he could not have written a line of his works. But it is arguable that he would have done better to go much further in the direction implied in his famous 'Anglo-Catholic and Royalist' declaration. He could not have developed into a Socialist, but he might have developed into the last apologist of aristocracy.

Neither feudalism nor indeed Fascism is[6] necessarily deadly to poets, though both are to prose-writers. The thing that is really deadly to both is Conservatism of the half-hearted modern kind.

It is at least imaginable that if Eliot had followed wholeheartedly the anti-democratic, anti-perfectionist strain in himself he might have struck a new vein comparable to his earlier one. But the negative, Pétainism, which turns its eyes to the past, accepts defeat, writes off earthly happiness as impossible, mumbles about prayer and repentance and thinks it a spiritual advance to see life as 'a pattern of living worms in the guts of the women of Canterbury'—that, surely, is the least hopeful road a poet could take.

6. The original text has 'is not'.

Letter to the Eastern Service Director

unpublished, 15 OCTOBER 1942

Weekly News Commentary

With reference to the suggestion that I should write and broadcast the weekly news review in English over my own name, i.e. George Orwell. The four speakers who are at present doing this in rotation have contracts up to November 7th, after which I will gladly take this on. But there are one or two points which it would be better to define clearly beforehand.

If I broadcast as George Orwell I am as it were selling my literary reputation, which so far as India is concerned probably arises chiefly from books of anti-imperialist tendency, some of which have been banned in India. If I gave broadcasts which appeared to endorse unreservedly the policy of the British government I should quite soon be written off as 'one more renegade' and should probably miss my potential public, at any rate among the student population. I am not thinking about my personal reputation, but clearly we should defeat our own object in these broadcasts if I could not preserve my position as an independent and more or less 'against the government' commentator. I would therefore like to be sure in advance that I can have reasonable freedom of speech. I think this weekly commentary is only likely to be of value if I can make it from an anti-fascist rather than imperialist standpoint and avoid mention of subjects on which I could not conscientiously agree with current Government policy.

I do not think this is likely to cause trouble, as the chief difficulty is over Indian internal politics, which we rarely mention in our weekly news commentaries. These commentaries have always followed what is by implication a 'left' line, and in fact have contained very little that I would not sign with my own name. But I can imagine situations arising in which I should have to say that I could not in honesty do the commentary for that week, and I should like the position to be defined in advance.

[Signed] Eric Blair

Orwell's memorandum was sent by Rushbrook Williams, the Eastern Service Director, to R.A. Rendall, Assistant Controller, Overseas Service, with this handwritten note:

Confidential: Subject: 'George Orwell' to broadcast?

Mr Brander has suggested that as Blair does in effect write the News Commentary for India (weekly) he should deliver it himself and thus enable us to 'cash in' on the popularity of 'George Orwell' in India. I mentioned this to Mr Blair, and the result is this characteristically honest and straight-forward note.

On the points that Mr Blair raises, I see no difficulty in practice. He and I can, by discussion, always arrange a *modus vivendi*. In fact, I feel strongly inclined to try the experiment.

Is there any difficulty about a Corporation employee broadcasting under a pen-name? [If the matter has to be referred to the Establishment side, may I suggest that Blair's memo. should *not* be forwarded? It was written for my own eye (and I know he would like you to see it also): but to people who do not know him as you and I do, it might be misleading!]

The Eastern Service Director, Rushbrook Williams, and the Assistant Controller for the Overseas Service, R. A. Rendall, both agreed that broadcasts should be made over Orwell's own name. The first such broadcast was No. 48, 21 November 1942.

Broadcast: Extracts from *Answering You*

BBC *and* Mutual Broadcasting System, New York, 18 OCTOBER 1942

The extracts from this two-way broadcast give only Orwell's contributions, in context. There are gaps in the transcript (represented by ellipses) where, presumably, what was said could not be heard to be transcribed; there is no indication that the censor cut anything. The programme was purportedly repeated on 19 October in North American and Eastern Services, but not noted in 'Programmes as Broadcast' (the BBC's record of broadcasts made).

NEW YORK STUDIO: Master of Ceremonies: Peter Donald, radio raconteur 'Can you top this?'
LONDON STUDIO: Master of Ceremonies: Colin Wills

Speakers	*Speakers*
Howard Dietz, playwright	George Strauss, M.P.
Madame Lee Ya Ching, Chinese woman pilot	George Orwell, author of 'Down and Out in Paris and London'
Pat Mulhearne, editor of 'Hobo News'	Commander Pauline Gower, A.T.A.
	Aircraftwoman Dean, W.A.A.F.
	W. Vaughan Thomas of 'John Londoner'

ANNOUNCER: This is London, England. And you're about to hear the British programme *Answering You*—65th edition. Again questioners in a New York Studio address themselves directly to speakers in London and they are ready and waiting with our Master of Ceremonies, Mr. Colin Wills, Australian War Commentator.

After the introductions, Pat Mulhearne asked the first question:

MULHEARNE: After the first war General Pershing said that the American hobo was one of the best fighters under his command. He said that they can march further with a pack on their back, they could go for days without anything to eat, they could sleep in a 'bus, car or a trench—it didn't make any difference. And what is the British military opinion of this?
WILLS: Well Pat we haven't got any British military leaders right here in the studio but we've got a fellow who's a Sergeant in the Home

Guard—you know what that is. This Sergeant is George Orwell. He's also a bit of a poet and he's been a bit of a hobo in the English way. So George, will you tell him how the British hobo—if you can define such a person—gets on in the war.

ORWELL: Well you've got to remember that in England the whole set-up is a bit different. There isn't that big hobo community here that you've got in America. The reason is at bottom that England's a very small country—I suppose it's only about as big as one of the smaller American States. It's very thickly populated, there's a policeman at every corner, you can't live that sort of wild, free life found in . . . novels and so on. Of course that type exists in England but they generally tend to emigrate to Australia or Canada or somewhere. You see, people going on the road —as they call it here in England—is generally a direct result of poverty, particularly unemployment. The time when that population on the road was biggest in England was during the slump years when I suppose there were not less than a hundred thousand people living that sort of life in England. But I'm afraid that by American standards you'd find it a very peaceful, harmless, dull existence. They're extremely law-abiding and their life really consists of going from one casual ward to another, eat a very unpleasant meal of bread and margarine, sleep on a hard bed and go on to the next.

MULHEARNE: But how about their fighting qualities?

ORWELL: Well it's quite true that some of the best regiments in the British Army, particularly the Highland regiments—the Scotch regiments—are recruited from very poor quarters of big towns such as Glasgow. But not, I should have thought, from what you could possibly call the derelict community.

DONALD: Well any more questions on that theme?

MULHEARNE: Question number two. The American hobo you know is basically a skilled migratory farm worker, or what you'd call an apple-knocker. Now are the English hobos skilled in farm work? And what part are the English hobos playing in this war? Are they digging up a lot of scrap over there and so forth?

WILLS: Well, George here will answer that one too I think.

ORWELL: Well I think the chief fact about them as a result of the war is that they've diminished in numbers very much—they have sort of got jobs or are in the army. There is in England that nucleus of skilled or semi-skilled migratory farm labour. For instance hop-picking, potato-picking, even sheep-shearing is done largely by that type of labour. But very largely by the gypsies. Or apart from the gypsies there's other people who are not gypsies by blood but have adopted that way of life. They travel around from farm to farm according to the seasons, working for rather low wages. They're quite an important section of the community. But I think that's been somewhat interfered with by the war because now there's all sorts of voluntary labour, also Italian prisoners, schoolboys and whatnot.

Later, Dietz asked about the democratizing effect of the war. Strauss replied at length on the theme that 'war is a great leveller', and he quoted figures given by the Chancellor of the Exchequer that, whereas in 1938 there were 7,000 people with an income of over $24,000 net per year, there were only 80 in 1942. He concluded, 'Those modifications will go on, and as the war goes on, will get more level.' Orwell was asked to respond.

ORWELL: Well, I can't altogether agree with Strauss about the decrease in big incomes, I know that's what the statistics say but that's not what I see when on occasion I put my nose inside an expensive hotel.

WILLS: You ought to put your nose inside a British restaurant.[1]

ORWELL: . . . war, two years during which at any rate there has been a good . . .[2] in people's thoughts, is that people are still thinking in terms of what they call going back to normal after the war. For example, it's a fact that the average man working in a factory is afraid of mass unemployment after the war. I do agree with what you might call mechanical changes that have been brought about by war rationing and lack of consumption goods and so on, but that to have any real deep effect without any structural changes is dependent on the war going on for some years. I think we must conclude that a change is happening in England but it's happening in a very peaceful manner—sort of twilight sleep.

1. He was referring to officially sponsored restaurants, often in temporary quarters, which provided a basic hot meal at a very modest price.
2. The transcript is defective here.

Broadcast: 'Imaginary Interview: George Orwell and Jonathan Swift'

BBC, 6 NOVEMBER 1942

ORWELL: My edition of Swift's works was printed some time between 1730 and 1740. It's in twelve small volumes, with calf covers a bit the worse for wear. It's not too easy to read, the ink is faded and the long S's are a nuisance, but I prefer it to any modern edition I've seen. When I open it and smell the dusty smell of old paper and see the woodcut illustrations and the crooked capital letters, I almost have the feeling that I can hear Swift speaking to me. I've a vivid picture of him in my mind's eye, with his knee-breeches and his three-cornered hat, and the snuff box and the spectacles he wrote about in *Gulliver's Travels*, though I don't believe I've ever seen a portrait of him. There's something in his way of writing that seems to tell you what his voice was like. For instance, here's one of his 'Thoughts on Various Subjects': 'When a true Genius appears in the world . . .'

SWIFT [*with contempt*]: 'When a true Genius appears in the world, you may know him by this infallible sign: that all the *Dunces* are in Confederacy against him'.

ORWELL: So you *did* wear a wig, Dr. Swift. I've often wondered.

SWIFT: So you have the first collected edition of my works?

ORWELL: Yes. I bought them for five shillings at a farmhouse auction.

SWIFT: I warn you to beware of all *modern* editions, even of my *Travels*. I have suffered from such damned dishonest editors as I believe no other writer ever had. It has been my especial misfortune to be edited usually by clergymen-who-thought me a disgrace to their cloth. They were tinkering with my writings long before Dr. Bowdler was ever born or thought of.

ORWELL: You see, Dr. Swift, you have put them in a difficulty. They know you are our greatest prose writer, and yet you used words and raised subjects that they couldn't approve of. In a way I don't approve of you myself.

SWIFT: I am desolated, sir.

ORWELL: I believe *Gulliver's Travels* has meant more to me than any other book ever written. I can't remember when I first read it, I must have been eight years old at the most, and it's lived with me ever since so that I suppose a year has never passed without my re-reading at least part of it.

SWIFT: I am vastly gratified.

ORWELL: And yet even I can't help feeling that you laid it on a bit too thick. You were too hard on humanity, and on your own country.

SWIFT: H'm!

ORWELL: For instance, here's a passage that has always stuck in my memory —also stuck in my gizzard, a little. It's at the end of Chapter VI in the second Book of Gulliver's Travels. Gulliver has just given the King of Brobdingnag a long description of life in England. The King listens to him and then picks him up in his hand, strokes him gently and says—wait a moment, I've got the book here. But perhaps you remember the passage yourself.

SWIFT: Oh, ay. 'It does not appear, from all you have said, how any one virtue is required toward the procurement of any one station among you; much less that men were ennobled on account of their *virtue*; [*voice up*] that priests were advanced for their *piety* or *learning*, soldiers, for their conduct or valour; judges, for their integrity; senators, for the love of their country; or counsellors for their wisdom . . . [*Quieter*] By what I have gathered from your own relation, and the answers I have with much pains wringed and extorted from you, I cannot but conclude the bulk of your natives to be the most pernicious race of little odious vermin that nature [*crescendo*] ever suffered to crawl upon the surface of the earth.'

ORWELL: I'd allow you 'pernicious' and 'odious' and 'vermin', Dr. Swift, but I'm inclined to cavil at 'most'. 'The *most* pernicious'. Are we in this island really worse than the *rest* of the world?

SWIFT: No. But I know you better than I know the rest of the world. When I wrote, I went upon the principle that if a lower kind of animal existed than you I could not imagine it.

ORWELL: That was 200 years ago. Surely you must admit that we have made a certain amount of progress since then?

SWIFT: Progress in quantity, yes. The buildings are taller and the vehicles move faster. Human beings are more numerous and commit greater follies. A battle kills a million where it used to kill a thousand. And in the matter of great men, as you still call them, I admit that your age outdoes mine. Whereas previously some petty tyrant was considered to have reached the highest point of human fame if he laid waste a single province and pillaged half a dozen towns, [*with ironic pleasure*] your great men nowadays can devastate whole *continents* and condemn entire races of men to *slavery*.

ORWELL: I was coming to that. One thing I feel inclined to urge in favour of my country is that we don't produce great men and don't like war. Since your day something has appeared called totalitarianism.

SWIFT: A new thing?

ORWELL: It isn't strictly new, it's merely been made practicable by modern weapons and modern methods of communication. Hobbes and other seventeenth-century writers predicted it. You yourself wrote about it with extraordinary foresight. There are passages in Part III of Gulliver's Travels that give me the feeling that I'm reading an account of the Reichstag Fire trial. But I'm thinking particularly of a passage in Part IV where the Houyhnhnm who is Gulliver's master is telling him about the habits and customs of the Yahoos. It appears that each tribe of Yahoos had a Dictator, or Fuehrer and this Dictator liked to surround himself with yes-men. The Houyhnhnm says:

SWIFT [quiet]: 'He had heard, indeed, some curious Houyhnhnms observe, that in most herds there was a sort of ruling Yahoo, who was always more *deformed* in body, and *mischievous* in disposition, than any of the rest. That this leader had usually a [tenderly] favourite, as like himself as he could get, whose employment was to lick his master's feet and [lico-rously] drive the female Yahoos to his *kennel*; for which he was now and then rewarded with a piece of ass's flesh. This favourite is hated by the whole herd, and therefore, to protect himself, keeps always near the person of his leader. He usually continues in office till a worse can be found; but the very moment he is discarded, his successor, at the head of all the Yahoos in that district, young and old, male and female, come in a body, and—'

ORWELL: We shall have to leave out that bit.

SWIFT: Thank you, Dr. Bowdler.

ORWELL: I remember that passage whenever I think of Goebbels or Ribbentrop, or for that matter Monsieur Laval. But looking at the world as a whole, do you find that the human being is *still* a Yahoo?

SWIFT: I had a good view of the people of London on my way here, and I assure you that I could remark very little difference. I saw round me the same hideous faces, unshapely bodies and ill-fitting clothes that could be seen in London two hundred years ago.

ORWELL: But the town had changed, even if the people had not?

SWIFT: Oh, it has grown prodigiously. Many a green field where Pope and I used to stroll after dinner on summer evenings is now a warren of bricks and mortar, for the kennelling of Yahoos.

ORWELL: But the town is a great deal safer, more orderly, than it was in your day. One can walk about nowadays without the fear of getting one's throat cut, even at night. You ought to admit some improvement there, though I suppose you won't. Besides, it's cleaner. In your day there were still lepers in London, not to mention the Plague. We have baths fairly frequently nowadays, and women don't keep their hair up for a month at a time and carry little silver goads to scratch their heads with. Do you remember writing a poem called 'A Description of a Lady's Dressing Room'?

> And Betty otherwise employed,
> Stole in, and took a strict survey
> Of all the litter as it lay:
> Whereof, to make the matter clear,
> An inventory follows here.

ORWELL: Unfortunately I don't think the inventory is suitable for broadcasting.

SWIFT: Poor Dr. Bowdler!

ORWELL: But the point is, would you sign that poem nowadays? Tell me candidly, do we stink as we used to?

SWIFT: Certainly the smells are different. There was a new one I remarked as I came through the streets—(sniffs)—

ORWELL: It's called petrol. But don't you find that the mass of the people are more intelligent than they were, or at least better educated? How about the newspapers and the radio? Surely they have opened people's minds a little? There are very few people in England now who can't read, for instance.

SWIFT: That is why they are so easily deceived. [*Voice up*] Your ancestors two hundred years ago were full of barbarous superstitions, but they would not have been so credulous as to believe [*gentle*] your daily newspapers. As you seem to know my works, perhaps you will remember another little thing I wrote, an 'Essay upon Genteel and Ingenious Conversation?'

ORWELL: Of course I remember it well. It's a description of fashionable ladies and gentlemen talking—an appalling stream of drivel which goes on and on for six hours without stopping.

SWIFT: On my way here I looked in at some of your fashionable clubs and suburban coffee shops, and listened to the conversation. I half believed that that little Essay of mine was being parodied. If there was any change, it was only that the English tongue had lost something of its earthy natural quality.

ORWELL: How about the scientific and technical achievements of the last two hundred years—railway trains, motor cars, aeroplanes and so forth? Doesn't that strike you as an advance?

SWIFT: I also passed through Cheapside on my way here. It has almost ceased to exist. Round St. Paul's there is only an acre of ruins. The Temple has been almost wiped out, and the little church outside it is only a shell. I am speaking only of the places I knew, but it is the same all over London, I believe. That is what your machines have done for you.

ORWELL: I am getting the worst of this argument, but I still feel, Dr. Swift, that there is something deeply deficient in your outlook. You remember what the king of Brobdingnag said when Gulliver described cannons and gunpowder to him?

SWIFT: 'The king was struck with horror at the description I had given of those terrible engines, and the proposal I had made. He was amazed, how so *impotent* and *grovelling* an insect as I (these were his expressions) could entertain such inhuman ideas, and in so familiar a manner as to appear wholly unmoved at all the scenes of blood and desolation, which I had painted as the common effects of those destructive machines; whereof, he said, some evil genius, enemy to mankind, must have been the first contriver. As for himself, he protested, that although few things delighted him so much as new discoveries in art or in nature, yet he would rather lose half his kingdom than be privy to such a secret, which he commanded me, as I valued my life, never to mention any more.'

ORWELL: I suppose the king would have spoken even more forcibly about tanks or mustard gas. But I can't help feeling that his attitude, and yours, show a certain lack of curiosity. Perhaps the most brilliant thing you ever wrote was the description of the scientific academy in part III of *Gulliver's Travels*. But after all you were wrong. You thought the whole process of scientific research was absurd, because you could not believe that any tangible result would ever come out of it. But after all the results have come. Modern machine civilisation is there, for good or evil. And the poorest person nowadays is better off, so far as physical comfort goes, than a nobleman in Saxon times, or even in the reign of Queen Anne.

SWIFT: Has that added anything to true wisdom or true refinement? Let me remind you of another saying of mine: 'The greatest Inventions were produced in the Times of Ignorance; as the use of the Compass,

Gunpowder and Printing; and by the dullest nations, as the Germans.'

ORWELL: I see now where it is that we part company, Dr. Swift. I believe that human society, and therefore human nature, can change. You don't. Do you still hold to that, after the French Revolution and the Russian Revolution?

SWIFT: You know very well what is my final word. I wrote it on the last page of Gulliver's Travels, but I will speak it again. 'My reconcilement to the Yahoo kind in general might not be so difficult if they would be content with those vices and follies only, which nature has entitled them to. I am not in the least provoked at the sight of a lawyer, a pickpocket, a colonel, a fool, a lord, a gamester, a politician, a whore-master, a physician, an evidence, a suborner, an attorney, a traitor, or the like: this is all according to the due course of things: but when I behold a lump of deformity and diseases both in body and mind, smitten with *pride*, it immediately breaks all the measures of my patience; neither shall I be ever able to comprehend how such an animal . . .' [*voice fading*]

ORWELL: Ah, he's fading out! Dr. Swift! Dr. Swift! Is that your last word?

SWIFT: [*voice a little stronger then finally fading out*]: Neither shall I ever be able to comprehend how such an animal and such a vice could tally together. And therefore I here entreat those who have any tincture of this absurd vice, that they will not presume to come in my sight.

ORWELL: He's gone. I didn't get much change out of him. He was a great man, and yet he was partially blind. He could only see one thing at a time. His vision of human society is so penetrating, and yet in the last analysis it's false. He couldn't see what the simplest person sees, that life is worth living and human beings, even if they're dirty and ridiculous, are mostly decent. But after all, if he could have seen that I suppose he couldn't have written Gulliver's Travels. Ah well, let him rest in peace in Dublin, where, in the words of his epitaph, 'Savage indignation can no longer lacerate his heart'.

SWIFT: *Ubi saeva indignatio ulterius cor lacerare nequit.*[1]

1. Swift's epitaph: 'Where fierce indignation can no longer tear the heart'.

'Background of French Morocco'[1]

Tribune, 20 NOVEMBER 1942

As you travel in the train from Spanish into French Morocco you pass for a while through a strip of territory which resembles my own mental picture of the Russian collective farms. Black earth, with here and there a tractor plough crawling across it, stretches away to the horizon on either side of the line, and every few miles there is a neat cluster of limewashed cottages and agricultural buildings. This is the fertile coastal belt, watered by the winds from the Atlantic and producing a million tons of wheat annually. Needless to say, the Arabs do not own an inch of it. It is all owned by a French syndicate which works it with gang labour. The Arabs, the vast majority of whom are small peasants, cultivate a dried-up, treeless soil on which they grow barley, lucerne and various fruits and vegetables. They live chiefly on barley and the milk of miserable goats which graze on cacti, and whose daily yield is a quarter of a pint per head.

The general poverty of the country is startling, and probably worse than anything to be seen in India. Beggars are as common as flies. Children are herding goats or sheep by the time they are six, and are often doing a full day's work at carpentering or blacksmithing when they are twelve. Most of the transport of the country is done by tiny donkeys, which cost ten shillings each and are worked to death within a few years. Bigger than England in size, Morocco barely supports a population of seven millions, and even if not under alien rule it would still be desperately poor, because of its lack of water. There are no considerable rivers, and until you come to the Atlas Mountains there are no wild trees at all, except in a few areas where the French have started reafforestation. The French settlers cultivate the land successfully and grow first-rate oranges and olives and a rather inferior wine, but this depends on having sufficient capital to dig wells and storage tanks. Apart from its agricultural and animal products the country has not much in the way of natural wealth, though the Atlas Mountains, which are not fully explored, no doubt contain minerals.

1. United States forces landed in French Morocco on 8 November 1942. The Resident-General, M. Noguès, surrendered on 11 November. It was this that prompted Orwell's article. Following the Casablanca Conference attended by Churchill, Roosevelt, and de Gaulle in January 1943, Churchill persuaded Roosevelt to spend a short time with him in Marrakech (which Churchill called 'the Paris of the Sahara'), where Orwell had spent the winter of 1938–39.

There are some 200,000 Europeans in Morocco, French or Frenchified Spanish. The seaport of Casablanca has a white proletariat of perhaps 70,000. Of the rest of the population about 5 millions would be Arabs, 100,000 Jews, and the rest chiefly Chleuh, a rather primitive Berber people inhabiting the Atlas. Except for Casablanca the big towns are really enormous villages where the peasants come to sell their beasts and buy cooking pots, nails, etc. Everything is made by hand with tools which have not altered since Biblical times. The Moroccan handicrafts, especially the pottery and the blankets, are some of the finest in the world, and have held their own against European or Japanese imports because of the miserable wages paid to the people who make them. A highly-skilled potter or carpenter earns round about a penny an hour. Except for agriculture the Jews do the same work as the Arabs, and seem on average to be somewhat poorer.

I may have seemed to paint a picture of general misery, but I must record that in 1938 and 1939 the people in Morocco struck me as being happier than, for instance, the people in London. One saw everywhere the most shocking destitution and drudgery, but also, on the whole, one saw happy faces and magnificent bodies. The Chleuh, even poorer than the Arabs of the plains, were one of the most debonair peoples I have seen. One must remember that Morocco is still almost entirely in the feudal stage, barely touched by industrialism with its conveniences and its discontents. The French took the country over in 1906, but they did not complete its conquest till 1934. The Arabs are not French citizens (for them this has the advantage that military service is not compulsory), and the country is ruled indirectly, through the Sultan, who is the creature of the French but towards whom the Arabs have a feudal loyalty. The excellent motor roads have carried a thin trickle of French culture from the Mediterranean shore to the southern slopes of the Atlas, but the mass of the people are untouched by it. Hardly any Arabs speak French correctly and few Frenchmen bother to learn Arabic.

The European population is made up of three quite distinct strata. At the top there are the well-to-do business men, bureaucrats and army officers, forming a society similar to that of Anglo-India, but probably stupider and certainly more reactionary. Then there are the small settlers, shopkeepers and minor officials, who look down on the Arabs and treat them as children; and then the white proletariat, who do not perhaps despise the Arabs but tend to keep aloof from them. Even very petty official jobs are done by Frenchmen, so that there are probably more white officials in Morocco, with its 7 million inhabitants than in India, with its 350 millions. The normal French attitude towards the Arabs is patronising, though not unkindly. Even in 1939 the country was ripe for Fascism. Almost the whole of the Press was pro-Franco—one of the principal papers was run by Doriot's party—*Gringoire* and *Candide*[2] were the favourite reading of the army officers, and the petite bourgeoisie were anti-Semitic. The left-wing parties had little footing in the country, even in Casablanca. The attitude of the Arabs towards the French occupation was rather difficult to gauge. Although the conquest was comparatively recent it seemed to have left no scars behind, and the absence of race-hatred was very striking. Wherever one went one met with friendliness, though no servility—even the beggars were not really servile. The Arabs have probably transferred some of their feudal feeling to the French régime, and the French have found it easy to recruit an excellent merce-nary army of the colonial type. But towards the poorer classes of French the attitude of the Arabs appeared to have an undercurrent of good natured contempt. They were very much nicer human beings than these petty functionaries and shopkeepers, and perhaps they were aware of it. It would be absurd to expect a revolutionary movement of anything like the European type to arise in Morocco, but a violent nationalist move-ment, non-existent three years ago, could probably arise quite suddenly. The French defeat by Germany may have paved the way for it.

It now seems as though the United Nations are going to have control of Morocco, and what they ought to do with it is clear enough in general terms.[3] A country like Morocco cannot be genuinely independent, because it cannot defend itself; it must be under some kind of tutelage, and it must have the loan of European technical experts; but to free the Arabs from economic exploitation would be very simple, and would hurt nobody except a few wealthy men in Paris and Casablanca. There is no need to interfere with the small French settler, who improves the soil and does little harm. But the big syndicates which have absorbed all the best land

2. Jacques Doriot (1898–1945), a Communist who turned to Fascism and led the Parti Populaire Français which the Germans financed. *Gringoire* and *Candide* had circulations in the 1930s of over 600,000 and 350,000 respectively. They were described by Eugen Weber as virulent, right-wing publications, anti-semitic and sympathetic to Mussolini (*The Hollow Years*, pp. 105 and 128).

3. On 4 December, *Tribune* published a letter from Cecily Mackworth arguing that Morocco should be treated no differently from France's other possessions in Africa and that the French had 'a better chance of bringing peace and prosperity to Morocco than the impersonal government of the United Nations'.

and given themselves a monopoly of the wine and tobacco trades should be expropriated forthwith. Above all, that strip of fertile soil down the west coast should be given back to the peasants. The buildings and the machinery for collective farms are already there; but even if the land were split up into small holdings the possession of it by the Arabs themselves would raise the standard of living perceptibly. It would be very easy for us and the Americans to do this, our own interests not being directly involved. Such a deed would echo round the world and cause convulsions in Franco's colony next door. But when one tries to imagine it actually happening, and then looks at the faces of the people who rule us, one remembers rather sadly that the age of miracles is over.

Review: V.K. Narayana Menon, *The Development of William Butler Yeats*

Horizon, JANUARY 1943

One thing that Marxist criticism has not succeeded in doing is to trace the connection between 'tendency' and literary style. The subject-matter and imagery of a book can be explained in sociological terms, but its texture seemingly cannot. Yet some such connection there must be. One knows, for instance, that a Socialist would not write like Chesterton or a Tory imperialist like Bernard Shaw, though *how* one knows is not easy to say. In the case of Yeats, there must be some kind of connection between his wayward, even tortured style of writing and his rather sinister vision of life. Mr. Menon is chiefly concerned with the esoteric philosophy underlying Yeats's work, but the quotations which are scattered all through his interesting book serve to remind one how artificial Yeats's manner of writing was. As a rule, this artificiality is accepted as Irishism, or Yeats is even credited with simplicity because he used short words, but in fact one seldom comes on six consecutive lines of his verse in which there is not an archaism or an affected turn of speech. To take the nearest example:

> Grant me an old man's Frenzy,
> My self must I remake
> Till I am Timon and Lear
> Or that William Blake
> Who beat upon the wall
> Till Truth obeyed his call.

The unnecessary 'that' imports a feeling of affectation, and the same tendency is present in all but Yeats's best passages. One is seldom long away from a suspicion of 'quaintness', something that links up not only with the 'nineties, the Ivory Tower and the 'calf covers of pissed-on green', but also with Rackham's drawings, Liberty art-fabrics and the *Peter Pan* never-never land, of which, after all, *The Happy Townland* is merely a more appetising example. This does not matter, because, on the whole, Yeats gets away with it, and if his straining after effect is often irritating it can also produce phrases ('the chill, footless years',[1] 'the mackerel-crowded seas') which suddenly overwhelm one like a girl's face seen across a room. He is an exception to the rule that poets do not use poetical language:

> How many centuries spent
> The sedentary soul
> In toils of measurement
> Beyond eagle or mole,
> Beyond hearing or seeing,
> Or Archimedes' guess,
> To raise into being
> That loveliness?[2]

Here he does not flinch from a squashy vulgar word like 'loveliness', and after all it does not seriously spoil this wonderful passage. But the same tendencies, together with a sort of raggedness which is no doubt intentional, weaken his epigrams and polemical poems. For instance (I am quoting from memory), the epigram against the critics who damned *The Playboy of the Western World*:

> Once when midnight smote the air
> Eunuchs ran through Hell and met
> On every crowded street to stare,
> Upon great Juan riding by;
> Even like these to rail and sweat,
> Staring upon his sinewy thigh.

The power which Yeats has within himself gives him the analogy ready made and produces the tremendous scorn of the last line, but even in this short poem there are six or seven unnecessary words. It would probably have been deadlier if it had been neater.

Mr. Menon's book is incidentally a short biography of Yeats, but he is above all interested in Yeats's philosophical 'system', which in his opinion supplies the subject-matter of more of Yeats's poems than is generally

---

1. Dr Bartek Zborski pointed out to the editor that this first quotation is not from Yeats but William Sharp (Fiona MacLeod), 'The End of Aodh-of-the-Songs'.
2. From the First Musician's opening speech of the play *The Only Jealousy of Emer*, Allt and Alspach, 788.

recognized. This system is set forth fragmentarily in various places, and at full length in *A Vision*, a privately printed book which I have never read but which Mr. Menon quotes from extensively. Yeats gave conflicting accounts of its origin, and Mr. Menon hints pretty broadly that the 'documents' on which it was ostensibly founded were imaginary. Yeats's philosophical system, says Mr. Menon, 'was at the back of his intellectual life almost from the beginning. His poetry is full of it. Without it his later poetry becomes almost completely unintelligible.' As soon as we begin to read about the so-called system we are in the middle of a hocus-pocus of Great Wheels, gyres, cycles of the moon, reincarnation, disembodied spirits, astrology, and what-not. Yeats hedges as to the literalness with which he believed in all this, but he certainly dabbled in spiritualism and astrology and in earlier life had made experiments in alchemy. Although almost buried under explanations, very difficult to understand, about the phases of the moon, the central idea of his philosophical system seems to be our old friend, the cyclical universe, in which everything happens over and over again. One has not, perhaps, the right to laugh at Yeats for his mystical beliefs—for I believe it could be shown that *some* degree of belief in magic is almost universal—but neither ought one to write such things off as mere unimportant eccentricities. It is Mr. Menon's perception of this that gives his book its deepest interest. 'In the first flush of admiration and enthusiasm,' he says, 'most people dismissed the fantastical philosophy as the price we have to pay for a great and curious intellect. One did not quite realize where he was heading. And those who did, like Pound and perhaps Eliot, approved the stand that he finally took. The first reaction to this did not come, as one might have expected, from the politically minded young English poets. They were puzzled because a less rigid or artificial system than that of *A Vision* might not have produced the great poetry of Yeats's last days.' It might not, and yet Yeats's philosophy has some very sinister implications, as Mr. Menon points out.

Translated into political terms, Yeats's tendency is Fascist. Throughout most of his life, and long before Fascism was ever heard of, he had had the outlook of those who reach Fascism by the aristocratic route. He is a great hater of democracy, of the modern world, science, machinery, the concept of progress—above all, of the idea of human equality. Much of the imagery of his work is feudal, and it is clear that he was not altogether free from ordinary snobbishness. Later these tendencies took clearer shape and led him to 'the exultant acceptance of authoritarianism as the only solution. Even violence and tyranny are not necessarily evil because

the people, knowing not evil and good, would become perfectly acquies-
cent to tyranny. . . . Everything must come from the top. Nothing can
come from the masses.' Not much interested in politics, and no doubt
disgusted by his brief incursions into public life, Yeats nevertheless makes
political pronouncements. He is too big a man to share the illusions of
Liberalism, and as early as 1920 he foretells in a justly famous passage
('The Second Coming') the kind of world that we have actually moved
into. But he appears to welcome the coming age, which is to be 'hierarchical, masculine, harsh, surgical', and he is influenced both by Ezra Pound
and by various Italian Fascist writers. He describes the new civilization
which he hopes and believes will arrive: 'an aristocratic civilisation in its
most completed form, every detail of life hierarchical, every great man's
door crowded at dawn by petitioners, great wealth everywhere in a few
men's hands, all dependent upon a few, up to the Emperor himself, who
is a God dependent on a greater God, and everywhere, in Court, in the
family, an inequality made law.' The innocence of this statement is as
interesting as its snobbishness. To begin with, in a single phrase, 'great
wealth in a few men's hands', Yeats lays bare the central reality of Fascism,
which the whole of its propaganda is designed to cover up. The merely
political Fascist claims always to be fighting for justice; Yeats, the poet,
sees at a glance that Fascism means injustice, and acclaims it for that very
reason. But at the same time he fails to see that the new authoritarian
civilisation, if it arrives, will not be aristocratic, or what he means by
aristocratic. It will not be ruled by noblemen with Van Dyck faces, but
by anonymous millionaires, shiny-bottomed bureaucrats and murdering
gangsters. Others who have made the same mistake have afterwards
changed their views, and one ought not to assume that Yeats, if he had
lived longer, would necessarily have followed his friend Pound, even in
sympathy. But the tendency of the passage I have quoted above is obvious,
and its complete throwing overboard of whatever good the past two
thousand years have achieved is a disquieting symptom.

How do Yeats's political ideas link up with his leaning towards
occultism? It is not clear at first glance why hatred of democracy and a
tendency to believe in crystal-gazing should go together. Mr. Menon only
discusses this rather shortly, but it is possible to make two guesses. To
begin with, the theory that civilisation moves in recurring cycles is one
way out for people who hate the concept of human equality. If it is true
that 'all this', or something like it, 'has happened before', then science
and the modern world are debunked at one stroke and progress becomes

for ever impossible. It does not much matter if the lower orders are getting above themselves, for, after all, we shall soon be returning to an age of tyranny. Yeats is by no means alone in this outlook. If the universe is moving round on a wheel, the future must be foreseeable, perhaps even in some detail. It is merely a question of discovering the laws of its motion, as the early astronomers discovered the solar year. Believe that, and it becomes difficult not to believe in astrology or some similar system. A year before the war, examining a copy of *Gringoire*, the French Fascist weekly, much read by army officers, I found in it no less than thirty-eight advertisements of clairvoyants. Secondly, the very concept of occultism carries with it the idea that knowledge must be a secret thing, limited to a small circle of initiates. But the same idea is integral to Fascism. Those who dread the prospect of universal suffrage, popular education, freedom of thought, emancipation of women, will start off with a predilection towards secret cults. There is another link between Fascism and magic in the profound hostility of both to the Christian ethical code.

No doubt Yeats wavered in his beliefs and held at different times many different opinions, some enlightened, some not. Mr. Menon repeats for him Eliot's claim that he had the longest period of development of any poet who has ever lived. But there is one thing that seems constant, at least in all of his work that I can remember, and that is his hatred of modern Western civilisation and desire to return to the Bronze Age, or perhaps to the Middle Ages. Like all such thinkers, he tends to write in praise of ignorance. The Fool in his remarkable play, *The Hour-Glass*, is a Chestertonian figure, 'God's fool', the 'natural born innocent', who is always wiser than the wise man. The philosopher in the play dies on the knowledge that all his lifetime of thought has been wasted (I am quoting from memory again):

> The stream of the world has changed its course,
> And with the stream my thoughts have run
> Into some cloudy, thunderous spring
> That is its mountain-source:
> Ay, to a frenzy of the mind,
> That all that we have done's undone,
> Our speculation but as the wind.

Beautiful words, but by implication profoundly obscurantist and reactionary; for if it is really true that a village idiot, as such, is wiser than a philosopher, then it would be better if the alphabet had never been invented. Of course, all praise of the past is partly sentimental, because we do not live in the past. The poor do not praise poverty. Before you can despise the machine, the machine must set you free from brute labour. But that is not to say that Yeats's yearning for a more primitive and more hierarchical age was not sincere. How much of all this is traceable to mere snobbishness, product of Yeats's own position as an impoverished offshoot of the aristocracy, is a different question. And the connection between his obscurantist opinions and his tendency towards 'quaintness' of language remains to be worked out; Mr. Menon hardly touches upon it.

This is a very short book and I would greatly like to see Mr. Menon go ahead and write another book on Yeats, starting where this one leaves off.[3] 'If the greatest poet of our times is exultantly ringing in an era of Fascism, it seems a somewhat disturbing symptom', he says on the last page, and leaves it at that. It *is* a disturbing symptom, because it is not an isolated one. By and large the best writers of our time have been reactionary in tendency, and though Fascism does not offer any real return to the past, those who yearn for the past will accept Fascism sooner than its probable alternatives. But there are other lines of approach, as we have seen during the past two or three years. The relationship between Fascism and the literary intelligentsia badly needs investigating, and Yeats might well be the starting-point. He is best studied by someone like Mr. Menon, who can approach a poet primarily as a poet, but who also knows that a writer's political and religious beliefs are not excrescences to be laughed away, but something that will leave their mark even on the smallest detail of his work.[4]

Orwell's review attracted considerable comment; one comment published anonymously in the Times Literary Supplement *(as was then its practice) accused him of a 'Political itch'. A later deputy editor of the* Times Literary Supplement, *Alan Hollinghurst, was able to identify that critic as Charles Morgan (1894–1958). Orwell's reply was published on 6 March 1943:*

---

3. He did not write a longer book on Yeats; indeed, the British Library lists no other book by Narayana Menon.
4. Some passages quoted by Orwell differ from those in the Variorum Edition (1957). Details are given in *CW*, XIV, 289.

Sir,—I am sorry to have annoyed your reviewer by pointing out that W. B. Yeats had Fascist tendencies, but I should be glad if you would allow me to answer him, because he has misrepresented what I said besides attacking me for several incompatible reasons.

In the first place he accuses me of a 'political itch' and appears to feel that there was something vulgar, not to say sacrilegious, in even noticing that Yeats had political tendencies. In the article he refers to I was criticizing a book which dealt quite largely with Yeats's Fascist leanings, but in any case it will not do to claim, as your reviewer seems to do, that poetry exists in a sort of water-tight or rather thought-tight world of its own. A writer's political and religious beliefs will always colour his aesthetic achievements, and to trace the connexion is one necessary function of criticism. A little later than this your reviewer drops his thesis that politics are irrelevant to poetry and defends Yeats against the charge of being a Fascist. He repeats my statement that 'Yeats's philosophy has some very sinister implications' as though it were a sort of wicked blasphemy, and entirely omits mention of the quotations with which I backed it up. But apart from these quotations, the facts are notorious. Did not Yeats write a 'marching song' for O'Duffy's Blueshirts? Your reviewer then accuses me of applying something called the 'Jargon Rule' and seems to suggest that I only admire writers who are politically 'left.' But I specifically said in my article, what I have been saying for years, that on the whole the best writers of our time have been reactionary in tendency: and I used Yeats himself as an instance.

Finally, your reviewer forgets all about my 'political itch' and suddenly goes for me because after all I have aesthetic preferences. My particular offence is to dislike the word 'loveliness,' which leads to a whole paragraph in which I am charged with wishing to 'impoverish the language' in order to 'establish the exclusive abracadabra of a sect.' May I suggest that the whole art of writing consists in preferring some words to others? It could be argued that no word is inherently ugly, but it is beyond question that certain words become vulgarized by association, and I object to a word like 'loveliness' because in our own age it inevitably calls up a picture of pink sunsets, Dorothy Lamour, soft-centre chocolates, &c. If your reviewer is so attached to 'loveliness' I wonder what he thinks of T. E. Brown's 'lovesome'? I stand by my statement that on the whole poets do not use poetical language.   GEO. ORWELL

Broadcast: 'Victories at Rostov and Kharkov'[1]

News Review 57, BBC, 20 FEBRUARY 1943

I don't need to tell you what are the big events of the week. Anyone who is listening to this broadcast will have heard of the capture by the Red Army of Rostov and Kharkov. This is a very great victory, probably the most important single event in the whole course of the Russo–German War. The capture of Kharkov, which the Russians failed to achieve last winter, is even more important than the re-capture of Rostov. Kharkov is not only a great industrial city but a great railway junction at which all the communications of the Ukraine cross. The Germans have not only lost heavily in territory, men and materials, but they're going to lose more, for one Army is all but cut off on the shores of the Sea of Azov and another somewhere in the rear of Rostov is threatened by the same fate. The Russians are not only driving westward from Rostov but another column has struck southward from the neighbourhood of Krasnoarmeisk and is moving more or less in the direction of Mariupol on the northern shore of the Sea of Azov.

The Germans in that area will have to get out quickly if they're not going to suffer the same destruction as has already happened to the German Sixth Army at Stalingrad and threatens the Army which is isolated in the Caucasus. Last year, when the Russians re-took Rostov, they did not get further westward than Taganrog, about 50 miles to the west, and the Germans were able to hold on to the Crimean Peninsula. This year, the Russian offensive is much more far-reaching in its effects and it is generally believed that the Germans will have to go back to the line of the Dnieper, thus leaving themselves in a position considerably worse than they were before their 1942 campaign started. Some observers including Dr Beneš, President of Czechoslovakia, even think that they will retreat as far as the river Dneister, which means standing on the borders of Poland and Roumania and abandoning the whole of the Russian territory which they have over-run. This may be an over-optimistic forecast but at any rate enough has happened already to make it undisguisably clear to the German man in the street that the 1942 campaign, with all its enormous losses, has been fought for exactly nothing.

1. This was the first typescript Orwell produced after his return from illness. There are a number of typographical errors and these have been silently corrected.

You can imagine, even if you haven't read, the sort of dope that is being handed out to the German masses to explain away the mistakes of their leaders. Hitler himself has been silent and apparently in retirement for some weeks past but his underlings, particularly Goebbels, have been very active. What Goebbels says to the German people is not of great importance to us but it is important to examine the propaganda line which is being handed out to the world at large because this propaganda is intended to deceive and weaken us and it is as well to be armed against it in advance.

Briefly, the main line now being followed is the Bolshevik bogey. It is being put out crudely by the German propagandists and somewhat more subtly by those of Italy and other satellite States. According to Goebbels's broadcasts, Europe is now faced with the fearful danger of a Communist invasion, which will not stop at its Eastern borders but sweep as far as the English channel and beyond, engulfing Britain as well as the other European countries. The Germans, it now appears, only took up arms in order to defend Europe from this Bolshevik peril, and by allying themselves with the Bolsheviks, Britain and the United States have betrayed European civilisation. All the talk which the Germans were uttering about the need for living space, or Lebensraum as it is called, and the divine right of Germany to rule the world, appears to have been forgotten for the time being. Germany's war is purely defensive, so Dr. Goebbels says. It can be seen, quite clearly, of course, that the real drift of these speeches is to appeal to those sections in Britain and America who are frightened of seeing Soviet Russia become too powerful and might be willing to consider a compromise peace. This is augmented by the Italian publicists, who are openly talking about a compromise, and the duty of Britain to collaborate with the Axis powers against the Bolshevik danger.

All this is foredoomed to failure because the anti-Russian sentiment on which the Axis propagandists seem to be playing is almost non-existent in the Anglo-Saxon countries. So far as Britain is concerned, Soviet Russia was never more popular than at this moment. But we ought not to under-rate the danger of Fascist propaganda which has scored such great triumphs in the past. Even if the anti-Bolshevik line of thought does not achieve much in Britain, it may find listeners among the wealthier classes all over Europe and in addition the hints which have been dropped by the Italian propagandists may be followed up later by very attractive-sounding peace offers. Towards India, of course, German propaganda will take a different line. The talk about defending Western civilisation is only for European consumption. To India the propaganda line will be that Soviet Russia is the Ally of Great Britain and therefore shares the responsibility for any grievances which the Indian Nationalists have, or believe they have. We can best deal with these propaganda campaigns, if we start with the knowledge that they are in essence, simply strategic manoeuvres and take no more account of the truth than a military commander does when he disposes his army so as to deceive the enemy.

Broadcast: 'Jack London'[1]

Landmarks in American Literature, BBC, 5 MARCH 1943

We are approaching the end of our survey of American literature, and as we get nearer our own time the landmarks are more difficult to distinguish. Who are the great American writers of the past fifty years? It is not an easy question to answer, especially if we exclude a novelist like Henry James, who lived most of his time in Europe and actually became a British citizen. But there are certain American writers whose names have gone round the world, and who therefore, apart from all questions of greatness, do possess a representative value. Such a writer is Jack London, whose books have been read by the million in all parts of the world, especially in Germany and Russia. Today, therefore George Orwell is going to talk to you about the significance of Jack London. There is no need for me to introduce George Orwell—he is the Talks Producer in this programme and his voice is more familiar to you than mine. But apart from producing these broadcasts, he is, as you probably know, the author of *The Road to Wigan Pier*, *Burmese Days*, and several critical studies which show fine penetration and an independent judgment.

Jack London, like Edgar Allan Poe, is one of those writers who have a bigger reputation outside the English-speaking world than inside it—but indeed, more so than Poe, who is at any rate taken seriously in England and America, whereas most people, if they remember Jack London at all, think of him as a writer of adventure stories not far removed from penny dreadfuls.

Now, I myself don't share the rather low opinion of Jack London which is held in this country and America, and I can claim to be in good company, for another admirer of Jack London's work was no less a person than Lenin, the central figure of the Russian Revolution. After Lenin's death his widow, Nadeshda Krupskaya, wrote a short biography of him, at the end of which she describes how she used to read stories to Lenin when

---

1. This talk exists in two versions: as originally broadcast on 5 March 1943 and as printed in BBC Pamphlet No. 3, published by the Oxford University Press, Bombay, 1946, with Orwell's authority. The broadcast typescript, reproduced here, omits short passages which are recorded in *CW*, XV, 7–8.

he was paralysed and slowly dying. On the last day of all, she says, she began to read him Dickens's *Christmas Carol*, but she could see that he didn't like it; what she calls Dickens's 'bourgeois sentimentality' was too much for him. So she changed over to Jack London's story 'Love of Life', and that was almost the last thing that Lenin ever heard. Krupskaya adds that it is a very good story. It *is* a good story, but here I want only to point to this rather queer conjunction between a writer of thrillers—stories about Pacific islands and the goldfields of the Klondike, and also about burglars, prizefighters and wild animals—and the greatest revolutionary of modern times. I don't know with certainty what first interested Lenin in Jack London's work, but I should expect that it was London's political or quasi-political writings. For London was among other things an ardent socialist and probably one of the first American writers to pay any attention to Karl Marx. His reputation in continental Europe is largely founded on that, and in particular on a rather remarkable book of political prophecy, *The Iron Heel*. It is a curious fact that London's political writings have almost escaped attention in his own country and Britain. Ten or fifteen years ago, when *The Iron Heel* was widely read and admired in France and Germany, it was out of print and almost unobtainable in Britain, and even now, though an English edition of it exists, few people have heard of it.

This has several reasons, and one of them is that Jack London was an extremely prolific writer. He was one of those writers who make a point of producing a fixed amount every day—a thousand words in his case—and in his short life (he was born in 1876 and died in 1916) he produced an immense number of books, of very different types. If you examine Jack London's work as a whole, you find that there are three distinct strains in it, which don't at first sight appear to have any connexion with one another. The first is a rather silly one about which I don't want to say much, and that is a worship of animals. This produced his best-known books, *White Fang* and *The Call of the Wild*. Sentimentality about animals is something almost peculiar to the English-speaking peoples, and it isn't altogether an admirable trait. Many thoughtful people in Britain and America are ashamed of it, and Jack London's short stories would probably have received more critical attention if he hadn't also written *White Fang* and *The Call of the Wild*. The next strain to notice in Jack London is his love of brutality and physical violence and, in general, what is known as 'adventure'. He is a sort of American version of Kipling, essentially an active, non-contemplative writer. By choice he wrote about such people as goldminers, sea-captains, trappers and cowboys, and he wrote his best work of all about tramps, burglars, prizefighters and the other riff-raff of great American cities. To this side of him belongs that story I've already mentioned, 'Love of Life', and I shall have more to say about it, because it produced nearly all of his work that is still worth reading. But on top of this there is also that other strain, his interest in sociology and in economic theory, which led him in *The Iron Heel* to make a very remarkable prophecy of the rise of Fascism.

Well, now let me return to 'Love of Life' and the other short stories which are Jack London's greatest achievement. He is essentially a short-story writer, and though he did produce one interesting novel, *The Valley of the Moon*, his especial gift is his power of describing isolated, brutal incidents. I use the word 'brutal' advisedly. The impression one brings away from Jack London's best and most characteristic stories is an impression of terrible cruelty. Not that Jack London himself was a cruel man or enjoyed the thought of pain—on the contrary he was even too much of a humanitarian, as his animal stories show—but his vision of life is a cruel one. He sees the world as a place of suffering, a place of struggle against a blind, cruel destiny. That is why he likes writing about the frozen polar regions, where Nature is an enemy against which man has to fight for his life. The story 'Love of Life' describes an incident which is typical of Jack London's peculiar vision. A gold-prospector who has missed the trail somewhere in the frozen wastes of Canada is struggling desperately towards the sea, slowly dying of starvation but kept going simply by the force of his will. A wolf, also dying of hunger and disease, is creeping after the man, hoping that sooner or later he will grow weak enough for it to attack him. They go on and on, day after day, till when they come within sight of the sea each is crawling on his belly, too weak to stand up. But the man's will is the stronger, and the story ends not by the wolf eating the man but the man eating the wolf. That is a typical Jack London incident, except that it has in some sense a happy ending. And if you analyse the subject-matter of any of his best stories you find the same kind of picture. The best story he ever wrote is called 'Just Meat'. It describes two burglars who have just got away with a big haul of jewellery. As soon as they get home with the swag it occurs to each of them that if he killed the other he would have the whole lot. As it happens they each poison one another at the same meal, and with the same poison —strychnine. They have a little mustard which might save one or other of them if used as an emetic; and the story ends with the two men writhing in agonies on the floor and feebly struggling with one another for the last cup of mustard. Another very good story describes the execution of a Chinese convict in one of the French islands in the Pacific. He is to be executed for a murder committed in the prison. It happens that the prison governor, by a slip of the pen, has written down the wrong name, and consequently it is the wrong prisoner who is taken out of his cell. His guards do not discover this till they have got him to the place of execution, which is twenty miles from the prison. The guards are uncertain what to do, but it hardly seems worth the trouble of going all the way back, so they solve the question by guillotining the wrong man. I could give further instances, but all I am anxious to establish is that Jack London's most characteristic work always deals with cruelty and disaster: Nature and Destiny are inherently evil things against which man has to struggle with nothing to back him up except his own courage and strength.

Now it is against this background that Jack London's political and sociological writings have to be seen. As I have said, Jack London's reputation in Europe depends on *The Iron Heel*, in which—in the year 1910 or thereabouts—he foretold the rise of Fascism. It's no use pretending that *The Iron Heel* is a good book, as a book. It's a very poor book, much below Jack London's average, and the developments it foretells aren't even particularly close to what has actually happened in Europe. But Jack London did foresee one thing which socialists of nearly all schools had astonishingly failed to foresee, and that was that when the working-class movements took on formidable dimensions and looked like dominating the world, the capitalist class *would hit back*. They wouldn't simply lie down and let themselves be expropriated, as so many socialists had imagined. Karl Marx, indeed, had never suggested that the change-over from Capitalism to Socialism would happen without a struggle, but he did proclaim that this change was *inevitable*, which his followers, in most cases, took as meaning that it would be *automatic*. Till Hitler was firmly in the saddle it was generally taken for granted that Capitalism could not defend itself, because of what are generally called its internal contradictions.

Most socialists not only did not foresee the rise of Fascism but did not even grasp that Hitler was dangerous till he had been about two years in power. Now Jack London would not have made this mistake. In his book he describes the growth of powerful working-class movements, and then the boss class organizing itself, hitting back, winning the victory and proceeding to set up an atrocious despotism, with the institution of actual slavery, which lasts for hundreds of years. Who now will dare to say that something like this hasn't happened over great areas of the world, and may not continue to happen unless the Axis is defeated? There is more in *The Iron Heel* than this. In particular there is Jack London's perception that hedonistic societies cannot endure, a perception which isn't common among what are called progressive thinkers. Outside Soviet Russia left-wing thought has generally been hedonistic, and the weaknesses of the Socialist Movement spring partly from this. But Jack London's main achievement was to foresee, some twenty years before the event, that the menaced capitalist class would counter-attack and not quietly die because the writers of Marxist textbooks told it to die.

Why could a mere story-teller like Jack London foresee this when so many learned sociologists could not? I think I have answered that question in what I said just now about the subject-matter of Jack London's stories. He could foresee the rise of Fascism, and the cruel struggles which would have to be gone through, because of the streak of brutality which he had in himself. If you like to exaggerate a little, you might say that he could understand Fascism because he had a fascist strain himself. Unlike the ordinary run of Marxist thinkers, who had neatly worked it out on paper that the capitalist class was bound to die of its own contradictions, he knew that the capitalist class was tough and would hit back; he knew that because he himself was tough. That is why the subject-matter of Jack London's stories is relevant to his political theories. The best of them deal with prison, the prize-ring, the sea and the frozen wastes of Canada—that is, with situations where toughness is everything. That is an unusual background for a socialist writer. Socialist thought has suffered greatly from having grown up almost entirely in urban industrialized societies and leaving some of the more primitive sides of human nature out of account. It was Jack London's understanding of the primitive that made him a better prophet than many better-informed and more logical thinkers.

I haven't time to speak at length about Jack London's other political and sociological writings, some of which are better, as books, than *The Iron Heel*. I will only shortly mention *The Road*, his reminiscences of the time when he was a tramp in America, one of the best books of its kind ever written, and *The People of the Abyss*, which deals with the London slums—its facts are out of date now, but various later books of the same kind were inspired by it. There is also *The Jacket*, which is a book of stories but contains at the beginning a remarkable description of life in an American prison. But it is as a story-writer that Jack London best deserves to be remembered, and if you can get hold of a copy I earnestly beg you to read the collection of short stories published under the title *When God Laughs*. The best of Jack London is there, and from some half-dozen of those stories you can get an adequate idea of this gifted writer who has been, in a way, so popular and influential but has never in my opinion had the literary reputation that was due to him.

Orwell's last *News Review for India*, 59

BBC, 13 MARCH 1943

At the start and end of this broadcast Orwell speaks of bringing these commen-
taries to a conclusion. This has misled some commentators to imagine that he
was delivering his last message to India and the East because he had been excluded
from participation in direct propaganda. This is a false conclusion. Orwell is
speaking only of the end of this particular series. He continued to prepare scripts
for translation into a number of Indian languages and later would write – and
deliver – newsletters in English which were directed at Japanese-occupied Malaya
and Indonesia.

As this is the last News Commentary that I shall do in this series I would
like to end up with a general review of the World situation rather than
a survey of the week's news. As a matter of fact there has not been a
great deal that is new to comment on this week. The big events of the
week have been the Russian capture of Vyasma on the central Front, the
German counter-attacks against Kharkov on the Southern Front,—from
this morning's news it is evident that Kharkov is in danger—the Germans
claim to be already in the City and the unsuccessful German attack in
the southern part of Tunisia, but the situation has not fundamentally
changed. Even the Red Army's recapture of Vyasma, important though
it is, could be foreseen, as probable when Rzhev fell. So, let me use my
time, this week, in trying to give a comprehensive picture of the whole
war and trying to predict in very general outlines what is likely to happen.
    If you look at the war, as a whole, there are six factors which really
count, four of them military, and two political. Of course, they're not
separable from one another, but one can see the situation more clearly
by listing them separately. The first factor is the failure of the Germans
to carry out their full plans in Russia. The second factor is the coming
Anglo-American attack on Continental Europe. The third factor is the
war of the German U-boats against the United Nations lines of supply.
The fourth factor is the Japanese offensive in the Far East and its slowing
down for reasons which we are not yet quite sure about. The fifth factor
is the failure of the Nazi New Order in Europe, and the sixth is the attempt
of the Japanese in the Far East to set up a New Order designed to benefit
only themselves, like that of the Germans in Europe.
    The first of these factors is the most important, because Germany is

the main enemy and the Japanese cannot really continue to fight alone if Germany goes out—they might manage to prolong the war for several years. If you look at the map of Russia, you can see that however much territory they've over-run, the Germans have totally failed in what was probably their most urgent war aim and are likely to fail in their secondary one. Their primary war aim was to capture the oil-fields of the Caucasus. It was for this reason that the Germans decided to attack Soviet Russia, probably as far back as the winter of 1940. Since Britain had failed to collapse, like France, they saw they were in for a long war, and it was absolutely necessary for them to have bigger supplies of oil than they could get from European sources and from synthetic production. Secondly, they had to have food, which meant that they had to have the fertile lands of the Ukraine. Europe is capable, or nearly capable, of feeding itself, but not if a large proportion of its manpower is making weapons of war for the German army instead of producing food. In peace-time, Europe could import food from the Americas, but with Britain blockading Germany at sea, the Ukraine was an absolute necessity for the German war machine. As everybody knows, the Germans have failed to get to the Caucasus, but they still hold the greater part of Ukraine. It is probably a mistake in spite of the defeats they have had in the last few months to imagine that they will give this up without fighting. They would probably regard the Dneiper river and a line containing the whole of Poland and the Baltic States, as the last Frontier, to which they could afford to retreat. Probably they will try to stand on the defensive on this line and muster their forces to meet the Allied attack from the west, but this strategy puts them in a dilemma. If they give up the Ukraine, they have not the food resources to carry on the war indefinitely. If they hold on to it, they're defending an immensely long Frontier, inevitably tying up a bigger army than they can afford to use. We don't really know what the German casualties have been in the two Russian winters, but certainly they have been large and the total mobilisation orders in Germany, together with endless attempts to make the European populations work harder, shows that the German man power position is becoming serious. Broadly, one can say, that by provoking both Britain and Soviet Russia, and the United States, against them, the Germans have made sure that they cannot win and can only hope, at best, for a stalemate. We may expect them, therefore, during this year to make violent political offensives aimed at sowing dissension among the United Nations. They will try to play on American fear of Bolshevism, Russian suspicion of Western capitalism, and Anglo-American jealousy, and they probably calculate that they have better chances along those lines than on purely military action.

The second and third factors, the Anglo–American attack on Europe, and the submarine war, cannot be considered separately. Much the best chance the Germans have of staving off an attack from the West is to sink so many ships that the United Nations, not only cannot transport a big force oversea, but what is more important, keep it supplied. When one realises that one infantry soldier needs about seven tons of supplies, one realises what an attack against Europe means in terms of shipping. Even if the Germans could not stave off an attack from the West altogether they might keep the United Nations embarrassed until the attack started too late to finish the war this year. In that case, the stalemate the Germans are probably hoping for, will become more likely of attainment. The campaign in Tunisia really has the same object, that is, to keep a big Allied Army tied up in Africa, and prevent it crossing the sea to Europe. I don't care to predict too much about the results of these German delaying tactics because there're two things we don't yet know. First of all, naturally, we don't know what is the Allied plan of attack. Secondly, we don't know the real facts about the shipping situation because the Governments of the United Nations, probably justifiably, don't publish figures of shipping losses, but we do know certain facts from which inferences can be drawn, and on the whole, they're hopeful. The first is that the United Nations succeeded in transporting a large army to Africa, evidently to the surprise of the Germans, and are transporting an American Army which grows every day across the Atlantic to Britain. The second is that the food situation, which is probably an index of the shipping situation, has not deteriorated in Britain during the past two years. The third is the enormous expansion of the American shipbuilding industry, and the fourth the growing improvement in the methods—surface ships, aeroplanes and bombing of bases,—of dealing with the submarine. The U-boats have been the Germans' strongest card hitherto, but there is no strong reason for thinking that they will be able to slow down Allied preparations indefinitely.

We don't know enough about Japanese strategy to be certain whether they've been seriously crippled by the blows they've had in the past eight months, or whether they've slowed down their campaigns according to some definite plan. All we do know is that a year ago they over-ran very rapidly the countries bordering the south-west Pacific and since then have made no progress but on the contrary have lost some valuable bases and an enormous amount of war material. Japan's weakest spot, like that of Britain, is shipping. They have certainly lost an immense quantity, both war ships and merchant ships, at a time when they need ships more and more in order to keep their island possessions running. Moreover, they've nothing like the power of replacement of the highly industrialised states. It is safe to say that the United States can build more ships in a month than Japan can in a year. And in aeroplane construction the margin is even greater. It seems likely, therefore, that if the Japanese did not go on to attack India and Australia, as everyone expected, it was not because they did not want to but because they could not. On the other hand, we ought not to assume that they will collapse quickly when Germany is finished with. The Japanese cannot afford to retreat from the mainland of Asia any more than the Germans can afford to give up Eastern Europe. If they did so, their industrial and military power would decline rapidly. We may expect, therefore, that the Japanese will defend every inch of what they have got and in the past few months they have shown how obstinately they can fight. But probably Japanese grand strategy, like that of Germany, is now aiming at a stalemate. They perhaps calculate that if they can consolidate their position where they are, the United Nations will be too war weary to go on fighting when Germany is defeated, and might be willing to make terms on the basis of everyone keeping what he has got. Of course, the real object of this would be to renew the war at the first favourable opportunity and we ought to be on our guard against Japanese peace-talk, no less than against German.

As to the political factors, there is no need to talk any longer about the failure of the Nazi New Order in Europe. By this time, it stinks in the nose of the whole world. But it is important to realise that Japanese aims and methods are essentially similar, and that the Japanese New Order or, as they call it, the Greater East Asia Co-Prosperity Sphere, will have the same appearance when the necessary time-lag has elapsed. The Japanese are plundering the lands under their control and it does not make very much difference if in one place they plunder by naked violence and in another by means of a faked paper money which will not buy anything. They must plunder Asia, even if they did not wish to do so, because they cannot afford to do otherwise. They must have the food and raw materials of the occupied countries and they cannot give anything of corresponding value in return. In order to pay for the goods they seize, they would have to turn their factories over to producing cheap consumption goods, which would be impossible without slowing down their war industries. The same essential situation exists in Europe, but less crudely because the countries over-run by the Germans are more industrialised. It is as certain as anything can well be that within a fairly short time, the Malays, Burmese and other peoples now under Japanese rule will find out all about their so-called protectors and realise that these people who were making such golden promises a year ago are simply a hoard of locusts eating their countries naked. But just how soon that will happen is a more difficult question and I do not intend to be able to answer it exactly. At present, comparatively little news comes to us from Japanese occupied territory, but we have one great and unimpeachable source of evidence and that is, China. The war in China began five years before it began in the rest of Asia and there are innumerable eye witness accounts of the way the Japanese have behaved. By almost universal agreement it is a regime of naked robbery with all the horrors of massacre, torture and rape on top of that. The same will happen, or has already happened, to all the lands unfortunate enough to fall under Japanese rule. Perhaps the best answer to the propaganda which the Japanese put out to India and other places is simply the three words LOOK AT CHINA. And since I am now bringing these weekly Commentaries to an end I believe those three words LOOK AT CHINA are the best final message I can deliver to India.

'Not Enough Money: A Sketch of George Gissing'

Tribune, 2 APRIL 1943

All books worth reading 'date,' and George Gissing, perhaps the best novelist England has produced, is tied more tightly than most writers to a particular place and time. His world is the grey world of London in the 'eighties, with its gas lamps flickering in the everlasting fog, its dingy overcoats and high-crowned bowler hats, its Sunday gloom tempered by drunkenness, its unbearable 'furnished apartments,' and, above all, its desperate struggle against poverty by a middle class which was poor chiefly because it had remained 'respectable.' It is hard to think of Gissing without thinking of a hansom cab. But he did much more than preserve an atmosphere which, after all, is also preserved in the early *Sherlock Holmes* stories, and it is as a novelist that he will be remembered, even more than as an interpreter of the middle-class view of life.

When I suggest that Gissing is the best novelist we have produced I am not speaking frivolously. It is obvious that Dickens, Fielding and a dozen others are superior to him in natural talent, but Gissing is a 'pure' novelist, a thing that few gifted English writers have been. Not only is he genuinely interested in character and in telling a story, but he has the great advantage of feeling no temptation to burlesque. It is a weakness of nearly all the characteristic English novelists, from Smollett to Joyce, that they want to be 'like life' and at the same time want to get a laugh as often as possible. Very few English novels exist throughout on the same plane of probability. Gissing solves this problem without apparent difficulty, and it may be that his native pessimism was a help to him. For though he certainly did not lack humour, he did lack high spirits, the instinct to play the fool which made Dickens, for instance, as unable to pass a joke as some people are to pass a pub. And it is a fact that *The Odd Women*, to name only one, is more 'like life' than the novels of bigger but less scrupulous writers.

At this date Gissing's best-known book is probably *The Private Papers of Henry Ryecroft*, written towards the end of his life when his worst struggles with poverty were over. But his real masterpieces are three novels, *The Odd Women*, *Demos* and *New Grub Street*, and his book on Dickens. In an article of this length I cannot even summarise the plots of the novels, but their central theme can be stated in three words – 'not enough money.' Gissing is the chronicler of poverty, not working-class poverty (he despises and perhaps hates the working class) but the cruel, grinding, 'respectable' poverty of underfed clerks, downtrodden governesses and bankrupt tradesmen. He believed, perhaps not wrongly, that poverty causes more suffering in the middle class than in the working class. *The Odd Women*, his most perfect and also his most depressing novel, describes the fate of middle-class spinsters flung on to the world with neither money nor vocational training. *New Grub Street* records the horrors of free-lance journalism, even worse then than now. In *Demos* the money theme enters in a somewhat different way. The book is a story of the moral and intellectual corruption of a working-class Socialist who inherits a fortune. Writing as he was in the 'eighties, Gissing shows great prescience, and also a rather surprising knowledge of the inner workings of the Socialist movement. But the usual shabby-genteel motif is present in the person of the heroine, pushed into a hateful marriage by impoverished middle-class parents. Some of the social conditions Gissing describes have passed away, but the general atmosphere of his books is still horribly intelligible, so much so that I have sometimes thought that no professional writer should read *New Grub Street* and no spinster *The Odd Women*.

What is interesting is that with all his depth of understanding Gissing has no revolutionary tendency. He is frankly anti-Socialist and anti-democratic. Understanding better than almost anyone the horror of a money-ruled society, he has little wish to change it, because he does not believe that the change would make any real difference. The only worth-while objective, as he sees it, is to make a purely personal escape from the misery of poverty and then proceed to live a civilised, aesthetically decent life. He is not a snob, he does not wish for luxury or great wealth, he sees the spuriousness of the aristocracy and he despises beyond all other types the go-getting, self-made business man; but he does long for an untroubled, studious life, the kind of life that cannot be lived on less than about £400 a year. As for the working class, he regards them as savages, and says so with great frankness. However wrong he may have been in his outlook, one cannot say of him that he spoke in ignorance, for he himself came of very poor parents, and circumstances forced him to live much of his life among the poorest of the working class. His reactions are worth studying, even at this date. Here was a humane, intelligent man, of scholarly tastes, forced into intimacy with the London poor, and his conclusion was simply this: these people are savages who must on no account be allowed political power. In a more excusable form it is the ordinary reaction of the lower-middle-class man who is near enough to the working class to be afraid of them. Above all, Gissing grasped that the middle classes suffer more from economic insecurity than the working class, and are more ready to take action against it. To ignore that fact has been one of the major blunders of the Left, and from this sensitive novelist who loved Greek tragedies, hated politics and began writing long before Hitler was born, one can learn something about the origins of Fascism.

Review: Tangye Lean, *Voices in the Darkness*

Tribune, 30 APRIL 1943

Anyone who has had to do propaganda to 'friendly' countries must envy the European Service of the B.B.C. They are playing on such an easy wicket! People living under a foreign occupation are necessarily hungry for news, and by making it a penal offence to listen in to Allied broadcasts the Germans have ensured that those broadcasts will be accepted as true. There, however, the advantage of the B.B.C.'s European Service ends. If heard it will be believed, except perhaps in Germany itself, but the difficulty is to be heard at all, and still more, to know what to say. With these difficulties Mr. Tangye Lean's interesting book is largely concerned.

First of all there are the physical and mechanical obstacles. It is never very easy to pick up a foreign station unless one has a fairly good radio set, and every hostile broadcast labours under the enormous disadvantage that its time and wavelength cannot be advertised in the Press. Even in England, where there is no sort of ban on listening, few people have even heard of the German 'freedom' stations such as the New British and the Workers' Challenge. There is also jamming, and above all there is the Gestapo. All over Europe countless people have been imprisoned or sent to concentration camps, and some have been executed, merely for listening to the B.B.C. In countries where surveillance is strict it is only safe to listen on earphones, which may not be available, and in any case the number of workable radio sets is probably declining for want of spare parts. These physical difficulties themselves lead on to the big and only partly soluble question of what it is safe to say. If your probable audience have got to risk their necks to hear you at all, and have also got to listen, for instance, at midnight in some draughty barn, or with earphones under the bedclothes, is it worthwhile to attempt propaganda, or must you assume that nothing except 'hard' news is worth broadcasting? Or again, does it pay to do definitely inflammatory propaganda among people whom you are unable to help in a military sense? Or again, is it better from a propaganda point of view to tell the truth or to spread confusing rumours and promise everything to everybody? When it is a case of addressing the enemy and not the conquered populations, the basic question is always whether to cajole or to threaten. Both the British and the German radios have havered between the two policies. So far as truthfulness of news goes the B.B.C. would compare favourably with any non-neutral radio.

On the other doubtful points its policy is usually a compromise, sometimes a compromise that makes the worst of both worlds, but there is little question that the stuff which is broadcast to Europe is on a higher intellectual level than what is broadcast to any other part of the world. The B.B.C. now broadcasts in over 30 European languages, and nearly 50 languages in all—a complex job, when one remembers that so far as Britain is concerned the whole business of foreign radio propaganda has had to be improvised since 1938.

Probably the most useful section of Mr. Tangye Lean's book is a careful analysis of the radio campaign the Germans did during the Battle of France. They seem to have mixed truth and falsehood with extraordinary skill, giving strictly accurate news of military events but, at the same time, spreading wild rumours calculated to cause panic. The French radio hardly seems to have told the truth at any moment of the battle, and much of the time it simply gave no news at all. During the period of the phoney war the French had countered the German propaganda chiefly by means of jamming, a bad method, because it either does not work or, if it does work, gives the impression that something is being concealed. During the same period the Germans had sapped the morale of the French Army by clever radio programmes which gave the bored troops some light entertainment and, at the same time, stirred up Anglo-French jealousy and cashed in on the demagogic appeal of the Russo–German pact. When the French transmitter stations fell into their hands the Germans were ready with programmes of propaganda and music which they had prepared long beforehand—a detail of organisation which every invading army ought to keep in mind.

The Battle of France went so well for the Germans in a military sense that one may be inclined, when reading Mr. Tangye Lean's account, to overrate the part that radio played in their victory. A question Mr. Tangye Lean glances at but does not discuss at length is whether propaganda can ever achieve anything on its own, or whether it merely speeds up processes that are happening already. Probably the latter is the case, partly because the radio itself has had the unexpected effect of making war a more truthful business than it used to be. Except in a country like Japan, insulated by its remoteness and by the fact that the people have no shortwave sets, it is very difficult to conceal bad news, and if one is being reasonably truthful at home, it is difficult to tell very big lies to the enemy. Now and again a well-timed lie (examples are the Russian troops who passed through England in 1914, and the German Government's order to destroy all dogs in June, 1940) may produce a great effect, but in general propaganda cannot fight against the facts, though it can colour and distort them. It evidently does not pay, for any length of time, to say one thing and do another; the failure of the German New Order, not to take examples nearer home, has demonstrated this.

It would be a good thing if more books like Mr. Tangye Lean's describing the B.B.C. and other organs of propaganda from the inside, were available to the general public. Even well-informed people, when they attack the B.B.C. or the M.O.I., usually demand the impossible while ignoring the really serious faults of British propaganda. Two recent debates in Parliament on this subject brought out the fact that not a single member seemed to know what does or does not happen in the B.B.C. This book should help towards a better understanding, though about half a dozen others along roughly the same lines are needed.

'Three Years of Home Guard: Unique Symbol of Stability'

The Observer, 9 MAY 1943

Late in 1941 Cyril Connolly suggested to David Astor (1912–2001) that he ask Orwell if he would be interested in writing for the distinguished Sunday newspaper, The Observer, *at the time owned by Astor's father. The paper's left-wing bent appealed to Orwell and he not only accepted but Astor and Orwell became close friends. Astor told the editor that contrary to common belief Orwell was a very amusing companion with a fine sense of humour. Indeed, he told the editor that, if he, Astor, were depressed, he would telephone Orwell and persuade him to meet him for a drink because he knew he would quickly cheer him up. Astor served in the Royal Marines, 1940–45, was foreign editor of the paper, 1946–48, and editor, 1948–75. He arranged for Orwell to be buried at All Saints church, Sutton Courtney, Berkshire (see 'Orwell's Death').*

It is close on three years since the eager amateurs of the L.D.V.[1] doctored shotgun cartridges with candle-grease and practised grenade-throwing with lumps of concrete, and the value of the Home Guard as a fighting force can now be fairly accurately estimated.

Although it has never fought, its achievement has not been negligible. In the early days the Germans, to judge by their broadcasts, took the Home Guard more seriously than it took itself, and it must at all times have been part of the reason for their failure to invade Britain. If it were even five per cent. of the reason it would not have done so badly for a part-time and unpaid army.

The Home Guard has passed through three fairly well-defined phases. The first was frankly chaotic, not only because in the summer of 1940 the Home Guard had few weapons and no uniforms, but because it was enormously larger than anyone had expected.

An appeal over the radio, probably intended to produce fifty thousand volunteers, produced a million within a few weeks, and the new force had to organise itself almost unhelped. Since opinions differed about the probable form of a German invasion, it organised itself in innumerable different ways.

By the middle of 1941 the Home Guard was a coherent and standardised force, seriously interested in street-fighting and camouflage, and reasonably

1. L.D.V.: Local Defence Volunteers – the title the Home Guard was first given.

well armed with rifles and machine-guns. By 1942 it had Sten guns and sub-artillery as well, and was beginning to take over some of the anti-aircraft defences. This third phase, in which the Home Guard is definitely integrated with both the regular Army and Civil Defence, has its own problems, some not easily soluble.

During the past year it has been assumed that if the Continent is invaded the Home Guard will partly replace the Regular forces in these islands, and the result has been the tendency to train it for mobile warfare. This has been made easier by the fall in the average age of the Home Guard. But in some ways the results have not been happy. With a part-time and frequently-changing personnel, it is doubtful wisdom to imitate the training of Regular soldiers, and, in any case, the Home Guard could not be made fully mobile even if transport existed for it.

Most of its members are also workers, and even in the case of invasion the economic life would have to be carried on in any area where fighting was not actually happening.

If Britain is ever invaded the Home Guard will in practice fight only in its own areas and in smallish units. The steady tightening of discipline and the increasing contact with the Regular Army have been enormous advantages; but as a strategic plan it would probably have been better to stick to the original idea of purely local defence, and thus make use of the only advantage the amateur soldier has over the professional—that is, intimate knowledge of the ground he is fighting on.

But though the Home Guard has come to look and to be much more like an army than it was, its early days have left their mark on it. The training schools started by Tom Wintringham and others in the summer of 1940 did invaluable work in spreading an understanding of the nature of total war and an imaginative attitude towards military problems.

Even the then lack of weapons had its advantages, for it led to much experimenting in garages and machine shops, and several of the anti-tank weapons now in use are partly the result of Home Guard researches.

Socially, the Home Guard is not quite what it was at the beginning. Membership has changed rapidly with the call-up, and its tendency has been to settle into the accepted English class pattern. This was perhaps inevitable in an unpaid army in which it is difficult to do the work of an officer without having a car and a telephone.

But if its internal atmosphere is not truly democratic, at least it is friendly. And it is very typical of Britain that this vast organisation, now three years old, has had no conscious political development whatever. It has neither developed into a People's Army like the Spanish Government militias, as some hoped at the beginning, nor into an S.A., as others feared or professed to fear. It has been held together not by any political creed, but simply by inarticulate patriotism.

Its mere existence—the fact that in the moment of crisis it could be called into being by a few words over the air, the fact that somewhere near two million men have rifles in their bedrooms and the authorities contemplate this without dismay—is the sign of a stability unequalled in any other country of the world.

Extract from 'London Letter', 23 May 1943(?): Unexpected Shortages

Partisan Review, JULY–AUGUST 1943

Life goes on much as before. I don't notice that our food is any different, but the food situation is generally considered to be worse. The war hits one a succession of blows in unexpected places. For a long time razor blades were unobtainable, now it is boot polish. Books are being printed on the most villainous paper and in tiny print, very trying to the eyes. A few people are wearing wooden-soled shoes. There is an alarming amount of drunkenness in London. The American soldiers seem to be getting on better terms with the locals, perhaps having become more resigned to the climate etc. Air raids continue, but on a pitiful scale. I notice that many people feel sympathy for the Germans now that it is they who are being bombed—a change from 1940, when people saw their houses tumbling about them and wanted to see Berlin scraped off the map.

'Literature and the Left'

Tribune, 4 JUNE 1943

'When a man of true Genius appears in the World, you may know him
by this infallible Sign, that all the Dunces are in Conspiracy against him.'[1]
So wrote Jonathan Swift, 200 years before the publication of *Ulysses*.

If you consult any sporting manual or year book you will find many
pages devoted to the hunting of the fox and the hare, but not a word
about the hunting of the highbrow. Yet this, more than any other, is the
characteristic British sport, in season all the year round and enjoyed by
rich and poor alike, with no complications from either class-feeling or
political alignment.

For it should be noted that in its attitude towards 'highbrows'—that
is, towards any writer or artist who makes experiments in technique—the
Left is no friendlier than the Right. Not only is 'highbrow' almost as much
a word of abuse in the *Daily Worker* as in *Punch*, but it is exactly those
writers whose work shows both originality and the power to endure that
Marxist doctrinaires single out for attack. I could name a long list of
examples, but I am thinking especially of Joyce, Yeats, Lawrence and Eliot.
Eliot, in particular, is damned in the left-wing press almost as automatically and perfunctorily as Kipling—and that by critics who only a few
years back were going into raptures over the already forgotten masterpieces of the Left Book Club.

If you ask a 'good party man' (and this goes for almost any party of
the Left) what he objects to in Eliot, you get an answer that ultimately
reduces to this. Eliot is a reactionary (he has declared himself a royalist,
an Anglo-Catholic, etc.), and he is also a 'bourgeois intellectual,' out of
touch with the common man: therefore he is a bad writer. Contained in
this statement is a half-conscious confusion of ideas which vitiates nearly
all politico-literary criticism.

To dislike a writer's politics is one thing. To dislike him because he
forces you to think is another, not necessarily incompatible with the first.
But as soon as you start talking about 'good' and 'bad' writers you are

---

1. More correctly quoted in 'Imaginary Interview: George Orwell and Jonathan Swift',
    2 November 1942 (see page 192); Orwell is doubtless quoting from memory as was
    often his custom. The correct reading is: 'When a true Genius appears in the World,
    you may know him by this Sign, that the Dunces are all in confederacy against him'
    (*Thoughts on Various Subjects, Miscellanies*, volume 1, 1728).

tacitly appealing to literary tradition and thus dragging in a totally different set of values. For what is a 'good' writer? Was Shakespeare 'good'? Most people would agree that he was. Yet Shakespeare is, and perhaps was even by the standards of his own time, reactionary in tendency; and he is also a difficult writer, only doubtfully accessible to the common man. What, then, becomes of the notion that Eliot is disqualified, as it were, by being an Anglo-Catholic royalist who is given to quoting Latin?

Left Wing literary criticism has not been wrong in insisting on the importance of subject-matter. It may not even have been wrong, considering the age we live in, in demanding that literature shall be first and foremost propaganda. Where it has been wrong is in making what are ostensibly literary judgments for politics ends. To take a crude example, what Communist would dare to admit in public that Trotsky is a better writer than Stalin—as he is, of course? To say 'X is a gifted writer, but he is a political enemy and I shall do my best to silence him' is harmless enough. Even if you end by silencing him with a tommy-gun you are not really sinning against the intellect. The deadly sin is to say 'X is a political enemy: therefore he is a bad writer.' And if anyone says that this kind of thing doesn't happen, I answer merely: look up the literary pages of the Left Wing press, from the *News Chronicle* to the *Labour Monthly*, and see what you find.

There is no knowing just how much the Socialist movement has lost by alienating the literary intelligentsia. But it has alienated them, partly by confusing tracts with literature, and partly by having no room in it for a humanistic culture. A writer can vote Labour as easily as anyone else, but it is very difficult for him to take part in the Socialist movement *as a writer*. Both the book-trained doctrinaire and the practical politician will despise him as a 'bourgeois intellectual,' and will lose no opportunity of telling him so. They will have much the same attitude towards his work as a golfing stockbroker would have. The illiteracy of politicians is a special feature of our age—as G. M. Trevelyan put it, 'In the seventeenth century Members of Parliament quoted the Bible, in the eighteenth and nineteenth centuries, the classics, and in the twentieth century nothing'—and its corollary is the literary impotence of writers. In the years following the last war the best English writers were reactionary in tendency, though most of them took no direct part in politics. After them, about 1930, there came a generation of writers who tried very hard to be actively useful in the Left Wing movement. Numbers of them joined the Communist Party, and got there exactly the same reception as they would have got in the

Conservative Party. That is, they were first regarded with patronage and suspicion, and then, when it was found that they would not or could not turn themselves into gramophone records, they were thrown out on their ears. Most of them retreated into individualism. No doubt they still vote Labour but their talents are lost to the movement; and—a more sinister development—after them there comes a new generation of writers who, without being strictly non-political, are outside the Socialist movement from the start. Of the very young writers who are now beginning their careers, the most gifted are pacifists; a few may even have a leaning towards Fascism. There is hardly one to whom the mystique of the Socialist move-ment appears to mean anything. The ten-year-long struggle against Fascism seems to them meaningless and uninteresting, and they say so frankly. One could explain this in a number of ways, but the contemptuous attitude of the Left towards 'bourgeois intellectuals' is likely to be part of the reason.

Gilbert Murray relates somewhere or other that he once lectured on Shakespeare to a Socialist debating society. At the end he called for ques-tions in the usual way, to receive as the sole question asked: 'Was Shakespeare a capitalist?' The depressing thing about this story is that it might well be true. Follow up its implications, and you perhaps get a glimpse of the reason why Céline wrote *Mea Culpa*[2] and Auden is watching his navel in America.

2. *Mea Culpa* (1936) was written after a visit to the USSR, which he found abhorrent.

'The Detective Story'

Fontaine, 17 NOVEMBER 1943

This article was published originally in French as 'Grandeur et décadence du roman policier anglais' in a cumulative issue of Fontaine, *37–40, of some 500 pages. It later appeared as a book,* Aspects de la Littérature Anglaise (1918–1945), *dropping some articles, adding several others, and making changes to some, those to Orwell's essay being of little significance. The issue was attacked as Roman Catholic propaganda even before it was published but that was fiercely contradicted by J.B. Brunius in* Tribune. *Given Orwell's antipathy to Roman Catholicism it would be surprising were he to participate in such propaganda. Orwell had a facility for languages. Although his articles were translated for him into French, he corresponded with his translators – R.N. Raimbault and Yvonne Davet – in French, although accents were often omitted (in part because he was using an English-language typewriter).*

It was between 1920 and 1940 that the majority of detective stories were written and read, but this is precisely the period that marks the decline of the detective story as a literary genre. Throughout these troubled and frivolous years, 'crime stories' as they were called (this title includes the detective story proper as well as the 'thriller' where the author follows the conventions of Grand Guignol), were in England a universal palliative equal to tea, aspirins, cigarettes and the wireless. These works were mass-produced, and it is not without some surprise that we find that their authors include professors of political economy and Roman Catholics as well as Anglican priests. Any amateur who had never dreamed of writing a novel felt capable of tackling a detective story, which requires only the haziest knowledge of toxicology and a plausible alibi to conceal the culprit. Yet soon the detective story started to get more complicated; it demanded more ingenuity if its author were to satisfy the reader's constantly growing appetite for violence and thirst for bloodshed. The crimes became more sensational and more difficult to unravel. It is nevertheless a fact that in this multitude of later works there is hardly anything worth re-reading.

Things were not always like this. Entertaining books are not necessarily bad books. Between 1880 and 1920 we had in England three specialists in the detective novel who showed undeniably artistic qualities. Conan Doyle of course belonged to this trio, together with two writers who are not his equal, but who should not be despised: Ernest Bramah and R. Austin

Freeman. The *Memoirs* and the *Adventures of Sherlock Holmes, Max Carrados* and *The Eyes of Max Carrados* by Bramah, *The Eye of Osiris* and *The Singing Bone* by Freeman are, together with the two or three short stories of Edgar Allan Poe which inspired them, the classics of English detective fiction. We can find in each of these works a quality of style, and even better an *atmosphere*, which we do not usually find in contemporary authors (Dorothy Sayers, for example, or Agatha Christie or Freeman Wills Croft). The reasons for this are worth examining.

Even today, more than half a century after his first appearance, Sherlock Holmes remains one of the most popular characters in the English novel. His slim, athletic build, his beaky nose, his crumpled dressing gown, the cluttered rooms of his Baker Street flat with their alcoves and test tubes, the violin, the tobacco in the Indian slipper, the bullet marks on the walls, all this is part of the intellectual furniture of the Englishman who knows his authors. Moreover the exploits of Sherlock Holmes have been translated into some twenty languages, from Norwegian to Japanese. The other two authors I mentioned, Ernest Bramah and R. Austin Freeman, never reached such a wide public, but both of them created unforgettable characters. Freeman's Dr Thorndyke is the laboratory detective, the forensic scientist who solves the mystery with his microscope and camera. As for Ernest Bramah's Max Carrados, he is blind, but his blindness only serves to sharpen his other senses, and he is all the better because of it. If we seek to determine why we are drawn to these three authors, we are led to a preliminary observation of a purely technical nature, one which emphasises the weakness of the modern detective story and of all English short stories of the past twenty years.

We can see that the vintage detective story (from Poe to Freeman) is much more *dense* than the modern novel. The dialogue is richer, the digressions more frequent. If the stories of Conan Doyle or Poe had been written yesterday, it is doubtful whether any editor would have accepted them. They are too long for the compact magazines of today, and their interminable opening scenes run counter to the current fad for economy.

Yet it is by accumulating details which at first seem superfluous that Conan Doyle, like Dickens before him, gains his most striking effects. If you set out to examine the Sherlock Holmes stories, you find that the eccentricities and the perspicacity of a character are principally revealed in episodes which do not form an integral part of the plot. Holmes is especially distinguished by his method of 'reasoning by deduction' which amazes the good Doctor Watson. We can see an example at the beginning of *The Blue Carbuncle*. Holmes only has to examine a bowler hat found in the street to give a detailed—and, as subsequent events prove, exact—description of its owner. Yet the hat incident has only the vaguest connection with the main events; several episodes are preceded by six or seven pages of conversation which do not claim to be anything but digressions pure and simple. These conversations act as a vehicle to demonstrate Holmes's genius and Watson's naivety.

Ernest Bramah and R. Austin Freeman also write with the same contempt for conciseness. It is largely thanks to their digressions that their stories are literary works and not mere 'puzzles'.

The vintage detective story is not necessarily founded on a mystery, and it is worth reading even if it does not end with a surprise or a sensational revelation. The most annoying thing about the writers of modern detective stories is their constant, almost painful effort to hide the culprit's identity—and this convention is doubly annoying because it soon palls on a reader, who eventually finds the intricacies of concealment grotesque. On the other hand, in several of Conan Doyle's stories and in Poe's famous story *The Purloined Letter*, the perpetrator of the crime is known at the outset. How will he react? How, in the end, will he be brought to justice? That is what is so intriguing. Austin Freeman sometimes has the audacity to describe the crime first in minute detail, then merely explains how the mystery was solved. In the earlier stories, the crime is not necessarily sensational or ingeniously contrived. In the modern detective story the key incident is almost always a murder (the formula hardly changes: a corpse, a dozen suspects, each with a watertight alibi); but the earlier stories often deal with petty crimes, perhaps the culprit is no more than a third-rate thief. There may even turn out to be neither culprit nor crime. Many of the mysteries investigated by Holmes fade away in the broad light of day. Bramah wrote ten or twenty stories, of which only two or three deal with a murder. The authors can indulge themselves like this because the success of their work depends, not on the unmasking of the criminal, but in the interest the reader finds in an account of the methods of detection so dear to Holmes, Thorndyke or Carrados. These characters appeal to the imagination, and the reader, if he reacts as he is meant to, transforms them into intellectual giants.

It is now possible for us to make a fundamental distinction between the two schools of detective story – the old and the new.

The earlier writers believed in their own characters. They made their detectives into exceptionally gifted individuals, demi-gods for whom they felt a boundless admiration. Against our present-day background of world wars, mass unemployment, famines, plague and totalitarianism, crime has lost much of its savour; we know far too much about its social and economic causes to look upon the ordinary detective as a benefactor of mankind. Nor is it easy for us to consider as an end in itself the mental gymnastics demanded of us by this kind of work. Sitting in the darkness that accompanies him everywhere, Poe's Dupin uses his mental faculties without ever thinking of action; because of this, he does not arouse in us quite the admiration which Poe feels for him. *The Mystery of Marie Roget*, a typical example of pure mental acrobatics, demanding from its reader the agility of a crossword-puzzle addict, could only have appeared in a more leisured age. In the Sherlock Holmes stories you catch the author taking evident pleasure in this display of virtuosity, which seems totally detached from the plot. It is the same with *Silver Blaze, The Musgrave Ritual, The Dancing Men*, or the sort of episode that allows Holmes to deduce the life-history of a passer-by from his appearance, or to astound Watson by guessing what he is thinking at that very moment. And yet the work which these detectives were striving to accomplish was obviously important for their creators. During the peaceful years at the close of the last century, Society seemed mainly composed of law-abiding people, whose security was disturbed only by the criminal. In his contemporaries' eyes, Dr Moriarty was as demoniac a figure as Hitler is today. The man who defeated Moriarty became a knight errant or a national hero. And when Conan Doyle, sending Holmes to his death at the end of *The Memoirs*,[1] allows Watson to echo the words of Plato's farewell to Socrates, there is no fear of his seeming ridiculous.[2]

1. Doyle had intended to finish his Sherlock Holmes series with *The Memoirs*, but his readers protested so vehemently that he felt obliged to carry on. Letters poured in from all over the world, and some were said to threaten Doyle with violence if he did not carry on with Holmes's adventures. So *The Memoirs* was followed by several more volumes. Yet the earlier ones are the best [Orwell's footnote].

2. In the last paragraph of 'The Final Problem', at the end of *The Memoirs of Sherlock Holmes*, Watson, who is looking for Holmes, finds a 'small square of paper' held down by Holmes's cigarette case at 'the fall of Reichenbach'. The note asks Watson to 'tell Inspector Patterson that the papers which he needs to convict the gang are in a pigeon-hole, done up in a blue envelope and inscribed "Moriarty".' Dr Watson's final words describing Holmes as 'him whom I shall ever regard as the best and the wisest man whom I have ever known' echo Plato's in the *Phaedo* on Socrates, 'Such was the end, Echecrates, of our friend, whom I may truly call the wisest, and justest, and best of all men whom I have ever known' (L. J. Hunt to the editor, quoting Jowett's translation).

Among modern writers, there are only two who seem to us to believe in their detectives: G. K. Chesterton and Edgar Wallace. Yet their motives are not as disinterested as those of Doyle or Freeman. Wallace, an extraordinarily prolific and gifted writer in a morbid genre, was inspired by his own private form of sadism which there is no time to analyse here. Chesterton's hero, Father Brown, is a Catholic priest used by Chesterton as an instrument of religious propaganda. In the other detective stories, at least in those I have read, I can see either a comic side, or a rather unconvincing effort on the author's part to create an atmosphere of horror around crimes which he himself has great difficulty in finding horrific. And then, to achieve their aims, the detectives in contemporary novels rely first and foremost on luck and intuition. They are less intellectual than the heroes of Poe, Doyle, Freeman or Bramah. It is clear that for the earlier writers, Holmes, Thorndyke and many others are all the prototype of the man of science, or, rather, of omniscience, who owes everything to logic and nothing to chance. Chesterton's Father Brown possesses almost magical powers. Holmes is a nineteenth-century rationalist. In creating this character Conan Doyle faithfully reproduced his contemporaries' idea of a scientist.

In the last century the detective was always a bachelor. That must be taken as further proof of his superiority. The modern detective also has a marked taste for celibacy (a wife does rather complicate matters in a detective story), but the celibacy of Holmes and Thorndyke is of a particularly monkish kind. It is stated categorically that neither of them is interested in the opposite sex. It is felt that the wise man should not be married, just as the Saint must practise celibacy. The wise man should have a complementary character beside him—the fool. The contrast accentuates the wise man's good qualities. This role is reserved for the police chief whose problems are solved by Dupin in *The Purloined Letter*. Jarvis, the fool who seconds Dr Thorndyke, lacks depth, but Mr Carlyle, Max Carrados's friend, is a well-rounded character. As for Watson, whose imbecility is almost chronic, he is a more lifelike character than Holmes himself. It is by design, and not accidental, that the early detectives are amateurs rather than police officers. It fell to Edgar Wallace to set the fashion for the professional Scotland Yard officer. This respect for the amateur is characteristically British. We can see in Sherlock Holmes a certain resemblance to one of his contemporaries, Raffles, the gentleman thief, the English counterpart of Arsène Lupin. Yet the unofficial role of the early sleuth serves once again to reveal superior gifts. In the early Sherlock Holmes stories and in some Dr Thorndyke adventures, the police are clearly hostile to outside investigators. The professionals constantly make mistakes and do not hesitate to accuse innocent people. Holmes's analytical genius and Thorndyke's encyclopaedic knowledge only shine more brightly against the background of humdrum official routine.

In this brief study I have only been able to write at length about one group of writers and I have not discussed foreign writers or American novelists apart from Poe. Since 1920 the output of detective stories has been enormous and the war has not slowed it down, yet, for the reasons I have tried to stress, the magic wand of yesteryear has lost its power. There is more ingenuity in the modern novel, but the authors seem incapable of creating an atmosphere. First place among modern writers should probably go to the brooding Edgar Wallace, more likely to terrorize his reader than to guide him through a jungle of complex problems. Mention must be made of Agatha Christie, who handles dialogue elegantly and shows artistry in laying false trails. The much vaunted short stories of Dorothy Sayers would probably have attracted little attention if the author had not had the bright idea of making her detective the son of a Duke. As for the works of the other contemporary writers, Freeman Wills Croft, G. D. H. and Margaret Cole, Ngaio Marsh and Philip Macdonald, they have scarcely more relevance to literature than a crossword puzzle.

It is not difficult to imagine that a novel conceived as a pure intellectual exercise, like *The Gold Bug*, might appear again one day. But it is unlikely to reappear as a detective story. I have already said, and this seems to me a significant fact, that the best detective story writers could exploit small-scale crimes. It is hard to believe that the game of cops and robbers could still inspire writers of the stature of Conan Doyle, let alone Poe. The detective story as we know it belonged to the nineteenth century, above all to the end of the nineteenth century. It belonged to the London of the eighties and nineties, to that gloomy and mysterious London where men in high-domed bowler hats slipped out into the flickering light of the gas lamps, where the bells of hansom cabs jingled through perpetual fogs; it belonged to the period when English public opinion was more deeply stirred by the exploits of Jack the Ripper[3] than by the problems of Irish Home Rule or the Battle of Majuba.[4]

3. The London counterpart of Landru who was loose in the London capital at the time, and who struck terror into the whole nation [*Orwell's footnote*].
4. At the Battle of Majuba, 1881, General Pietrus Jacobus Joubert (1831–1900) routed the British forces in the First Boer War.

Review: H.N. Brailsford, *Subject India*

New Statesman and Nation, 20 NOVEMBER 1943

If there is one point in the Indian problem that cannot be disputed—or, at any rate, is not disputed, outside the ranks of the British Conservative Party—it is that Britain ought to stop ruling India as early as possible. But this is a smaller basis of agreement than it sounds, and the answers to literally every other question are always coloured by subjective feelings. Mr. Brailsford is better equipped than the majority of writers on India in that he is not only aware of his own prejudices but possesses enough background knowledge to be unafraid of the 'experts.' Probably he has not been very long in India, perhaps he does not even speak any Indian language, but he differs from the vast majority of English left-wingers in having bothered to visit India at all, and in being more interested in the peasants than in the politicians.

As he rightly says, the great, central fact about India is its poverty. From birth to death, generation after generation, the peasant lives his life in the grip of the landlord or the money-lender—they are frequently the same person—tilling his tiny patch of soil with the tools and methods of the Bronze Age. Over great areas the children barely taste milk after they are weaned, and the average physique is so wretched that ninety-eight pounds is a normal weight for a full-grown man. The last detailed survey to be taken showed that the average Indian income was Rs.62 (about £4 13s. od.) per annum: in the same period the average British income was £94. In spite of the drift to the towns that is occurring in India as elsewhere, the condition of the industrial workers is hardly better than that of the peasants. Brailsford describes them in the slums of Bombay, sleeping eight to a tiny room, with three water taps among four hundred people, and working a twelve-hour day, three hundred and sixty five days a year, for wages of around seven and sixpence a week. These conditions will not be cured simply by the removal of British rule, but neither can they be seriously improved while the British remain, because British policy, largely unconscious, is to hamper industrialization and preserve the status quo. The worst barbarities from which Indians suffer are inflicted on them not by Europeans but by other Indians—the landlords and money-lenders, the bribe-taking minor officials, and the Indian capitalists who exploit their working people with a ruthlessness quite impossible in the West since the rise of trade unionism. But although the business community, at any rate, tends to be anti-British and is involved in the Nationalist movement, the privileged classes really depend on British arms. Only when the British have gone will what Brailsford calls the latent class war be able to develop.

Brailsford is attempting exposition rather than moral judgment, and he gives no very definite answer to the difficult question of whether, in balance, the British have done India more good than harm. As he points out, they have made possible an increase of population without making it possible for that population to be properly fed. They have saved India from war, internal and external, at the expense of destroying political liberty. Probably their greatest gift to India has been the railway. If one studies a railway map of Asia, India looks like a piece of fishing-net in the middle of a white tablecloth. And this network of communications has not only made it possible to check famines by bringing food to the afflicted areas—the famine now raging in India would hardly have been a famine at all by the standards of a hundred years ago—but to administer India as a unit, with a common system of law, internal free trade and freedom of movement, and even, for the educated minority, a lingua franca in the English language. India is potentially a nation, as Europe, with its smaller population and great racial homogeneity, is not. But since 1910 or thereabouts the British power has acted as a dead hand. Often loosely denounced as 'fascist,' the British régime in India is almost the exact opposite of Fascism, since it has never developed the notion of positive government at all. It has remained an old fashioned despotism, keeping the peace, collecting its taxes, and for the rest letting things slide, with hardly the faintest interest in how its subjects lived or what they thought, so long as they were outwardly obedient. As a result—to pick just one fact out of the thousands one could choose—the whole subcontinent, in this year of 1943, is incapable of manufacturing an automobile engine. In spite of all that can be said on the other side, this fact alone would justify Brailsford in his final conclusion: 'Our day in India is over; we have no creative part to play.'

Brailsford is justifiably bleak about the future. He sees that the handing over of power is a complicated process which cannot be achieved quickly, especially in the middle of a war, and that it will solve nothing in itself. There is still the problem of India's poverty and ignorance to be solved, and the struggle between the landlords, big business, and the labour movement to be fought out. And there is also the question of how, if at all, a backward agricultural country like India is to remain independent in a world of power politics. Brailsford gives a good account of the current political situation, in which he struggles very hard not to be engulfed by the prevailing left-wing orthodoxy. He writes judiciously about the tortuous character of Gandhi; comes nearer to being fair to Cripps than most English commentators have been—Cripps, indeed, has been the whipping-boy of the left, both British and Indian—and rightly emphasises the importance of the Indian princes, who are often forgotten and who present a much more serious difficulty than the faked-up quarrel between Hindus and Moslems. At this moment India is such a painful subject that it is hardly possible to write a really good book about it. English books are either dishonest or irresponsible; American books are ignorant and self-righteous; Indian books are coloured by spite and an inferiority complex. Well aware of the gaps in his knowledge and the injustices he is bound to commit, Brailsford has produced not only a transparently honest but—what is much rarer in this context—a good-tempered book. Nearly all books written about the British Empire in these days have the air of being written *at* somebody—either a Blimp, or a Communist, or an American, as the case may be. Brailsford is writing primarily for the ordinary British public, the people who before all others have the power and the duty to do something about India, and whose conscience it is first necessary to move. But it is a book that the American public might find useful too. Perhaps it is worth uttering the warning that—owing to war-time conditions—there are many misprints, and as some of them have crept into the statistics these are apt to be misleading.

Broadcast: 'Your Questions Answered: Wigan Pier'[1]

London Calling, BBC, 2 DECEMBER 1943

Your Questions Answered *was, in effect, a successor to* Answering You *(see page 189). These were Orwell's only appearances on such programmes.*

WILLS: I am going to try some more of these trick questions on somebody else in another programme. And now we've got time for just one more question, asked by Sergeant Salt and Signalman McGrath serving in India. They say: 'How long is the Wigan Pier and what is the Wigan Pier?' Well, if anybody ought to know, it should be George Orwell who wrote a book called 'The Road to Wigan Pier.' And here's what he's got to say on the subject.

ORWELL: Well, I am afraid I must tell you that Wigan Pier doesn't exist. I made a journey specially to see it in 1936, and I couldn't find it. It did exist once, however, and to judge from the photographs it must have been about twenty feet long.

Wigan is in the middle of the mining areas, and though it's a very pleasant place in some ways its scenery is not its strong point. The landscape is mostly slag-heaps, looking like the mountains of the moon, and mud and soot and so forth. For some reason, though it's not worse than fifty other places, Wigan has always been picked on as a symbol of the ugliness of the industrial areas. At one time, on one of the little muddy canals that run round the town, there used to be a tumble-down wooden jetty; and by way of a joke someone nicknamed this Wigan Pier. The joke caught on locally, and then the music-hall comedians get hold of it, and they are the ones who have succeeded in keeping Wigan Pier alive as a by-word, long after the place itself had been demolished.

WILLS: And so Signalman Salt and Sergeant McGrath, if you meant to

---

1. The script in the Orwell Archive for Number 25 of the BBC radio programme *Your Questions Answered* states that it was broadcast on Thursday, 2 December 1943, from 1830 to 1845 GMT in the General Overseas Service and repeated on the next day from approximately 1310 to 1315 using disc SOX23536. This timing is clearly wrong. 'London Calling' gives both transmissions and the time for the second as 1310–1340. There is no indication in the *Radio Times* that the programme was broadcast in the United Kingdom between 28 November and 4 December 1943. The compère was Colin Wills.

floor the experts with a question about Wigan Pier, you'll have to try again with something else! Now our time's up for this week but we'll be back again on the air at the same time next week to answer some more of your questions.

Extract from 'As I Please', 1: Anglo-American Relations in Wartime

Tribune, 3 DECEMBER 1943

Orwell's last day at the BBC was Tuesday 23 November 1943. He started writing letters on Tribune*'s headed paper on Monday 29 November and it is likely that that was the day he began work as its literary editor.*

In addition to organising book reviews for the journal, one of Orwell's principal contributions to Tribune *was a personal column, 'As I Please': a random causerie, sometimes deeply serious, often light-hearted. He wrote eighty 'As I Please' columns. The first appeared on 3 December 1943 and the last on 4 April 1947. Raymond Postgate had contributed to a short series entitled 'As I Please' in* Controversy *in 1939. Jon Kimche (who had shared a flat with Orwell at Booklovers' Corner in 1934–35) told the editor that it was he who suggested to Orwell that he use that title for his series.*

Aneurin Bevan (nominally editor of Tribune*) gave Orwell free rein in 'As I Please'. As a result, 'Protests were frequent, both at the frivolous use he made of his column and at his frequent attacks on the Soviet Communist Party.' Bevan defended Orwell, without whose support Orwell 'might not have lasted —even though the circulation manager coolly reported that those who wrote in regularly threatening to cancel their subscriptions were rarely subscribers' (Crick, 445–46).*

In most instances only selections are reproduced from individual 'As I Please' columns. Very occasionally one or two of the very many letters that readers sent in to Orwell in response to his column and his reviews are reproduced. All the columns in full and most of the letters from readers will be found in the Complete Works.

Anglo-American Relations in Wartime
Scene in a tobacconist's shop. Two American soldiers sprawling across the counter, one of them just sober enough to make unwanted love to the two young women who run the shop, the other at the stage known as 'fighting drunk.' Enter Orwell in search of matches. The pugnacious one makes an effort and stands upright.

Soldier: 'Wharrishay is, perfijious Albion. You heard that? Perfijious Albion. Never trust a Britisher. You can't trust the b——s.'

Orwell: 'Can't trust them with what?'

Soldier: 'Wharrishay is, down with Britain. Down with the British. You wanna do anything 'bout that? Then you can —— well do it.' (Sticks his face out like a tomcat on a garden wall.)

Tobacconist: 'He'll knock your block off if you don't shut up.'

Soldier: 'Wharrishay is, down with Britain.' (Subsides across the counter again. The tobacconist lifts his head delicately out of the scales.)

This kind of thing is not exceptional. Even if you steer clear of Piccadilly with its seething swarms of drunks and whores, it is difficult to go anywhere in London without having the feeling that Britain is now Occupied Territory. The general consensus of opinion seems to be that the only American soldiers with decent manners are the Negroes. On the other hand the Americans have their own justifiable complaints—in particular, they complain of the children who follow them night and day, cadging sweets.

Does this sort of thing matter? The answer is that it might matter at some moment when Anglo-American relations were in the balance, and when the still powerful forces in this country which want an understanding with Japan were able to show their faces again. At such moments popular prejudice can count for a great deal. Before the war there was no popular anti-American feeling in this country. It all dates from the arrival of the American troops, and it is made vastly worse by the tacit agreement never to discuss it in print.

Seemingly it is our fixed policy in this war not to criticise our allies, nor to answer their criticisms of us. As a result things have happened which are capable of causing the worst kind of trouble sooner or later. An example is the agreement by which American troops in this country are not liable to British courts for offences against British subjects—practically 'extra-territorial rights.' Not one English person in ten knows of the existence of this agreement; the newspapers barely reported it and refrained from commenting on it. Nor have people been made to realise the extent of anti-British feeling in the United States. Drawing their picture of America from films carefully edited for the British market, they have no notion of the kind of thing that Americans are brought up to believe about us. Suddenly to discover, for instance, that the average American thinks the U.S.A. had more casualties than Britain in the last war comes as a shock, and the kind of shock that can cause a violent quarrel. Even such a fundamental difficulty as the fact that an American soldier's pay is five times that of a British soldier has never been properly ventilated. No sensible person wants to whip up Anglo-American jealousy. On the contrary, it is just because one does want a good relationship between the two countries that one wants plain speaking. Our official soft-soaping policy does us no good in America, while in this country it allows dangerous resentments to fester just below the surface.

Amongst the letters received from readers were these two:

I cannot speak for London, but I can assure you that Mr. Orwell's 'popular anti-American feeling' does not extend to this military centre [Salisbury], where we have probably seen more American soldiers than any other provincial town.

The American authorities are surely not to be blamed for giving their men decent pay; we should give our fighting men equally good payment, not expect others to descend to our own miserable level. Piccadilly at night may be disgusting, but due to our social system there were whores there long before the Americans landed. Drunkenness too was not exactly unknown.

Let us have plain-speaking by all means, but before we criticise Uncle Sam's representatives in this country, let us be perfectly sure that the sons of John Bull are all behaving like perfect little gentlemen in the towns and villages of Italy.

'Unity'

Mr. Orwell's remarks on two drunk U.S. boys in a cigar store—your issue of December 3rd—in my opinion is plainly dirty. It strikes me as 'cakes and coffee' lines (penny a line or better).

If the incident did occur the boys would be from tank towns (small towns on the prairie, consisting of half a dozen houses, a grain elevator, and a water tank used by the railway engines), and they would not have words like 'perfidious' and 'Albion' in their vocabulary.

Such writings as the paragraphs in question can do no good, but plenty of harm. To me they sound prejudiced; cut 'em out, George—help not hinder.

W.T. Grose.

Extract from 'As I Please', 2: Skin Colour and Living Standards; Insulting Nicknames

Tribune, 10 DECEMBER 1943

Skin Colour and Living Standards

One of the big unmentionable facts of politics is the differential standard of living. An English working-man spends on cigarettes about the same sum as an Indian peasant has for his entire income. It is not easy for Socialists to admit this, or at any rate to emphasise it. If you want people to rebel against the existing system, you have got to show them that they are badly off, and it is doubtful tactics to *start* by telling an Englishman on the dole that in the eyes of an Indian coolie he would be next door to a millionaire. Almost complete silence reigns on this subject, at any rate at the European end, and it contributes to the lack of solidarity between white and coloured workers. Almost without knowing it—and perhaps without wanting to know it—the white worker exploits the coloured worker, and in revenge the coloured worker can be and is used against the white. Franco's Moors in Spain were only doing more dramatically the same thing as is done by half-starved Indians in Bombay mills or Japanese factory-girls sold into semi-slavery by their parents. As things are, Asia and Africa are simply a bottomless reserve of scab labour.

The coloured worker cannot be blamed for feeling no solidarity with his white comrades. The gap between their standard of living and his own is so vast that it makes any differences which may exist in the West seem negligible. In Asiatic eyes the European class struggle is a sham. The Socialist movement has never gained a real foothold in Asia or Africa, or even among the American Negroes: it is everywhere side-tracked by nationalism and race-hatred. Hence the spectacle of thoughtful Negroes getting ready to vote for Dewey,[1] and Indian Congressmen preferring their own capitalists to the British Labour Party. There is no solution until the living-standards of the thousand million people who are not 'white' can be forced up to the same level as our own. But as this might mean

1. Thomas Edmund Dewey (1902–1971), Governor of New York for three successive terms (1942–54), was the Republican Party's Presidential candidate in 1944 and 1948; he lost both elections. He might well have attracted votes 'of thoughtful Negroes' because, as special prosecutor and district attorney, he won seventy-two of seventy-three prosecutions of racketeers involved in organised crime in New York.

temporarily *lowering* our own standards the subject is systematically avoided by Left and Right alike.

Insulting Nicknames

Is there anything that one can do about this, as an individual? One can at least remember that the colour problem exists. And there is one small precaution which is not much trouble, and which can perhaps do a little to mitigate the horrors of the colour war. That is to avoid using insulting nicknames. It is an astonishing thing that few journalists, even in the Left-wing press, bother to find out which names are and which are not resented by members of other races. The word 'native,' which makes any Asiatic boil with rage, and which has been dropped even by British officials in India these ten years past, is flung about all over the place. 'Negro' is habitually printed with a small n, a thing most Negroes resent. One's information about these matters needs to be kept up to date. I have just been carefully going through the proofs of a reprinted book of mine,[2] cutting out the word 'Chinaman' wherever it occurred and substituting 'Chinese.' The book was written less than a dozen years ago, but in the intervening time 'Chinaman' has become a deadly insult. Even 'Mahomedan' is now beginning to be resented: one should say 'Moslem.' These things are childish, but then nationalism is childish. And after all we ourselves do not actually like being called 'Limeys' or 'Britishers.'

2. *Burmese Days*, Penguin Books, published in May 1944. Orwell was alerted to the provision of an initial capital for 'Negro' by Cedric Dover during the proofing of *Talking to India*. Orwell had returned the proofs of *Burmese Days* to Penguin Books on 21 November 1943. Dover (1904–1971) was born of Eurasian parents in Calcutta and broadcast for the BBC Overseas Service under Orwell's direction. He was an entomologist and wrote on sociological and political topics.

Extracts from 'London Letter', 15 January 1944: Parliament[1]; London in Wartime

Partisan Review, Spring 1944

Parliament

When I was working with the BBC I sometimes had to go and listen to a debate in the Commons. The last time I had been there was about ten years previously, and I was very much struck by the deterioration that seemed to have taken place. The whole thing now has a mangy, forgotten look. Even the ushers' shirt fronts are grimy. And it is noticeable now that, except from the places they sit in (the opposition always sits on the Speaker's left), you can't tell one party from another. It is just a collection of mediocre-looking men in dingy, dark suits, nearly all speaking in the same accent and all laughing at the same jokes. I may say, however, that they don't look such a set of crooks as the French Deputies used to look. The most striking thing of all is the lack of attendance. It would be very rare indeed for 400 members out of the 640 to turn up. The House of Lords, where they are now sitting, only has seating accommodation for about 250, and the old House of Commons (it was blitzed) cannot have been much larger. I attended the big debate on India after Cripps came back. At the start there were a little over 200 members present, which rapidly shrank to about 45. It seems to be the custom to clear out, presumably to the bar, as soon as any important speech begins, but the House fills up again when there are questions or anything else that promises a bit of fun. There is a marked family atmosphere. Everyone shouts with laughter over jokes and allusions which are unintelligible to anyone not an MP, nicknames are used freely, violent political opponents pal up over drinks. Nearly any member of long standing is corrupted by this kind of thing sooner or later. Maxton,[2] the ILP MP, twenty years ago an inflammatory orator whom the ruling classes hated like poison, is now the pet of the House, and Gallacher,[3]

---

1. The sub-heading Parliament was added by *Partisan Review*. London in Wartime was added by the editor.
2. James Maxton (1885–1946), Independent Labour MP, 1922–46; Chairman of the Independent Labour Party (ILP), 1926–31, 1934–39.
3. William Gallacher (1881–1965), Communist MP, 1935–50, was the sole representative of his party in Parliament, 1935–45, but was then joined by Phil Piratin (who also lost his seat in 1950). Gallacher was Chairman of the Clyde Workers' Committee during World War I and a member of the Communist International from 1920.

the Communist MP, is going the same road. Each time I have been in the House recently I have found myself thinking the same thought—that the Roman Senate still existed under the later Empire.

I don't need [to] indicate to you the various features of capitalism that make democracy unworkable. But apart from these, and apart from the dwindling prestige of representative institutions, there are special reasons why it is difficult for able men to find their way into Parliament. To begin with, the out-of-date electoral system grossly favors the Conservative Party. The rural areas, where, on the whole, people vote as the landlords tell them to, are so much over-represented, and the industrial areas so much under-represented that the Conservatives consistently win a far higher proportion of seats than their share in the total vote entitles them to. Secondly, the electorate seldom have a chance to vote for anyone except the nominees of the party machines. In the Conservative Party safe seats are peddled round to men rich enough to 'keep up' the seat (contributions to local charities, etc.), and no doubt to pay an agreed sum into the party funds as well. Labour Party candidates are selected for their political docility, and a proportion of the Labour MP's are always elderly trade-union officials who have been allotted a seat as a kind of pension. Naturally, these men are even more slavishly obedient to the party machine than the Tories. To any MP who shows signs of independent thought the same threat is always applied—'We won't support you at the next election.' In practice a candidate cannot win an election against the opposition of his own party machine, unless the inhabitants of that locality have some special reason for admiring him personally. But the party system has destroyed the territorial basis of politics. Few MP's have any connection with their constituency, even to the extent of living there: many have never seen it till they go down to fight their first election. At this moment Parliament is more than usually unrepresentative because, owing to the war, literally millions of people are disenfranchised. There has been no register of voters since 1939, which means that no one under 25, and no one who has changed his place of residence, now has a vote; for practical purposes the men in the forces are disenfranchised as well. On the whole, the people who have lost their votes are those who would vote against the Government. It is fair to add that in the general mechanics of an election in England there is no dirty work—no intimidation, no miscounting of votes or direct bribery, and the ballot is genuinely secret.

The feeling that Parliament has lost its importance is very widespread. The electorate are conscious of having no control over their MP's; the

MP's are conscious that it is not they who are directing affairs. All major decisions, whether to go to war, whether to open a second front, and where, which power to go into alliance with, and so forth, are taken by an Inner Cabinet which acts first and announces the fait accompli after- wards. Theoretically, Parliament has the power to overthrow the Government if it wishes, but the party machines can usually prevent this. The average MP, or even a minor member of the Government, has no more information about what is going on than any reader of the *Times*. There is an extra hurdle for any progressive policy in the House of Lords, which has supposedly been shorn of its powers but still has the power of obstruction. In all, only two or three bills thrown out by the Lords have ever been forced through by the Commons. Seeing all this, people of every political colour simply lose interest in Parliament, which they refer to as 'the talking shop.' One cannot judge from wartime, but for years before the war the percentage of the electorate voting had been going down. Sixty percent was considered a high vote. In the big towns many people do not know the name of their MP or which constituency they live in. A social survey at a recent election showed that many adults now don't know the first facts about British electoral procedures—e.g., don't know that the ballot is secret.

Nevertheless, I myself feel that Parliament has justified its existence during the war, and I even think that its prestige has risen slightly in the last two or three years. While losing most of its original powers it has retained its power of criticism, and it is the only remaining place in which one is free, theoretically as well as practically, to utter literally any opinion. Except for sheer personal abuse (and even that has to be something fairly extreme), any remark made in Parliament is privileged. The Government has, of course, devices for dodging awkward questions, but can't dodge all of them. However, the importance of Parliamentary criticism is not so much its direct effect on the Government as its effect on public opinion. For what is said in Parliament cannot go altogether unreported. The newspapers, even the *Times*, and the BBC probably do tend to play down the speeches of opposition members, but cannot do so very grossly because of the existence of Hansard, which publishes the Parliamentary debates verbatim. The effective circulation of Hansard is small (2 or 3 thousand), but so long as it is available to anyone who wants it, a lot of things that the Government would like to suppress get across to the public. This critical function of Parliament is all the more noticeable because intel- lectually this must be one of the worst Parliaments we have ever had.

Outside the Government, I do not think there can be thirty able men in the House, but that small handful have managed to give every subject from dive bombers to 18B[4] an airing. As a legislative body Parliament has become relatively unimportant, and it has even less control over the executive than over the Government. But it still functions as a kind of uncensored supplement to the radio—which, after all, is something worth preserving.

London in Wartime
Well, no more news. I am afraid I have written rather a lot already. It is a foul winter, not at all cold, but with endless fogs, almost like the famous 'London fogs' of my childhood. The blackout seems to get less and not more tolerable as the war goes on. Food is much as usual, but wine has almost vanished and whisky can only be bought by the nip, unless you have influential pals. There are air-raid alarms almost every night, but hardly any bombs. There is much talk about the rocket guns[5] with which the Germans are supposedly going to bombard London. A little while before the talk was of a four-hundred ton bomb which was to be made in the form of an enormous glider and towed across by fleets of German airplanes. Rumours of this kind have followed one another since the beginning of the war, and are always firmly believed in by numbers of people, evidently fulfilling some obscure psychological need.

Yours ever, George Orwell

4. Regulation 18b, under the Emergency Powers (Defence) Act, enabled aliens to be imprisoned on grounds that they might give aid and comfort to the enemy.
5. The rumours were to be proved true. V-1 rockets were launched on London on the night of 13–14 June 1944, a week after D-Day. The first V-2 was launched against Paris on 6 September 1944 and on London on 8 September.

Extracts from 'As I Please', 8: The BBC; On Being Negative – Woolworth's Roses

Tribune, 21 JANUARY 1944

The BBC

When the B.B.C. is attacked in the press, the attack is usually so ignorant that it is impossible to meet it. Some time ago I wrote to a well-known Irish writer,[1] now living in England, asking him to broadcast. He sent me an indignant refusal, which incidentally revealed that he did not know (*a*) that there is a Broadcasting Corporation in India, (*b*) that Indians broadcast every day from London, and (*c*) that the B.B.C. broadcasts in Oriental languages. If people don't even know that much, of what use are their criticisms of the B.B.C. likely to be? To quite a large extent the B.B.C. is blamed for its virtues while its real faults are ignored. Everyone complains, for instance, about the Kensingtonian accent of B.B.C. news-readers, which has been carefully selected *not* in order to cause annoyance in England, but because it is a 'neutral' accent which will be intelligible wherever English is spoken. Yet how many people are aware that millions of public money are squandered in broadcasting to countries where there is virtually no audience?[2]

Here is a little catechism for amateur radio critics.

You say you don't like the present programmes. Have you a clear idea of what kind of programmes you *would* like? If so, what steps have you taken towards securing them?

In your opinion, are the B.B.C. news bulletins truthful? Are they more or less truthful than those of other belligerent countries? Have you checked this by comparison?

Have you any ideas about the possibilities of the radio play, the short story, the feature, the discussion? If so, have you bothered to find out which of your ideas are technically feasible?

Do you think the B.B.C. would benefit by competition? Give your opinion of commercial broadcasting.

---

1. Unidentified. It was unlikely to be Bernard Shaw, who allowed extracts of his work to be broadcast, or O'Casey, who did a broadcast for Orwell on 5 September 1943 (though no correspondence with him survives from Orwell's time at the BBC).
2. Orwell probably has the BBC service to India in mind. There was one radio to 3,875 people in India compared with 1 to 5.36 in England then, and broadcasts to India had to be made in several languages.

Who controls the B.B.C.? Who pays for it? Who directs its policy? How does the censorship work?

What do you know of B.B.C. propaganda to foreign countries, hostile, friendly or neutral? How much does it cost? Is it effective? How would it compare with German propaganda? Add some notes on radio propaganda in general.

I could extend this considerably, but if even a hundred thousand people in England could give definite answers to the above questions it would be a big step forward.

On Being Negative – Woolworth's Roses

A correspondent reproaches me with being 'negative' and 'always attacking things.' The fact is that we live in a time when causes for rejoicing are not numerous. But I like praising things, when there is anything to praise, and I would like here to write a few lines—they have to be retrospective, unfortunately—in praise of the Woolworth's Rose.

In the good days when nothing in Woolworth's cost over sixpence, one of their best lines was their rose bushes. They were always very young plants, but they came into bloom in their second year, and I don't think I ever had one die on me. Their chief interest was that they were never, or very seldom, what they claimed to be on their labels. One that I bought for a Dorothy Perkins turned out to be a beautiful little white rose with a yellow heart, one of the finest ramblers I have ever seen. A polyantha rose labelled yellow turned out to be deep red. Another, bought for an Albertine, was like an Albertine, but more double, and gave astonishing masses of blossom. These roses had all the interest of a surprise packet, and there was always the chance that you might happen upon a new variety which you would have the right to name John Smithii or something of that kind.

Last summer I passed the cottage where I used to live before the war.[3] The little white rose, no bigger than a boy's catapult when I put it in, had grown into a huge vigorous bush, the Albertine or near-Albertine was smothering half the fence in a cloud of pink blossom. I had planted both of those in 1936. And I thought, 'All that for sixpence!' I do not know how long a rose bush lives; I suppose ten years might be an average life. And

3. Orwell's Albertine (or 'near-Albertine') was still flourishing at The Stores, Wallington, Hertfordshire, some fifty years later; see Pam Dajda, 'Careful restoration of Orwell's "awful" cottage,' *Cambridge Weekly News*, 24 November 1988.

throughout that time a rambler will be in full bloom for a month or six weeks each year, while a bush rose will be blooming, on and off, for at least four months. All that for sixpence—the price, before the war, of ten Players or a pint and a half of mild, or a week's subscription to the *Daily Mail*, or about twenty minutes of twice-breathed air in the movies!

Orwell's delight in sixpenny roses from Woolworth's brought forth this rebuke, printed on 4 February under the heading 'Sentimentality':

What a pity that the desultory paragraphs of 'As I Please' are so uneven in character! After some interesting and instructive remarks on the nature of amateur radio-criticism it would seem that the remaining printing space had been allocated to Godfrey Winn rather than to George Orwell. It is unfortunate that *Tribune*, which has done much, consciously or unconsciously, to nourish a high standard of literary taste among its readers, should publish such a passage, instinct as it is, with bourgeois nostalgia, and in which sentiment gives place to sickly sentimentality. Obviously the meanest rose that blows has hardly 'thoughts that lie too deep for tears' for Orwell, who addresses himself to the readers of best sellers and sentimentalised films, rather than to those who appreciate and enjoy good writing. Let him remember that the former type of reading public are singularly few in number amongst regular readers of *Tribune*.

Eileen E. Purber

Orwell replied:

I am interested to learn that being fond of flowers is a sign of 'bourgeois nostalgia.' If so we are all bourgeois. One of the outstanding characteristics of the working class of this country is their love of flowers, which not only accounts for the window boxes where nasturtiums try to flourish in the smokiest parts of London, but leads the agricultural labourer to spend his spare hours of daylight in cultivating his garden, sometimes even growing roses to the exclusion of vegetables. Or is 'bourgeois' meant to apply to the extravagance of spending sixpence on a rosebush—this in a country where few working men spend less than a shilling a day on cigarettes?

Extract from 'As I Please', 9: Ezra Pound

Tribune, 28 JANUARY 1944

A correspondent has sent us a letter in defence of Ezra Pound,[1] the American poet who transferred his allegiance to Mussolini some years before the war and has been a lively propagandist on the Rome radio. The substance of his claim is that (*a*) Pound did not sell himself simply for money, and (*b*) that when you get hold of a true poet you can afford to ignore his political opinions.

Now, of course, Pound did not sell himself solely for money. No writer ever does that. Anyone who wanted money before all else would choose some more paying profession. But I think it probable that Pound did sell himself partly for prestige, flattery and a professorship. He had a most venomous hatred for both Britain and the U.S.A., where he felt that his talents had not been fully appreciated, and obviously believed that there was a conspiracy against him throughout the English-speaking countries. Then there were several ignominious episodes in which Pound's phoney erudition was shown up, and which he no doubt found it hard to forgive. By the mid-thirties Pound was singing the praises of 'the Boss' (Mussolini) in a number of English papers, including Mosley's quarterly, *British Union* (to which Vidkun Quisling[2] was also a contributor). At the time of the Abyssinian war Pound was vociferously anti-Abyssinian. In 1938 or there-abouts the Italians gave him a chair at one of their universities, and some time after war broke out he took Italian citizenship.

Whether a poet, as such, is to be forgiven his political opinions is a different question. Obviously one mustn't say 'X agrees with me: therefore he is a good writer,' and for the last ten years honest literary criticism has largely consisted in combating this outlook. Personally I admire several writers (Céline, for instance) who have gone over to the Fascists, and many others whose political outlook I strongly object to. But one has the right to expect ordinary decency even of a poet. I never listened to Pound's broadcasts, but I often read them in the B.B.C. Monitoring Report, and

1. Paul Potts (1911–90) (author of *Dante Called You Beatrice*, which includes a moving tribute to Orwell, 'Don Quixote on a Bicycle') wrote in defence of Ezra Pound, who was then facing trial for collaboration with the enemy, in *Tribune*, 28 January 1944.
2. Vidkun Quisling (1887–1945), Norwegian Fascist who led the Norwegian puppet government during the German occupation of Norway. He was executed for treason; his name was widely applied to collaborators.

they were intellectually and morally disgusting. Anti-Semitism, for instance, is simply not the doctrine of a grown-up person. People who go in for that kind of thing must take the consequences. But I do agree with our correspondent in hoping that the American authorities do not catch Pound and shoot him, as they have threatened to do. It would establish his reputation so thoroughly that it might be a hundred years before anyone could determine dispassionately whether Pound's much-debated poems are any good or not.

Extract from 'As I Please', 11: Anti-Semitism

Tribune, 11 FEBRUARY 1944

There are two journalistic activities that will always bring you a come-back. One is to attack the Catholics and the other is to defend the Jews. Recently I happened to review some books dealing with the persecution of the Jews in medieval and modern Europe.[1] The review brought me the usual wad of anti-Semitic letters, which left me thinking for the thousandth time that this problem is being evaded even by the people whom it concerns most directly.

The disquieting thing about these letters is that they do not all come from lunatics. I don't greatly mind the person who believes in the Protocols of the Elders of Zion, nor even the discharged army officer who has been shabbily treated by the Government and is infuriated by seeing 'aliens' given all the best jobs. But in addition to these types there is the small business or professional man who is firmly convinced that the Jews bring all their troubles upon themselves by underhand business methods and complete lack of public spirit. These people write reasonable, well-balanced letters, disclaim any belief in racialism, and back up everything they say with copious instances. They admit the existence of 'good Jews,' and usually declare (Hitler says just the same in *Mein Kampf*) that they did not start out with any anti-Jewish feeling but have been forced into it simply by observing how Jews behave.

The weakness of the Left-wing attitude towards anti-Semitism is to approach it from a rationalistic angle. Obviously the charges made against Jews are not true. They cannot be true, partly because they cancel out, partly because no one people could have such a monopoly of wickedness. But simply by pointing this out one gets no further. The official Left-wing view of anti-Semitism is that it is something 'got up' by the ruling classes in order to divert attention away from the real evils of society. The Jews, in fact, are scapegoats. This is no doubt correct, but it is quite useless as an argument. One does not dispose of a belief by showing that it is irra-tional. Nor is it any use, in my experience, to talk about the persecution of the Jews in Germany. If a man has the slightest disposition towards anti-Semitism, such things bounce off his consciousness like peas off a

1. Joshua Trachtenberg's *The Devil and the Jews* and Edmond Fleg's *Why I Am Jew, The Observer,* 30 January 1944.

steel helmet. The best argument of all, if rational arguments were ever of any use, would be to point out that the alleged crimes of the Jews are only possible because we live in a society which rewards crime. If all Jews are crooks, let us deal with them by so arranging our economic system that crooks cannot prosper. But what good is it to say that kind of thing to the man who believes as an article of faith that Jews dominate the Black Market, push their way to the front of queues and dodge military service?

We could do with a detailed enquiry into the causes of anti-Semitism, and it ought not to be vitiated in advance by the assumption that those causes are wholly economic. However true the 'scapegoat' theory may be in general terms, it does not explain why the Jews rather than some [other] minority group are picked on, nor does it make clear what they are a scapegoat *for*. A thing like the Dreyfus Case, for instance, is not easily translated into economic terms. So far as Britain is concerned, the important things to find out are just what charges are made against the Jews, whether anti-Semitism is really on the increase (it may actually have decreased over the past thirty years), and to what extent it is aggravated by the influx of refugees since about 1938.

One not only ought not to assume that the causes of anti-Semitism are economic in a crude, direct way (unemployment, business jealousy, etc.), one also ought not to assume that 'sensible' people are immune to it. It flourishes especially among literary men, for instance. Without even getting up from this table to consult a book I can think of passages in Villon, Shakespeare, Smollett, Thackeray, H. G. Wells, Aldous Huxley, T. S. Eliot and many another which would be called anti-Semitic if they had been written since Hitler came to power. Both Belloc and Chesterton flirted, or something more than flirted, with anti-Semitism, and other writers whom it is possible to respect have swallowed it more or less in its Nazi form. Clearly the neurosis lies very deep, and just what it is that people hate when they say that they hate a non-existent entity called 'the Jews' is still uncertain. And it is partly the fear of finding out how wide-spread anti-Semitism is that prevents it from being seriously investigated.

Extract from 'As I Please', 12: The Equalising Effect of Clothes Rationing

Tribune, 18 FEBRUARY 1944

A correspondent reproaches me for wanting to see clothes rationing continue until we are all equally shabby; though she adds that clothes rationing hasn't, in fact, had an equalising effect. I will quote an extract from her letter:—

'I work in a very exclusive shop just off Bond Street. . . . When I, shivering in my 25/- utility frock, serve these elegant creatures in sables, fur caps and fur-lined boots, who regard me uncomprehendingly when I say 'Good morning, it's very cold to-day, madam' (very stupid of me—after all, how should they know?), I do not wish to see them deprived of their lovely and warm attire, but rather that such attire was available to me, and for all . . . We should aim not at reducing the present highest standard of living, but at raising any and everything less than the highest. It is a malicious and mean-spirited attitude that wishes to drag Etonians and Harrovians from their fortunate positions of eminence and force them down the mines. Rather, in the present reshuffling of society we should seek to make these places accessible to all.'

I answer, first of all, that although clothes rationing obviously bears hardest on those who don't possess large stocks of clothes already, it *has* had a certain equalising effect, because it has made people uneasy about appearing too smart. Certain garments, such as men's evening dress, have practically disappeared; also it is now considered permissible to wear almost any clothes for almost any job. But my original point was that if clothes rationing goes on long enough even wealthy people will have worn out their extra stocks of clothes, and we shall all be somewhere near equal.

But is it not the case that we ought always to aim at levelling 'up' and not levelling 'down'? I answer that in some cases you can't level 'up.' You can't give everyone a Rolls Royce car. You can't even give everyone a fur coat, especially in war time. As to the statement that everyone ought to go to Eton or Harrow, it is meaningless. The whole value of those places, from the point of view of the people who go there, is their exclusiveness. And since certain luxuries—high-powered cars, for instance, fur coats, yachts, country houses and what-not—obviously can't be distributed to everybody, then it is better that nobody should have them. The rich lose almost as much by their wealth as the poor lose by their poverty. Doesn't my correspondent bring that out when she speaks of those ignorant rich women who cannot even imagine what a cold morning means to a person without an overcoat?

Extracts from 'As I Please', 14: Life after Death; Decay in Christian Belief

Tribune, 3 MARCH 1944

Life After Death

I do not know whether, officially, there has been any alteration in Christian doctrine. Father Knox and my correspondent would seem to be in disagreement about this. But what I do know is that belief in survival after death—the individual survival of John Smith, still conscious of himself as John Smith—is enormously less widespread than it was. Even among professing Christians it is probably decaying; other people, as a rule, don't even entertain the possibility that it might be true. But our forefathers, so far as we know, did believe in it. Unless all that they wrote about it was intended to mislead us, they believed it in an exceedingly literal, concrete way. Life on earth, as they saw it, was simply a short period of preparation for an infinitely more important life beyond the grave. But that notion has disappeared, or is disappearing, and the consequences have not really been faced.

Decay in Christian Belief

Western civilisation, unlike some Oriental civilisations, was founded partly on the belief in individual immortality. If one looks at the Christian religion from the outside, this belief appears far more important than the belief in God. The Western conception of good and evil is very difficult to separate from it. There is little doubt that the modern cult of power-worship is bound up with the modern man's feeling that life here and now is the only life there is. If death ends everything, it becomes much harder to believe that you can be in the right even if you are defeated. Statesmen, nations, theories, causes are judged almost inevitably by the test of material success. Supposing that one can separate the two phenomena, I would say that the decay of the belief in personal immortality has been as important as the rise of machine civilisation. Machine civilisation has terrible possibilities, as you probably reflected the other night when the ack-ack guns started up: but the other thing has terrible possibilities too, and it cannot be said that the Socialist movement has given much thought to them.

I do not want the belief in life after death to return, and in any case it is not likely to return. What I do point out is that its disappearance has left a big hole, and that we ought to take notice of that fact. Reared for thousands of years on the notion that the individual survives, man has got to make a considerable psychological effort to get used to the notion that the individual perishes. He is not likely to salvage civilisation unless he can evolve a system of good and evil which is independent of heaven and hell. Marxism, indeed, does supply this, but it has never really been popularised. Most Socialists are content to point out that once Socialism has been established we shall be happier in a material sense, and to assume that all problems lapse when one's belly is full. But the truth is the opposite: when one's belly is empty, one's only problem is an empty belly. It is when we have got away from drudgery and exploitation that we shall really start wondering about man's destiny and the reason for his existence. One cannot have any worthwhile picture of the future unless one realises how much we have lost by the decay of Christianity. Few Socialists seem to be aware of this. And the Catholic intellectuals who cling to the letter of the Creeds while reading into them meanings they were never meant to have, and who snigger at anyone simple enough to suppose that the Fathers of the Church meant what they said, are simply raising smokescreens to conceal their own disbelief from themselves.

Extract from 'As I Please', 15: Dickens and Country Life

Tribune, 10 MARCH 1944

One of the big gaps in Dickens is that he writes nothing, even in a burlesque spirit, about country life. Of agriculture he does not even pretend to know anything. There are some farcical descriptions of shooting in the *Pickwick Papers*, but Dickens, as a middle-class radical, would be incapable of describing such amusements sympathetically. He sees field-sports as primarily an exercise in snobbishness, which they already were in the England of that date. The enclosures, industrialism, the vast differentiation of wealth, and the cult of the pheasant and the red deer, had all combined to drive the mass of the English people off the land and make the hunting instinct, which is probably almost universal in human beings, seem merely a fetish of the aristocracy. Perhaps the best thing in *War and Peace* is the description of the wolf hunt. In the end it is the peasant's dog that outstrips those of the nobles and gets the wolf; and afterwards Natasha finds it quite natural to dance in the peasant's hut.

To see such scenes in England you would have had to go back a hundred or two hundred years, to a time when difference in status did not mean any very great difference in habits. Dickens's England was already dominated by the 'Trespassers will be Prosecuted' board. When one thinks of the accepted Left Wing attitude towards hunting, shooting and the like, it is queer to reflect that Lenin, Stalin and Trotsky were all of them keen sportsmen in their day. But then they belonged to a large empty country where there was no necessary connection between sport and snobbishness, and the divorce between country and town was never complete. The society which almost any modern novelist has as his material is very much meaner, less comely and less carefree than Tolstoy's, and to grasp this has been one of the signs of talent.[1] Joyce would have been falsifying the facts if he had made the people in *Dubliners* less disgusting than they

---

1. In a letter published by *Tribune* on 24 March 1944, N. and J. A. Turnbull considered that Orwell gave a 'very misleading picture of Tolstoy', particularly with regard to 'hunting and similar barbarities which Mr. Orwell seems to regard as desirable'. They also took exception to his statement that 'the hunting instinct is probably universal in human beings'. There was, they wrote, a connection between 'such savage survivals and the bloodstained condition of the earth today—a connection which Tolstoy did not fail to appreciate'.

are. But the natural advantage lay with Tolstoy: for, other things being equal, who would not rather write about Peter and Natasha than about furtive seductions in boarding-houses or drunken Catholic business-men celebrating a 'retreat'?

Letter to Victor Gollancz

unpublished, 19 MARCH 1944

Dear Mr Gollancz,

I have just finished a book [*Animal Farm*] and the typing will be completed in a few days. You have the first refusal of my fiction books, and I think this comes under the heading of fiction. It is a little fairy story, about 30,000 words, with a political meaning. But I must tell you that it is—I think—completely unacceptable politically from your point of view (it is anti-Stalin). I don't know whether in that case you will want to see it. If you do, of course I will send it along, but the point is that I am not anxious, naturally, for the MS to be hanging about too long. If you think that you would like to have a look at it, in spite of its not being politically O.K., could you let either me or my agent (Christy & Moore) know? Moore will have the MS. Otherwise, could you let me know that you *don't* want to see it, so that I can take it elsewhere without wasting time?

Yours sincerely, [Signed] Eric Blair

'As I Please', 18: On Revenge Killings

Tribune, 31 MARCH 1944

The other day I attended a Press conference at which a newly arrived Frenchman, who was described as an 'eminent jurist'—he could not give his name or other specifications because of his family in France—set forth the French point of view on the recent execution of Pucheu.[1] I was surprised to note that he was distinctly on the defensive, and seemed to think that the shooting of Pucheu was a deed that would want a good deal of justification in British and American eyes. His main point was that Pucheu was not shot for political reasons, but for the ordinary crime of 'collaborating with the enemy,' which has always been punishable by death under French law.

An American correspondent asked the question: 'Would collaborating with the enemy be equally a crime in the case of some petty official—an inspector of police, for example?' 'Absolutely the same,' answered the Frenchman. As he had just come from France he was presumably voicing French opinion, but one can assume that in practice only the most active collaborators will be put to death. Any really big-scale massacre, if it really happened, would be quite largely the punishment of the guilty by the guilty. For there is much evidence that large sections of the French population were more or less pro-German in 1940 and only changed their minds when they found out what the Germans were like.

I do not want people like Pucheu to escape, but a few very obscure quislings, including one or two Arabs, have been shot as well, and this whole business of taking vengeance on traitors and captured enemies raises questions which are strategic as well as moral. The point is that if we shoot too many of the small rats now we may have no stomach for dealing with the big ones when the time comes. It is difficult to believe that the Fascist regimes can be thoroughly crushed without the killing of the responsible individuals, to the number of some hundreds or even thousands in each country. But it could well happen that all the truly guilty people will escape in the end, simply because public opinion has

---

1. Pierre Pucheu, formerly Vichy Minister of the Interior, fled to North Africa and was shot on the orders of General de Gaulle. Further trials followed; General Blanc was condemned to death and Colonel Magnin sentenced to solitary confinement for twenty years.

been sickened beforehand by hypocritical trials and cold-blooded executions.

In effect this was what happened in the last war. Who that was alive in those years does not remember the maniacal hatred of the Kaiser that was fostered in this country? Like Hitler in this war, he was supposed to be the cause of all our ills. No one doubted that he would be executed as soon as caught and the only question was what method would be adopted. Magazine articles were written in which the rival merits of boiling in oil, drawing and quartering and breaking on the wheel were carefully examined. The Royal Academy exhibitions were full of allegorical pictures of incredible vulgarity, showing the Kaiser being thrown into Hell. And what came of it in the end? The Kaiser retired to Holland and (though he had been 'dying of cancer' in 1915) lived another twenty-two years, one of the richest men in Europe.

So also with all the other 'war criminals.' After all the threats and promises that had been made, no war criminals were tried: to be exact, a dozen people or so were put on trial, given sentences of imprisonment and soon released. And though, of course, the failure to crush the German military caste was due to the conscious policy of the Allied leaders, who were terrified of revolution in Germany, the revulsion of feeling in ordinary people helped to make it possible. They did not want revenge when it was in their power. The Belgian atrocities, Miss Cavell,[2] the U-boat captains who had sunk passenger ships without warning and machine-gunned the survivors—somehow it was all forgotten. Ten million innocent men had been killed and no one wanted to follow it up by killing a few thousand guilty ones.

Whether we do or don't shoot the Fascists and quislings who happen to fall into our hands is probably not very important in itself. What is important is that revenge and 'punishment' should have no part in our policy or even in our day-dreams. Up to date, one of the mitigating features of this war is that in this country there has been very little hatred. There has been none of the nonsensical racialism that there was last time —no pretence that all Germans have faces like pigs, for instance. Even the word 'Hun' has not really popularised itself. The Germans in this

---

2. Nurse Edith Cavell (1865–1915), executed by the Germans in Brussels for assisting Allied soldiers to escape from occupied Belgium. A Belgian, Philippe Baucq, who had acted as a guide, was also shot. Her execution was regarded as particularly shameful. A statue to her memory, inscribed with her last words, 'Patriotism is not enough', stands in St Martin's Place, London, WC2.

country, mostly refugees, have not been well treated, but they have not been meanly persecuted as they were last time. In the last war it would have been very unsafe, for instance, to speak German in a London street. Wretched little German bakers and hairdressers had their shops sacked by the mob. German music fell out of favour, even the breed of dachshunds almost disappeared because no one wanted to have a 'German dog.' And the weak British attitude in the early period of German rearmament had a direct connection with those follies of the war years.

Hatred is an impossible basis for policy, and curiously enough it can lead to over-softness as well as to over-toughness. In the war of 1914–18 the British people were whipped up into a hideous frenzy of hatred, they were fed on preposterous lies about crucified Belgian babies and German factories where corpses were made into margarine and then as soon as the war stopped they suffered the natural revulsion, which was all the stronger because the troops came home, as British troops usually do, with a warm admiration for the enemy. The result was an exaggerated pro-German reaction which set in about 1920 and lasted till Hitler was well in the saddle. Throughout those years all 'enlightened' opinion (see any number of the Daily Herald before 1929, for instance) held it as an article of faith that Germany bore no responsibility for the war. Treitschke,[3] Bernhardi,[4] the Pan-Germans, the 'Nordic' myth, the open boasts about 'Der Tag'[5] which the Germans had been making from 1900 onwards—all this went for nothing. The Versailles Treaty was the greatest infamy the

3. Heinrich Gotthard von Treitschke (1834–1896; spelt 'Tretschke' in 'As I Please'), German historian and writer on political science, advocated German power politics and believed in the total authority of the state unfettered by a parliament (though he was a member of the Reichstag, 1871–84). He was a prolific writer, though he did not live to complete his major work, a history of Germany.

4. Friedrich von Bernhardi (1849–1930), General of Cavalry from 1901. He wrote several books on army organisation, tactics, and the deployment of cavalry. Orwell may have come across his writing through translations of his work or The New Bernhardi, 'World Power or Downfall', which was published in English in 1915. He regarded war as a biological necessity and is credited with the expression 'Might is Right'.

5. 'Der Tag' is in quotation marks because, in all probability, it refers to the use of these words as an after-dinner toast to the day when Germany would achieve what Bernhardi called 'Weltmacht' – 'World Power' in his own translation (for, as he wrote, 'I never thought of world dominion by Germany,' The New Bernhardi, 41). James Barrie (creator of Peter Pan) wrote a propaganda play called Der Tag in 1914. Peter Buitenhuis describes it as almost as great a fiasco as Barrie's recent lecture tour of the United States (The Great War of Words, 111). It opened at the London Coliseum, 21 December 1914, and was published in New York in 1914 and 1919.

world had ever seen: few people had even heard of Brest-Litovsk.[6] All this was the price of that four years' orgy of lying and hatred.

Anyone who tried to awaken public opinion during the years of Fascist aggression from 1933 onwards knows what the after-effects of that hate-propaganda were like. 'Atrocities'[7] had come to be looked on as synonymous with 'lies.' But the stories about the German concentration camps were atrocity stories: therefore they were lies—so reasoned the average man. The left-wingers who tried to make the public see that Fascism was an unspeakable horror were fighting against their own propaganda of the past fifteen years.

That is why—though I would not save creatures like Pucheu even if I could—I am not happy when I see trials of 'war criminals,' especially when they are very petty criminals and when witnesses are allowed to make inflammatory political speeches. Still less am I happy to see the Left associating itself with schemes to partition Germany, enrol millions of Germans in forced labour gangs and impose reparations which will make the Versailles reparations look like a bus fare. All these vindictive daydreams, like those of 1914–18, will simply make it harder to have a realistic post-war policy. If you think *now* in terms of 'making Germany pay,' you will quite likely find yourself praising Hitler in 1950. Results are what matter, and one of the results we want from this war is to be quite sure that Germany will not make war again. Whether this is best achieved by ruthlessness or generosity I am not certain: but I am quite certain that either of these will be more difficult if we allow ourselves to be influenced by hatred.

6. Orwell points to the harsh treatment the Germans meted out to Russia in the Treaty of Brest-Litovsk, March 1918. The Soviets were forced to recognise the independence of Poland, Estonia, Latvia, Lithuania, Georgia, and the Ukraine; allow German occupation of Belorussia; cede territories to Turkey (Germany's ally); and were required to pay a heavy indemnity. Trotsky was the chief Soviet negotiator. The treaty was nullified with the cessation of hostilities on the Western Front. Much fuller details of the personalities and issues raised in notes 3, 4, and 6 will be found in CW, XVI, 139–40.
7. It may be no more than coincidence, but Orwell's placing of 'Atrocities' within quotation marks, as he usually did for titles of books, could be significant. What he says – that most atrocity stories (and many of the worst ones, such as shooting babies from cannon) were lies – was well-enough understood when he wrote this article. However, on the back cover of The New Bernhardi (see n. 4 on page 272) were advertisements for several books, ranging from Is the Kaiser Insane? to Our Regiments and Their Glorious Deeds; the sixth and last was Official Book of the German Atrocities, told by Victims and Eye-Witnesses, being 'The complete verbatim Report of the Belgian, French, and Russian Commissions of Enquiry. Published by Authority.'

Extract from 'As I Please', 21: Why Borrow Foreign Words?

Tribune, 21 APRIL 1944

One mystery about the English language is why, with the biggest vocabulary in existence, it has to be constantly borrowing foreign words and phrases. Where is the sense, for instance, of saying *cul de sac* when you mean blind alley? Other totally unnecessary French phrases are *joie de vivre, amour propre, reculer pour mieux sauter, raison d'être, vis-à-vis, tête-à-tête, au pied de la lettre, esprit de corps*. There are dozens more of them. Other needless borrowings come from Latin (though there is a case for 'i.e.' and 'e.g.,' which are useful abbreviations), and since the war we have been much infested by German words, *Gleichschaltung, Lebensraum, Weltanschauung, Wehrmacht, Panzerdivisionen* and others being flung about with great freedom. In nearly every case an English equivalent already exists or could easily be improvised. There is also a tendency to take over American slang phrases without understanding their meaning. For example, the expression 'barking up the wrong tree' is fairly widely used, but inquiry shows that most people don't know its origin nor exactly what it means.

Sometimes it is necessary to take over a foreign word, but in that case we should anglicise its pronunciation, as our ancestors used to do. If we really need the word 'café' (we got on well enough with 'coffee house' for two hundred years), it should either be spelled 'caffay' or pronounced 'cayfe.' 'Garage' should be pronounced 'garridge.' For what point is there in littering our speech with fragments of foreign pronunciation, very tiresome to anyone who does not happen to have learned that particular language?

And why is it that most of us never use a word of English origin if we can find a manufactured Greek one? One sees a good example of this in the rapid disappearance of English flower names. What until twenty years ago was universally called a snapdragon is now called an antirrhinum, a word no one can spell without consulting a dictionary. Forget-me-nots are coming more and more to be called myosotis. Many other names, Red Hot Poker, Mind Your Own Business, Love Lies Bleeding, London Pride, are disappearing in favour of colourless Greek names out of botany textbooks. I had better not continue too long on this subject, because last time I mentioned flowers in this column an indignant lady wrote in to say that flowers are bourgeois.

But I don't think it a good augury for the future of the English language that 'marigold' should be dropped in favour of 'calendula,' while the pleasant little Cheddar Pink loses its name and becomes merely Dianthus Cæsius.[1]

---

1. Orwell clearly had an affection for the Cheddar Pink. They featured in his garden at Barnhill, Jura.

Extract from 'As I Please', 23: I.A. Richards's *Practical Criticism*

Tribune, 5 MAY 1944

For anyone who wants a good laugh I recommend a book which was published about a dozen years ago, but which I only recently succeeded in getting hold of. This is I. A. Richards's *Practical Criticism*.

Although mostly concerned with the general principles of literary criticism, it also describes an experiment that Mr. Richards made with, or one should perhaps say *on*, his English students at Cambridge. Various volunteers, not actually students but presumably interested in English literature, also took part. Thirteen poems were presented to them, and they were asked to criticise them. The authorship of the poems was not revealed, and none of them was well enough known to be recognised at sight by the average reader. You are getting, therefore, specimens of literary criticism not complicated by snobbishness of the ordinary kind.

One ought not to be too superior, and there is no need to be, because the book is so arranged that you can try the experiment on yourself. The poems, unsigned, are all together at the end, and the authors' names are on a fold-over page which you need not look at till afterwards. I will say at once that I only spotted the authorship of two, one of which I knew already, and though I could date most of the others within a few decades, I made two bad bloomers, in one case attributing to Shelley a poem written in the nineteen-twenties. But still, some of the comments recorded by Dr. Richards are startling. They go to show that many people who would describe themselves as lovers of poetry have no more notion of distinguishing between a good poem and a bad one than a dog has of arithmetic.

For example, a piece of completely spurious bombast by Alfred Noyes gets quite a lot of praise. One critic compares it to Keats. A sentimental ballad from *Rough Rhymes of a Padre*, by 'Woodbine Willie,'[1] also gets quite a good Press. On the other hand, a magnificent sonnet by John Donne gets a distinctly chilly reception. Dr. Richards records only three

1. G. A. Studdert Kennedy (1883–1929), described in *G. A. Studdert Kennedy by his Friends* (1929) as 'an Army Chaplain of unconventional manners and speech', was 'an effective platform speaker', and also a model parish priest in Worcester. His nickname came from his generous distribution of a particular brand of cigarettes, Woodbines, to soldiers in the front line after becoming an army chaplain in December 1915. His *Rough Rhymes of a Padre* went into several editions (the sixth in 1918).

favourable criticisms and about a dozen cold or hostile ones. One writer says contemptuously that the poem 'would make a good hymn,' while another remarks, 'I can find no other reaction except disgust.' Donne was at that time at the top of his reputation and no doubt most of the people taking part in this experiment would have fallen on their faces at his name. D. H. Lawrence's poem *The Piano* gets many sneers, though it is praised by a minority. So also with a short poem by Gerard Manley Hopkins. 'The worst poem I have ever read,' declares one writer, while another's criticism is simply 'Pish-posh!'

However, before blaming these youthful students for their bad judgment, let it be remembered that when some time ago somebody published a not very convincing fake of an eighteenth-century diary, the aged critic, Sir Edmund Gosse,[2] librarian of the House of Lords, fell for it immediately. And there was also the case of the Parisian art critics of I forget which 'school,' who went into rhapsodies over a picture which was afterwards discovered to have been painted by a donkey with a paintbrush tied to its tail.[3]

2. Sir Edmund Gosse (1849–1928), literary scholar with a particular knowledge of Scandinavian literature, did much to promote the work of Ibsen in England. He also wrote prolifically on English literature and published several volumes of poetry. The work for which he is still remembered is *Father and Son*, published anonymously in 1907, which records his relations with his father, an eminent zoologist and Plymouth Brother.

3. In March 1910 an art critic, Roland Dorgelès arranged with two friends to borrow a donkey called Aliboron – Lola to his friends – from a local innkeeper. He tied a paintbrush to its tail and dipped the brush in a can of paint. He then had Lola walk over a prepared canvas several times. The resulting 'masterpiece', *Sunset over the Adriatic* (54 x 80 cm), was exhibited at the Salon des Indépendents and the canvas can still be seen at the Espace culturel Paul Bédu, Milly-la-Forêt.

Extract from 'As I Please', 26: *The Matrimonial Post*

Tribune, 26 MAY 1944

The May number of the *Matrimonial Post and Fashionable Marriage Advertiser* contains advertisements from 191 men seeking brides and over 200 women seeking husbands. Advertisements of this type have been running in a whole series of magazines since the 'sixties or earlier, and they are nearly always very much alike. For example:

'Bachelor, age 25, height 6 ft. 1 in., slim, fond of horticulture, animals, children, cinema, etc., would like to meet lady, age 27 to 35, with love of flowers, nature, children, must be tall, medium build, Church of England.' The general run of them are just like that, though occasionally a more unusual note is struck. For instance:

'I'm 29, single, 5 ft. 10 in., English, large build, kind, quiet, varied intellectual interests, firm moral background (registered unconditionally as absolute C.O.), progressive, creative, literary inclinations. A dealer in rare stamps, income variable but quite adequate. Strong swimmer, cyclist, slight stammer occasionally. Looking for the following rarity, amiable, adaptable, educated girl, easy on eye and ear, under 30, Secretary type or similar, mentally adventurous, immune to mercenary and social incentives, bright sense of genuine humour, a reliable working partner. Capital unimportant, character vital.'

The thing that is and always has been striking in these advertisements is that nearly all the applicants are remarkably eligible. It is not only that most of them are broad-minded, intelligent, home-loving, musical, loyal, sincere and affectionate, with a keen sense of humour and, in the case of women, a good figure; in the majority of cases they are financially O.K. as well. When you consider how fatally easy it is to get married, you would not imagine that a 36-year-old bachelor, 'dark hair, fair complexion, slim build, height 6 ft., well-educated and of considerate, jolly and intelligent disposition, income £1,000 per annum and capital,' would need to find himself a bride through the columns of a newspaper. And ditto with 'Adventurous young woman, Left-wing opinions, modern outlook' with 'fairly full but shapely figure, medium colour curly hair, grey-blue eyes, fair skin, natural colouring, health exceptionally good, interested in music, art, literature, cinema, theatre, fond of walking, cycling, tennis, skating and rowing.' Why does such a paragon have to advertise?

It should be noted that the *Matrimonial Post* is entirely above-board and checks up carefully on its advertisers.

What these things really demonstrate is the atrocious loneliness of people living in big towns. People meet for work and then scatter to widely separated homes. Anywhere in inner London it is probably exceptional to know even the names of the people who live next door.

Years ago I lodged for a while in the Portobello Road.[1] This is hardly a fashionable quarter, but the landlady had been lady's maid to some woman of title and had a good opinion of herself. One day something went wrong with the front door and my landlady, her husband and myself were all locked out of the house. It was evident that we should have to get in by an upper window, and as there was a jobbing builder next door I suggested borrowing a ladder from him. My landlady looked somewhat uncomfortable.

'I wouldn't like to do that,' she said finally. 'You see we don't know him. We've been here fourteen years, and we've always taken care not to know the people on either side of us. It *wouldn't do*, not in a neighbour-hood like this. If you once begin talking to them they get familiar, you see.'

So we had to borrow a ladder from a relative of her husband's, and carry it nearly a mile with great labour and discomfort.

---

1. In 1927 Orwell went to live at 22 Portobello Road, next door to Ruth Pitter, who found him these lodgings; his landlady was Mrs Edwin Craig. The builder lived at number 20. The three houses are illustrated in Thompson, p. 23.

Extract from 'As I Please', 28: On the Perversion of Book Reviewing

Tribune, 11 JUNE 1944

Arthur Koestler's recent article in *Tribune*[1] set me wondering whether the book racket will start up again in its old vigour after the war, when paper is plentiful and there are other things to spend your money on.

Publishers have got to live, like anyone else, and you cannot blame them for advertising their wares, but the truly shameful feature of literary life before the war was the blurring of the distinction between advertisement and criticism. A number of the so-called reviewers, and especially the best known ones, were simply blurb writers. The 'screaming' advertisement started some time in the nineteen-twenties, and as the competition to take up as much space and use as many superlatives as possible became fiercer, publishers' advertisements grew to be an important source of revenue to a number of papers. The literary pages of several well-known papers were practically owned by a handful of publishers, who had their quislings planted in all the important jobs. These wretches churned forth their praise—'masterpiece,' 'brilliant,' 'unforgettable' and so forth—like so many mechanical pianos. A book coming from the right publishers could be absolutely certain not only of favourable reviews, but of being placed on the 'recommended' list which industrious book-borrowers would cut out and take to the library the next day.

If you published books at several different houses you soon learned how strong the pressure of advertisement was. A book coming from a big publisher, who habitually spent large sums on advertisement, might get fifty or seventy-five reviews: a book from a small publisher might get only twenty. I knew of one case where a theological publisher, for some reason, took it into his head to publish a novel. He spent a great deal of money on advertising it. It got exactly four reviews in the whole of England, and the only full-length one was in a motoring paper, which seized the opportunity to point out that the part of the country described

---

1. In *Tribune*, 28 April 1944, Arthur Koestler (1905–83; novelist and friend of Orwell) had written an article in the form of a letter to a young corporal who had written to ask for advice as to which book reviewers could be taken as reliable guides. Koestler pointed out the dismal standards of criticism prevailing in most of the press.

in the novel would be a good place for a motoring tour. This man was not in the racket, his advertisements were not likely to become a regular source of revenue to the literary papers, and so they just ignored him.

Even reputable literary papers could not afford to disregard their advertisers altogether. It was quite usual to send a book to a reviewer with some such formula as, 'Review this book if it seems any good. If not, send it back. We don't think it's worthwhile to print simply damning reviews.'

Naturally, a person to whom the guinea or so that he gets for the review means next week's rent is not going to send the book back. He can be counted on to find something to praise, whatever his private opinion of the book may be.

In America even the pretence that hack-reviewers read the books they are paid to criticise has been partially abandoned. Publishers, or some publishers, send out with review copies a short synopsis telling the reviewer what to say. Once, in the case of a novel of my own, they misspelt the name of one of the characters. The same misspelling turned up in review after review. The so-called critics had not even glanced into the book—which, nevertheless, most of them were boosting to the skies.

Review: Hilda Martindale, CBE, *From One Generation to Another*

Manchester Evening News, 29 JUNE 1944

The Manchester Evening News was founded in 1868 and has had an off-on relationship with the Manchester Guardian (now the Guardian). The papers were reunited in the 1920s and the News remained part of the Guardian Media Group until 2010. Although it has suffered like so many newspapers from the competition of other media outlets it was in Orwell's day one of the major – and vigorous – provincial newspapers. In the main it took an independent liberal approach but was not so liberal when it rejected Orwell's review of Harold Laski's Faith, Reason and Civilization *which he submitted on 13 March 1944, because, Orwell believed, of its 'Anti-Stalin implications' and a fear of offending the Soviets. However he still continued to write for the paper and worked as its correspondent in France and Germany in 1945 (see, for example, 'The French* Believe We Have Had a Revolution' *on page 335).*

To become a factory inspector does not sound a very thrilling achievement, but its unusualness depends partly on the sex of the person in question, and also on the date. Miss Hilda Martindale was one of the first women factory inspectors to be appointed in this country, and afterwards held one of the highest posts in her department. Behind that rather prosaic statement there lies a story of feminine struggle stretching far back into the nineteenth century—for Miss Martindale is almost more interested in her mother's history than her own.[1]

At the beginning of her book there is a photograph of her mother in old age; a grim but handsome face, belonging obviously to a woman of character. Miss Spicer (as her maiden name was) had been born into a wealthy nonconformist family, and like her near-contemporary, Florence Nightingale, she became dissatisfied in early adult life with the idle

---

1. Hilda Martindale, CBE (1875–1952), a civil servant, was born into a great Liberal-Nonconformist family, but her father and one sister (there were three children, not two, as Orwell says; the surviving sister became one of the first women surgeons) died before she was born. She was appointed deputy chief inspector after years of devoted work against opposition and with little support from the magistracy. She also fought for equal opportunities for women in the Civil Service. When, some years after her retirement in 1937, a woman became principal assistant secretary in charge of all general establishment work, she wrote, 'Now indeed my desire was fulfilled.' She also did much to establish the Home Office Industrial Museum (*DNB*).

meaningless existence that a woman of the richer classes was then expected to lead.

This dissatisfaction persisted in spite of a happy marriage and the birth of two children, and she became one of the pioneers of the women's suffrage movement. Her great aim in life was to see men and women regarded as the same kind of animal—once, when approached by a clergyman who was opening a home for fallen women, she told him that if he opened a home for fallen men she would subscribe to it—and to make it possible for girls to follow any profession that suited them instead of being tied down to a few 'ladylike' pursuits.

Among the innumerable girls to whom she gave help and advice was an eager, intelligent, overworked shop assistant of 16 named Margaret Bondfield.[2] Mrs. Martindale did not live long enough to see female suffrage become a reality, but unlike some of her fellow-workers she did not lose her faith in the Liberal party.

The Liberals, from Gladstone onwards, tended to be tepid or evasive on the subject of female emancipation, and it was out of disappointment with the behaviour of the Liberal Government that the 'militant' suffragette movement arose. It is interesting to learn that as early as the 'nineties female suffrage was opposed inside the Liberal party on the ground that if women were given votes they would vote Conservative.

Miss Hilda Martindale's official career began about 1895. Much the most interesting thing in her book is the revelation that the kind of sweating and child labour that we associate with the early days of the Industrial Revolution persisted in England till almost the beginning of the last war. At different times she was investigating conditions in the pottery trade, the textile industries, the dressmaking trade, and many others, both in England and in Ireland, and everywhere she found atrocious things happening.

In the Potteries, for instance, children as young as 12 worked long hours carrying lumps of clay weighing 60 or 70 pounds, while among adults lead poisoning was extremely common and was regarded as something unavoidable, like the weather. In Ireland the highly skilled lace-makers earned round about a penny an hour, and the Truck Act which had been

---

2. Margaret Bondfield (1873–1953), trade union leader and first woman cabinet minister, as Minister of Labour in Ramsay MacDonald's second administration, 1929. She was the first woman Privy Councillor.

passed 70 years earlier[3] was flagrantly disregarded. Lace-making was a cottage industry, and orders were farmed out to an 'agent' who in most cases was also the local shopkeeper and publican. As far as possible he paid his work people in goods instead of money, grossly overcharging for everything, and kept them permanently in debt to him.

The prosecutions which Miss Martindale instituted generally failed, because no one dared to give evidence against the 'agent.' But the worst sweating of all seems to have happened in the workshops of 'court' dressmakers in London. When some urgent order, for a wedding or something of the kind, had to be completed the sempstresses might be kept on the job for 60 or 70 hours continuously. The laws against Sunday work and child labour were a dead letter. If a factory inspector arrived unexpectedly the girls were simply bundled into an attic, or anywhere else where they would be out of sight, and the employer was able to declare that no law was being infringed.

The enormous supplies of cheap female labour that were available made it very difficult to combat these conditions. Any girl who complained against her employer knew that she would be dismissed, and Miss Martindale had to proceed chiefly on the evidence of anonymous letters.

On one occasion she received information that the girls in a certain shop were being kept at work on Sunday. When she arrived there she was assured that the girls were all at their homes, and was shown round the empty workrooms. She promptly jumped into a hansom cab and made a tour of all the girls' homes, the addresses of which she had procured beforehand.

They were, in fact, all at work, and had been hidden somewhere or other while Miss Martindale made her visit. Miss Martindale is convinced that industrial conditions have enormously improved over the last 40 years, and when one reads of her experiences—especially when one reads the pathetic ill-spelt letters she used to receive from working girls—it is impossible not to agree.

Wages, working hours, protection against accident and industrial diseases and also the treatment of children are very different from what they were 40 years ago, although there has been no basic change in the economic system. Miss Martindale thinks that the improvement, at any rate so far as women are concerned, dates from the last war, when women

3. The Truck Acts were passed in 1831, 1887, and 1896 and were designed to stop the practice of paying employees' wages in goods instead of money.

for the first time were employed in large numbers in industry including trades previously reserved for men, and made their first acquaintance with trade unions.

It was, incidentally, the Boer War that had first made the Government realise that the national physique was deteriorating as a result of industrial conditions, and the present war has probably worked another improvement in the status of labour.

Evidently war has its compensations since military efficiency is not compatible with underfeeding, overwork, or even illiteracy.

Parts of this book are rather slow going, but it is an informative book, and a remarkably good-tempered one. Herself a feminist and the daughter of an even more ardent feminist, Miss Martindale has none of that bitter anti-masculine feeling that feminist writers used to have. Her own career, and the self-confidence and independence of outlook that she evidently showed from the very start, bear out her claim that women are the equals of men in everything except physical strength.

The Orwells Bombed Out

28 JUNE 1944

On 28 June 1944, Orwell and his wife were bombed out of their flat in Mortimer Crescent. They first moved into Inez Holden's house, 106 George Street, London, W.1; Inez Holden was away, ill. In a letter to Leonard Moore, 3 October 1944, Orwell described 27b Canonbury Square, London, N.1 as 'my permanent address'. In the intervening weeks he gave his address as care of the Tribune office.

In her Summer Journal, on p. 245, Inez Holden wrote: 'George [Orwell] telephoned. He had been planning to get his books up from the country [Wallington] for some time. At last he managed it, but now his house has been broken up by blast. The place is no longer habitable, but he goes each day to rummage in the rubble to recover as many books as possible and wheel them away in a wheelbarrow. He makes this journey from Fleet Street during his lunch hour.' Mortimer Crescent to the Tribune office in Fleet Street is about four miles each way.

Extract from 'As I Please', 32: The Flying Bomb

Tribune, 7 JULY 1944

Life in the civilised world.
(The family are at tea.)
Zoom-zoom-zoom!
'Is there an alert on?'
'No, it's all clear.'
'I thought there was an alert on.'
Zoom-zoom-zoom!
'There's another of those things coming!'
'It's all right, it's miles away.'
Zoom-zoom-ZOOM!
'Look out, here it comes! Under the table, quick!'
Zoom-zoom-zoom!
'It's all right, it's getting fainter.'
Zoom-zoom-ZOOM!
'It's coming back!'
'They seem to kind of circle round and come back again. They've
    got something on their tails that makes them do it. Like a torpedo.'
ZOOM-ZOOM-ZOOM!
'Christ! It's bang overhead!'
Dead silence.
'Now get *right* underneath. Keep your head well down. What a
    mercy baby isn't here!'
'Look at the cat! He's frightened too.'
'Of course animals *know*. They can feel the vibrations.'
BOOM!
'It's all right, I told you it was miles away.'
(Tea continues.)[1]

1. Orwell is describing the V-1 (Vergeltungswaffe-1; Revenge Weapon-1) or 'buzz-bomb' or
   'doodlebug', as it was nicknamed. These flying bombs had no pilot and carried about
   2,000 lbs. (900 kg.) of explosives. Their design was started secretly in 1936. The first was
   fired on the night of 13–14 June 1944, seven days after the Normandy landings and
   continued intermittently until the end of March 1945. In all, 9,251 were fired at southern
   England. Of these, 4,621 were destroyed, 630 being shot down by the RAF. About 5,500
   people were killed and some 16,000 injured; damage was considerable but not of a kind
   to undermine war production. The buzz of the bomb cut out as the bomb lost power
   and fell silently to earth to explode on impact. Crown Film made a 14-minute film, *The
   Eighty Days*, directed by Humphrey Jennings, in 1944 which dramatically shows the V-1
   attacks on London and the South-East. Its commentary was spoken by the American,
   Ed Murrow (1908–65), the American broadcasting journalist. The reactions of those
   being bombed were sometimes from earlier films of air-raids.

Extract from 'London Letter', 24 July 1944: Highly Unpopular Subjects

Partisan Review, Fall 1944

Other highly unpopular subjects are postwar mobility of labour, postwar continuation of food rationing, etc., and the war against Japan. People will, I have no doubt, be ready to go on fighting until Japan is beaten, but their capacity for simply *forgetting* these years of warfare that lie ahead is surprising. In conversation, 'When the war stops' invariably means when Germany packs up. The last Mass Observation report shows a considerable recrudescence of 1918 habits of thought. Everyone expects not only that there will [be] a ghastly muddle over demobilization, but that mass unemployment will promptly return. No one wants to remember that we shall have to keep living for years on a wartime basis and that the switch-over to peacetime production and the recapture of lost markets may entail as great an effort as the war itself. Everyone wants, above all things, a rest. I overhear very little discussion of the wider issues of the war, and I can't discern much popular interest in the kind of peace we should impose on Germany. The newspapers of the Right and Left are outdoing one another in demanding a vindictive peace. Vansittart is now a back number; indeed the more extreme of his one-time followers have brought out a pamphlet denouncing him as pro-German.

The Communists are using the slogan, 'Make Germany Pay' (the diehard Tory slogan of 1918) and branding as pro-Nazi anyone who says either that we should make a generous peace or that publication of reasonable peace-terms would hasten the German collapse. The peace-terms that they and other Russophiles advocate are indeed simply a worse version of the Versailles Treaty against which they yapped for twenty years. Thus the dog returns to his vomit, or more exactly to somebody else's vomit. But once again, I can't see that ordinary people want anything of the kind, and if past wars are any guide the troops will all come home pro-German. The implications of the fact that the common people are Russophile but don't want the sort of peace that the Russians are demanding haven't yet sunk in, and leftwing journalists avoid discussing them. The Soviet government now makes direct efforts to interfere with the British press. I suppose that for sheer weariness and the instinct to support Russia at all costs the man-in-the-street might be brought to approve of an unjust peace, but there would be a rapid pro-German reaction, as last time.

Extract from 'As I Please', 37: The Colour Bar

Tribune, 11 AUGUST 1944

A few days ago a West African wrote to inform us that a certain London dance hall had recently erected a 'colour bar,' presumably in order to please the American soldiers who formed an important part of its clientele. Telephone conversations with the management of the dance hall brought us the answers: (a) that the 'colour bar' had been cancelled, and (b) that it had never been imposed in the first place; but I think one can take it that our informant's charge had some kind of basis. There have been other similar incidents recently. For instance, during last week a case in a magistrate's court brought out the fact that a West Indian Negro working in this country had been refused admission to a place of entertainment when he was wearing Home Guard uniform. And there have been many instances of Indians, Negroes and others being turned away from hotels on the ground that 'we don't take coloured people.'

It is immensely important to be vigilant against this kind of thing, and to make as much public fuss as possible whenever it happens. For this is one of those matters in which making a fuss can achieve something. There is no kind of legal disability against coloured people in this country, and, what is more, there is very little popular colour feeling. (This is not due to any inherent virtue in the British people, as our behaviour in India shows. It is due to the fact that in Britain itself there is no colour problem.)

The trouble always arises in the same way. A hotel, restaurant or what-not is frequented by people who have money to spend and who object to mixing with Indians or Negroes. They tell the proprietor that unless he imposes a colour bar they will go elsewhere. They may be a very small minority, and the proprietor may not be in agreement with them, but it is difficult for him to lose good customers; so he imposes the colour bar. This kind of thing cannot happen when public opinion is on the alert and disagreeable publicity is given to any establishment where coloured people are insulted. Anyone who knows of a provable instance of colour discrimination ought always to expose it. Otherwise the tiny percentage of colour-snobs who exist among us can make endless mischief, and the British people are given a bad name which, as a whole, they do not deserve.

In the nineteen-twenties, when American tourists were as much a part of the scenery of Paris as tobacco kiosks and tin urinals, the beginnings of a colour bar began to appear even in France. The Americans spent money like water; and restaurant proprietors and the like could not afford to disregard them. One evening, at a dance in a very well-known café, some Americans objected to the presence of a Negro who was there with an Egyptian woman. After making some feeble protests, the proprietor gave in, and the Negro was turned out.

Next morning there was a terrible hullabaloo and the cafe proprietor was hauled up before a Minister of the Government and threatened with prosecution. It had turned out that the offended Negro was the Ambassador of Haiti. People of that kind can usually get satisfaction, but most of us do not have the good fortune to be ambassadors, and the ordinary Indian, Negro or Chinese can only be protected against petty insult if other ordinary people are willing to exert themselves on his behalf.

Review: Marie Paneth, *Branch Street*

The Observer, 13 AUGUST 1944

A valuable piece of sociological work has been done by Mrs. Marie Paneth, the Austrian authoress, whose book, *Branch Street*, recently published by Allen and Unwin, brought to light some rather surprising facts about the slum conditions still existing here and there in the heart of London.

For nearly two years Mrs. Paneth has been working at a children's play centre in a street which she chooses to conceal under the name of Branch Street. Though not far from the centre of London it happens to be a 'bad' quarter, and it is quite clear from her descriptions that when she first went there the children were little better than savages. They did, indeed, have homes of sorts, but in behaviour they resembled the troops of 'wild children' who were a by-product of the Russian civil war. They were not only dirty, ragged, undernourished and unbelievably obscene in language and corrupt in outlook, but they were all thieves, and as intractable as wild animals.

A few of the girls were comparatively approachable, but the boys simply smashed up the play centre over and over again, sometimes breaking in at night to do the job more thoroughly, and at times it was even dangerous for a grown-up to venture among them single-handed.

It took a long time for this gentle, grey-haired lady, with her marked foreign accent, to win the children's confidence. The principle she went on was never to oppose them forcibly if it could possibly be avoided, and never to let them think that they could shock her. In the end this seems to have worked, though not without some very disagreeable experiences. Mrs. Paneth believes that children of this kind, who have had no proper home life and regard grown-ups as enemies, are best treated on the 'libertarian' principles evolved by Homer Lane, Mr. A. S. Neill, and others.

Though not a professional psychologist, Mrs. Paneth is the wife of a doctor, and has done work of this kind before. During the last war she worked in a children's hospital in Vienna and later in a children's play centre in Berlin. She describes the 'Branch Street' children as much the worst she has encountered in any country. But, speaking as a foreign observer, she finds that nearly all English children have certain redeeming traits: she instances the devotion which even the worst child will show in looking after a younger brother or sister.

It is also interesting to learn that these semi-savage children, who see nothing wrong in stealing and flee at the very sight of a policeman, are all deeply patriotic and keen admirers of Mr. Churchill.

It is clear from Mrs. Paneth's account that *Branch Street* is simply a forgotten corner of the nineteenth century existing in the middle of a comparatively prosperous area. She does not believe that the conditions in which the children live have been made much worse by the war. (Incidentally, various attempts to evacuate these children were a failure: they all came under the heading of 'unbilletable.')

It is impossible to talk to her or read her book without wondering how many more of these pockets of corruption exist in London and other big towns. Mrs. Paneth has managed to keep in touch with some of the children who were previously under her care and have now gone to work. With such a background they have neither the chance of a worth-while job nor, as a rule, the capacity for steady work. At best they find their way into some blind-alley occupation, but are more likely to end up in crime or prostitution.

The surprise which this book caused in many quarters is an indication of how little is still known of the underside of London life. The huge slum areas that existed within living memory have been cleared up, but in a smaller way there is obviously still a great deal to do. Mrs. Paneth was astonished and gratified that her book, which casts a very unfavourable light on this country, received no hostile criticism.

Probably that is a sign that public opinion is becoming more sensitive to the problem of the neglected child. In any case it would be difficult to read the book without conceiving an admiration for its author, who has carried out a useful piece of civilising work with great courage and infinite good-temper.

But *Branch Street* still exists, and it will go on creating wild and hopeless children until it has been abolished and rebuilt along with the other streets that have the same atmosphere.[1]

1. The review was headed – presumably by a sub-editor at *The Observer* – 'The Children Who Cannot be Billeted'.

Extract from 'As I Please', 40: The Warsaw Uprising

Tribune, 1 SEPTEMBER 1944

As the German Army retreated through Poland pursued by the Soviet Army, the Polish Home Army, under General Tadeusz Komorowski (known as 'Bor'), though desperately ill-equipped, attempted to liberate Warsaw from its German occupiers. It fought bitterly from 1 August 1944, literally even 'rising from the cellars'. In addition to a burning desire for their freedom, the Poles in Warsaw were anxious to ensure that the Soviet-backed Polish Committee of National Liberation was not imposed as the new government of Poland.

Despite their having reached the River Vistula, and the Red Air Force being only a few minutes' flying time away from Warsaw, the Soviets offered their Polish 'allies' no help despite Winston Churchill's desperate pleas on behalf of the Poles. Stalin described the Poles who had risen against the Germans as 'a handful of criminals'. Despite the lack of Soviet support, Churchill authorised the Polish Air Force, the RAF, and the South African Air Force, all flying from Italy, to make over two-hundred low-level drops. Churchill begged President Roosevelt to join in but Roosevelt was anxious not to upset the Soviets before the Yalta Conference and did not consider it would be advantageous to the overall war effort to go to the help of the Poles. In the end the US air force, having had permission to refuel in Soviet airfields, made a single drop.

Probably upwards of 200,000 Poles were killed in the course of the Uprising and the Germans deliberately destroyed some 60 per cent of Warsaw's buildings during and after it.

Tribune of 11 August 1944 devoted an editorial to 'Who Deserted Warsaw?' and Orwell's contribution followed. This prompted a very lively correspondence. Only two letters from that are reproduced here. The first is by a hard-line supporter of the Soviets, Douglas Goldring, and the other by Orwell's friend, the novelist and anti-Communist, Arthur Koestler (1905–83), who makes the telling comparison of the Soviets' behaviour with that of the Germans at Lidice.

The Warsaw Uprising

It is not my primary job to discuss the details of contemporary politics, but this week there is something that cries out to be said. Since, it seems, nobody else will do so, I want to protest against the mean and cowardly attitude adopted by the British press towards the recent rising in Warsaw.

As soon as the news of the rising broke, the *News Chronicle* and kindred papers adopted a markedly disapproving attitude. One was left with the general impression that the Poles deserved to have their bottoms smacked for doing what all the Allied wirelesses had been urging them to do for years past, and that they would not be given and did not deserve to be given any help from outside. A few papers tentatively suggested that arms and supplies might be dropped by the Anglo-Americans, a thousand miles away: no one, so far as I know, suggested that this might be done by the Russians, perhaps twenty miles away. The *New Statesman*, in its issue of August 18, even went so far as to doubt whether appreciable help could be given from the air in such circumstances. All or nearly all the papers of the Left were full of blame for the '*émigré*' London Government which had 'prematurely' ordered its followers to rise when the Red Army was at the gates. This line of thought is adequately set forth in a letter to last week's *Tribune* from Mr. G. Barraclough. He makes the following specific charges:—

(1) The Warsaw rising was 'not a spontaneous popular rising,' but was 'begun on orders from the soi-disant Polish Government in London.'

(2) The order to rise was given 'without consultation with either the British or Soviet Governments,' and 'no attempt was made to co-ordinate the rising with Allied action.'

(3) The Polish resistance movement is no more united round the London Government than the Greek resistance movement is united round King George of the Hellenes. (This is further emphasised by frequent use of the words '*émigré*,' 'soi-disant,' etc., applied to the London Government.)

(4) The London Government precipitated the rising in order to be in possession of Warsaw when the Russians arrived, because in that case 'the bargaining position of the *émigré* Government would be improved.' The London Government, we are told, 'is ready to betray the Polish people's cause to bolster up its own tenure of precarious office,' with much more to the same effect.

No shadow of proof is offered for any of these charges, though (1) and (2) are of a kind that could be verified and may well be true. My own guess is that (2) is true and (1) partly true. The third charge makes nonsense of the first two. If the London Government is not accepted by the mass of the people in Warsaw, why should they raise a desperate insurrection on its orders? By blaming Sosnokowski and the rest for the rising, you are automatically assuming that it is to them that the Polish people look for guidance. This obvious contradiction has been repeated in paper after paper, without, so far as I know, a single person having the honesty to point it out. As for the use of such expressions as '*émigré*,' it is simply a rhetorical trick. If the London Poles are *émigrés*, so are the Polish National Committee of Liberation, besides the 'free' Governments of all the occupied countries. Why does one become an *émigré* by emigrating to London and not by emigrating to Moscow?

Charge No. (4) is morally on a par with the *Osservatore Romano's* suggestion that the Russians held up their attack on Warsaw in order to get as many Polish resisters as possible killed off. It is the unproved and unprovable assertion of a mere propagandist who has no wish to establish the truth, but is simply out to do as much dirt on his opponent as possible. And all that I have read about this matter in the press— except for some very obscure papers and some remarks in *Tribune*, the *Economist* and the *Evening Standard*—is on the same level as Mr. Barraclough's letter.

Now, I know nothing of Polish affairs and even if I had the power to do so I would not intervene in the struggle between the London Polish Government and the Moscow National Committee of Liberation. What I am concerned with is the attitude of the British intelligentsia, who cannot raise between them one single voice to question what they believe to be Russian policy, no matter what turn it takes, and in this case have had the unheard-of meanness to hint that our bombers ought not to be sent to the aid of our comrades fighting in Warsaw. The enormous majority of Left-wingers who swallow the policy put out by the *News Chronicle*, etc., know no more about Poland than I do. All they know is that the Russians object to the London Government and have set up a rival organisation, and so far as they are concerned that settles the matter. If tomorrow Stalin were to drop the Committee of Liberation and recognise the London Government, the whole British intelligentsia would flock after him like a troop of parrots. Their attitude towards Russian foreign policy is not 'Is this policy right or wrong?' but 'This is Russian policy: how can we make it appear right?' And this attitude is defended, if at all, solely on grounds of power. The Russians are powerful in Eastern Europe, we are not: therefore we must not oppose them. This involves the principle, of its nature alien to Socialism, that you must not protest against an evil which you cannot prevent.

I cannot discuss here why it is that the British intelligentsia, with few exceptions, have developed a nationalistic loyalty towards the U.S.S.R. and are dishonestly uncritical of its policies. In any case, I have discussed it elsewhere. But I would like to close with two considerations which are worth thinking over.

First of all, a message to English Left-wing journalists and intellectuals generally. 'Do remember that dishonesty and cowardice always have to be paid for. Don't imagine that for years on end you can make yourself the boot-licking propagandist of the Soviet regime, or any other regime, and then suddenly return to mental decency. Once a whore, always a whore.'

Secondly, a wider consideration. Nothing is more important in the world today than Anglo-Russian friendship and co-operation, and that will not be attained without plain speaking. The best way to come to an agreement with a foreign nation is *not* to refrain from criticising its policies, even to the extent of leaving your own people in the dark about them. At present, so slavish is the attitude of nearly the whole British press that ordinary people have very little idea of what is happening, and may well be committed to policies which they will repudiate in five years' time. In a shadowy sort of way we have been told that the Russian peace terms are a super-Versailles, with partition of Germany, astronomical reparations, and forced labour on a huge scale. These proposals go practically uncriticised, while in much of the Left-wing press hack-writers are even hired to extol them. The result is that the average man has no notion of the enormity of what is proposed. I don't know whether, when the time comes, the Russians will really want to put such terms into operation. My guess is that they won't. But what I do know is that if any such thing were done, the British and probably the American public would never support it when the passion of war had died down. Any flagrantly unjust peace settlement will simply have the result, as it did last time, of making the British people unreasonably sympathetic with the victims. Anglo-Russian friendship depends upon there being a policy which both countries can agree upon, and this is impossible without free discussion and genuine criticism *now*. There can be no real alliance on the basis of 'Stalin is always right.' The first step towards a real alliance is the dropping of illusions.

An extremely vigorous correspondence followed. These are but two fairly typical examples:

George Orwell's experiences in the Spanish war, in which he served in a 'Trotskyite' formation, seem to have roused in him a pathological hatred not only of the U.S.S.R. but of all the Left-wing intellectuals who do not share his opinions.

In the course of a sort of papal encyclical, arrogantly addressed 'to English Left-wing journalists and intellectuals *generally*,' he exhorts us to 'remember that dishonesty and cowardice always have to be paid for. Don't imagine that for years on end you can make yourself the boot-licking propagandist of the Soviet régime, or any other régime, and then suddenly return to mental decency. Once a whore, always a whore.'

Apart from two or three independent dailies and one Sunday paper, the 'Left-wing Press' in this country means, for practical purposes, the *New Statesman*, *Tribune* and the *Daily Worker*. If we omit *Tribune* and discount the *Daily Worker*, which Mr. Orwell would probably regard as prostituted to Moscow, it only leaves the *New Statesman* as a possible field for those 'hack-writers,' hired to extol Russian policies at the expense of their honour, to whom he refers.

It happens that the *New Statesman*, whose chastity I have hitherto considered above suspicion, deals editorially in last week's issue with the Warsaw tragedy and also prints a long cable from its correspondent in Poland. The leader gives an impartial résumé of the most authoritative information at present available, while the message cabled from Lublin contains a full report of the interview which British and American correspondents have had with Morawski, General Rola-Zymierski and other members of the Polish Committee of Liberation. As both these statements contradict Mr. Orwell's unfounded assertions, the hired 'hack-writers' responsible for them must be, by his definition, cowardly boot-licking whores, guilty of what he describes as 'unheard of meanness.'

Evidently my old-fashioned ideas of what constitutes 'mental decency' conflict with Mr. Orwell's. I consider his article a disgrace to the profession he has so recently condescended to join and an insult to readers of *Tribune*.

As for nearly 30 years I have had the honour to belong to the group of writers to whom his 'message' is addressed, I should like to add a word of warning to any beginners who may be taken in by his exposure of our venality. If they want to sell their virtue profitably they should turn not Left but Right. It is Catholic Fascist boot-licking and *Anti*-Soviet propaganda that produce the big money—and the Mayfair invitations to meet Foreign Office high-ups and fascinating Polish Counts.

Douglas Goldring[1]

In your last issue John Armstrong, in defence of Russian policy, quotes from my novel, *Darkness at Noon*, a passage extolling the virtues of the old Bolshevik Guard. Mr. Armstrong, an excellent painter and political nitwit, seems not to have realised that the theme of the book he quotes is the liquidation of that old guard by Russia's present rulers, and that praise of the victim aggravates the charge against the killer.

I don't believe in polemics in correspondence columns, but as I have been quoted in defence of the Russian attitude towards the Warsaw *maquis*, you will permit me to say that I consider it as one of the major infamies of this war which, though committed by different methods, will rank for the future historian on the same ethical level with Lidice.[2]

Arthur Koestler

1. Douglas Goldring (1887–1960), journalist, editor, university teacher, 1925–27, critic, and novelist. In his notes about fellow-travellers, Orwell had little respect for Goldring, describing him as probably venal. Note Goldring's reference to Orwell's 'exposure of our venality.'
2. The Czech village of Lidice was 'removed from the map' and its population shot or incarcerated in concentration camps (where most died) in revenge for the assassination of Reinhard Heydrich, Reich 'Protector' in Czechoslovakia. The Crown Film Unit's *The Silent Village* (1943), directed by Humphrey Jennings, movingly tells this story and, to bring it home to British viewers, sets it in a Welsh mining village. It was filmed in the village of Cwmgiedd in the Upper Swansea Valley about half a mile from Ystradgynlais. The opening section of life before the arrival of the Nazis mainly has dialogue spoken in Welsh – without subtitles.

Extract from 'As I Please', 42: A Paris Taxi-Driver

Tribune, 15 SEPTEMBER 1944

About the end of 1936, as I was passing through Paris on the way to Spain, I had to visit somebody at an address I did not know, and I thought that the quickest way of getting there would probably be to take a taxi. The taxi-driver did not know the address either. However, we drove up the street and asked the nearest policeman, whereupon it turned out that the address I was looking for was only about a hundred yards away. So I had taken the taxi-driver off the rank for a fare which in English money was about threepence.

The taxi-driver was furiously angry. He began accusing me, in a roaring voice and with the maximum of offensiveness, of having 'done it on purpose.' I protested that I had not known where the place was, and that I obviously would not have taken a taxi if I had known. 'You knew very well!' he yelled back at me. He was an old, grey, thick-set man, with ragged grey moustaches and a face of quite unusual malignity. In the end I lost my temper, and, my command of French coming back to me in my rage, I shouted at him, 'You think you're too old for me to smash your face in. Don't be too sure!' He backed up against the taxi, snarling and full of fight, in spite of his sixty years.

Then the moment came to pay. I had taken out a ten-franc note. 'I've no change!' he yelled as soon as he saw the money. 'Go and change it for yourself!'

'Where can I get change?'

'How should I know? That's your business.'

So I had to cross the street, find a tobacconist's shop and get change. When I came back I gave the taxi-driver the exact fare, telling him that after his behaviour I saw no reason for giving him anything extra; and after exchanging a few more insults we parted.

This sordid squabble left me at the moment violently angry, and a little later saddened and disgusted. 'Why do people have to behave like that?' I thought.

But that night I left for Spain. The train, a slow one, was packed with Czechs, Germans, Frenchmen, all bound on the same mission. Up and down the train you could hear one phrase repeated over and over again, in the accents of all the languages of Europe—*là-bas* (down there). My third-class carriage was full of very young, fair-haired, underfed Germans in suits of incredible shoddiness—the first *ersatz* cloth I had seen—who rushed out at every stopping-place to buy bottles of cheap wine and later fell asleep in a sort of pyramid on the floor of the carriage. About halfway down France the ordinary passengers dropped off. There might still be a few nondescript journalists like myself, but the train was practically a troop train, and the countryside knew it. In the morning, as we crawled across southern France, every peasant working in the fields turned round, stood solemnly upright and gave the anti-Fascist salute. They were like a guard of honour, greeting the train mile after mile.

As I watched this, the behaviour of the old taxi-driver gradually fell into perspective. I saw now what had made him so unnecessarily offensive. This was 1936, the year of the great strikes, and the Blum government was still in office. The wave of revolutionary feeling which had swept across France had affected people like taxi-drivers as well as factory workers. With my English accent I had appeared to him as a symbol of the idle, patronising foreign tourists who had done their best to turn France into something midway between a museum and a brothel. In his eyes an English tourist meant a bourgeois. He was getting a bit of his own back on the parasites who were normally his employers. And it struck me that the motives of the polyglot army that filled the train, and of the peasants with raised fists out there in the fields, and my own motive in going to Spain, and the motive of the old taxi-driver in insulting me, were at bottom all the same.

'London Letter', October 1944(?): I Have Tried to Tell the Truth: errors and mistakes

Partisan Review, Winter 1944–45

Dear Editors,

It is close on four years since I first wrote to you, and I have told you several times that I would like to write one letter which should be a sort of commentary on the previous ones. This seems to be a suitable moment.

Now that we have seemingly won the war and lost the peace, it is possible to see earlier events in a certain perspective, and the first thing I have to admit is that up to at any rate the end of 1942 I was grossly wrong in my analysis of the situation. It is because, so far as I can see, everyone else was wrong too that my own mistakes are worth commenting on.

I have tried to tell the truth in these letters, and I believe your readers have got from them a not too distorted picture of what was happening at any given moment. Of course there are many mistaken predictions (e.g., in 1941 I prophesied that Russia and Germany would go on collaborating and in 1942 that Churchill would fall from power), many generalizations based on little or no evidence, and also, from time to time, spiteful or misleading remarks about individuals. For instance, I particularly regret having said in one letter that Julian Symons 'writes in a vaguely Fascist strain'—a quite unjustified statement based on a single article which I probably misunderstood. But this kind of thing results largely from the lunatic atmosphere of war, the fog of lies and misinformation in which one has to work and the endless sordid controversies in which a political journalist is involved. By the low standards now prevailing I think I have been fairly accurate about facts. Where I have gone wrong is in assessing the relative importance of different *trends*. And most of my mistakes spring from a political analysis which I had made in the desperate period of 1940 and continued to cling to long after it should have been clear that it was untenable.

The essential error is contained in my very first letter, written at the end of 1940, in which I stated that the political reaction which was already visibly under weigh 'is not going to make very much ultimate difference.' For about eighteen months I repeated this in various forms again and again. I not only assumed (what is probably true) that the drift of popular feeling was towards the Left, but that it would be quite impossible to win the war without democratizing it. In 1940 I had written, 'Either we turn this into a revolutionary war, or we lose it,' and I find myself repeating this word for word as late as the middle of 1942. This probably coloured my judgment of actual events and made me exaggerate the depth of the political crisis in 1942, the possibilities of Cripps as a popular leader and of Common Wealth as a revolutionary party, and also the socially level-ling process occurring in Britain as a result of the war. But what really matters is that I fell into the trap of assuming that 'the war and the revolution are inseparable.' There were excuses for this belief, but still it was a very great error. For after all we have not lost the war, unless appearances are very deceiving, and we have not introduced Socialism. Britain is moving towards a planned economy, and class distinctions tend to dwindle, but there has been no real shift of power and no increase in genuine democracy. The same people still own all the property and usurp all the best jobs. In the United States the development appears to be *away* from Socialism. The United States is indeed the most powerful country in the world, and the most capitalistic. When we look back at our judgments of a year or two ago, whether we 'opposed' the war or whether we 'supported' it, I think the first admission we ought to make is that *we were all wrong*.

Among the British and American intelligentsia, using the word in a wide sense, there were five attitudes towards the war:

(1) The war is worth winning at any price, because nothing could be worse than a Fascist victory. We must support any regime which will oppose the Nazis.

(2) The war is worth winning at any price, but in practice it cannot be won while capitalism survives. We must support the war, and at the same time endeavour to turn it into a revolutionary war.

(3) The war cannot be won while capitalism survives, but even if it could, such a victory would be worse than useless. It would merely lead to the establishment of Fascism in our own coun-tries. We must overthrow our own government before lending our support to the war.

(4) If we fight against Fascism, under no matter what government, we shall inevitably go Fascist ourselves.

(5) It is no use fighting, because the Germans and the Japanese are bound to win anyway.

Position (1) was taken by radicals everywhere, and by Stalinists after the entry of the USSR. Trotskyists of various colours took either position (2) or position (4). Pacifists took position (4) and generally used (5) as an additional argument. (1) merely amounts to saying, 'I don't like Fascism,' and is hardly a guide to political action: it does not make any prediction about what will happen. But the other theories have all been completely falsified. The fact that we were fighting for our lives has not forced us to 'go Socialist,' as I foretold that it would, but neither has it driven us into Fascism. So far as I can judge, we are somewhat further away from Fascism than we were at the beginning of the war. It seems to me very important to realize that we have been wrong, and say so. Most people nowadays, when their predictions are falsified, just impudently claim that they have been justified, and squeeze the facts accordingly. Thus many people who took the line that I did will in effect claim that the revolution has already happened, that class privilege and economic injustice can never return, etc., etc. Pacifists claim with even greater confidence that Britain is already a Fascist country and indistinguishable from Nazi Germany, although the very fact that they are allowed to write and agitate contradicts them. From all sides there is a chorus of 'I told you so,' and complete shamelessness about past mistakes. Appeasers, Popular Front-ers, Communists, Trotskyists, Anarchists, Pacifists, all claim—and in almost exactly the same tone of voice— that *their* prophecies and no others have been borne out by events. Particularly on the Left, political thought is a sort of masturbation fantasy in which the world of facts hardly matters.

But to return to my own mistakes. I am not here concerned with correcting those mistakes, so much as with explaining why I made them. When I suggested to you that Britain was on the edge of drastic political changes, and had already made an advance from which there could be no drawing back, I was not trying to put a good face on things for the benefit of the American public. I expressed the same ideas, and much more violently, in books and articles only published at home. Here are a few samples:

'The choice is between Socialism and defeat. We must go forward, or perish.' 'Laissez-faire capitalism is dead.' 'The English revolution started several years ago, and it began to gather momentum when the troops came back from Dunkirk.' 'With its present social structure England cannot survive.' 'This war, unless we are defeated, will wipe out most of the existing class privileges.' 'Within a year, perhaps even within six months, if we are still unconquered, we shall see the rise of something that has never existed before, a specifically *English* Socialist movement.' 'The last thing the British ruling class wants is to acquire fresh territory.' 'The real quarrel of the Fascist powers with British imperialism is that they know that it is disintegrating.' 'The war will bankrupt the majority of the public schools if it continues for another year or two.' 'This war is a race between the consolidation of Hitler's empire and the growth of democratic consciousness.'

And so on and so on. How could I write such things? Well, there is a clue in the fact that my predictions, especially about military events, were by no means always wrong. Looking back through my diaries and the news commentaries[1] which I wrote for the BBC over a period of two years, I see that I was often right as against the bulk of the left-wing intelligentsia. I was right to the extent that I was not defeatist, and after all the war has not been lost. The majority of left-wing intellectuals, whatever they might say in print, were blackly defeatist in 1940 and again in 1942. In the summer of 1942, the turning-point of the war, most of them held it as an article of faith that Alexandria would fall and Stalingrad would not. I remember a fellow broadcaster, a Communist saying to me with a kind of passion, 'I would bet you anything, *anything*, that Rommel will be in Cairo in a month.' What this person really meant, as I could see at a glance, was, 'I *hope* Rommel will be in Cairo in a month.' I myself didn't hope anything of the kind, and therefore I was able to see that the chances of holding on to Egypt were fairly good. You have here an example of the wish-thinking that underlies almost all political prediction at present.

I could be right on a point of this kind, because I don't share the average English intellectual's hatred of his own country and am not

1. From the way that Orwell expresses this, it would seem that he kept some, at least, of the scripts he wrote for the Eastern Service Newsletters, just as he kept his diaries.

dismayed by a British victory. But just for the same reason I failed to form a true picture of political developments. I hate to see England either humiliated or humiliating anybody else. I wanted to think that we would not be defeated, and I wanted to think that the class distinctions and imperialist exploitation of which I am ashamed would not return. I over-emphasized the anti-Fascist character of the war, exaggerated the social changes that were actually occurring; and under-rated the enormous strength of the forces of reaction. This unconscious falsification coloured all my earlier letters to you, though perhaps not the more recent ones.

So far as I can see, all political thinking for years past has been vitiated in the same way. People can foresee the future only when it coincides with their own wishes, and the most grossly obvious facts can be ignored when they are unwelcome. For example, right up to May of this year the more disaffected English intellectuals refused to believe that a Second Front would be opened. They went on refusing while, bang in front of their faces, the endless convoys of guns and landing craft rumbled through London on their way to the coast. One could point to countless other instances of people hugging quite manifest delusions because the truth would be wounding to their pride. Hence the absence of reliable political prediction. To name just one easily isolated example: Who foresaw the Russo–German pact of 1939? A few pessimistic Conservatives foretold an agreement between Germany and Russia, but the wrong kind of agreement, and for the wrong reasons. So far as I am aware, no intellectual of the Left, whether Russophile or Russophobe, foresaw anything of the kind. For that matter, the Left as a whole failed to foresee the rise of Fascism and failed to grasp that the Nazis were dangerous even when they were on the verge of seizing power. To appreciate the danger of Fascism the Left would have had to admit its own shortcomings, which was too painful: so the whole phenomenon was ignored or misinterpreted, with disastrous results.

The most one can say is that people can be fairly good prophets when their wishes are realizable. But a truly objective approach is almost impossible, because in one form or another almost everyone is a nationalist. Left-wing intellectuals do not think of themselves as nationalists, because as a rule they transfer their loyalty to some foreign country, such as the USSR, or indulge it in a merely negative form, in hatred of their own country and its rulers. But their outlook is essentially nationalist, in that they think entirely in terms of power politics and competitive prestige. In looking at any situation they do not say, 'What are the facts? What are the probabilities,' but, 'How can I make it appear to myself and others that my faction is getting the better of some rival faction?' To a Stalinist it is *impossible* that Stalin could ever be wrong, and to a Trotskyist it is equally impossible that Stalin could ever be right. So also with Anarchists, Pacifists, Tories or what-have-you. And the atomization of the world, the lack of any real contact between one country and another, makes delusions easier to preserve. To an astonishing extent it is impossible to discover what is happening outside one's own immediate circle. An illustration of this is that no one, so far as I know, can calculate the casualties in the present war within ten millions. But one expects governments and newspapers to tell lies. What is worse, to me, is the contempt even of intellectuals for objective truth so long as their own brand of nationalism is being boosted. The most intelligent people seem capable of holding schizophrenic beliefs, of disregarding plain facts, of evading serious questions with debating-society repartees, or swallowing baseless rumours and of looking on indifferently while history is falsified. All these mental vices spring ultimately from the nationalistic habit of mind, which is itself, I suppose, the product of fear and of the ghastly emptiness of machine civilization. But at any rate it is not surprising that in our age the followers of Marx have not been much more successful as prophets than the followers of Nostradamus.

I believe that it is possible to be more objective than most of us are, but that it involves a *moral* effort. One cannot get away from one's own subjective feelings, but at least one can know what they are and make allowance for them. I have made attempts to do this, especially latterly, and for that reason I think the later ones among my letters to you, roughly speaking from the middle of 1942 onwards, give a more truthful picture of developments in Britain than the earlier ones. As this letter has been largely a tirade against the left-wing intelligentsia, I would like to add, without flattery, that judging from such American periodicals as I see, the mental atmosphere in the USA is still a good deal more breathable than it is in England.

I began this letter three days ago. World-shaking events are happening all over the place, but in London nothing new.[2] The change-over from the blackout to the so-called dim-out[3] has made no difference as yet. The streets are still inky dark. On and off it is beastly cold and it looks as though fuel will be very short this winter. People's tempers get more and more ragged, and shopping is a misery. The shopkeepers treat you like dirt, especially if you want something that happens to be in short supply at the moment. The latest shortages are combs and teats for babies' feeding bottles. Teats have been actually unprocurable in some areas, and what do exist are made of reconditioned rubber. At the same time contraceptives are plentiful and made of good rubber. Whisky is rarer than ever, but there are more cars on the roads, so the petrol situation must have let up a little. The Home Guard has been stood down and firewatching greatly reduced. More U.S. soldiers have looked me up, using PR as an introduction. I am always most happy to meet any reader of PR. I can generally be got at the *Tribune*, but failing that my home number is CAN 3751.

George Orwell

---

2. At this point, Orwell's reference to the V-2 appears to have been censored.
3. In the autumn of 1944, strict blackout regulations were relaxed, and a low level of lighting was permitted, since manned bombing flights were then rare. V-1s and V-2s did not depend on direct land sightings.

Extract from 'As I Please', 49: On the Rudeness of Shopkeepers

Tribune, 24 NOVEMBER 1944

There have been innumerable complaints lately about the rudeness of shopkeepers. People say, I think with truth, that shopkeepers appear to take a sadistic pleasure in telling you that they don't stock the thing you ask for. To go in search of some really rare object, such as a comb or a tin of boot polish, is a miserable experience. It means trailing from shop to shop and getting a series of curt or actually hostile negatives. But even the routine business of buying the rations and the bread is made as difficult as possible for busy people. How is a woman to do her household shopping if she is working till six every day while most of the shops shut at five? She can only do it by fighting round crowded counters during her lunch hour. But it is the snubs that they get when they ask for some article which is in short supply that people dread most. Many shopkeepers seem to regard the customer as a kind of mendicant and to feel that they are conferring a favour on him by selling him anything. And there are other justified grievances—for instance, the shameless overcharging on uncontrolled goods such as secondhand furniture and the irritating trick, now very common, of displaying in the window goods which are not on sale.

But before blaming the shopkeeper for all this, there are several things one ought to remember. To begin with, irritability and bad manners are on the increase everywhere. You have only to observe the behaviour of normally longsuffering people like 'bus conductors to realise this. It is a neurosis produced by the war. But, in addition, many small independent shopkeepers (in my experience you are treated far more politely in big shops) are people with a well-founded grievance against society. Some of them are in effect the ill-paid employees of wholesale firms, others are being slowly crushed by the competition of the chain stores, and they are often treated with the greatest inconsiderateness by the local authorities. Sometimes a rehousing scheme will rob a shopkeeper of half his customers at one swoop. In war time this may happen even more drastically owing to bombing and the call-up. And war has other special irritations for the shopkeeper. Rationing puts a great deal of extra work on to grocers, butchers, etc., and it is very exasperating to be asked all day long for articles which you have not got.

But after all, the main fact is that at normal times both the shop assistant and the independent shopkeeper are downtrodden. They live to the tune of 'the customer is always right.' In peace time, in capitalist society, everyone is trying to sell goods which there is never enough money to buy, whereas in war time money is plentiful and goods scarce. Matches, razor blades, torch batteries, alarm clocks and teats for babies' feeding bottles are precious rarities, and the man who possesses them is a powerful being, to be approached cap in hand. I don't think one can blame the shopkeeper for getting a bit of his own back, when the situation is temporarily reversed. But I do agree that the behaviour of some of them is disgusting, and that when one is treated with more than normal haughtiness it is a duty to the rest of the public not to go to that shop again.

Extract from 'As I Please', 50: The V2[1]

Tribune, 4 DECEMBER 1944

V2 (I am told that you can now mention it in print so long as you just call it V2 and don't describe it too minutely) supplies another instance of the contrariness of human nature. People are complaining of the sudden unexpected wallop with which these things go off. 'It wouldn't be so bad if you got a bit of warning,' is the usual formula. There is even a tendency to talk nostalgically of the days of V1. The good old doodlebug did at least give you time to get under the table, etc., etc. Whereas, in fact, when the doodlebugs were actually dropping, the usual subject of complaint was the uncomfortable waiting period before they went off. Some people are never satisfied. Personally, I am no lover of V2, especially at this moment when the house still seems to be rocking from a recent explosion, but what most depresses me about these things is the way they set people talking about the next war. Every time one goes off I hear gloomy references to 'next time,' and the reflection: 'I suppose they'll be able to shoot them across the Atlantic by that time.' But if you ask who will be fighting whom when this universally expected war breaks out, you get no clear answer. It is just war in the abstract—the notion that human beings could ever behave sanely having apparently faded out of many people's memories.

---

1. The V-1 (or flying bomb, nicknamed the doodlebug) was followed by another 'Vergeltungswaffe' or 'revenge weapon', the V-2. This was a genuine rocket. Its chief designer, Wernher von Braun (1912–77), was a member of the Nazi Party and the production of the V-2s was said to have killed more slave labourers than people at whom it was eventually aimed. The first rockets were fired at Paris on 6 September 1944. On the 8th, the first of some 3,000 were launched at England and a similar number fell on Belgium. After the war von Braun was recruited for the US Space Agency and played a major role in enabling space travel to be accomplished.

Review: L.A.G. Strong, *Authorship*

Manchester Evening News, 11 JANUARY 1945

It is said to be the practice of the sterner religious orders to discourage proselytes, and Mr. L. A. G. Strong goes on rather the same principle in his advice to aspiring authors. Himself a highly successful writer of novels, short stories and radio scripts and with experience as a teacher in a school of journalism, he makes it clear from the outset that this profession is not an easy one. It has to be learned like any other, it entails endless work, and you are unlikely ever to make very much money out of it.

Indeed, Mr. Strong records that he himself was writing for fifteen years before literature became his main source of livelihood, and of the first forty manuscripts he sent out thirty-nine came back.

Most of the books (and they are numberless) on 'How To Become An Author' are quite worthless. They are worthless because they are written by people who regard writing simply as a way of making money. Everything is wrong in this approach.

To begin with, writing is not a lucrative profession (a novelist who made as much as the average country doctor would be doing very well indeed), and even on its lowest levels it has to be practised for its own sake.

And secondly most of the self-styled teachers of journalism are the worst possible guides, even from a commercial point of view, because they are unable to put their own precepts into practice. If they really knew how to make money out of journalism they would be doing it, instead of selling their secret to others.

However Mr. Strong is a very exceptional man, and his advice is well worth listening to. He is a successful writer, but he happens to be such a fast worker that he has time to run journalistic courses as a side-line.

He knows that literature is a trade as well as an art, but, unlike the vast majority of teachers, he also understands the nature of creation and realises that even hack journalism needs sincerity as well as competence. Over and over again he says in different ways, 'don't falsify. Even from a financial point of view it doesn't pay.'

In his early days one of those kind friends who take it upon them to advise young writers said to him, 'Write what they want first. Then, when you have made a name, write what you want.'

Mr. Strong adds, 'I repudiated the advice as damnable, and I repudiate it even more passionately to-day . . . my own experience is all on the side of honesty. Once, for a short time, when I was very hard up, I tried desperately to write what I thought the public wanted.

'The result was a disastrous failure. I never sold a line of it . . . insincerity is no substitute for talent.

'The sincere writer, however small his gift, has a better chance of success than the faker.'

In these and other similar passages, Mr. Strong is not referring merely to æsthetic faking. There is also the political pressure that is put so strongly upon many journalists to-day. Some topics are practically unmentionable, and the cult of the 'happy ending' is mixed up with the desire to present society in the rosiest possible light.

The correspondence tutors employed by schools of journalism frequently warn their pupils that anything 'unpleasant' or 'controversial' is difficult to sell. Mr. Strong's comment on all such false counsellors is 'tell them to go where they belong.'

But this is not to say that he despises or ignores the business side of the writing profession.

To begin with, every writer, however unusual his gifts may be, must learn to be readable. He must learn, by practice and apprenticeship, how to arrange his material and make his meaning unmistakably clear.

Mr Strong insists, and perhaps over-insists, that in a short article or story it is better to 'concentrate on one point only and never attempt to make more.'

Again, a writer must be ready to fall in with the wishes of editors and publishers on any question where his intellectual honesty is not involved. He must submit to having his articles cut when they are too long, and he must realise that one cannot write in the same style for a daily paper, a weekly review, and a technical magazine.

And he must study his market and not, for instance, 'send a women's magazine an article about Rugby football, or a yachting magazine an article on white mice.'

Submissions quite as silly as this are made every day, and many a promising novel has found its way to the dustbin because its author sent it to the wrong kind of publisher and then gave up hope when it came back to him.

Mr Strong gives some useful technical notes on the novel, the article, and the short story, and advises the budding writer not to despise that thankless and ill-paid job, lecturing.

He does, however, discourage the beginner from attempting the play or the film. There is, he considers, not one chance in ten thousand that a play written by a beginner will be produced.

Whereas a publisher risks a few hundred pounds on a book, a theatrical manager has to risk tens of thousands, and naturally he prefers to deal with writers who have already made a name for themselves in some other way.

The films are even more inaccessible. Indeed, the biggest film companies, it seems, make a practice of returning all unsolicited manuscripts unopened.

The radio is a much more promising field for the beginner. Its special technique, different from that of ordinary writing, has to be learned, but the demand for scripts is so large that there is comparatively little prejudice against newcomers.

Mr Strong ends with some notes on literary agents (useful to the writer of books, but less so to the free-lance journalist), schools of journalism, publishers, honest and otherwise, and contracts.

This is a useful little book. No book can teach you to write if you have not the initial gift, but at least you can learn how to use language simply, how to avoid unnecessary technical errors, how to market your writings, and how to dodge the innumerable crooks who haunt the fringes of the literary profession.

Mr. Strong never loses sight of the need to make a living but his advice carries all the more weight because he knows that the desire for money is not the ultimate motive of any writer worth reading.

Extracts from 'As I Please', 57: Huns and Other Such Names; A V-1 Explosion; The Three Super-states of the Future

Tribune, 2 FEBRUARY 1945

Huns and Other Such Names

I have just been re-reading, with great interest, an old favourite of my boyhood, *The Green Curve*, by 'Ole Luk-Oie.' 'Ole Luk-Oie' was the pseudonym of Major Swinton (afterwards General Swinton),[1] who was, I believe, one of the rather numerous people credited with the invention of the tank. The stories in this book, written about 1908, are the forecasts of an intelligent professional soldier who had learned the lessons of the Boer War and the Russo–Japanese War, and it is interesting to compare them with what actually happened a few years later.

One story, written as early as 1907 (at which date no aeroplane had actually risen off the ground for more than a few seconds), describes an air raid. The aeroplanes carry eight-pounder bombs! Another story, written in the same year, deals with a German invasion of England, and I was particularly interested to notice that in this story the Germans are already nicknamed 'Huns.' I had been inclined to attribute the use of the word 'Hun,' for German, to Kipling, who certainly used it in the poem that he published during the first week of the last war.[2]

In spite of the efforts of several newspapers, 'Hun' has never caught on in this war, but we have plenty of other offensive nicknames. Someone could write a valuable monograph on the use of question-begging names and epithets, and their effect in obscuring political controversies. It would bring out the curious fact that if you simply accept and apply to yourself a name intended as an insult, it may end by losing its insulting character. This appears to be happening to 'Trotskyist,' which is already dangerously close to being a compliment. So also with 'Conchy' during the last war. Another example is 'Britisher.' This word was used for years as a term of

---

1. Major-General Sir Ernest Dunlop Swinton (1868–1951), Professor of Military History, Fellow of All Souls College, Oxford. In addition to his stories, he wrote and translated a number of military histories. As Ole (Old) Luk-Oie he published *The Green Curve* (1909) and *The Great Tab Dope* (1915).
2. Ironically, the twentieth-century use of 'Hun' derives from a speech by Kaiser Wilhelm II to German troops sailing for China in 1900. Kipling is cited by the OED as referring to the 'shameless Hun' in *The Times*, 22 December 1902. Kipling's poem, 'For all we have and are' (1914), has as its fourth line, 'The Hun is at the gate!'

opprobrium in the Anglophobe American Press. Later on, Northcliffe and others, looking round for some substitute for 'Englishman' which should have an Imperialistic and jingoistic flavour, found 'Britisher' ready to hand, and took it over. Since then the word has had an aura of gutter patriotism, and the kind of person who tells you that 'what these natives need is a firm hand,' also tells you that he is 'proud to be a Britisher'—which is about equivalent to a Chinese Nationalist describing himself as a 'Chink.'

A V-1 Explosion

A not-too-distant explosion shakes the house, the windows rattle in their sockets, and in the next room the 1964 class[3] wakes up and lets out a yell or two. Each time this happens I find myself thinking, 'Is it possible that human beings can continue with this lunacy very much longer?' You know the answer, of course. Indeed, the difficulty nowadays is to find anyone who thinks that there will *not* be another war in the fairly near future.

The Three Super-states of the Future

Germany, I suppose, will be defeated this year, and when Germany is out of the way Japan will not be able to stand up to the combined power of Britain and the U.S.A. Then there will be a peace of exhaustion, with only minor and unofficial wars raging all over the place, and perhaps this so-called peace may last for decades. But after that, by the way the world is actually shaping, it may well be that war will *become permanent*. Already, quite visibly and more or less with the acquiescence of all of us, the world is splitting up into the two or three huge super-states forecast in James Burnham's *Managerial Revolution*. One cannot draw their exact boundaries as yet, but one can see more or less what areas they will comprise. And if the world does settle down into this pattern, it is likely that these vast states will be permanently at war with one another, though it will not necessarily be a very intensive or bloody kind of war. Their problems, both economic and psychological, will be a lot simpler if the doodlebugs are more or less constantly whizzing to and fro.

If these two or three super-states do establish themselves, not only will each of them be too big to be conquered, but they will be under no necessity to trade with one another, and in a position to prevent all contact between their nationals. Already, for a dozen years or so, large areas of the

---

3. '1964 class' is presumably a reference to Richard, Orwell's adopted son, then nine months old, who would be twenty in 1964, the age of a graduating class.

earth have been cut off from one another, although technically at peace.

Some months ago, in this column, I pointed out that modern scientific inventions have tended to prevent rather than increase international communication. This brought me several angry letters from readers, but none of them were able to show that what I had said was false. They merely retorted that if we had Socialism, the aeroplane, the radio, etc., would not be perverted to wrong uses. Very true, but then we haven't Socialism. As it is, the aeroplane is primarily a thing for dropping bombs and the radio primarily a thing for whipping up nationalism. Even before the war there was enormously less contact between the peoples of the earth than there had been thirty years earlier, and education was perverted, history rewritten and freedom of thought suppressed to an extent undreamed of in earlier ages. And there is no sign whatever of these tendencies being reversed.

Maybe I am pessimistic. But, at any rate those are the thoughts that cross my mind (and a lot of other people's too, I believe) every time the explosion of a V-bomb booms through the mist.[4]

4. This section includes several ideas developed in *Nineteen Eighty-Four*.

'In Defence of P.G. Wodehouse'[1]

Windmill, 1945

The Windmill *ran from 1944–48 at first as an annual and then more frequently. Twelve numbers were published. It published essays, stories and verse and was edited by Reginald Moore and Edward Lane, the latter being a pseudonym for the lesbian, Kay Dick (1915–2001). D.J. Taylor explains in* Orwell: The Life *that Orwell contributed his essay on Wodehouse because 'susceptible to the entreaties of literary friends he thought needed encouraging' (p. 344). Kay Dick had evidently asked Orwell for a story for her journal because on 26 September 1945 Orwell wrote telling her he had no ideas at that moment. He may well have sent her this essay instead of a story (see* A Life in Letters, *p. 273).*

When the Germans made their rapid advance through Belgium in the early summer of 1940, they captured, among other things, Mr. P. G. Wodehouse,[2] who had been living throughout the early part of the war in his villa at Le Touquet, and seems not to have realised until the last moment that he was in any danger. As he was led away into captivity, he is said to have remarked, 'Perhaps after this I shall write a serious book.' He was placed for the time being under house arrest, and from his subsequent statements it appears that he was treated in a fairly friendly way, German officers in the neighbourhood frequently 'dropping in for a bath or a party'.[3]

Over a year later, on 25th June 1941, the news came that Wodehouse had been released from internment and was living at the Adlon Hotel in Berlin. On the following day the public was astonished to learn that he had agreed to do some broadcasts of a 'non-political' nature over the

---

1. The essay was reprinted in *Critical Essays* (1946) and *Dickens, Dali & Others* (1946). The text reproduced here is from *Critical Essays*, which (with *Dickens, Dali & Others*) has a few sentences not included in the *Windmill*.
2. P.G. Wodehouse (1881–1975), author, dramatist, and lyricist. In 1940, when France was overrun by the Germans, he was interned. In the summer of 1941 he gave an interview in Berlin for the CBS network to be broadcast to the United States (then neutral), and recorded five talks which were broadcast to the United States and to Britain (see *n.* 4 below). He was immediately vilified in Britain as a traitor. The texts of the broadcasts were published by *Encounter*, reprinted in *Performing Flea: A Self-Portrait in Letters* (Penguin Books, 1961). After the war Wodehouse lived in virtual self-exile in the United States, but his work remained very popular. Six weeks before he died, he was knighted.
3. Wodehouse denied this; see Sproat, 42–43.

German radio. The full texts of these broadcasts are not easy to obtain at this date, but Wodehouse seems to have done five of them between 26th June and 2nd July, when the Germans took him off the air again. The first broadcast, on 26th June, was not made on the Nazi radio but took the form of an interview with Harry Flannery, the representative of the Columbia Broadcasting System, which still had its correspondents in Berlin. Wodehouse also published in the *Saturday Evening Post* an article which he had written while still in the internment camp.

The article and the broadcasts dealt mainly with Wodehouse's experiences in internment, but they did include a very few comments on the war. The following are fair samples:

> I never was interested in politics. I'm quite unable to work up any kind of belligerent feeling. Just as I'm about to feel belligerent about some country I meet a decent sort of chap. We go out together and lose any fighting thoughts or feelings.

> A short time ago they had a look at me on parade and got the right idea; at least they sent us to the local lunatic asylum. And I have been there forty-two weeks. There is a good deal to be said for internment. It keeps you out of the saloon and helps you to keep up with your reading. The chief trouble is that it means you are away from home for a long time. When I join my wife I had better take along a letter of introduction to be on the safe side.

> In the days before the war I had always been modestly proud of being an Englishman, but now that I have been some months resident in this bin or repository of Englishmen I am not so sure. . . . The only concession I want from Germany is that she gives me a loaf of bread, tells the gentlemen with muskets at the main gate to look the other way, and leaves the rest to me. In return I am prepared to hand over India, an autographed set of my books, and to reveal the secret process of cooking sliced potatoes on a radiator. This offer holds good till Wednesday week.

The first extract quoted above caused great offence. Wodehouse was also censured for using (in the interview with Flannery) the phrase 'whether Britain wins the war or not', and he did not make things better by describing in another broadcast the filthy habits of some Belgian prisoners among whom he was interned. The Germans recorded this broadcast and repeated it a number of times. They seem to have supervised his talks very lightly, and they allowed him not only to be funny about the discomforts of internment but to remark that 'the internees at Trost camp all fervently believe that Britain will eventually win'. The general upshot of the talks, however, was that he had not been ill-treated and bore no malice.

These broadcasts caused an immediate uproar in England. There were questions in Parliament, angry editorial comments in the press, and a stream of letters from fellow-authors, nearly all of them disapproving, though one or two suggested that it would be better to suspend judgment, and several pleaded that Wodehouse probably did not realise what he was doing. On 15th July, the Home Service of the B.B.C. carried an extremely violent Postscript by 'Cassandra' of the *Daily Mirror*, accusing Wodehouse of 'selling his country'. This postscript made free use of such expressions as 'Quisling' and 'worshipping the Führer'. The main charge was that Wodehouse had agreed to do German propaganda as a way of buying himself out of the internment camp.

'Cassandra's' Postscript caused a certain amount of protest, but on the whole it seems to have intensified popular feeling against Wodehouse. One result of it was that numerous lending libraries withdrew Wodehouse's books from circulation. Here is a typical news item:

> Within twenty-four hours of listening to the broadcast of Cassandra, the *Daily Mirror* columnist, Portadown (North Ireland) Urban District Council banned P. G. Wodehouse's books from their public library. Mr. Edward McCann said that Cassandra's broadcast had clinched the matter. Wodehouse was funny no longer. (*Daily Mirror*.)

In addition the B.B.C. banned Wodehouse's lyrics from the air and was still doing so a couple of years later. As late as December 1944 there were demands in Parliament that Wodehouse should be put on trial as a traitor.

There is an old saying that if you throw enough mud some of it will stick, and the mud has stuck to Wodehouse in a rather peculiar way. An impression has been left behind that Wodehouse's talks (not that anyone remembers what he said in them) showed him up not merely as a traitor but as an ideological sympathiser with Fascism. Even at the time several letters to the press claimed that 'Fascist tendencies' could be detected in his books, and the charge has been repeated since. I shall try to analyse the mental atmosphere of those books in a moment, but it is important to realise that the events of 1941 do not convict Wodehouse of anything worse than stupidity. The really interesting question is how and why he could be so stupid. When Flannery met Wodehouse (released, but still under guard) at the Adlon Hotel in June 1941, he saw at once that he was dealing with a political innocent, and when preparing him for their broadcast interview he had to warn him against making some exceedingly unfortunate remarks, one of which was by implication slightly anti-Russian. As it was, the phrase 'whether England wins or not' did get through.[4] Soon after the interview Wodehouse told him that he was also going to broadcast on the Nazi radio, apparently not realising that this action had any special significance. Flannery comments in his *Assignment to Berlin* (1942):

> By this time the Wodehouse plot was evident. It was one of the best Nazi publicity stunts of the war, the first with a human angle. . . . Plack (Goebbels's assistant) had gone to the camp near Gleiwitz to see Wodehouse, found that the author was completely without political sense, and had an idea. He suggested to Wodehouse that in return for being released from the prison camp he write a series of broadcasts about his experiences; there would be no censorship and he would put them on the air himself. In making that proposal Plack showed that he knew his man. He knew that Wodehouse made fun of the English in all his stories and that he seldom wrote in any other way, that he was still living in the period about which he wrote and had no conception of Nazism and all it meant. Wodehouse was his own Bertie Wooster.

The striking of an actual bargain between Wodehouse and Plack seems to be merely Flannery's own interpretation. The arrangement may have been of a much less definite kind, and to judge from the broadcasts themselves, Wodehouse's main idea in making them was to keep in touch with his public and—the comedian's ruling passion—to get a laugh. Obviously they are not the utterances of a Quisling of the type of Ezra

4. In an interview with a British journalist, Hubert Cole (*Illustrated*, 7 December 1946), Wodehouse maintained that this statement, which appeared in his interview, was written by Flannery: 'He wrote the whole script, including the words you mention, and I read them without realising their intention. I did not even notice them at the time' (Sproat, 58).

Pound or John Amery,[5] nor, probably, of a person capable of understanding the nature of Quislingism. Flannery seems to have warned
Wodehouse that it would be unwise to broadcast, but not very forcibly.
He adds that Wodehouse (though in one broadcast he refers to himself
as an Englishman) seemed to regard himself as an American citizen. He
had contemplated naturalisation, but had never filled in the necessary
papers. He even used, to Flannery, the phrase, 'We're not at war with
Germany'.

I have before me a bibliography of P. G. Wodehouse's works. It names
round about fifty books, but is certainly incomplete. It is as well to be
honest, and I ought to start by admitting that there are many books by
Wodehouse—perhaps a quarter or a third of the total—which I have not
read. It is not, indeed, easy to read the whole output of a popular writer
who is normally published in cheap editions. But I have followed his work
fairly closely since 1911, when I was eight years old, and am well acquainted
with its peculiar mental atmosphere—an atmosphere which has not, of
course, remained completely unchanged, but shows little alteration since
about 1925. In the passage from Flannery's book which I quoted above
there are two remarks which would immediately strike any attentive reader
of Wodehouse. One is to the effect that Wodehouse 'was still living in the
period about which he wrote', and the other that the Nazi Propaganda
Ministry made use of him because he 'made fun of the English'. The
second statement is based on a misconception to which I will return
presently. But Flannery's other comment is quite true and contains in it
part of the clue to Wodehouse's behaviour.

A thing that people often forget about P. G. Wodehouse's novels is how
long ago the better-known of them were written. We think of him as in
some sense typifying the silliness of the nineteen-twenties and nineteen-
thirties, but in fact the scenes and characters by which he is best remembered had all made their appearance before 1925. Psmith first appeared in
1909, having been foreshadowed by other characters in earlier school-
stories. Blandings Castle, with Baxter and the Earl of Emsworth both in
residence, was introduced in 1915. The Jeeves-Wooster cycle began in 1919,

5. John Amery (1912–1945), right-wing politician and son of Leo Amery, who was
a Conservative and patriotic MP and Secretary of State for India 1940–45. John Amery,
an ardent admirer of Hitler, broadcast from Germany during the war urging British
subjects in captivity to fight for Germany against England and Russia, and made public
speeches throughout occupied Europe on behalf of the German regime. He was
executed for treason in December 1945.

both Jeeves and Wooster having made brief appearances earlier. Ukridge appeared in 1924. When one looks through the list of Wodehouse's books from 1902 onwards, one can observe three fairly well-marked periods. The first is the school-story period. It includes such books as *The Gold Bat, The Pothunters*, etc., and has its high-spot in *Mike* (1909). *Psmith in the City*, published in the following year, belongs in this category, though it is not directly concerned with school life. The next is the American period. Wodehouse seems to have lived in the United States from about 1913 to 1920, and for a while showed signs of becoming Americanised in idiom and outlook. Some of the stories in *The Man with Two Left Feet* (1917) appear to have been influenced by O. Henry, and other books written about this time contain Americanisms (*e.g.* 'highball' for 'whisky and soda') which an Englishman would not normally use *in propria persona*. Nevertheless, almost all the books of this period—*Psmith, Journalist; The Little Nugget; The Indiscretions of Archie; Piccadilly Jim* and various others —depend for their effect on the *contrast* between English and American manners. English characters appear in an American setting, or *vice versa*: there is a certain number of purely English stories, but hardly any purely American ones. The third period might fitly be called the country-house period. By the early nineteen-twenties Wodehouse must have been making a very large income, and the social status of his characters moved upwards accordingly, though the Ukridge stories form a partial exception. The typical setting is now a country mansion, a luxurious bachelor flat or an expensive golf club. The schoolboy athleticism of the earlier books fades out, cricket and football giving way to golf, and the element of farce and burlesque becomes more marked. No doubt many of the later books, such as *Summer Lightning*, are light comedy rather than pure farce, but the occasional attempts at moral earnestness which can be found in *Psmith, Journalist; The Little Nugget; The Coming of Bill; The Man with Two Left Feet* and some of the school stories, no longer appear. Mike Jackson has turned into Bertie Wooster. That, however, is not a very startling metamorphosis, and one of the most noticeable things about Wodehouse is his *lack* of development. Books like *The Gold Bat* and *Tales of St. Austin's*, written in the opening years of this century, already have the familiar atmosphere. How much of a formula the writing of his later books had become one can see from the fact that he continued to write stories of English life although throughout the sixteen years before his internment he was living at Hollywood and Le Touquet.

Mike, which is now a difficult book to obtain in an unabridged form, must be one of the best 'light' school stories in English. But though its incidents are largely farcical, it is by no means a satire on the public-school system, and *The Gold Bat*, *The Pothunters*, etc., are even less so. Wodehouse was educated at Dulwich, and then worked in a bank and graduated into novel-writing by way of very cheap journalism. It is clear that for many years he remained 'fixated' on his old school and loathed the unromantic job and the lower-middle-class surroundings in which he found himself. In the early stories the 'glamour' of public-school life (house matches, fagging, teas round the study fire, etc.) is laid on fairly thick, and the 'play the game' code of morals is accepted with not many reservations. Wrykyn, Wodehouse's imaginary public school, is a school of a more fashionable type than Dulwich, and one gets the impression that between *The Gold Bat* (1904) and *Mike* (1909) Wrykyn itself has become more expensive and moved farther from London. Psychologically the most revealing book of Wodehouse's early period is *Psmith in the City*. Mike Jackson's father has suddenly lost his money, and Mike, like Wodehouse himself, is thrust at the age of about eighteen into an ill-paid subordinate job in a bank. Psmith is similarly employed, though not from financial necessity. Both this book and *Psmith, Journalist* (1915) are unusual in that they display a certain amount of political consciousness. Psmith at this stage chooses to call himself a Socialist—in his mind, and no doubt in Wodehouse's, this means no more than ignoring class distinctions—and on one occasion the two boys attend an open-air meeting on Clapham Common and go home to tea with an elderly Socialist orator, whose shabby-genteel home is described with some accuracy. But the most striking feature of the book is Mike's inability to wean himself from the atmosphere of school. He enters upon his job without any pretence of enthusiasm, and his main desire is not, as one might expect, to find a more interesting and useful job, but simply to be playing cricket. When he has to find himself lodgings he chooses to settle at Dulwich, because there he will be near a school and will be able to hear the agreeable sound of the ball striking against the bat. The climax of the book comes when Mike gets the chance to play in a county match and simply walks out of his job in order to do so. The point is that Wodehouse here sympathises with Mike: indeed he identifies himself with him, for it is clear enough that Mike bears the same relation to Wodehouse as Julien Sorel to Stendhal. But he created many other heroes essentially similar. Through the books of this and the next period there passes a whole series of young men to whom playing games and 'keeping fit' are a sufficient lifework. Wodehouse is almost incapable of imagining a desirable job. The great thing is to have money of your own, or, failing that, to find a sinecure. The hero of *Something Fresh* (1915) escapes from low-class journalism by becoming physical-training instructor to a dyspeptic millionaire: this is regarded as a step up, morally as well as financially.

In the books of the third period there is no narcissism and no serious interludes, but the implied moral and social background has changed much less than might appear at first sight. If one compares Bertie Wooster with Mike, or even with the rugger-playing prefects of the earliest school stories, one sees that the only real difference between them is that Bertie is richer and lazier. His ideals would be almost the same as theirs, but he fails to live up to them. Archie Moffam, in *The Indiscretions of Archie* (1921), is a type intermediate between Bertie and the earlier heroes: he is an ass, but he is also honest, kind-hearted, athletic and courageous. From first to last Wodehouse takes the public-school code of behaviour for granted, with the difference that in his later, more sophisticated period he prefers to show his characters violating it or living up to it against their will:

'Bertie! You wouldn't let down a pal?'

'Yes, I would.'

'But we were at school together, Bertie.'

'I don't care.'

'The old school, Bertie, the old school!'

'Oh, well—dash it!'

Bertie, a sluggish Don Quixote, has no wish to tilt at windmills, but he would hardly think of refusing to do so when honour calls. Most of the people whom Wodehouse intends as sympathetic characters are para-sites, and some of them are plain imbeciles, but very few of them could be described as immoral. Even Ukridge is a visionary rather than a plain crook. The most immoral, or rather un-moral, of Wodehouse's characters is Jeeves, who acts as a foil to Bertie Wooster's comparative high-mindedness and perhaps symbolises the widespread English belief that intelligence and unscrupulousness are much the same thing. How closely Wodehouse sticks to conventional morality can be seen from the fact that nowhere in his books is there anything in the nature of a sex joke. This is an enormous sacrifice for a farcical writer to make. Not only are there no dirty jokes, but there are hardly any compromising situations: the horns-on-the-forehead motif is almost completely avoided. Most of the full-length books, of course, contain a 'love interest', but it is always at the light-comedy level: the love affair, with its complications and its idyllic scenes, goes on and on, but, as the saying goes, 'nothing happens'. It is significant that Wodehouse, by nature a writer of farces, was able to collaborate more than once with Ian Hay,[6] a serio-comic writer and an exponent (vide *Pip*, etc.) of the 'clean-living Englishman' tradition at its silliest.

In *Something Fresh* Wodehouse had discovered the comic possibilities of the English aristocracy, and a succession of ridiculous but, save in a very few instances, not actually contemptible barons, earls and what-not followed accordingly. This had the rather curious effect of causing Wodehouse to be regarded, outside England, as a penetrating satirist of English society. Hence Flannery's statement that Wodehouse 'made fun of the English', which is the impression he would probably make on a German or even an American reader. Some time after the broadcasts from Berlin I was discussing them with a young Indian Nationalist who defended Wodehouse warmly. He took it for granted that Wodehouse *had* gone over to the enemy, which from his own point of view was the right thing to do. But what interested me was to find that he regarded Wodehouse as an anti-British writer who had done useful work by showing up the British aristocracy in their true colours. This is a mistake that it would be very difficult for an English person to make, and is a good instance of the way in which books, especially humorous books, lose their finer nuances when they reach a foreign audience. For it is clear enough that Wodehouse is *not* anti-British, and not anti-upper class either. On the contrary, a harmless old-fashioned snobbishness is perceptible all through his work. Just as an intelligent Catholic is able to see that the blasphemies of Baudelaire or James Joyce are not seriously damaging to the Catholic faith, so an English reader can see that in creating such characters as Hildebrand Spencer Poyns de Burgh John Hanneyside Coombe-Crombie, 12th Earl of Dreever, Wodehouse is not really attacking the social hierarchy. Indeed, no one who genuinely despised titles would write of them so much. Wodehouse's attitude towards the English social system is the same as his attitude towards the public-school moral code—a mild facetiousness covering an unthinking acceptance. The Earl of Emsworth is funny because an earl ought to have more dignity, and Bertie Wooster's helpless dependence on Jeeves is funny partly because the servant ought not to

---

6. Ian Hay (John Hay Beith, 1876–1952), novelist and dramatist. Wodehouse and Hay collaborated on the plays *A Damsel in Distress* (1928) and *Baa, Baa, Black Sheep* (1929).

be superior to the master. An American reader can mistake these two, and others like them, for hostile caricatures, because he is inclined to be Anglophobe already and they correspond to his preconceived ideas about a decadent aristocracy. Bertie Wooster, with his spats and his cane, is the traditional stage Englishman. But, as any English reader would see, Wodehouse intends him as a sympathetic figure, and Wodehouse's real sin has been to present the English upper classes as much nicer people than they are. All through his books certain problems are consistently avoided. Almost without exception his moneyed young men are unassuming, good mixers, not avaricious: their tone is set for them by Psmith, who retains his own upper-class exterior but bridges the social gap by addressing everyone as 'Comrade'.

But there is another important point about Bertie Wooster: his out-of-dateness. Conceived in 1917 or thereabouts, Bertie really belongs to an epoch earlier than that. He is the 'knut' of the pre-1914 period, celebrated in such songs as 'Gilbert the Filbert' or 'Reckless Reggie of the Regent's Palace'. The kind of life that Wodehouse writes about by preference, the life of the 'clubman' or 'man about town', the elegant young man who lounges all the morning in Piccadilly with a cane under his arm and a carnation in his buttonhole, barely survived into the nineteen-twenties. It is significant that Wodehouse could publish in 1936 a book entitled *Young Men in Spats*. For who was wearing spats at that date? They had gone out of fashion quite ten years earlier. But the traditional 'knut', the 'Piccadilly Johnny', *ought* to wear spats, just as the pantomime Chinese ought to wear a pigtail. A humorous writer is not obliged to keep up to date, and having struck one or two good veins, Wodehouse continued to exploit them with a regularity that was no doubt all the easier because he did not set foot in England during the sixteen years that preceded his internment. His picture of English society had been formed before 1914, and it was a naïve, traditional and, at bottom, admiring picture. Nor did he ever become genuinely Americanised. As I have pointed out, spontaneous Americanisms do occur in the books of the middle period, but Wodehouse remained English enough to find American slang an amusing and slightly shocking novelty. He loves to thrust a slang phrase or a crude fact in among Wardour Street English ('With a hollow groan Ukridge borrowed five shillings from me and went out into the night'), and expressions like 'a piece of cheese' or 'bust him on the noggin' lend themselves to this purpose. But the trick had been developed before he made any American contacts, and his use of garbled quotations is a common device of English writers running back to Fielding. As Mr. John Hayward has pointed out,[7] Wodehouse owes a good deal to his knowledge of English literature and especially of Shakespeare. His books are aimed, not, obviously, at a highbrow audience, but at an audience educated along traditional lines. When, for instance, he describes somebody as heaving 'the kind of sigh that Prometheus might have heaved when the vulture dropped in for its lunch', he is assuming that his readers will know something of Greek mythology. In his early days the writers he admired were probably Barry Pain, Jerome K. Jerome, W. W. Jacobs, Kipling and F. Anstey, and he has remained closer to them than to the quick-moving American comic writers such as Ring Lardner or Damon Runyon. In his radio interview with Flannery, Wodehouse wondered whether 'the kind of people and the kind of England I write about will live after the war', not realising that they were ghosts already. 'He was still living in the period about which he wrote,' says Flannery, meaning, probably, the nineteen-twenties. But the period was really the Edwardian age, and Bertie Wooster, if he ever existed, was killed round about 1915.

If my analysis of Wodehouse's mentality is accepted, the idea that in 1941 he consciously aided the Nazi propaganda machine becomes untenable and even ridiculous. He *may* have been induced to broadcast by the promise of an earlier release (he was due for release a few months later, on reaching his sixtieth birthday), but he cannot have realised that what he did would be damaging to British interests. As I have tried to show, his moral outlook has remained that of a public-school boy, and according to the public-school code, treachery in time of war is the most unforgivable of all the sins. But how could he fail to grasp that what he did would be a big propaganda score for the Germans and would bring down a torrent of disapproval on his own head? To answer this one must take two things into consideration. First, Wodehouse's complete lack—so far as one can judge from his printed works—of political awareness. It is nonsense to talk of 'Fascist tendencies' in his books. There are no post-1918 tendencies at all. Throughout his work there is a certain uneasy awareness of the problem of class distinctions, and scattered through it at various dates there are ignorant though not unfriendly references to Socialism. In *The Heart of a Goof* (1926) there is a rather silly story about a Russian novelist, which seems to have been inspired by the factional

---

7. 'P. G. Wodehouse', by John Hayward (*The Saturday Book*, 1942). In a footnote Orwell states, 'I believe this is the only full-length critical essay on Wodehouse.'

struggle then raging in the U.S.S.R. But the references in it to the Soviet system are entirely frivolous and, considering the date, not markedly hostile. That is about the extent of Wodehouse's political consciousness, so far as it is discoverable from his writings. Nowhere, so far as I know, does he so much as use the word 'Fascism' or 'Nazism'. In left-wing circles, indeed in 'enlightened' circles of any kind, to broadcast on the Nazi radio, to have any truck with the Nazis whatever, would have seemed just as shocking an action before the war as during it. But that is a habit of mind that had been developed during nearly a decade of ideological struggle against Fascism. The bulk of the British people, one ought to remember, remained anæsthetic to that struggle until late into 1940. Abyssinia, Spain, China, Austria, Czechoslovakia—the long series of crimes and aggressions had simply slid past their consciousness or were dimly noted as quarrels occurring among foreigners and 'not our business'. One can gauge the general ignorance from the fact that the ordinary Englishman thought of 'Fascism' as an exclusively Italian thing and was bewildered when the same word was applied to Germany. And there is nothing in Wodehouse's writings to suggest that he was better informed, or more interested in politics, than the general run of his readers.

The other thing one must remember is that Wodehouse happened to be taken prisoner at just the moment when the war reached its desperate phase. We forget these things now, but until that time feelings about the war had been noticeably tepid. There was hardly any fighting, the Chamberlain government was unpopular, eminent publicists like Lloyd George and Bernard Shaw[8] were hinting that we should make a compromise peace as quickly as possible, trade union and Labour Party branches all over the country were passing anti-war resolutions. Afterwards, of course, things changed. The Army was with difficulty extricated from Dunkirk, France collapsed, Britain was alone, the bombs rained on London, Goebbels announced that Britain was to be 'reduced to degradation and poverty'. By the middle of 1941 the British people knew what they were up against and feelings against the enemy were far fiercer than before. But Wodehouse had spent the intervening year in internment, and his captors seem to have treated him reasonably well. He had missed the

8. The words 'like Lloyd George and Bernard Shaw' were set in page proof, but excised. The excision was probably due to in-house censorship, for fear of libel. Lloyd George, World War I Prime Minister, died in 1945, but George Bernard Shaw did not die until 1950, and until his death a libel action could have been launched. It seems likely that Orwell intended these words to be included, and so they have been restored.

turning-point of the war, and in 1941 he was still reacting in terms of 1939. He was not alone in this. On several occasions about this time the Germans brought captured British soldiers to the microphone, and some of them made remarks at least as tactless as Wodehouse's. They attracted no attention, however. And even an outright Quisling like John Amery was afterwards to arouse much less indignation than Wodehouse had done.[9]

But why? Why should a few rather silly but harmless remarks by an elderly novelist have provoked such an outcry? One has to look for the probable answer amid the dirty requirements of propaganda warfare.

There is one point about the Wodehouse broadcasts that is almost certainly significant—the date. Wodehouse was released two or three days before the invasion of the U.S.S.R., and at a time when the higher ranks of the Nazi party must have known that the invasion was imminent. It was vitally necessary to keep America out of the war as long as possible, and in fact, about this time, the German attitude towards the U.S.A. did become more conciliatory than it had been before. The Germans could hardly hope to defeat Russia, Britain and the U.S.A. in combination, but if they could polish off Russia quickly—and presumably they expected to do so—the Americans might never intervene. The release of Wodehouse was only a minor move, but it was not a bad sop to throw to the American isolationists. He was well known in the United States, and he was—or so the Germans calculated—popular with the Anglophobe public as a caricaturist who made fun of the silly-ass Englishman with his spats and his monocle. At the microphone he could be trusted to damage British prestige in one way or another, while his release would demonstrate that the Germans were good fellows and knew how to treat their enemies chivalrously. That presumably was the calculation, though the fact that Wodehouse was only broadcasting for about a week suggests that he did not come up to expectations.

But on the British side similar though opposite calculations were at work. For the two years following Dunkirk, British morale depended largely upon the feeling that this was not only a war for democracy but a war which the common people had to win by their own efforts. The upper classes were discredited by their appeasement policy and by the

9. The words 'And even an outright Quisling . . . had done' were not in *Windmill*. Examples of interviews with Allied soldiers captured in April 1941 after the failure of the campaign in Greece, with their photographs, can be found in *Signal* (1940–45), the German propaganda magazine circulated outside Germany.

disasters of 1940, and a social levelling process appeared to be taking place. Patriotism and left-wing sentiments were associated in the popular mind, and numerous able journalists were at work to tie the association tighter. Priestley's 1940 broadcasts, and 'Cassandra's' articles in the *Daily Mirror*, were good examples of the demagogic propaganda flourishing at that time. In this atmosphere, Wodehouse made an ideal whipping-boy. For it was generally felt that the rich were treacherous, and Wodehouse—as 'Cassandra' vigorously pointed out in his broadcast—was a rich man. But he was the kind of rich man who could be attacked with impunity and without risking any damage to the structure of society. To denounce Wodehouse was not like denouncing, say, Beaverbrook. A mere novelist, however large his earnings may happen to be, is not *of* the possessing class. Even if his income touches £50,000 a year he has only the outward semblance of a millionaire. He is a lucky outsider who has fluked into a fortune—usually a very temporary fortune—like the winner of the Calcutta Derby Sweep. Consequently, Wodehouse's indiscretion gave a good propaganda opening. It was a chance to 'expose' a wealthy parasite without drawing attention to any of the parasites who really mattered.

In the desperate circumstances of the time, it was excusable to be angry at what Wodehouse did, but to go on denouncing him three or four years later—and more, to let an impression remain that he acted with conscious treachery—is not excusable.[10] Few things in this war have been more morally disgusting than the present hunt after traitors and Quislings. At best it is largely the punishment of the guilty by the guilty. In France, all kinds of petty rats—police officials, penny-a-lining journalists, women who have slept with German soldiers—are hunted down while almost without exception the big rats escape. In England the fiercest tirades against Quislings are uttered by Conservatives who were practising appeasement in 1938 and Communists who were advocating it in 1940. I have striven to show how the wretched Wodehouse—just because success and expatriation had allowed him to remain mentally in the Edwardian age—became the *corpus vile* in a propaganda experiment, and I suggest that it is now time to regard the incident as closed. If Ezra Pound is caught and shot by the American authorities, it will have the effect of establishing

10. For thirty-five years, successive British governments kept Wodehouse's file under seal as an 'official secret'. This included the MI5 interrogation report. The suspicion of Wodehouse's treachery was allowed to stand unanswered authoritatively (Sproat, 104). The papers were released in October 1999; see Iain Sproat, 'In all innocence', *Times Literary Supplement*, 29 October 1999, pp. 14–15.

his reputation as a poet for hundreds of years; and even in the case of Wodehouse, if we drive him to retire to the United States and renounce his British citizenship, we shall end by being horribly ashamed of ourselves. Meanwhile, if we really want to punish the people who weakened national morale at critical moments, there are other culprits who are nearer home and better worth chasing.

'Paris Puts a Gay Face on Its Miseries'

The Observer, 25 FEBRUARY 1945

One Paris correspondent after another has dilated on the food shortage, but it can hardly be mentioned too often. It is the dominant factor in most people's lives, and by diverting attention from larger issues—perhaps even by rousing resentment against Britain and the United States—it is capable of directly affecting the political situation.

Every newspaper one looks at contains complaints about food distribution. One must realise that for two months the average Parisian has not seen butter, and for far longer than that he has never had enough of anything except vegetables and a blackish bread, which probably contains rye and barley.

The tiny meat ration is often unobtainable, sugar is very scarce, coffee (even in the form of roasted acorns) is almost non-existent, and cigarettes are costly rarities unless you happen to be friends with an American soldier.

A litre of the coarsest wine, if you can get hold of it, costs the equivalent of eight shillings. More serious is the lack of milk, even tinned milk, for the children. And there is no coal for domestic purposes. There is gas for cooking at certain hours, but the gas situation has presumably not been improved by the recent flooding of the Seine, which has made it impossible for the coal barges to pass under the bridges.

With all this, the first remark of every newcomer is that Paris manages to put a very good face upon its miseries. In the centre of the town, where American money oozes in all directions and a lively Black Market flourishes, it would almost be possible to imagine that nothing is wrong. There are no taxis and the streets are only half lit, but the girls are as carefully made up as ever, and the hat shops and jewellery stores have almost their ancient glitter. Out in the working-class suburbs things are naturally worse. Glassless windows are common, many of the cafés are shut, the food shops have a miserable appearance.

A grocer's window will sometimes contain nothing at all except a list of the goods which are out of stock. Yet even in the poorest quarters the surface aspect of things is less bad than I would have expected. Paris is not dingier or more neglected than present-day London, and considerably less battered. And in several days of wandering to and fro in all kinds of quarters I have not yet seen a barefooted person, and not many who were conspicuously ragged. Probably half the women have stockings, and though wooden shoes are common they do not predominate.

The signs of privation are obvious enough if one knows where to look for them. The children of five or six look fairly sturdy, but the very young babies are terribly pale. The pigeons, once so numerous in Paris streets, have almost completely disappeared. They have been eaten. When a plane tree on the sidewalk is lopped, one sees elegantly dressed women waiting to collect bundles of twigs for firewood. Yet the people carry themselves with a peculiar dignity which they perhaps learned under the German occupation. On the Metro they eye your foreign uniform with an air that seems to say, 'We know you are well fed and have plenty of cigarettes. We know, you are the possessor of soap, and even of coffee. But let us pretend we are on an equal footing.'

It is an interesting fact that there are almost no beggars—certainly far fewer than there were before the war. One is not even asked for cigarettes, though if one offers a cigarette spontaneously it is accepted with pathetic gratitude.

Almost as soon as I set foot in Paris I returned, as anyone would, to the quarters I had known best in the days before the war. Round Notre Dame it was almost the same as ever. The little bookstalls along the river bank were just the same, the print-sellers were even selling the same prints: the innumerable anglers were still catching nothing, the menders of mattresses were as busy as ever on the quays.

Further south, in the Latin Quarter, things were more changed. The various foreign colonies, even including the Arabs who used to do most of the navvy work of Paris, seemed all to have disappeared.

In the big Montparnasse cafés, instead of a cosmopolitan mob of artists, there sat middle-class French families thriftily sipping at glasses of fruit juice. The Panthéon had been spattered by machine-gun bullets. In the old quarter between the Boulevard Saint Michel and the Rue Monge I could at first find only one shop (an undertaker's) which was in exactly the same position as before.

Then, to my delight, I came upon a little bistro which I used to know and which had not changed hands. The proprietor welcomed me with open arms, refused to take more than half the cigarettes I offered him, and brought out a bottle of something that was very drinkable though it was not what its label declared it to be.

Across the street the tiny hotel where I used once to live[1] was boarded up and partly ruinous. It appeared empty. But as I came away, from behind the broken window pane of what used to be my own room, I saw two hungry-looking children peeping out at me, just like wild animals.[2]

1. Orwell lived in a small hotel in the rue du Pot de Fer, the eastern end of which is less than 200 metres west of the rue Monge at Place Monge Metro station.
2. This article, like others in the series, had sub-headings (e.g. 'Streets Half Lit', 'Pale Babies', and 'The Little Bistro'). These are almost certainly the work of a sub-editor (as is the shortness of the paragraphs) and have not been included here or elsewhere.

'The French Believe We Have Had a Revolution'

Manchester Evening News, 20 MARCH 1945

So far as one can judge from casual conversations and from the Press, Britain's reputation has never stood higher in France than it does now. The attitude of the average man is not only friendlier than General de Gaulle's speeches would lead one to suppose but it is also far friendlier than one would infer from what might be called the mechanics of the situation.

For four years France was subjected to a barrage of anti-British propaganda, some of it extremely skilful, and at the same time Britain was driven by military necessity to bomb French cities, sink French ships, and commit other acts of war which the average man could hardly be blamed for resenting at the time when they happened. But on top of this, the invasion and the subsequent campaigns have seriously disrupted the economic life of the country. It is generally agreed that in the later period of the occupation France was better off in a physical sense than she is now, in spite of the huge-scale looting practised by the Germans.

The transport system has not yet recovered from the invasion, and the heaviest fighting took place in some of the best agricultural areas, upsetting first the hay harvest, then the grain harvest, and resulting in enormous losses of livestock. One gets some idea of what this means when one sees butter, almost unobtainable in any legal way, being black-marketed at something over £2 a pound. It is the same with many other foodstuffs, and thanks to the lack of locomotives the fuel situation in the big towns is catastrophic. Paris shivered through the winter of 1940, under the Germans, and shivered again through the winter of 1944, under the Anglo-Americans. Moreover it is realised that the food crisis has been accentuated in recent months by the diversion of Allied shipping to the Pacific.

Yet there seems to be remarkably little resentment. No doubt the forces that supported Vichy are still there, under the surface, but the only body of expressed opinion that could be possibly called anti-British is that of the Communists. The Communists are to some extent politically hostile to Britain because they see in Britain the likeliest leader of the 'western bloc' which it is the object of Soviet policy to prevent. The ordinary man is pro-British both personally and politically, and if asked why, he gives two reasons, one rather trivial, the other more serious and possibly containing in it the seeds of future misunderstanding.

The first reason is that the British troops have on the whole been better ambassadors for their country than the Americans. The comparison is not really a fair one, because the British are here in comparatively small numbers. The bulk of the British forces are in Belgium, and the vast majority of the soldiers who throng the streets of Paris are Americans. Most of them have come from several months in the unbearable conditions of the front line, and they have a large accumulation of pay in their pockets and only a few hours in which to spend it. But the other reason for the present friendly attitude of the French towards Britain is a flattering but somewhat exaggerated estimate of British political achievement during the war.

Frenchmen are much impressed not only by the obstinacy with which Britain continued the struggle in 1940 but by the national unity she displayed. They say with truth that in the moment of crisis Britain had no fifth column and not even any great bitterness of feeling between classes. But to a surprising extent they are inclined to mistake the surface changes of war-time Britain for an actual social revolution, accomplished by common consent. The word 'revolution' is used again and again in connection with Britain's present-day development, both in conversation and in print.

Frenchmen who might be expected to take a more cynical view are to be heard saying that class privilege is no longer rampant in England, that large incomes have been taxed out of existence, and that private capitalism has in effect given way to a centralised economy. And they remark with admiration that all this has been achieved without bloodshed, almost without friction, in the middle of a struggle for existence.

To anyone who knows how little real structural change has taken place in Britain during the war, these eulogies are rather disconcerting. Curiously enough they are repeated by Frenchmen who have visited war-time Britain, and perhaps spent several years there. The mistake made, in many cases, seems to be to confuse patriotism with social enlightenment. Without a doubt the general *behaviour* in Britain during the war has been good. All classes have been willing to sacrifice either their lives or their comfort, rationing has been equitable and efficient, profiteering and black-marketing have never been a major problem, industrial production has soared in spite of every kind of difficulty, and women have flung themselves into the war effort to an unprecedented extent. Frenchmen compare these phenomena with the much more discouraging things that have happened in their own country, and are apt not to realise that the essential social structure of Britain has remained almost unchanged and may reassert itself when the danger has passed.

There are other current misconceptions—in particular, the failure of nearly all Frenchmen to grasp the British attitude towards Germany and the peace settlement. Few Frenchmen realise how unwilling the British people will be to maintain a permanent army of occupation in Germany, or to support any settlement that would make such an army necessary. Not many Frenchmen understand the extent to which Britain's policy is conditioned by her close association with the U.S.A., and hardly any realise that Britain can never act internationally without considering the Dominions.

The present relations between France and Britain are good, but the possible sources of discord are many, and they could do with more illumination than they are getting at present.

France looks hopefully towards Britain as the land of true democracy, the country that has been able to recover from its past mistakes without civil disturbance, without dictatorship, and without infringing intellectual liberty. This picture is not altogether false, but it could be the cause of serious disappointment, and it would be well if more Frenchmen were able to distinguish between the real social changes that have taken place in Britain and the temporary expedients that have been forced upon a country fighting for its life.

Letter to *Tribune*: 'The Polish Trial'

unpublished, 26(?) JUNE 1945

This letter was set up in type but, according to Orwell's marginal note on the galley slip, 'withdrawn because Tribune *altered attitude in following week'.*

I read with some disappointment your comment on the trial of the sixteen Poles in Moscow,[1] in which you seemed to imply that they had behaved in a discreditable manner and deserved punishment.

Early in the proceedings I formed the opinion that the accused were technically guilty: only, just what were they guilty of? Apparently it was merely of doing what everyone thinks it right to do when his country is occupied by a foreign power—that is, of trying to keep a military force in being, of maintaining communication with the outside world, of committing acts of sabotage and occasionally killing people. In other words, they were accused of trying to preserve the independence of their country against an unelected puppet government, and of remaining obedient to a government which at that time was recognised by the whole world except the U.S.S.R. The Germans during their period of occupation could have brought exactly the same indictment against them, and they would have been equally guilty.

It will not do to say that the efforts of the Poles to remain independent 'objectively' aided the Nazis, and leave it at that. Many actions which Left-wingers do not disapprove of have 'objectively' aided the Germans. How about E.A.M., for instance?[2] They also tried to keep their military force in being, and they, too, killed Allied soldiers—British in this case—and they were not even acting under the orders of a government which was recognised by anyone as legal. But what of it? We do not disapprove

1. The British had called for a meeting of the leaders of the Polish underground to discuss the implementation of the Yalta decisions on the formation of a Polish Government of National Unity. The preliminary meeting was to be held in Moscow and a further meeting was planned for London. However, when the Poles reached Moscow they were put on trial.

2. E.A.M. (Ethnikon Apeleftherotikon Metopon), the National Liberation Front, was formed in Greece in 1941 after the German invasion. It started as a true resistance movement with nearly the whole population as members. By early 1942 it was discovered that it was in fact a Communist-organised movement. A national guerrilla army was then formed to fight the Germans, but found itself also fighting the E.A.M. When the British returned to Greece in 1945, they also found themselves fighting the E.A.M.

of their action, and if sixteen E.A.M. leaders were now brought to London and sentenced to long terms of imprisonment we should rightly protest.

To be anti-Polish and pro-Greek is only possible if one sets up a double standard of political morality, one for the U.S.S.R. and the other for the rest of the world. Before these sixteen Poles went to Moscow they were described in the Press as political delegates, and it was stated that they had been summoned there to take part in discussions on the formation of a new government. After their arrest all mention of their status as political delegates was dropped from the British Press—an example of the kind of censorship that is necessary if this double standard is to be made acceptable to the big public. Any well-informed person is aware of similar instances. To name just one: at this moment speakers up and down the country are justifying the Russian purges on the ground that Russia 'had no quislings,' at the same time as any mention of the considerable numbers of Russian troops, including several generals, who changed sides and fought for the Germans is being suppressed by cautious editors. This kind of whitewashing may be due to a number of different motives, some of them respectable ones, but its effect on the Socialist movement can be deadly if it is long continued.

When I wrote in your columns I repeatedly said that if one criticises this or that Russian action one is not obliged to put on airs of moral superiority. Their behaviour is not worse than that of capitalist governments, and its actual results may often be better. Nor is it likely that we shall alter the behaviour of the rulers of the U.S.S.R. by telling them that we disapprove of them. The whole point is the effect of the Russian mythos on the Socialist movement *here*. At present we are all but openly applying the double standard of morality. With one side of our mouths we cry out that mass deportations, concentration camps, forced labour and suppression of freedom of speech are appalling crimes, while with the other we proclaim that these things are perfectly all right if done by the U.S.S.R. or its satellite states: and where necessary we make this plausible by doctoring the news and cutting out unpalatable facts. One cannot possibly build up a healthy Socialist movement if one is obliged to condone no matter what crime when the U.S.S.R. commits it. No one knows better than I do that it is unpopular to say anything anti-Russian *at this moment*. But what of it? I am only 42, and I can remember the time when it was as dangerous to say anything pro-Russian as it is to say anything anti-Russian now. Indeed, I am old enough to have seen working class audiences booing and jeering at speakers who had used the word Socialism.

These fashions pass away, but they can't be depended on to do so unless thinking people are willing to raise their voices against the fallacy of the moment. It is only because over the past hundred years small groups and lonely individuals have been willing to face unpopularity that the Socialist movement exists at all.

George Orwell

Response to 'Orwell and the Stinkers'

Tribune, 27 JULY 1945

Orwell's letter is a response to an accusation by J.E. Miller in Million.[1]

I can hardly ask you to publish whole chapters of a book in your correspondence columns, but anyone who cares to look up the relevant passages in *The Road to Wigan Pier* will see that your correspondent, Mr. J. E. Miller, has misrepresented me seriously and, I think, intentionally.

He accuses me of 'violently abusing' the working class and of thinking them 'smelly,' etc., because of such statements as (*a*) the working classes as a whole are dirtier than the bourgeoisie; (*b*) the habit of washing all over is a recent one in Europe and was more recently adopted by the working class; and (*c*) the English are dirtier than the Japanese. All of these are simply statements of well-known and easily observed facts which it would be merely dishonest to deny. Of course, the working classes, as a whole, are dirtier than the bourgeoisie. How can they be otherwise? The average person in this country still lives in a house where there is not even a bathroom, let alone an adequate water supply. Again, it is perfectly well known that personal cleanliness is only a recently adopted habit in Europe and, like most innovations, reached the poorer classes last. Well within the last ten years I have heard elderly or middle-aged miners and farm labourers maintain that hot baths are 'weakening.' And, of course, the English are dirtier than the Japanese or several other Oriental peoples. Thousands of observers would confirm this. Every Indian, for example, washes his teeth elaborately every day. Who would dare to say the same of the English? If I had *not* made the remarks objected to, while I was discussing the question at all, I should simply have been misstating known facts.

But what I was discussing in this chapter of *Wigan Pier* was the theory taught to us as children that the working classes are, as it were, smelly by nature. We were taught that the 'lower classes' (as it was usual to call them) had a different smell from ourselves, and that it was a nasty smell; we were taught just the same about Jews, Negroes and various other

---

1. *Million* ran for three issues. It was undated; they are assigned to 1943–45. It was published in Glasgow and carried one of two subtitles: 'New Left Writing' or 'The People's Review'.

categories of human beings. In the book, I explained elaborately how I was taught this, how I accepted it, and how and why I afterwards got rid of it. Mr. Miller ignores all this and simply picks out isolated sentences which seem to support his thesis, a method by which anybody can be made to say anything.[2]

Since Mr. Miller has chosen to drag in Mr. Gollancz (no longer my publisher, by the way), I will add that I discussed these passages with Mr. Gollancz before the book was printed, and that he does not 'reproach' me in his preface but merely reinforced what I had said: that I had received a thoroughly snobbish education, which had left its mark on me but which I had done my best to struggle against.[3] After all, if the book had been simply the anti-working-class tirade that Mr. Miller seems to imply it was, why should it have been selected by the Left Book Club?

George Orwell

2. Orwell wrote, 'That was what we were taught – *the lower classes smell*'; see *CW*, V, 119; the italics are in the original. He then discussed this proposition on the following four pages. It was Somerset Maugham who unequivocally stated that the working man stank. Orwell quoted a dozen lines from Maugham's *On a Chinese Screen*, the only book, Orwell said, he knew in which this issue 'is set forth without humbug'. Maugham wrote, and Orwell quoted, 'I do not blame the working man because he stinks, but stink he does.'

3. Gollancz's Foreword is reprinted as an appendix to the *Complete Works* edition, Volume V. Although he thought Orwell was 'exaggerating violently', he went on, 'I know, in fact, of no other book in which a member of the middle class exposes with such complete frankness the shameful way in which he was brought up to think of large numbers of his fellow men. This section will be, I think, of the greatest value to middle-class and working-class members of the Left Book Club alike. . . .'

Review: Pierre Maillaud, *The English Way*

Manchester Evening News, 12 JULY 1945

At a time like the present, when the trouble in Syria[1] is still making headlines in the French Press, it is pleasant to be reminded that there are some Frenchmen who do not dislike us. But actually, friendly and even over-friendly though it is, M. Maillaud's book gives a truer picture of the contemporary French attitude towards England than one would gather from the utterances of certain public men.[2] Almost any Englishman who has been in France recently would agree that Anglophile feeling has never been so strong, and that now, if ever, is the moment for the two countries to move into closer partnership.

M. Maillaud's book, which is aimed at the British rather than the French public, is first and foremost a plea for Anglo-French co-operation and for an understanding of what that co-operation would mean.

However, it is also an analysis of English civilization and the English character, of the structure and peculiarities of British political parties, and of the policies and strategies that have been dictated by Britain's special position as a part of Europe and at the same time the centre of an extra-European empire. M. Maillaud has lived in England for the last fourteen or fifteen years and he knows our country quite exceptionally well. Throughout most of the war he was one of the small but brilliant team of French broadcasters who succeeded in making the B.B.C. the most trusted source of news in occupied France.

Probably the most valuable part of his book is his examination of British foreign policy between the wars. Politically he is himself a Liberal,

1. In 1945, Syria sought independence from French control. In May there were clashes between local people and French troops, and the French bombarded Damascus. The British, who, as a result of World War II, had forces in Syria, intervened. France was forced to evacuate its troops from Syria and Lebanon in 1946.
2. At the head of this review were reproduced photographs of ten prominent Frenchmen, each with a two-word description: Charles Boyer (actor), 'Latin romance'; Edouard Herriot (radical socialist politician), 'stubby provincial'; General Charles de Gaulle, 'rigid dignity'; Paul Reynaud (politician and prime minister), 'intellectual subtlety'; Maurice Chevalier (actor and singer), 'saucy wit'; Marshal Pétain, 'the Ancien regime'; Edouard Daladier (politician and premier), 'smooth shrewdness'; Jean Borotra (tennis champion), 'wiry vigour'; Georges Bidault (resistance leader and foreign minister), 'keen-eyed strength'; General De Lattre de Tassigny, 'ironic nonchalance'. These were probably not Orwell's descriptions.

and the qualities he most admires in England are respect for minorities and the ability to make deep changes without either shedding blood or losing touch with tradition. But with the detachment of a foreigner he is able to see that these qualities spring out of Britain's insular position, which is also a cause of ignorance and complacency.

British conduct of foreign affairs between 1930 and 1940 is not a thing to be proud of, and M. Maillaud does not spare it. He rightly points out the part played by sheer class feeling in the Conservative party's appeasement of Fascism, but he also emphasises—what is less popular to mention nowadays— the pacifism of the British working class and the unrealistic outlook of the Left-wing parties who demanded an active foreign policy but were unwilling to back it up with adequate armies.

It is important that as many foreign critics as possible should point this out, for few people are aware of the disastrous effects that were produced in Europe by the Labour party's opposition to conscription. But M. Maillaud is looking deeper than the surface and he sees that part of the trouble is that nearly all classes in England are guilty of xenophobia. The strip of water which has given them security has also given them a conscious or unconscious contempt for foreigners—especially, M. Maillaud adds, those who are 'noisiest and darkest-haired'—which leads to a lack of interest in foreign affairs and a too slow reaction to danger.

The appeasement policy was due partly to the apathy of the masses who, if they paid any attention to Europe at all, were inclined to prefer the Germans to the French. But it was also due in part to the British Government's need to consider the Dominions, who were none too willing to be mixed up in European quarrels.

The fact that M. Maillaud points this out is sufficient to stamp him as an exceptionally acute observer. Britain's special relationship with the United States, and the pull it exercises on British policy, is obvious enough, but there are very few Europeans indeed who realise that Australia and Canada are not simply provinces governed from Whitehall and that public opinion in those countries has to be considered when Britain makes any move in Europe.

M. Maillaud ends his book with an urgent plea to Britain to abandon the policy implied in the Teheran agreement (this book appears to have been written early in 1944) and to remember that she is part of Europe and that her main interests lie there. In 1940, he says, all Europe looked up to Britain as the defender of Western civilisation. But the special position then gained could be lost if Britain committed herself to a 'Big Four' policy which would tie her to Russia and America and force her to be indifferent to the fate of the smaller nations.

What he would like to see is a federation of all the Western European States—an attractive project, but one which is less likely of realisation now than it may have seemed when the book was written. However, the first step towards it would be a better understanding between Britain and France, and this book should at least help in achieving that.

'The Sporting Spirit'

Tribune, 14 DECEMBER 1945

Now that the brief visit of the Dynamo football team[1] has come to an end, it is possible to say publicly what many thinking people were saying privately before the Dynamos ever arrived. That is, that sport is an unfailing cause of ill-will, and that if such a visit as this had any effect at all on Anglo-Soviet relations, it could only be to make them slightly worse than before.

Even the newspapers have been unable to conceal the fact that at least two of the four matches played led to much bad feeling. At the Arsenal match, I am told by someone who was there, a British and a Russian player came to blows and the crowd booed the referee. The Glasgow match, someone else informs me, was simply a free-for-all from the start. And then there was the controversy, typical of our nationalistic age, about the composition of the Arsenal team. Was it really an all-England team, as claimed by the Russians, or merely a league team, as claimed by the British? And did the Dynamos end their tour abruptly in order to avoid playing an all-England team? As usual, everyone answers these questions according to his political predilections. Not quite everyone, however. I noted with interest, as an instance of the vicious passions that football provokes, that the sporting correspondent of the Russophile *News Chronicle* took the anti-Russian line and maintained that Arsenal was *not* an all-England team. No doubt the controversy will continue to echo for years in the footnotes of history books. Meanwhile the result of the Dynamos' tour, in so far as it has had any result, will have been to create fresh animosity on both sides.

---

1. Moscow Dynamo, a Russian soccer team, toured Britain in the autumn of 1945 and played a number of leading British clubs. 'Guest players' were allowed into teams at this time because of wartime conditions, but, even allowing for that, it was claimed that Britain's Arsenal team had been unduly strengthened. Orwell had been a successful participant in football and the Wall Game at Eton and had played soccer in Burma, so he was familiar with the rough-and-tumble of the game but he was also imbued with the Corinthian Spirit of 'fair play'. I happened to see this game with a friend whilst serving in the Royal Navy. Neither of us remembers it as especially violent though it was, perhaps, fractious. Orwell, as he says, did not see the game and relied upon reports. It is possible to see a few minutes of the game – and the enormous crowd of 92,000 – and also thirty-eight still pictures on the internet at: www.british pathe.com/video/dynamos-drew-with-rangers and for a commentary see: www.big soccer/commentary/threads/dynamo-moscow-1945-visit-to-the-uk

And how could it be otherwise? I am always amazed when I hear people saying that sport creates good will between the nations, and that if only the common peoples of the world could meet one another at football or cricket, they would have no inclination to meet on the battlefield. Even if one didn't know from concrete examples (the 1936 Olympic Games, for instance) that international sporting contests lead to orgies of hatred, one could deduce it from general principles.

Nearly all the sports practised nowadays are competitive. You play to win, and the game has little meaning unless you do your utmost to win. On the village green, where you pick up sides and no feeling of local patriotism is involved, it is possible to play simply for the fun and the exercise: but as soon as the question of prestige arises, as soon as you feel that you and some larger unit will be disgraced if you lose, the most savage combative instincts are aroused. Anyone who has played even in a school football match knows this. At the international level sport is frankly mimic warfare. But the significant thing is not the behaviour of the players but the attitude of the spectators: and, behind the spectators, of the nations who work themselves into furies over these absurd contests, and seriously believe—at any rate for short periods—that running, jumping and kicking a ball are tests of national virtue.

Even a leisurely game like cricket, demanding grace rather than strength, can cause much ill-will, as we saw in the controversy over body-line bowling and over the rough tactics of the Australian team that visited England in 1921. Football, a game in which everyone gets hurt and every nation has its own style of play which seems unfair to foreigners, is far worse. Worst of all is boxing. One of the most horrible sights in the world is a fight between white and coloured boxers before a mixed audience. But a boxing audience is always disgusting, and the behaviour of the women, in particular, is such that the Army, I believe, does not allow them to attend its contests. At any rate, two or three years ago, when Home Guards and regular troops were holding a boxing tournament, I was placed on guard at the door of the hall, with orders to keep the women out.

In England, the obsession with sport is bad enough, but even fiercer passions are aroused in young countries where games-playing and nationalism are both recent developments. In countries like India or Burma, it is necessary at football matches to have strong cordons of police to keep the crowd from invading the field. In Burma, I have seen the supporters of one side break through the police and disable the goalkeeper of the opposing side at a critical moment. The first big football match that was played in Spain, about fifteen years ago, led to an uncontrollable riot. As soon as strong feelings of rivalry are aroused, the notion of playing the game according to the rules always vanishes. People want to see one side on top and the other side humiliated, and they forget that victory gained through cheating or through the intervention of the crowd is meaningless. Even when the spectators don't intervene physically, they try to influence the game by cheering their own side and 'rattling' opposing players with boos and insults. Serious sport has nothing to do with fair play. It is bound up with hatred, jealousy, boastfulness, disregard of all rules and sadistic pleasure in witnessing violence: in other words it is war minus the shooting.

Instead of blah-blahing about the clean, healthy rivalry of the football field and the great part played by the Olympic Games in bringing the nations together, it is more useful to inquire how and why this modern cult of sport arose. Most of the games we now play are of ancient origin, but sport does not seem to have been taken very seriously between Roman times and the Nineteenth century. Even in the English public schools the games cult did not start till the later part of the last century. Dr. Arnold, generally regarded as the founder of the modern public school, looked on games as simply a waste of time. Then, chiefly in England and the United States, games were built up into a heavily-financed activity, capable of attracting vast crowds and rousing savage passions, and the infection spread from country to country. It is the most violently combative sports, football and boxing, that have spread the widest. There cannot be much doubt that the whole thing is bound up with the rise of nationalism—that is, with the lunatic modern habit of identifying oneself with large power units and seeing everything in terms of competitive prestige. Also, organised games are more likely to flourish in urban communities where the average human being lives a sedentary or at least a confined life, and does not get much opportunity for creative labour. In a rustic community a boy or young man works off a good deal of his surplus energy by walking, swimming, snowballing, climbing trees, riding horses, and by various sports involving cruelty to animals, such as fishing, cock-fighting and ferreting for rats. In a big town one must indulge in group activities if one wants an outlet for one's physical strength or for one's sadistic impulses. Games are taken seriously in London and New York, and they were taken seriously in Rome and Byzantium: in the Middle Ages they were played, and probably played with much physical brutality, but they were not mixed up with politics nor a cause of group hatreds.

If you wanted to add to the vast fund of ill-will existing in the world at this moment, you could hardly do it better than by a series of football matches between Jews and Arabs, Germans and Czechs, Indians and British, Russians and Poles, and Italians and Jugoslavs, each match to be watched by a mixed audience of 100,000 spectators. I do not, of course, suggest that sport is one of the main causes of international rivalry; big-scale sport is itself, I think, merely another effect of the causes that have produced nationalism. Still, you do make things worse by sending forth a team of eleven men, labelled as national champions, to do battle against some rival team, and allowing it to be felt on all sides that whichever nation is defeated will 'lose face'.

I hope, therefore, that we shan't follow up the visit of the Dynamos by sending a British team to the U.S.S.R. If we must do so, then let us send a second-rate team which is sure to be beaten and cannot be claimed to represent Britain as a whole. There are quite enough real causes of trouble already, and we need not add to them by encouraging young men to kick each other on the shins amid the roars of infuriated spectators.[2]

2. The clubs met again on 24 May 1972 in the European Cup and the result was Rangers 3 Dynamo 2.

Review: 'Freedom and Happiness' [Yevgeny Zamyatin, *We*]

Tribune, 4 JANUARY 1946

Several years after hearing of its existence, I have at last got my hands on a copy of Zamyatin's *We*, which is one of the literary curiosities of this book-burning age. Looking it up in Gleb Struve's *25 Years of Soviet Russian Literature*, I find its history to have been this:

Zamyatin, who died in Paris in 1937, was a Russian novelist and critic who published a number of books both before and after the Revolution.[1] *We* was written about 1923, and though it is not about Russia and has no direct connection with contemporary politics—it is a fantasy dealing with the twenty-sixth century A.D.—it was refused publication on the ground that it was ideologically undesirable. A copy of the manuscript found its way out of the country, and the book has appeared in English, French and Czech translations, but never in Russian. The English translation was published in the United States, and I have never been able to procure a copy: but copies of the French translation (the title is *Nous Autres*) do exist, and I have at last succeeded in borrowing one.[2] So far as I can judge it is not a book of the first order, but it is certainly an unusual one, and it is astonishing that no English publisher has been enterprising enough to re-issue it.

The first thing anyone would notice about *We* is the fact—never pointed out, I believe—that Aldous Huxley's *Brave New World* must be partly derived from it. Both books deal with the rebellion of the primitive human spirit against a rationalised, mechanised, painless world, and both stories are supposed to take place about six hundred years hence. The atmosphere

---

1. Yevgeny Zamyatin (1884–1937), naval engineer and satirical author, was arrested in 1905 following his participation in the unsuccessful revolution against the Russian government; he was exiled but, in 1913, amnestied. *We* was written in 1920 (not 1923 as Orwell has it), but its publication was forbidden in Soviet Russia. An English translation was published in New York in 1924, with Zamyatin's consent, and it was published outside Russia, in Russian, by a White Russian émigré journal in 1927. For that, Zamyatin was attacked by the Association of Proletarian Writers in 1929. He was allowed to leave Russia in 1931 and settled in Paris, where he died.

2. The journalist Alan Moray Williams (1915–) lent Orwell a copy of the French translation of *We* (*Nous Autres*). Williams did not discount the possibility that Orwell may have heard of the book before he lent it to him. He himself might have referred to it, or Orwell could have come across it when he lived in Paris. However, Williams was sure that Orwell had not read *We* in any language until 1944.

of the two books is similar, and it is roughly speaking the same kind of society that is being described, though Huxley's book shows less political awareness and is more influenced by recent biological and psychological theories.

In the twenty-sixth century, in Zamyatin's vision of it, the inhabitants of Utopia have so completely lost their individuality as to be known only by numbers. They live in glass houses (this was written before television was invented), which enables the political police, known as the 'Guardians,' to supervise them more easily. They all wear identical uniforms, and a human being is commonly referred to either as 'a number' or 'a unif' (uniform). They live on synthetic food, and their usual recreation is to march in fours while the anthem of the Single State is played through loudspeakers. At stated intervals they are allowed for one hour (known as 'the sex hour') to lower the curtains round their glass apartments. There is, of course, no marriage, though sex life does not appear to be completely promiscuous. For purposes of love-making everyone has a sort of ration book of pink tickets, and the partner with whom he spends one of his allotted sex hours signs the counterfoil. The Single State is ruled over by a personage known as The Benefactor, who is annually re-elected by the entire population, the vote being always unanimous. The guiding principle of the State is that happiness and freedom are incompatible. In the Garden of Eden man was happy, but in his folly he demanded freedom and was driven out into the wilderness. Now the Single State has restored his happiness by removing his freedom.

So far the resemblance with *Brave New World* is striking. But though Zamyatin's book is less well put together—it has a rather weak and episodic plot which is too complex to summarise—it has a political point which the other lacks. In Huxley's book the problem of 'human nature' is in a sense solved, because it assumes that by pre-natal treatment, drugs and hypnotic suggestion the human organism can be specialised in any way that is desired. A first-rate scientific worker is as easily produced as an Epsilon semi-moron, and in either case the vestiges of primitive instincts, such as maternal feeling or the desire for liberty, are easily dealt with. At the same time no clear reason is given why society should be stratified in the elaborate way that is described. The aim is not economic exploitation, but the desire to bully and dominate does not seem to be a motive either. There is no power-hunger, no sadism, no hardness of any kind. Those at the top have no strong motive for staying at the top, and though everyone is happy in a vacuous way, life has become so pointless that it is difficult to believe that such a society could endure.

Zamyatin's book is on the whole more relevant to our own situation. In spite of education and the vigilance of the Guardians, many of the ancient human instincts are still there. The teller of the story, D-503, who, though a gifted engineer, is a poor conventional creature, a sort of Utopian Billy Brown of London Town, is constantly horrified by the atavistic impulses which seize upon him. He falls in love (this is a crime, of course) with a certain I-330 who is a member of an underground resistance movement and succeeds for a while in leading him into rebellion. When the rebellion breaks out it appears that the enemies of The Benefactor are in fact fairly numerous, and these people, apart from plotting the overthrow of the State, even indulge, at the moment when their curtains are down, in such vices as smoking cigarettes and drinking alcohol. D-503 is ultimately saved from the consequences of his own folly. The authorities announce that they have discovered the cause of the recent disorders: it is that some human beings suffer from a disease called imagination. The nerve-centre responsible for imagination has now been located, and the disease can be cured by X-ray treatment. D-503 undergoes the operation, after which it is easy for him to do what he has known all along that he ought to do —that is, betray his confederates to the police. With complete equanimity he watches I-330 tortured by means of compressed air under a glass bell:

> She looked at me, her hands clasping the arms of the chair, until her eyes were completely shut. They took her out, brought her to herself by means of an electric shock, and put her under the bell again. This operation was repeated three times, and not a word issued from her lips.
>
> The others who had been brought along with her showed themselves more honest. Many of them confessed after one application. Tomorrow they will all be sent to the Machine of the Benefactor.

The Machine of the Benefactor is the guillotine. There are many executions in Zamyatin's Utopia. They take place publicly, in the presence of the Benefactor, and are accompanied by triumphal odes recited by the official poets. The guillotine, of course, is not the old crude instrument but a much improved model which literally liquidates its victim, reducing him in an instant to a puff of smoke and a pool of clear water. The execution is, in fact, a human sacrifice, and the scene describing it is given deliberately the colour of the sinister slave civilisations of the ancient world. It is this intuitive grasp of the irrational side of totalitarianism—human sacrifice, cruelty as an end in itself, the worship of a Leader who is credited with divine attributes—that makes Zamyatin's book superior to Huxley's.

It is easy to see why the book was refused publication. The following conversation (I abridge it slightly) between D-503 and I-330 would have been quite enough to set the blue pencils working:

'Do you realise that what you are suggesting is revolution?'
'Of course, it's revolution. Why not?'
'Because there can't *be* a revolution. *Our* revolution was the last and there can never be another. Everybody knows that.'
'My dear, you're a mathematician: tell me, which is the last number?'
'What do you mean, the last number?'
'Well, then, the biggest number!'
'But that's absurd. Numbers are infinite. There can't be a last one.'
'Then why do you talk about the last revolution?'

There are other similar passages. It may well be, however, that Zamyatin did not intend the Soviet regime to be the special target of his satire. Writing at about the time of Lenin's death, he cannot have had the Stalin dictatorship in mind, and conditions in Russia in 1923 were not such that anyone would revolt against them on the ground that life was becoming too safe and comfortable. What Zamyatin seems to be aiming at is not any particular country but the implied aims of industrial civilisation. I have not read any of his other books, but I learn from Gleb Struve that he had spent several years in England and had written some blistering satires on English life. It is evident from *We* that he had a strong leaning towards primitivism. Imprisoned by the Czarist Government in 1906, and then imprisoned by the Bolsheviks in 1922 in the same corridor of the same prison, he had cause to dislike the political regime he had lived under, but his book is not simply the expression of a grievance. It is in effect a study of the Machine, the genie that man has thoughtlessly let out of its bottle and cannot put back again. This is a book to look out for when an English version appears.

'The Cost of Radio Programmes'

Tribune, 1 FEBRUARY 1946

In last week's *Observer*, Mr. W. E. Williams, discussing the recent raising of radio licences from ten shillings to a pound, made the pertinent remark that 'the trouble with British broadcasting is that it is far too cheap.' It seems to me that his remark is worth expanding, because the relationship between the amount of money brought in by a radio programme, and the amount of work that can be put into it, is not generally grasped. Nor is it realised that the badness of many radio programmes is due to the fact that to write and produce them better would be impossibly expensive.

Radio-listening costs at most a few pence a day, and if you like you can keep your radio turned on for the whole twenty-four hours. As it is what might be called a low-pressure entertainment, not giving you nearly such acute pleasure as you get from watching a film or drinking a glass of beer, most people feel that they pay quite a high enough price for it. Actually, the tiny price that they pay, measured against the heavy cost of the mechanical side of broadcasting, makes for a dull, cut-off-the-joint type of programme, and discourages innovation and experiment. This is best illustrated by plays, features and short stories, because it is especially in this type of programme that the vast possibilities of radio have remained unrealised.

The writer of a play or feature which is to take 30 minutes is usually paid about 30 guineas. He may get rather more if he is a 'name,' and he may get a small extra fee if his piece is re-broadcast: but, in general, 30 guineas is the most he can expect,[1] and he may get much less, since many programmes of this type are written by salaried employees who turn out several of them a week. Even if he is not a salaried employee, he is not likely to have much choice about his subject or his manner of treating it. The need to produce fresh programmes every day means that schedules have to be produced months in advance, and nothing can be accepted unless it fits in with some predetermined series. If you get a good idea for a novel or magazine article you can sit down and write it without consulting anyone else, and if you make a good job of it you

---

1. Orwell was paid £47 5s. for his 45-minute radio script for *The Voyage of the 'Beagle'*, with £5 5s. for 'additional research'.

can probably sell it. It would be no use going on this principle with a radio programme. Either it fits in somewhere or other, or it is unsaleable, however good it may be in itself.

When this play, story or whatever it may be, is ready, it will in all probability go on the air only once. It is, therefore, impossible to spend much time and money in producing it. What actually happens is that it is broadcast by a company of stock actors who are taking part in several totally different programmes every week. They may be given copies of their parts a day or two before they go on the air, but quite often they arrive in the studio without even having heard the name of the programme in which they are to take part. In any case, there is no question of their learning their parts by heart: they simply read them from the typewritten script. The rehearsals, for a 30-minute programme, will probably take four, or at most, six hours. There is no time for more, and to do more on any one day would simply exhaust the actors and producer to no purpose. Finally the programme goes on the air, and there is an end of it. If it is ever re-broadcast, it will probably not be by a fresh performance, in which the actors might improve on their first effort, but by a mechanical recording of the first one.

Now compare this with what happens in the case of a stage play. Writing a play is speculative. Most plays fail to reach the stage, and many of those that do get acted are a flop. Still, anyone who writes a play *hopes* that it will run for months and bring him several hundred pounds: also, he can choose his theme, and within limits he can even vary the length to suit himself. Even on a one-act play, therefore, he will probably do weeks or months of work, and he will shed a drop of sweat on every semi-colon. Before the play opens there will be weeks of careful rehearsal, and the actors will not only be word-perfect, but will have studied their parts and done their best to pack the utmost significance into every speech. Produced in this manner, the play can be *acted*, whereas the average radio programme is merely *read*. Yet how would it be possible to take all this trouble with a programme which is to be broadcast only once, and which the public pays for at a much lower rate than it pays for drinking water?

Criticism of the B.B.C., both in the press and by the general public, is usually unfavourable, but what most people appear to demand is simply a better version of the programmes they are getting already. They want better music, funnier jokes, more intelligent discussions, more truthful news. What is much less often pointed out is that the radio as a medium of literary expression has been very little studied. The microphone is a new instrument, and it ought to call into being a new attitude towards verse, drama and stories. Actually very little thought has been given to this subject, and still less concrete experiment. When an experimental programme does get broadcast, it is usually because there happens to be inside the B.B.C. some imaginative person who can pull the necessary wires and overcome bureaucratic opposition. There is nothing to tempt a free-lance writer into trying innovations.

If a radio play, for instance, could be performed night after night for months, like a stage play, it would be possible to spend more money and do more work on it; and the radio play, as an art-form, might then begin to be taken seriously. However, there is an obvious reason why the same programme cannot be broadcast over and over again. This being so, serious work along certain lines is only possible if commercial considerations are ignored. This means, first of all, setting aside one wavelength for uncompromisingly 'highbrow' programmes.[2] It is curious how strongly this idea is resisted, and by what people. Even Frederick Laws, of the *News Chronicle*, one of the best radio critics we have, has pronounced against it. Yet it is difficult to see how any genuinely new idea can be tested if every programme that goes on the air has to make an immediate appeal to millions, or at any rate, hundreds of thousands of people. There is enough fuss already over the meagre periods devoted to broadcasting poetry. In the long run, no doubt, anything that is good becomes popular; but any innovation, in any of the arts, needs protection during its experimental stage. It is significant that during the war the most intelligent— though not the most technically efficient—broadcasting has been done on the overseas' services, where no commercial consideration entered and, in many cases, a large audience was not aimed at.

The other thing that is needed is more facilities for experiment—not experiment in the technical side of radio, of which there is no doubt plenty already, but experiment on the problem of adapting existing literary forms to the air. Various difficulties which may in reality be quite simple

2. A 'Third Programme' for just this purpose was introduced by the BBC on 29 September 1946. The then Director-General of the BBC, Sir William Haley, said, 'Its whole content will be devoted to an audience that is not of one class but that is perceptive and intelligent' ('Breaking New Grounds in Radio', *The Listener*, 26 September 1946, Supplement, i), and, in another context, designed for the upper reaches of a community seen 'as a broadly based cultural pyramid slowly aspiring upwards' (*The Responsibilities of Broadcasting*, 10). See B. Paulu, *British Broadcasting in Transition* (1961), 148–50.

have never yet been overcome. To name just one (it is discussed in the introduction to Edward Sackville West's radio play, *The Rescue*): no one has yet discovered how to present a play or dramatised story in such a way that the audience can discover what is happening, without the use of a 'narrator' who ruins the dramatic effect. To solve such problems it would be necessary to make use of closed circuits and to employ teams of musicians, actors and producers—in other words, it would be necessary to spend a lot of money. But then oceans of money are spent already, and nearly all of it on rubbish.

The sort of competition that would be presented by 'sponsored' radio is not likely to have a beneficial effect on the B.B.C. It might tend to keep the B.B.C. up to the mark in the matter of brightness and efficiency, but people who are broadcasting in order to advertise Bile Beans or Player's Cigarettes are not going to aim at the minority public. If the possibilities latent in radio are ever realised, it will be because the people who have ideas get a chance to test them and are not choked off by being told that this or that 'would not fit in' or 'would not have a wide enough appeal.' Also, it should be possible to produce a radio programme with the same care and seriousness as is devoted to a stage play, and the writer should receive a large enough fee to encourage him to spend sufficient time on the work. All of which demands money, and might even, lamentable though that would be, mean raising the price of a radio licence by a few shillings more.

'Books v. Cigarettes'

Tribune, 8 FEBRUARY 1946

A couple of years ago a friend of mine, a newspaper editor, was fire-watching with some factory workers. They fell to talking about this newspaper, which most of them read and approved of, but when he asked them what they thought of the literary section, the answer he got was: 'You don't suppose we read that stuff, do you? Why, half the time you're talking about books that cost twelve and sixpence! Chaps like us couldn't spend twelve and sixpence on a book.' These, he said, were men who thought nothing of spending several pounds on a day trip to Blackpool.

This idea that the buying, or even the reading, of books is an expensive hobby and beyond the reach of the average person is so widespread that it deserves some detailed examination. Exactly what reading costs, reckoned in terms of pence per hour, is difficult to estimate, but I have made a start by inventorying my own books and adding up their total price. After allowing for various other expenses, I can make a fairly good guess at my expenditure over the last fifteen years.

The books that I have counted and priced are the ones I have here, in my flat. I have about an equal number stored in another place, so that I shall double the final figure in order to arrive at the complete amount. I have not counted oddments such as proof copies, defaced volumes, cheap paper-covered editions, pamphlets, or magazines, unless bound up into book form. Nor have I counted the kind of junky books —old school textbooks and so forth—that accumulate in the bottoms of cupboards. I have counted only those books which I have acquired voluntarily, or else would have acquired voluntarily, and which I intend to keep. In this category I find that I have 442 books, acquired in the following ways:—

Bought (mostly secondhand)	251
Given to me or bought with book tokens	33
Review copies and complimentary copies	143
Borrowed and not returned	10
Temporarily on loan	5
TOTAL	442

Now as to the method of pricing. Those books that I have bought, I have listed at their full price, as closely as I can determine it. I have also listed at their full price the books that have been given to me, and those that I have temporarily borrowed, or borrowed and kept. This is because book-giving, book-borrowing and book-stealing more or less even out. I possess books that do not strictly speaking belong to me, but many other people also have books of mine: so that the books I have not paid for can be taken as balancing others which I have paid for but no longer possess. On the other hand I have listed the review and complimentary copies at half price. That is about what I would have paid for them secondhand, and they are mostly books that I would only have bought secondhand, if at all. For the prices I have sometimes had to rely on guesswork, but my figures will not be far out. The costs were as follows:—

	£ s. d.
Bought	36 9 0
Gifts	10 10 6
Review copies, etc.	25 11 9
Borrowed and not returned	4 16 9
On loan	3 10 6
Shelves	2 0 0
	———
TOTAL	£82 17 6

Adding the other batch of books that I have elsewhere, it seems that I possess, altogether nearly 900 books, at a cost of £165 15s. This is the accumulation of about fifteen years—actually more, since some of these books date from my childhood: but call it fifteen years. This works out at £11 1s. a year, but there are other charges that must be added in order to estimate my full reading expenses. The biggest will be for newspapers and periodicals, and for this I think £8 a year would be a reasonable figure. Eight pounds a year covers the cost of two daily papers, one evening paper, two Sunday papers, one weekly review and one or two monthly magazines. This brings the figure up to £19 1s., but to arrive at the grand total one has to make a guess. Obviously one often spends money on books without afterwards having anything to show for it. There are library subscriptions, and there are also the books, chiefly Penguins and other cheap editions, which one buys and then loses or throws away. However, on the basis of my other figures, it looks as though £6 a year would be quite enough to add for expenditure of this kind. So my total reading expenses over the past fifteen years have been in the neighbourhood of £25 a year.

Twenty-five pounds a year sounds quite a lot until you begin to measure it against other kinds of expenditure. It is nearly 9s. 9d. a week, and at present 9s. 9d. is the equivalent of about 83 cigarettes (Players): even before the war it would have bought you less than 200 cigarettes. With prices as they now are, I am spending far more on tobacco than I do on books. I smoke six ounces a week, at half-a-crown an ounce, making nearly £40 a year. Even before the war, when the same tobacco cost 8d. an ounce, I was spending over £10 a year on it: and if I also averaged a pint of beer a day, at sixpence, these two items together will have cost me close on £20 a year. This was probably not much above the national average. In 1938 the people of this country spent nearly £10 per head per annum on alcohol and tobacco: however, 20 per cent. of the population were children under 15 and another 40 per cent. were women, so that the average smoker and drinker must have been spending much more than £10. In 1944, the annual expenditure per head on these items was no less than £23. Allow for the women and children as before, and £40 is a reasonable individual figure. Forty pounds a year would just about pay for a packet of Woodbines everyday and half a pint of mild six days a week —not a magnificent allowance. Of course, all prices are now inflated, including the price of books: still, it looks as though the cost of reading, even if you buy books instead of borrowing them and take in a fairly large number of periodicals, does not amount to more than the combined cost of smoking and drinking.

It is difficult to establish any relationship between the price of books and the value one gets out of them. 'Books' includes novels, poetry, textbooks, works of reference, sociological treatises and much else, and length and price do not correspond to one another, especially if one habitually buys books secondhand. You may spend ten shillings on a poem of 500 lines, and you may spend sixpence on a dictionary which you consult at odd moments over a period of twenty years. There are books that one reads over and over again, books that become part of the furniture of one's mind and alter one's whole attitude to life, books that one dips into but never reads through, books that one reads at a single sitting and forgets a week later: and the cost, in terms of money, may be the same in each case. But if one regards reading simply as a recreation, like going to the pictures, then it is possible to make a rough estimate of what it costs. If you read nothing but novels and 'light' literature, and bought every book that you read, you would be spending —allowing eight shillings as the price of a book, and four hours as the time spent in reading it—two shillings an hour. This is about what it costs to sit in one of the more expensive seats in the cinema. If you concentrated on more serious books, and still bought everything that you read, your expenses would be about the same. The books would cost more, but they would take longer to read. In either case you would still possess the books after you had read them, and they would be sale-able at about a third of their purchase price. If you bought only second-hand books, your reading expenses would, of course, be much less: perhaps sixpence an hour would be a fair estimate. And on the other hand if you don't buy books, but merely borrow them from the lending library, reading costs you round about a halfpenny on hour: if you borrow them from the public library, it costs you next door to nothing.

I have said enough to show that reading is one of the cheaper recrea-tions: after listening to the radio, probably *the* cheapest. Meanwhile, what is the actual amount that the British public spends on books? I cannot discover any figures, though no doubt they exist. But I do know that before the war this country was publishing annually about 15,000 books, which included reprints and schoolbooks. If as many as ten thousand copies of each book were sold—and even allowing for the schoolbooks, this is probably a high estimate—the average person was only buying, directly or indirectly, about three books a year. These three books taken together might cost £1, or probably less.

These figures are guesswork, and I should be interested if someone would correct them for me.[1] But if my estimate is anywhere near right,

---

1. Joyce A. Sharpey-Shafer (possibly related to the Professor of Physiology, Edinburgh University, b. 1850) took up Orwell's invitation to correct his figures in an unpublished letter dated 11 February 1946. She had found that she could not buy the books she wished to read at the low secondhand prices he quoted, and the average reader did not receive review and complimentary copies. Further, although women and children 'don't appear to need beer and cigarettes as much as men', did that mean he implied they did not need books either? Even as a non-smoker and non-drinker, she found indulging in books a very expensive hobby. She also commented on his suggestion in 'The Cost of Radio Programmes' (see p. 354) that a special wavelength be devoted to 'highbrow' radio programmes. This, she deplored. Note that the total Orwell calculates on page 359 is incorrect. It should be £82 18s 6d. That doubled would be £165 17s.

it is not a proud record for a country which is nearly 100 per cent. literate and where the ordinary man spends more on cigarettes than an Indian peasant has for his whole livelihood. And if our book-consumption remains as low as it has been, at least let us admit that it is because reading is a less exciting pastime than going to the dogs, the pictures or the pub, and not because books, whether bought or borrowed, are too expensive.

Review: Robert Tressall, *The Ragged-Trousered Philanthropists*[1]

Manchester Evening News, 25 APRIL 1946

This was Orwell's last review for the Manchester Evening News *until that published on 7 November 1946. On 2 May 1946, the newspaper printed this notice: 'Mr. George Orwell, who has been conducting the Life, People—and Books feature in the* Manchester Evening News *for the past two and a half years, has decided to take a rest from journalism for six months. He is retiring to a house he has taken in the Hebrides for this purpose.' Orwell's place was taken by Carl R. Fallas, a writer of short stories and articles, from 2 May until 31 October.*

When *The Ragged-Trousered Philanthropists*, which was reprinted as a Penguin about a year ago, was first published the term 'proletarian literature' had hardly been coined. In the last 15 years, on the other hand, we have heard rather too much of it and usually in a specialised and unsatisfactory sense.

A 'proletarian' book has come to mean not necessarily a book written by a member of the working class, and still less the kind of book that the average working man would willingly read, but the kind of book which in the opinion of middle-class intellectuals every right-minded worker ought to read. 'Proletarian literature' means books about industrial life written from an orthodox Marxist angle, and its most successful practitioners are people who have either never done any manual work or have long since abandoned it.

The Ragged-Trousered Philanthropists seldom gets a mention when this school of literature is discussed, though it has been reprinted often enough to make it describable as a popular book.

Robert Tressall, its author, was a house painter, who died prematurely (he is said to have committed suicide) in 1914 before his book was published.[2] He thus never left the ranks of the working class, and it is

---

1. The newspaper's title for this review was 'Legacy from a House Painter'; the book's title and author were not in display type.
2. Robert Tressall's real name was Robert Noonan, and 'Tressall' is properly 'Tressell'. He was born in 1870 and died of tuberculosis in 1911. Jessie Pope's edition was abridged. The complete text was not published until 1955, edited by F. C. Ball (New York 1962). Ball also wrote two excellent biographies of Tressell: *Tressell of Mugsborough* (1951) and *One of the Damned: The Life and Times of Robert Tressell* (1973).

interesting to speculate whether he would have wished to do so if he had lived on with the opportunity of becoming a successful writer.

Although his book is cast in story form it is in effect a day-to-day account of life in the building trade at a time (1913 or thereabouts) when sevenpence an hour was an accepted wage for a skilled man. One cannot say that it is a strictly 'objective' book—it does indeed contain a good deal of Socialist propaganda of a naïve idealistic kind—but it is essentially an honest book and valuable above all for the exactness of its observation.

Without sensationalism and almost without plot it sets out to record the actual detail of manual work and the tiny things almost unimaginable to any comfortably situated person which make life a misery when one's income drops below a certain level.

Here is a typical extract—a description of a workman stripping the walls and ceiling of a room before distempering it.

Although it was only a small room Joe had to tear into the work pretty hard all the time, for the ceiling seemed to have had two or three coats of whitewash which had never been washed off, and there were several thicknesses of paper on the walls. The difficulty of removing these papers was increased by the fact that the dado had been varnished. In order to get this off it had been necessary to soak it several times with strong soda water, and, although Joe was as careful as possible, he had not been able to avoid getting some of this stuff on his fingers. The result was that his nails were all burnt and discoloured and the flesh round them cracked and bleeding. However, he had got it all off at last and he was not sorry, for his right arm and shoulder were aching from the prolonged strain and in the palm of his right hand there was a blister as large as a shilling caused by the handle of the stripping knife.

It is pedestrian enough, and yet the accumulation of authentic details of this kind produces in the long run an extraordinarily vivid effect. Tressall is especially good at bringing out the importance of very small disasters.

He knows, for instance, all about the loss of sleep that can be entailed by not possessing a clock. But he also has another kind of realism which makes his book especially interesting and marks it off sharply from the 'proletarian literature' of to-day.

In the last twenty years or so books written from a Left-wing angle have usually idealised the working class. Tressall, although he pities his fellow-workers, also despises them and says so plainly. The word 'philanthropists' in the title of the book is ironical. The workers are 'philanthropists' because they are fools enough to support—out of charity, as it were —a worthless class of property-owners. They not only accept their fate like cattle but 'oppose and ridicule any suggestion of reform.' This last is the main theme of the book.

All the way through the thoughtful Socialistic workman Frank Owen (who is, no doubt, a portrait of Tressall himself) is shown arguing with his mates trying to make them see that the capitalist system is responsible for their miseries and being met not merely with apathy and ignorance but with downright ill-will.

With few exceptions they regard the social system as reasonably just and the division into rich and poor as inevitable, believe unemployment to be due to 'this here labour-saving machinery,' and are resentful when someone proposes—as they see it—to rob them of their chance of making a fortune by private enterprise.

Although the likeliest end for all of them is to die in the work-house, their outlook is essentially capitalistic, and Owen's private comment on them is, 'No wonder the rich despised them and looked upon them as dirt. They were despicable. They were dirt.'

The unfortunate Owen, discouraged by their ignorance and hostility, assails them with arguments taken out of penny tracts, using pedantic language, which irritates them all the more. These conversations make very pathetic reading. They remind one of the years of patient, unrewarded work by obscure people that has to be done before any new idea can get a footing among the great masses.

The pathos lies in the fact that nearly everything Owen says would now be regarded as a commonplace. When he says that machinery increases wealth and does not diminish it or that money is merely a token which has no value in itself he is greeted with jeers. To-day such ideas are accepted by almost everyone, thanks precisely to the efforts of thousands of unhonoured people like Owen himself.

Although the book ends with Owen, who is suffering from tuberculosis and sees no hope for his wife and child after he is gone, contemplating murder and suicide its effect is in some sense encouraging. For, after all, the particular kind of folly against which he struggled so unsuccessfully is no longer dominant. The 'Conservative working man' is almost a vanished type.

Tressall died before completing the book and the manuscript was afterwards put in order by Miss Jessie Pope. It is a book that everyone should read. Quite apart from its value as a piece of social history it leaves one with the feeling that a considerable novelist was lost in this young working-man whom society could not bother to keep alive.

Extracts from 'London Letter': early May 1946(?): Scarcity and Despair; The Literary Front – and Birth of the Third Programme

Partisan Review, Summer 1946

Scarcity and Despair

Politically there is not much else happening. There has been some slight activity on the part of the Mosleyites and other Fascist groups, but there is no sign that they have any mass following. The intellectual struggle between Stalinists and anti-Stalinists goes on and on, with frequent sensational defections from one side or the other. Wyndham Lewis, I am credibly informed, has become a Communist or at least a strong sympathiser, and is writing a book in praise of Stalin to balance his previous books in favor of Hitler. All who bother about politics are immersed in the day-to-day struggle over Trieste, Palestine, India, Egypt, the nationalisation of steel, the American loan, re-housing, the Health Service bill, and I do not know what else, but no thoughtful person whom I know has any hopeful picture of the future. The notion that a war between Russia and America is inevitable within the next few decades, and that Britain, in its unfavorable geographical position, is bound to be blown to pieces by atomic bombs, is accepted with a sort of vague resignation, rather as people accept the statement that sooner or later the sun will cool down and we shall all freeze to death. The general public seems to have forgotten about the atomic bomb, which seldom figures in the news. Everyone is intent on having a good time, so far as our reduced circumstances permit. Football matches are attended by enormous crowds, pubs and picture-houses are always packed, and motoring has revived to a surprising extent considering that petrol is still theoretically rationed, the 'basic' ration being only five gallons a month. Secondhand cars sell for fantastic prices,[1] and extraordinary objects, some of them twenty or thirty years old, are to be seen puffing along on the roads. The forgery of petrol coupons is said to have reached such a pitch that the authorities may actually give up rationing in despair. With some difficulty you can now buy a vacuum cleaner, but I still haven't seen a refrigerator for sale, and it would be impossible to furnish a house in even the barest way without spending

---

1. Some new cars were available. From 24 June 1946 Morris 2-door cars cost £270 and 4-door cars, £290.

hundreds of pounds and having to make do with a great deal of ugly and ill-made stuff. There is still, for instance, no crockery except the hideous 'utility' ware or secondhand sets at impossible prices. The general scarcity makes everyone competitive about small possessions, and when you succeed in buying something like a wristwatch or a fountain pen you boast of it for weeks afterwards. The snob note is definitely returning to the advertisements, and in spite of the all-round shabbiness one can feel a sort of quiet pressure to make people dress in a more formal manner again. The other day when I was passing St. Paul's some kind of ceremony was going on, and I was interested to see top hats in fairly large numbers, for the first time in six years or more. But they were rather mangy-looking top hats, and the aspect of the crowd was such that I could not tell whether the function was a wedding or a funeral.

The Literary Front – and Birth of the BBC Third Programme
Very little to report on the literary front. The newspapers are still at their reduced size and likely to remain so for some time to come, but there are constant rumours of the starting of two or three new evening papers and of a new weekly political review of the type of the *New Statesman* or *Tribune*. Books are as scarce and easy to sell as ever. Most of the time I can't even buy copies of my own books. Scissors-and-paste anthologies and miscellanies continue to appear in great numbers, and since I wrote to you last a whole lot more literary monthlies and quarterlies have come into being. Most of these are poor little things and unlikely to live long, but the kind of streamlined, high-powered, slickly got-up, semi-intellectual magazine which you are familiar with in the USA is now beginning to appear here also. Two recent examples are *Future* and *Contact*. Hatry, the financial wizard, who went into the book trade after he came out of prison, is said to be behind some of these new ventures.[2] Thoughtful people watch these developments with dismay, but it is clear that you can only get a large circulation for the kind of magazine in which the letterpress exists round the edges of photographs, and which gives the average reader the feeling of being 'advanced' without actually forcing him to

2. George Weidenfeld states in his autobiography that Orwell was here 'taking his revenge' on *Contact* because Weidenfeld and his literary editor, Philip Toynbee, had rejected 'Politics and the English Language'. However, Weidenfeld writes as if Orwell had referred specifically to *Contact* and not, more generally, to a batch of new ventures. He says the fraudster Clarence Hatry (1888–1965) did not finance *Contact*: 'I had never heard of, let alone met, the man' (*Remembering My Good Friends*, p. 129).

think. It is also well known that a great part of the British periodical press is hopelessly antiquated, and that if it does not modernise itself it may be suddenly supplanted by any magazines which the Americans may decide to start over here. The 'digest' type of magazine is more and more popular, and even the Central Office of Information (previously the M.O.I.) runs magazines of this type in numerous languages for distribution in Europe. In the BBC what may possibly turn out to be an important change is taking place. After years of struggle it has been decided to set aside one wavelength for intelligent programmes. One of the great troubles of broadcasting in this country has been that no programme is regarded as economic unless it can appeal to millions of people, and that anything in the smallest degree highbrow provokes storms of indignation from ordinary radio users, who claim that the time they pay for is being wasted on stuff that can only appeal to a small minority. Also, as the BBC is a chartered corporation and, during the war, has been heavily subsidised by the government, it is subject to a great deal of ignorant and hostile criticism in Parliament, of which its directors are terrified. If the highbrow stuff is isolated in the separate wavelength where the average listener who keeps his radio tuned in to the Home Service for twenty-three hours a day need not be bored by it, much of the criticism will drop off and the more intelligent people inside the BBC may get a free hand. As I well know, there are in the BBC, mostly in its lower ranks, many gifted people who realise that the possibilities of radio have not yet been explored and cannot be explored unless one is content with a minority audience. However, although it is claimed that the 'C' programmes (ie. those on the separate wavelength)[3] will be highly experimental and almost completely uncensored, the people ultimately in charge of them are still high-up permanent officials of the BBC, so it may be that no real change is contemplated.

I can't think of any more news. It is a beautiful spring, with everything in bloom very early. The railings round the parks have not been restored, but the statues are returning to their pedestals. London looks as shabby and dirty as ever, but even after an interval of a year the cessation of the blackout is still an acute pleasure.

George Orwell

3. This would become the Third Programme, which started on 29 September 1946.

'The Cost of Letters'

Horizon, SEPTEMBER 1946

In September 1946 Horizon *set this questionnaire on 'The Cost of Letters':*

1. How much do you think a writer needs to live on?
2. Do you think a serious writer can earn this sum by his writing, and if so, how?
3. If not, what do you think is the most suitable second occupation for him?
4. Do you think literature suffers from the diversion of a writer's energy into other employments or is enriched by it?
5. Do you think the State or any other institution should do more for writers?
6. Are you satisfied with your own solution of the problem and have you any specific advice to give to young people who wish to earn their living by writing?

Orwell replied:

1. At the present purchasing value of money, I think £10 a week after payment of income tax is a minimum for a married man, and perhaps £6 a week for an unmarried man. The *best* income for a writer, I should say—again at the present value of money—is about £1,000 a year. With that he can live in reasonable comfort, free from duns and the necessity to do hackwork, without having the feeling that he has definitely moved into the privileged class. I do not think one can with justice expect a writer to do his best on a working-class income. His first necessity, just as indispensable to him as are tools to a carpenter, is a comfortable, well-warmed room where he can be sure of not being interrupted; and, although this does not sound much, if one works out what it means in terms of domestic arrangements, it implies fairly large earnings. A writer's work is done at home, and if he lets it happen he will be subjected to almost constant interruption. To be protected against interruption always costs money, directly or indirectly. Then again, writers need books and periodicals in great numbers, they need space and furniture for filing papers, they spend a great deal on correspondence, they need at any rate part-time secretarial help, and most of them probably benefit by

travelling, by living in what they consider sympathetic surroundings, and by eating and drinking the things they like best and by being able to take their friends out to meals or have them to stay. It all costs money. Ideally I would like to see every human being have the same income, provided that it were a fairly high income: but so long as there is to be differentiation, I think the writer's place is in the middle bracket, which means, at present standards, round about £1,000 a year.

2. No. I am told that at most a few hundred people in Great Britain earn their living solely by writing books, and most of those are probably writers of detective stories, etc. In a way it is easier for people like Ethel M. Dell[1] to avoid prostitution than it is for a serious writer.

3. If it can be so arranged as not to take up the whole of his time, I think a writer's second occupation should be something non-literary. I suppose it would be better if it were also something congenial. But I can just imagine, for instance, a bank clerk or an insurance agent going home and doing serious work in his evenings; whereas the effort is too much to make if one has already squandered one's energies on semi-creative work such as teaching, broadcasting or composing propaganda for bodies such as the British Council.

4. Provided one's whole time and energies are not used up, I think it benefits. After all, one must make some sort of contact with the ordinary world. Otherwise, what is one to write about?

5. The only thing the State could usefully do is to divert more of the public money into buying books for the public libraries. If we are to have full Socialism, then clearly the writer must be State-supported, and ought to be placed among the better-paid groups. But so long as we have an economy like the present one, in which there is a great deal of State enterprise but also large areas of private capitalism, then the less truck a writer has with the State, or any other organized body, the better for him and his work. There are invariably strings tied to any kind of organized patronage. On the other hand, the old kind of private patronage, in which the writer is in effect the dependant of some individual rich man, is obviously undesirable. By far the best and least exacting patron is the big public. Unfortunately the British public won't at present spend money on books, although it reads more and more and its average of taste, I should say, has risen greatly in the last twenty years. At present,

---

1. See *Keep the Aspidistra Flying* for Gordon Comstock's views of Ethel M. Dell, *CW*, IV, 9–11.

372 | SEEING THINGS AS THEY ARE

I believe, the average British citizen spends round about £1 a year on books,[2] whereas he spends getting on for £25 on tobacco and alcohol combined. Via the rates and taxes he could easily be made to spend more without even knowing it—as, during the war years, he spent far more than usual on radio, owing to the subsidizing of the B.B.C. by the Treasury. If the Government could be induced simply to earmark larger sums for the purchase of books, without in the process taking over the whole book trade and turning it into a propaganda machine, I think the writer's position would be eased and literature might also benefit.

6. Personally I am satisfied, i.e. in a financial sense, because I have been lucky, at any rate during the last few years. I had to struggle desperately at the beginning, and if I had listened to what people said to me I would never have been a writer. Even until quite recently, whenever I have written anything which I took seriously, there have been strenuous efforts, sometimes by quite influential people, to keep it out of print. To a young writer who is conscious of having something in him, the only advice I can give is not to take advice. Financially, of course, there are tips I could give, but even those are of no use unless one has some kind of talent. If one simply wants to make a living by putting words on paper, then the B.B.C., the film companies, and the like are reasonably helpful. But if one wants to be primarily a *writer*, then, in our society, one is an animal that is tolerated but not encouraged—something rather like a house sparrow—and one gets on better if one realizes one's position from the start.[3]

2. For a later, much lower, estimate of 2d per week, see 'As I Please,' 65, 13 December 1946.
3. Reprinted in *Current British Thought*, No. 1, 1947. George Woodcock pursued this investigation in *Freedom—through Anarchism*, 19 October 1946. *Horizon*'s investigation would have been worthwhile, he wrote, had it been 'an objective study of the undoubtedly bad economic plight of many writers and the startling differences of income within this occupation. Unfortunately . . . the questionnaire and the majority of its answers seemed to regard the economic needs of the writer as something different from the needs of the people as a whole. In too many replies one saw the vision of a parasitic existence for the writer, elevated on a balloon of state or private patronage above the rest of the workers and consequently detached from their lives.' Some writers had protested – he singled out for praise Alex Comfort and D. S. Savage – but others thought they should be paid like high-income company directors: he mentioned Elizabeth Bowen (£3,500 a year) and Cyril Connolly (£5 a day); most who mentioned money suggested £1,000 or upwards, free of tax. He then offered a detailed analysis of earnings and expectations. 'A fortunate writer,' he said, 'will earn between £250 and £300 for a book which takes him more than a year to write.' He hoped to get £150 for a recent book.

Broadcast: 'The Written Word': The first sustained critical assessment of Orwell's journalism

BBC, 16 SEPTEMBER 1946

On 16 September 1946, in its series 'The Written Word', the BBC's Eastern Service broadcast a talk by Daniel George on Orwell. It is the first sustained critique of Orwell as an essayist. George was for many years chief reader for the publisher, Jonathan Cape. Cape had rejected Animal Farm *despite George's strong recommendation. The talk was produced by John Arlott. Daniel George and John Witty read the extracts from five essays and a review. It has only recently come to light and I am grateful to Richard Young for providing me with the text reproduced here. There are a dozen or so textual variants in the original; these have been corrected silently.*

Gradually rather than suddenly – over a period of twelve years or so – George Orwell has won for himself a prominent position among our English essayists. The essays themselves are only secondarily on literary matters. He is a social rather than a literary critic. He writes about what he has experienced rather than what he has read – and his experience has been extremely varied.

He was born in India in 1903. He was educated at Eton. He served in Burma in the Indian Imperial Police. He lived – precariously – in Paris. He schoolmastered in England. He worked in a bookshop. He fought for the Republicans in Spain and was wounded. He was a Home Guard and a BBC producer. He has written novels, short stories, sociological studies, satires, essays and literary criticism. One of his works has been chosen as 'the Book of the Month' in America. Except at the extremes of James Agate and A.L. Rowse, he has had few unfavourable critics. Mr. Agate says Orwell is an intellectual whose brow can be scaled only by a stepladder, so he abandons the climb. Mr Rowse also stigmatised him as an intellectual and reproves him for not sharing Mr Rowse's opinions. Just what an intellectual is has never been made very clear. It seems to be a term of abuse. But if it can mean a superior person with a contempt for the ordinary man's enjoyments, Orwell is certainly no intellectual. He never seems to suggest that he is more than an ordinary man himself. He once wrote: 'The intellectual *is* different from the ordinary man, but only in certain sections of his personality and even then not all the time.' He has even gone so far as to suggest that Mr T.S. Eliot must have a touch of the ordinary man in him because he has edited a selection of poems of Kipling.

But Orwell strikes no attitude, adopts no pose. He never proudly claims to be a lowbrow. All he appears to claim is common sense. His style is a common sense style, unadorned by tricks and graces. It represents the man himself – a man, one cannot help feeling, who assumed the garb of simplicity after some practice. He now wears it naturally. It is now natural, or at least habitual, for him to see things not so much from the point of view of, as on behalf of, a much lower social class than that to which by birth and education he belongs. The old Etonian speaks for the Islingtonian – oh, but not crudely, not in his language, and not, on the other hand, with too-too exquisite sympathy or with smart paradox. He sees no nobility in poverty and no advantage in lack of education, no point in bad taste, no virtue in humility.

What he does see, what he is continually re-discovering, is the inconsistencies of man – evidences of good in the bad and of the worst in the good, confirmation of the ancient dualism of body and soul. In an essay on Donald McGill[1] he writes, 'If you look into your own mind, which are you, Don Quixote or Sancho Panza? Almost certainly you are both. There is one part of you that wishes to be a hero or a saint, but another part of you is a little fat man who sees very clearly the advantages of staying alive with a whole skin.' Orwell suggests that there is a constant world-wide conspiracy to pretend that the lazy unheroic man in us does not exist. He does not, of course, plead that he should be warmly encouraged. 'When it comes to the pinch, human beings *are* heroic.' But the other self needs an outlet. 'On the whole, human beings want to be good, but not too good, and not quite all the time.' He is all for an occasional saturnalia, a harmless rebellion against virtue.

He arrives at this conclusion by way of a consideration of the vulgar picture postcard and its social significance. He finds that the humour is stereotyped – he might have said that it is in the English Chaucerian tradition, which still survives in the working classes. It is stereotyped because it is based on stability. It is unsophisticated because when you work for your living, humour is the only relief from the harsher facts

---

1. From 'The Art of Donald McGill', *Horizon*, September 1941, *CW*, XIII, 23–31. The quotations are from pp. 29 and 30. McGill (1875–1962) was probably the most talented of picture postcard artists, and his work is still appreciated today. The script has 'are heroic' for '*are* heroic'.

of life, and the humour has to be crude and unintellectual, not disguised by wit.

Most of Orwell's essays have a literary starting-point. But he quickly deserts literature for life and politics. His review, for example, of Dr V.K. Narayana Menon's book, *The Development of William Butler Yeats*,[2] develops into an examination not only of Yeats' tendency towards Fascist philosophy but of the connection between Fascism and mysticism. Here is what he says:

John Witty: 'It is not clear at first glance why hatred of democracy and a tendency to believe in crystal-gazing should go together. . . . To begin with, the theory that civilisation moves in recurring cycles is one way out for people who hate the concept of human equality. If it is true that "all this", or something like it, "has happened before", then science and the modern world are debunked at one stroke and progress becomes forever impossible. It does not matter much if the lower orders are getting above themselves, for, after all, we shall soon be returning to an age of tyranny. Yeats is by no means alone in this outlook. If the universe is moving round on a wheel the future must be foreseeable, perhaps even in some detail. It is merely a question of discovering the laws of its motion. Believe that, and it becomes difficult not to believe in astrology or some similar system. A year before the war, examining a copy of *Gringoire*, the French fascist weekly, much read by army officers, I found in it no less than thirty-eight advertisements for clairvoyants. Secondly, the very concept of occultism carries with it the idea that knowledge must be a secret thing, limited to a small circle of initiates. But the same idea is integral to Fascism.'

Daniel George: You may have noticed in that extract the extreme plausibility of George Orwell's style. It consists of a series of barely qualified statements, quietly and persuasively made. He never pauses to wonder whether the reader is accepting them or not. There is nothing argumentative about him and nothing that appears dogmatic. He is not seeking

2. Orwell reviewed V.K. Narayana Menon's study of Yeats twice. This passage is from his first review, *Horizon*, January 1943, *CW*, XIV, 282. The second review is reproduced in this collection (page 202). Orwell engaged Menon on a number of occasions to broadcast to India.

the reader's agreement; he takes that for granted – as in his observations about cricket:[3]

John Witty: 'Cricket is not in reality a very popular game in England – it is nowhere near so popular as football, for instance – but it gives expression to a well-marked trait in the English character, the tendency to value "form" or "style" more highly than success. In the eyes of any true cricket-lover it is possible for an innings of ten runs to be "better" (i.e. more elegant) than an innings of a hundred runs: cricket is also one of the very few games in which an amateur can excel the professional. It is a game of forlorn hopes and sudden dramatic changes of fortune, and its rules are so ill-defined that their interpretation is partly an ethical business. When Larwood, for instance, practised body-line bowling in Australia he was not actually breaking any rule: he was merely doing something that was "not cricket". Since cricket takes up a lot of time and is rather an expensive game to play, it is predominantly an upper-class game, but for the whole nation it is bound up with such concepts as "good form", "playing the game", etc., and it has declined in popularity just as the tradition of "don't hit a man when he's down" has declined. It is not a twentieth-century game, and nearly all modern-minded people dislike it.'

Daniel George: Passages like the two you have heard, in which there are at least questionable assertions, can be found in all George Orwell's books. They are disturbing because they are not wilful exaggerations; there is enough of truth in them to make it certain that he himself sincerely believes them. All his work is based on his own maxim, that, above a quite low level, literature is an attempt to influence the viewpoint of one's contemporaries, by recording experience. His work is a record of his own experience and observations.

Comparatively little of it is in the set form of the essay. There is nothing in the style of Lamb's whimsicality or even of Hazlitt's garrulous irascibility. His subjects are as often sociological and political as they are literary. His last book is called *Critical Essays,* and it is made up of studies of Charles Dickens, Rudyard Kipling, W.B. Yeats, P.G. Wodehouse, Salvador Dali, Arthur Koestler and other writers, with the addition of articles on

---

3. From 'Raffles and Miss Blandish', *Horizon*, October 1944; *CW* XVI, 347–8. Orwell reviewed Edmund Blunden's *Cricket Country*, in the *Manchester Evening News* a month or two earlier – 20 April 1944; *CW*, XVI, 161–3. In this he shows himself rather more sympathetic to the game, especially the village green variety. On several occasions between 1939 and 1942 he refers to the annual Eton v. Harrow game.

popular Boys'Weeklies and comic picture postcards. All of these become, sooner or later, but *chiefly,* moralizings upon modern tendencies in thought and behaviour, and all illustrate his dislike – almost his fear – of a totalitarian system of government.

The only essay which exhibits anything like playfulness is 'Some Thoughts on the Common Toad'. It was printed here in a periodical and has also appeared in America.[4] He begins:

John Witty: 'Before the swallow, before the daffodil, and not much later than the snowdrop, the common toad salutes the coming of spring after his own fashion, which is to emerge from a hole in the ground, where he has laid buried since the previous autumn, and crawl as rapidly as possible towards the nearest suitable patch of water. Something – some shudder in the earth, or perhaps merely a rise of a few degrees in the temperature – has told him it is time to wake up: though a few toads seem to sleep the clock round and miss out a year from time to time – at any rate, I have more than once dug them up alive and apparently well, in the middle of autumn.'

Daniel George: He goes on to say that at this period, after his long fast, the toad has a very spiritual look, like a strict Anglo-Catholic towards the end of Lent.

John Witty: 'His movements are languid but purposeful, his body is shrunken, and by contrast his eyes look abnormally large. This allows one to notice, what one might not at another time, that a toad has about the most beautiful eye of any living creature. It is like gold or more exactly it is like the golden-coloured semi-precious stone which one sometimes sees in signet rings, and which I think is called a chrysoberyl.'

Daniel George: He proceeds to describe the spawning of the toads and says it is one of the phenomena of Spring which most deeply appeals to him because the toad, unlike the skylark and the primrose, has never had much of a boost from poets. From there he passes on to consider the miracle of Spring, remarking that he has seen a kestrel flying over

4. 'Some Thoughts on the Common Toad', *Tribune,* 12 April 1946; *CW,* XVIII, 238–41. Its concluding thought is also worth quoting: 'Spring is still Spring . . . and neither the dictators nor the bureaucrats, deeply as they disapprove of the process, are able to prevent it.'

Deptford gasworks and a blackbird performing in the Euston Road. There must be hundreds of thousands if not millions of birds in London, he says, adding, characteristically: 'It is rather a pleasing thought that none of them pays a halfpenny rent.' And now we are given – equally characteristically – the moral of these musings:

John Witty: 'If a man cannot enjoy the return of Spring, why should he be happy in a labour-saving Utopia? What will he do with the leisure that the machine will give him? I have always suspected that if our economic and political problems are ever really solved, life will become simpler instead of more complex, and that the sort of pleasure one gets from finding the first primrose will loom larger than the sort of pleasure one gets from eating an ice to the tune of a Wurlitzer. I think that by retaining one's childhood love of such things as trees, fishes, butterflies and – to return to my first instance – toads, one makes a peaceful and decent future a little more probable, and that by preaching the doctrine that nothing is to be admired except steel and concrete, one merely makes it a little surer that human beings will have no outlet for their surplus energy except in hatred and leader-worship.'

Daniel George: Nothing, you say, very original in all that. Perhaps not. Perhaps it is a habit of Orwell's to re-state old truths in new contexts. If so, it is a remarkably effective habit. It can be seen that he is essentially serious-minded. He writes nothing that has not an immediate bearing on life in the present and future. And he is a passionate defender of intellectual liberty. What seems to distress him particularly is not that writers – daily journalists particularly – have often to distort or suppress truth but that they are losing faith in the virtue of personal integrity. 'Political writing in our time,' he says, 'consists almost entirely of prefabricated phrases bolted together like the pieces of a child's Meccano set. . . . To write in plain, vigorous language one has to think fearlessly, and if one thinks fearlessly one cannot be politically orthodox.'[5] In the same essay, which is called 'The Prevention of Literature' and appeared in a new periodical called *Polemic*, he insists that literature is doomed if liberty of thought perishes. 'Unless spontaneity enters at some point or another, literary creation is impossible, and language becomes ossified.' 'At some time in the future,' he goes on, 'we may learn to separate literary creation from intellectual honesty. At present we only

5. 'The Prevention of Literature', *Polemic*, January 1946; *CW*, XVII, 376.

know that imagination, like certain wild animals, will not breed in captivity.'

Orwell himself is not orthodox either in politics or literature. That is why he writes fearlessly, but, as I have tried to indicate, it is not a loud-voiced fearlessness. Insidious persuasion is his method. The method can be illustrated by a passage from the study of Charles Dickens.[6] He has pointed out that in every attack Dickens makes upon society he is always pointing to a change of spirit rather than a change of structure. Dickens might be no more than a cheer-up writer, a reactionary humbug, but he is more than that; and it is perhaps permissible to suggest that Orwell, understanding Dickens' attitude so well, has seen the effectiveness of the moral as well as the materialist critic.

John Witty: 'I said earlier that Dickens is not *in the accepted sense* a revolutionary writer. But it is not at all certain that a merely moral criticism of society may not be just as 'revolutionary' – and revolution, after all, means turning things upside down – as the politico-economic criticism which is fashionable at the moment. Blake was not a politician, but there is more understanding of the nature of capitalist society in a poem like "I wander through each charter'd street" than in three-quarters of Socialist literature. Progress is not an illusion: it happens, but it is slow and invariably disappointing. There is always a new tyrant waiting to take over from the old – generally not quite so bad, but still a tyrant. Consequently two viewpoints are always tenable. The one, how can you improve human nature until you have changed the system? The other, what is the use of changing the system before you have improved human nature? They appeal to different individuals, and they probably show a tendency to alternate in point of time. The moralist and the revolutionary are constantly undermining one another. Marx exploded a hundred tons of dynamite beneath the moralist position, and we are still living in the echo of that tremendous crash. But already somewhere or other, sappers are at work and fresh dynamite is being tamped into place to blow Marx at the moon. Then Marx, or somebody like him, will come back with yet more dynamite, and so the process continues, to an end we cannot yet foresee. The central problem – how to prevent power from being abused – remains unsolved. Dickens, who had not the vision to see that private property is an obstructive nuisance, had the vision to see that – "If men would behave decently the world would be decent" is not such a platitude as it sounds.'

6. 'Charles Dickens', 11 March 1940; *CW*, XII, 31.

'As I Please', 61: Polish Immigration; On Hanging

Tribune, 15 NOVEMBER 1946

Polish Immigration

As the clouds, most of them much larger and dirtier than a man's hand, come blowing up over the political horizon, there is one fact that obtrudes itself over and over again. This is that the Government's troubles, present and future, arise quite largely from its failure to publicise itself properly.

People are not told with sufficient clarity what is happening, and why, and what may be expected to happen in the near future. As a result, every calamity, great or small, takes the mass of the public by surprise, and the Government incurs unpopularity by doing things which any government, of whatever colour, would have to do in the same circumstances.

Take one question which has been much in the news lately but has never been properly thrashed out: the immigration of foreign labour into this country. Recently we have seen a tremendous outcry at the T.U.C. conference against allowing Poles to work in the two places where labour is most urgently needed—in the mines and on the land.

It will not do to write this off as something 'got up' by Communist sympathisers, nor on the other hand to justify it by saying that the Polish refugees are all Fascists who 'strut about' wearing monocles and carrying brief-cases.

The question is, would the attitude of the British trade unions be any friendlier if it were a question, not of alleged Fascists but of the admitted victims of Fascism?

For example, hundreds of thousands of homeless Jews are now trying desperately to get to Palestine. No doubt many of them will ultimately succeed, but others will fail. How about inviting, say, 100,000 Jewish refugees to settle in this country? Or what about the Displaced Persons numbering nearly a million, who are dotted in camps all over Germany, with no future and no place to go, the United States and the British Dominions having already refused to admit them in significant numbers? Why not solve their problem by offering them British citizenship?

It is easy to imagine what the average Briton's answer would be. Even before the war, with the Nazi persecutions in full swing, there was no popular support for the idea of allowing large numbers of Jewish refugees into this country: nor was there any strong move to admit the hundreds of thousands of Spaniards who had fled from Franco to be penned up behind barbed wire in France.

For that matter, there was very little protest against the internment of the wretched German refugees in 1940. The comments I most often overheard at the time were 'What did they want to come here for?' and 'They're only after our jobs.'

The fact is that there is strong popular feeling in this country against foreign immigration. It arises partly from simple xenophobia, partly from fear of undercutting in wages, but above all from the out-of-date notion that Britain is overpopulated and that more population means more unemployment.

Actually, so far from having more workers than jobs, we have a serious labour shortage which will be accentuated by the continuance of conscription, and which will grow worse, not better, because of the ageing of the population.

Meanwhile our birth-rate is still frighteningly low, and several hundred thousand women of marriageable age have no chance of getting husbands. But how widely are these facts known or understood?

In the end it is doubtful whether we can solve our problems without encouraging immigration from Europe. In a tentative way the Government has already tried to do this, only to be met by ignorant hostility, because the public has not been told the relevant facts beforehand. So also with countless other unpopular things that will have to be done from time to time.

But the most necessary step is not to prepare public opinion for particular emergencies, but to raise the general level of political understanding: above all, to drive home the fact, which has never been properly grasped, that British prosperity depends largely on factors outside Britain.

This business of publicising and explaining itself is not easy for a Labour Government, faced by a press which at bottom is mostly hostile. Nevertheless, there are other ways of communicating with the public, and Mr. Attlee and his colleagues might well pay more attention to the radio, a medium which very few politicians in this country have ever taken seriously.

On Hanging

There is one question which at first sight looks both petty and disgusting but which I should like to see answered. It is this. In the innumerable hangings of war criminals which have taken place all over Europe during the past few years, which method has been followed—the old method of strangulation, or the modern, comparatively humane method which is supposed to break the victim's neck at one snap?

A hundred years ago or more, people were hanged by simply hauling them up and letting them kick and struggle until they died, which might take a quarter of an hour or so. Later the drop was introduced, theoretically making death instantaneous, though it does not always work very well.

In recent years, however, there seems to have been a tendency to revert to strangulation. I did not see the news-film of the hanging of the German war criminals at Kharkov,[1] but the descriptions in the British press appeared to show that the older method was used. So also with various executions in the Balkan countries.

The newspaper accounts of the Nuremberg hangings were ambiguous. There was talk of a drop, but there was also talk of the condemned men taking ten or twenty minutes to die. Perhaps, by a typically Anglo-Saxon piece of compromise, it was decided to use a drop but to make it too short to be effective.

It is not a good symptom that hanging should still be the accepted form of capital punishment in this country. Hanging is a barbarous, inefficient way of killing anybody, and at least one fact about it—quite widely known, I believe—is so obscene as to be almost unprintable.[2]

Still, until recently we did feel rather uneasy on the subject, and we did have our hangings in private. Indeed, before the war public execution was a thing of the past in nearly every civilised country. Now it seems to be returning, at least for political crimes, and though we ourselves have not actually reintroduced it as yet, we participate at secondhand by watching the news films.

It is queer to look back and think that only a dozen years ago the abolition of the death penalty was one of those things that every enlightened person advocated as a matter of course, like divorce reform or the independence of India. Now, on the other hand, it is a mark of enlightenment not merely to approve of executions but to raise an outcry because there are not more of them.

1. On 19 December 1943, three Germans were found guilty of atrocities in the first 'war crimes trial' at Kharkov and hanged. A Ukrainian was also hanged.
2. This paragraph and the three preceding paragraphs were reprinted as a single paragraph within a box headed 'Hanging To-day' in the journal *The Plebs*, June 1947. The penultimate word of the first of these paragraphs, 'very,' was omitted. The 'obscene fact' to which Orwell is probably referring is defecation and, in men, ejaculation, on death.

Therefore it seems to me of some importance to know whether strangulation is now coming to be the normal practice. For if people are being taught to gloat not only over death but over a peculiarly horrible form of torture, it marks another turn on the downward spiral that we have been following ever since 1933.

'Riding Down from Bangor'

Tribune, 22 NOVEMBER 1946

The reappearance of *Helen's Babies,*[1] in its day one of the most popular books in the world—within the British Empire alone it was pirated by twenty different publishing firms, the author receiving a total profit of £40 from a sale of some hundreds of thousands or millions of copies—will ring a bell in any literate person over 35. Not that the present edition is an altogether satisfactory one. It is a cheap little book with rather unsuitable illustrations, various American dialect words appear to have been cut out of it, and the sequel, *Other People's Children,* which was often bound up with it in earlier editions, is missing. Still, it is pleasant to see *Helen's Babies* in print again. It had become almost a rarity in recent years, and it is one of the best of the little library of American books on which people born at about the turn of the century were brought up.

The books one reads in childhood, and perhaps most of all the bad and good-bad books, create in one's mind a sort of false map of the world, a series of fabulous countries into which one can retreat at odd moments throughout the rest of life, and which in some cases can even survive a visit to the real countries which they are supposed to represent. The pampas, the Amazon, the coral islands of the Pacific, Russia, land of birch-tree and samovar, Transylvania with its boyars and vampires, the China of Guy Boothby,[2] the Paris of du Maurier—one could continue the list for a long time. But one other imaginary country that I acquired early in life was called America. If I pause on the word 'America,' and, deliberately putting aside the existing reality, call up my childhood vision of it, I see two pictures—composite pictures, of course, from which I am omitting a good deal of the detail.

One is of a boy sitting in a whitewashed stone schoolroom. He wears braces and has patches on his shirt, and if it is summer he is barefooted. In the corner of the schoolroom there is a bucket of drinking water with a dipper. The boy lives in a farmhouse, also of stone and also whitewashed, which has a mortgage on it. He aspires to be President, and is expected to keep the woodpile full. Somewhere in the background of the picture, but

---

1. *Helen's Babies* by John Habberton (1842–1921) was first published in 1876.
2. Orwell is referring to *Dr Nikola* by Guy Boothby (1867–1905); which he described as a 'Tibetan thriller' and a first-rate 'boy's sixpenny thriller'.

completely dominating it, is a huge black Bible. The other picture is of a tall, angular man, with a shapeless hat pulled down over his eyes, leaning against a wooden paling and whittling at a stick. His lower jaw moves slowly but ceaselessly. At very long intervals he emits some piece of wisdom such as 'A women is the orneriest critter there is, 'ceptin' a mule,' or 'When you don't know a thing to do, don't do a thing'; but more often it is merely a jet of tobacco juice that issues from the gap in his front teeth. Between them those two pictures summed up my earliest impression of America. And of the two, the first—which, I suppose, represented New England, the other representing the South—had the stronger hold upon me.

The books from which these pictures were derived included, of course, books which it is still possible to take seriously, such as *Tom Sawyer* and *Uncle Tom's Cabin*, but the most richly American flavour was to be found in minor works which are now almost forgotten. I wonder, for instance, if anyone still reads *Rebecca of Sunnybrook Farm*, which remained a popular favourite long enough to be filmed with Mary Pickford in the leading part. Or how about the 'Katy' books by Susan Coolidge[3] (*What Katy Did at School*, etc.), which, although girls' books and therefore 'soppy,' had the fascination of foreignness? Louisa M. Alcott's *Little Women* and *Good Wives* are, I suppose, still flickeringly in print, and certainly they still have their devotees. As a child I loved both of them, though I was less pleased by the third of the trilogy, *Little Men*. That model school where the worst punishment was to have to whack the schoolmaster, on 'this hurts me more than it hurts you' principles, was rather difficult to swallow.

Helen's Babies belonged in much the same world as *Little Women*,[4] and must have been published round about the same date. Then there were Artemus Ward, Bret Harte, and various songs, hymns and ballads, besides poems dealing with the Civil War, such as *Barbara Frietchie* ('"Shoot if you must this old grey head, But spare your country's flag," she said')[5] and *Little Gifford of Tennessee*. There were other books so obscure that it hardly seems worth mentioning them, and magazine stories of which I remember

---

3. Susan Coolidge, pen name for Sarah Chauncey Woolsey, 1835–1905.
4. *Little Women* by Louisa M. Alcott (1832–1888) was published in 1868; *Good Wives*, described as 'being a sequel to *Little Women*', in 1869. They were published in a single volume in 1871 and since then they have been published together and separately, in England *Good Wives* as *Nice Wives* (1879) and *Little Women Wedded* (1937). The combined *Little Women* and *Good Wives* was followed by *Little Men* (1871) and *Jo's Boys* (1886), to make a trilogy.
5. The text has '*Fritchie*'; the quotation should read: 'Shoot, if you must, this old gray head.'

nothing except that the old homestead always seemed to have a mortgage on it. There was also *Beautiful Joe*, the American reply to *Black Beauty*, of which you might just possibly pick up a copy in a sixpenny box. All the books I have mentioned were written well before 1900, but something of the special American flavour lingered on into this century in, for instance, the Buster Brown coloured supplements, and even in Booth Tarkington's 'Penrod' stories, which will have been written round about 1910.[6] Perhaps there was even a tinge of it in Ernest Thompson Seton's animal books (*Wild Animals I Have Known*, etc.), which have now fallen from favour but which drew tears from the pre-1914 child as surely as *Misunderstood* had done from the children of a generation earlier.

Somewhat later my picture of nineteenth-century America was given greater precision by a song which is still fairly well known and which can be found (I think) in the *Scottish Students' Song Book*. As usual in these bookless days I cannot get hold of a copy, and I must quote fragments from memory. It begins:

> Riding down from Bangor
> On an Eastern train,
> Bronzed with weeks of hunting
> In the woods of Maine—
> Quite extensive whiskers,
> Beard, moustache as well—
> Sat a student fellow,
> Tall and slim and swell.

Presently an aged couple and a 'village maiden,' described as 'beautiful, petite,' get into the carriage. Quantities of cinders are flying about, and before long the student fellow gets one in his eye: the village maiden extracts it for him, to the scandal of the aged couple. Soon after this the train shoots into a long tunnel, 'black as Egypt's night.' When it emerges into the daylight again the maiden is covered with blushes, and the cause of her confusion is revealed when—

> There suddenly appeared
> A tiny little ear-ring
> In that horrid student's beard!

6. *Penrod* was published in 1914.

I do not know the date of the song, but the primitiveness of the train (no lights in the carriage, and a cinder in one's eye a normal accident) suggests that it belongs well back in the nineteenth century.

What connects this song with books like *Helen's Babies* is first of all a sort of sweet innocence—the climax, the thing you are supposed to be slightly shocked at, is an episode with which any modern piece of naughty-naughty would *start*—and, secondly, a faint vulgarity of language mixed up with a certain cultural pretentiousness. *Helen's Babies* is intended as a humorous, even a farcical book, but it is haunted all the way through by words like 'tasteful' and 'ladylike,' and it is funny chiefly because its tiny disasters happen against a background of conscious gentility. 'Handsome, intelligent, composed, tastefully dressed, without a suspicion of the flirt or the languid woman of fashion about her, she awakened to the utmost my every admiring sentiment'—thus is the heroine described, figuring elsewhere as 'erect, fresh, neat, composed, bright-eyed, fair-faced, smiling and observant.' One gets beautiful glimpses of a now-vanished world in such remarks as: 'I believe you arranged the floral decorations at St. Zephaniah's Fair last winter, Mr. Burton? 'Twas the most tasteful display of the season.' But in spite of the occasional use of ''twas,' and other archaisms—'parlour' for sitting-room, 'chamber' for bedroom, 'real' as an adverb, and so forth—the book does not 'date' very markedly, and many of its admirers imagine it to have been written round about 1900. Actually it was written in 1875, a fact which one might infer from internal evidence, since the hero, aged twenty-eight, is a veteran of the civil war.

The book is very short, and the story is a simple one. A young bachelor is prevailed on by his sister to look after her house and her two sons, aged five and three, while she and her husband go on a fortnight's holiday. The children drive him almost mad by an endless succession of such acts as falling into ponds, swallowing poison, throwing keys down wells, cutting themselves with razors, and the like, but also facilitate his engagement to 'a charming girl, whom, for about a year, I had been adoring from afar.' These events take place in an outer suburb of New York, in a society which now seems astonishingly sedate, formal, domesticated and, according to current conceptions, un-American. Every action is governed by etiquette. To pass a carriage full of ladies when your hat is crooked is an ordeal; to recognise an acquaintance in church is ill-bred; to become engaged after a ten-days' courtship is a severe social lapse. We are accustomed to thinking of American society as more crude, adventurous and, in a cultural sense, democratic than our own, and from writers like Mark

Twain, Whitman and Bret Harte, not to mention the cowboy and Red Indian stories of the weekly papers, one draws a picture of a wild anarchic world peopled by eccentrics and desperadoes who have no traditions and no attachment to one place. That aspect of nineteenth-century America did of course exist, but in the more populous eastern states a society similar to Jane Austen's seems to have survived longer than it did in England. And it is hard not to feel that it was a better kind of society than that which arose from the sudden industrialisation of the later part of the century. The people in *Helen's Babies* or *Little Women* may be mildly ridiculous, but they are uncorrupted. They have something that is perhaps best described as integrity, or good morale, founded partly on an unthinking piety. It is a matter of course that everyone attends church on Sunday morning and says grace before meals and prayers at bedtime: to amuse the children one tells them Bible stories, and if they ask for a song it is probably 'Glory, glory Hallelujah.' Perhaps it is also a sign of spiritual health in the light literature of this period that death is mentioned freely. 'Baby Phil,' the brother of Budge and Toddie, has died shortly before *Helen's Babies* opens, and there are various tear-jerking references to his 'tiny coffin.' A modern writer attempting a story of this kind would have kept coffins out of it.

English children are still Americanised by way of the films, but it would no longer be generally claimed that American books are the best ones for children. Who, without misgivings, would bring up a child on the coloured 'comics' in which sinister professors manufacture atomic bombs in underground laboratories while Superman whizzes through the clouds, the machine-gun bullets bouncing off his chest like peas, and platinum blondes are raped, or very nearly, by steel robots and fifty-foot dinosaurs? It is a far cry from Superman to the Bible and the woodpile. The earlier children's books, or books readable by children, had not only innocence but a sort of native gaiety, a buoyant, carefree feeling, which was the product, presumably, of the unheard-of freedom and security which nineteenth-century America enjoyed. That is the connecting link between books so seemingly far apart as *Little Women* and *Life on the Mississippi*. The society described in the one is subdued, bookish and home-loving, while the other tells of a crazy world of bandits, gold mines, duels, drunkenness and gambling hells: but in both one can detect an underlying confidence in the future, a sense of freedom and opportunity.

Nineteenth-century America was a rich, empty country which lay outside the main stream of world events, and in which the twin nightmares that beset nearly every modern man, the nightmare of unemployment and the nightmare of State interference, had hardly come into being. There were social distinctions, more marked than those of today, and there was poverty (in *Little Women*, it will be remembered, the family is at one time so hard up that one of the girls sells her hair to the barber), but there was not, as there is now, an all-prevailing sense of helplessness. There was room for everybody and if you worked hard you could be certain of a living—could even be certain of growing rich: this was generally believed, and for the greater part of the population it was even broadly true. In other words, the civilisation of nineteenth-century America was capitalist civilisation of its best. Soon after the Civil War the inevitable deterioration started. But for some decades at least, life in America was much better fun than life in Europe—there was more happening, more colour, more variety, more opportunity—and the books and songs of that period had a sort of bloom, a childlike quality. Hence, I think, the popularity of *Helen's Babies* and other 'light' literature, which made it normal for the English child of thirty or forty years ago to grow up with a theoretical knowledge of raccoons, woodchucks, chipmunks, gophers, hickory trees, water-melons and other unfamiliar fragments of the American scene.

Extract from 'As I Please', 62: Intelligence and Popularity of Newspapers

Tribune, 22 NOVEMBER 1946

In current discussions of the Royal Commission that is to inquire into the Press, the talk is always of the debasing influence exerted by owners and advertisers. It is not said often enough that a nation gets the newspapers it deserves. Admittedly, this is not the whole of the truth. When the bulk of the Press is owned by a handful of people, one has not much choice, and the fact that during the war the newspapers temporarily became more intelligent, without losing circulation, suggests that the public taste is not quite so bad as it seems. Still, our newspapers are not all alike; some of them are more intelligent than others, and some are more popular than others. And when you study the relationship between intelligence and popularity, what do you find?

Below I list in two columns our nine leading national daily papers. In the first column these are ranged in order of intelligence, so far as I am able to judge it: in the other they are ranged in order of popularity, as measured by circulation. By intelligence I do not mean agreement with my own opinions. I mean a readiness to present news objectively, to give prominence to the things that really matter, to discuss serious questions even when they are dull, and to advocate policies which are at least coherent and intelligible. As to the circulation, I may have misplaced one or two papers, as I have no recent figures, but my list will not be far out. Here are the two lists:—

INTELLIGENCE	POPULARITY
1. *Manchester Guardian.*	1. *Express.*
2. *Times.*	2. *Herald.*
3. *News Chronicle.*	3. *Mirror.*
4. *Telegraph.*	4. *News Chronicle.*
5. *Herald.*	5. *Mail.*
6. *Mail.*	6. *Graphic.*
7. *Mirror.*	7. *Telegraph.*
8. *Express.*	8. *Times.*
9. *Graphic.*	9. *Manchester Guardian.*

It will be seen that the second list is very nearly—not quite, for life is never so neat as that—the first turned upside down. And even if I have not ranged these papers in quite the right order, the general relationship holds good. The paper that has the best reputation for truthfulness, the *Manchester Guardian*, is the one that is not read even by those who admire it. People complain that it is 'so dull.' On the other hand countless people read the *Daily* —— while saying frankly that they 'don't believe a word of it.'

In these circumstances it is difficult to foresee a radical change, even if the special kind of pressure exerted by owners and advertisers is removed. What matters is that in England we do possess juridical liberty of the Press, which makes it possible to utter one's true opinions fearlessly in papers of comparatively small circulation. It is vitally important to hang on to that. But no Royal Commission can make the big-circulation Press much better than it is, however much it manipulates the methods of control. We shall have a serious and truthful popular Press when public opinion actively demands it. Till then, if the news is not distorted by businessmen it will be distorted by bureaucrats, who are only one degree better.[1]

There were two responses to this article. This is one:

The dropping of bombs very close to the N.C.L.C. office in Hampstead has given me an opportunity of studying the Scottish newspapers. May I therefore suggest that George Orwell should have added *The Scotsman* to the list of dailies that rank very high for intelligence. Its circulation is about the same, I should think, as the *Manchester Guardian's*.

J. P. M. Millar.

1. On 13 December Orwell offered some amendments to his lists. In terms of circulation, *The Mirror* should have been placed above the *Herald* and the *Mail* above the *News Chronicle*. He was unsure whether the *Graphic* 'was merely bottom of penny papers or bottom of the whole lot'. He had not included the *Daily Worker* because its circulation was small and it is 'doubtful whether it is a newspaper in quite the same sense as the others'. However, whereas it comes bottom in terms of popularity, in intelligence it ranks about level with the *Daily Telegraph*.

Extract from 'As I Please', 63: What is Dominant: a Desire for Power or for Wealth?

Tribune, 29 NOVEMBER 1946

It is not easy to find a direct economic explanation of the behaviour of the people who now rule the world. The desire for pure power seems to be much more dominant than the desire for wealth. This has often been pointed out, but curiously enough the desire for power seems to be taken for granted as a natural instinct, equally prevalent in all ages, like the desire for food. Actually it is no more natural, in the sense of being biologically necessary, than drunkenness or gambling. And if it has reached new levels of lunacy in our own age, as I think it has, then the question becomes: what is the special quality in modern life that makes a major human motive out of the impulse to bully others? If we could answer that question—seldom asked, never followed up—there might occasionally be a bit of good news on the front page of your morning paper.

However, it is always possible, in spite of appearances, that the age we live in is *not* worse than the other ages that have preceded it, nor perhaps even greatly different. At least this possibility occurs to me when I think of an Indian proverb which a friend of mine once translated:—

> In April was the jackal born,
> In June the rain-fed rivers swelled:
> 'Never in all my life,' said he,
> 'Have I so great a flood beheld.'[1]

---

1. In 'As I Please,' 70, 24 January 1947, Orwell wrote: 'A few weeks ago I quoted an Indian proverb in this column, and erroneously said that it had been translated by a friend of mine. Actually the verse I quoted comes from Kipling. This illustrates something I have pointed out elsewhere—that Kipling is one of those writers whom one quotes unconsciously.' Orwell is presumably referring to 'Rudyard Kipling', *Horizon*, February 1942, where he remarks that a vulgar thought, vigorously expressed is 'there . . . ready-made and, as it were, waiting for you. So the chances are that, having once heard this line, you will remember it.' The instance he quotes is: 'He travels the fastest who travels alone.' The verse appears in *The Second Jungle Book*, 'The Undertakers', as: 'In August was the Jackal born:/The Rains fell in September;/"Now such a fearful flood as this,"/Says he, "I can't remember!"'

'As I Please', 64: *Trilby* and Anti-Semitism; Authors' Decline; Four-letter Words

Tribune, 6 DECEMBER 1946

Trilby *and Anti-Semitism*

With great enjoyment I have just been re-reading *Trilby*, George du Maurier's justly popular novel,[1] one of the finest specimens of that 'good bad' literature which the English-speaking peoples seem to have lost the secret of producing. *Trilby* is an imitation of Thackeray, a very good imitation and immensely readable—Bernard Shaw, if I remember rightly, considered it to be *better* than Thackeray in many ways—but to me the most interesting thing about it is the different impressions one derives from reading it first before and then after the career of Hitler.

The thing that now hits one in the eye in reading *Trilby* is its anti-semitism. I suppose, although few people actually read the book now, its central story is fairly widely known, the name of Svengali having become a by-word, like that of Sherlock Holmes. A Jewish musician—not a composer, but a brilliant pianist and music-teacher—gets into his power an orphaned Irish girl, a painter's model, who has a magnificent voice but happens to be tone deaf. Having hypnotised her one day to cure an attack of neuralgia, he discovers that when she is in the hypnotic trance she can be taught to sing in tune.

Thereafter, for about two years, the pair of them travel from one European capital to another, the girl singing every night to enormous and ecstatic audiences, and never even knowing, in her waking life, that she is a singer. The end comes when Svengali dies suddenly in the middle of a concert and Trilby breaks down and is booed off the stage. That is the main story, though of course there is much else, including an unhappy love affair and three clean-living English painters who make a foil for Svengali's villainy.

There is no question that the book is anti-semitic. Apart from the fact that Svengali's vanity, treacherousness, selfishness, personal uncleanliness and so forth are constantly connected with the fact that he is a Jew, there are the illustrations. Du Maurier, better known for his drawings in *Punch* than for his writings, illustrated his own book, and he made Svengali into

---

1. *Trilby* (3 vols., 1894) by George du Maurier (1834–1896) was first published in *Harper's Magazine*.

a sinister caricature of the traditional type. But what is most interesting is the divergence of the anti-semitism of that date—1895, the period of the Dreyfus case—and that of today.

To begin with, du Maurier evidently holds that there are two kinds of Jew, good ones and bad ones, and that there is a racial difference between them. There enters briefly into the story another Jew, Glorioli, who possesses all the virtues and qualities that Svengali lacks. Glorioli is 'one of the Sephardim'—of Spanish extraction, that is—whereas Svengali, who comes from German Poland, is 'an Oriental Israelite Hebrew Jew.' Secondly, du Maurier considers that to have a dash of Jewish blood is an advantage. We are told that the hero, Little Billee, may have had some Jewish blood, of which there was a suggestion in his features, and 'fortunately for the world, and especially for ourselves, most of us have in our veins at least a minim of that precious fluid.' Clearly, this is not the Nazi form of anti-semitism.

And yet the tone of all the references to Svengali is almost unconsciously contemptuous, and the fact that du Maurier chose a Jew to play such a part is significant. Svengali, who cannot sing himself and has to sing, as it were through Trilby's lungs, represents that well-known type, the clever underling who acts as the brains of some more impressive person.

It is queer how freely du Maurier admits that Svengali is more gifted than the three Englishmen, even than Little Billee, who is represented, unconvincingly, as a brilliant painter. Svengali has 'genius,' but the others have 'character,' and 'character' is what matters. It is the attitude of the rugger-playing prefect towards the spectacled 'swot,' and it was probably the normal attitude towards Jews at that time. They were natural inferiors, but of course they were cleverer, more sensitive and more artistic than ourselves, because such qualities are of secondary importance. Nowadays the English are less sure of themselves, less confident that stupidity always wins in the end, and the prevailing form of anti-semitism has changed, not altogether for the better.

Authors' Decline

In last week's *Tribune* Mr. Julian Symons[2] remarked—rightly, I think—that Aldous Huxley's later novels are much inferior to his earlier ones. But he

---

2. Julian Symons reviewed for *Tribune*; he had recently taken over from Orwell as regular guest reviewer for the *Manchester Evening News*. The reference is to his article 'Aldous Revisited', *Tribune*, 29 November 1946.

might have added that this kind of falling-off is usual in imaginative writers, and that it only goes unnoticed when a writer is, so to speak, carried forward by the momentum of his earlier books. We value H.G. Wells, for example, for *Tono-Bungay, Mr. Polly, The Time Machine*, etc. If he had stopped writing in 1920 his reputation would stand quite as high as it does: if we knew him only by the books he wrote after that date, we should have rather a low opinion of him. A novelist does not, any more than a boxer or a ballet dancer, last for ever. He has an initial impulse which is good for three or four books, perhaps even for a dozen, but which must exhaust itself sooner or later. Obviously one cannot lay down any rigid rule, but in many cases the creative impulse seems to last for about 15 years: in a prose writer these 15 years would probably be between the ages of 30 and 45, or thereabouts. A few writers, it is true, have a much longer lease of life, and can go on developing when they are middle-aged or even old. But these are usually writers (examples: Yeats, Eliot, Hardy, Tolstoy) who make a sudden, almost violent change in their style, or their subject-matter, or both, and who may even tend to repudiate their earlier work.

Many writers, perhaps most, ought simply to stop writing when they reach middle age. Unfortunately our society will not let them stop. Most of them know no other way of earning a living, and writing, with all that goes with it—quarrels, rivalries, flattery, the sense of being a semi-public figure—is habit-forming. In a reasonable world a writer who had said his say would simply take up some other profession. In a competitive society he feels, just as a politician does, that retirement is death. So he continues long after his impulse is spent, and, as a rule, the less conscious he is of imitating himself, the more grossly he does it.

Four-letter Words

Early this year I met an American publisher who told me that his firm had just had a nine-months lawsuit from which it had emerged partially victorious, though out of pocket. It concerned the printing of a four-letter word which most of us use every day, generally in the present participle.

The United States is usually a few years ahead of Britain in these matters. You could print 'b——' in full in American books at a time when it had to appear in English ones as B dash. Recently it has become possible in England to print the word in full in a book, but in periodicals it still has to be B dash. Only five or six years ago it was printed in a well-known monthly magazine, but the last-minute panic was so great that a weary staff had to black the word out by hand.[3]

As to the other word, the four-letter one, it is still unprintable in periodicals in this country, but in books it can be represented by its first letter and a dash. In the United States this point was reached at least a dozen years ago. Last year the publishing firm in question tried the experiment of printing the word in full. The book was suppressed, and after nine months of litigation the suppression was upheld. But in the process an important step forward was made. It was ruled that you may now print the first and last letters of the word with two asterisks in between, clearly indicating that it had four letters. This makes it reasonably sure that within a few years the word will be printable in full.

So does progress continue—and it is genuine progress, in my opinion, for if only our half-dozen 'bad' words could be got off the lavatory wall and on to the printed page, they would soon lose their magical quality, and the habit of swearing, degrading to our thoughts and weakening to our language, might become less common.

3. In 'I had to go sick' by J. Maclaren Ross, the word 'bugger' was printed when the story was published in *Horizon*, August 1942, 126. In most copies it was then blacked out. A copy in Ian Angus's possession was missed. (Information from Diana Witherby and Janetta Parladé, who had to black out the offending word.)

Extract from 'As I Please', 65: Expenditure on Alcohol, Tobacco and Books; Soviet and US positions at United Nations

Tribune, 13 DECEMBER 1946

Expenditure on Alcohol, Tobacco and Books
Recently I received a copy of Sir Stanley Unwin's interesting and useful book, *The Truth about Publishing,* which has appeared in a number of editions from 1926 onwards, and has recently been expanded and brought up to date. I particularly value it because it assembles certain figures which one might have difficulty in finding elsewhere. A year or so ago, writing in *Tribune* on the cost of reading matter, I made a guess at the average yearly expenditure on books in this country, and put it at £1 a head. It seems that I was pitching it too high. Here are some figures of national expenditure in 1945:—

Alcoholic beverages	£685 millions
Tobacco	£548 millions
Books	£23 millions

In other words the average British citizen spends about 2d. a week on books, whereas he spends nearly 10 shillings on drink and tobacco.[1] I suppose this noble figure of 2d. would include the amount spent on school textbooks and other books which are bought, so to speak, involuntarily. Is it any wonder that when recently a questionnaire was sent out by *Horizon,* asking twenty-one poets and novelists how they thought a writer could best earn his living, not one of them said plainly that he might earn it by writing books?

Soviet and US positions at United Nations
When one reads the reports of UNO conferences, or international negotiations of any kind, it is difficult not to be reminded of *L'Attaque* and

---

1. In *Tribune,* 14 February 1947, Bernard Denvir, reviewing a selection of Honoré Daumier's work, referred to readers who objected to *Tribune's* reviewing high-priced books – the Daumier cost £2.2.0. Among the reasons he gave for so doing was that Orwell had 'several times pointed out in our columns, the total spent by the nation on books is still absurdly small—compared with the weekly volume of expenditure at the cinema and theatre'. In addition to Orwell's comments here, he also discussed this topic in 'Books *v.* Cigarettes', 8 February 1946.

similar war games that children used to play,[2] with cardboard pieces representing battleships, aeroplanes and so forth, each of which had a fixed value and could be countered in some recognised way. In fact, one might almost invent a new game called Uno, to be played in enlightened homes where the parents do not want their children to grow up with a militaristic outlook.

The pieces in this game are called the proposal, the *démarche*, the formula, the stumbling block, the stalemate, the deadlock, the bottleneck and the vicious circle. The object of the game is to arrive at a formula, and though details vary, the general outline of play is always much the same. First the players assemble, and somebody leads off with the proposal. This is countered by the stumbling block, without which the game could not develop. The stumbling block then changes into a bottleneck, or more often into a deadlock or a vicious circle. A deadlock and a vicious circle occurring simultaneously produce a stalemate, which may last for weeks. Then suddenly someone plays the *démarche*. The *démarche* makes it possible to produce a formula, and once the formula has been found the players can go home, leaving everything as it was at the beginning.

At the moment of writing, the front page of my morning paper has broken out into a pink rash of optimism. It seems that everything is going to be all right after all. The Russians will agree to inspection of armaments, and the Americans will internationalise the atomic bomb. On another page of the same paper are reports of events in Greece which amount to a state of war between the two groups of powers who are being so chummy in New York.

But while the game of deadlocks and bottlenecks goes on, another more serious game is also being played. It is governed by two axioms. One is that there can be no peace without a general surrender of sovereignty: the other is that no country capable of defending its sovereignty ever surrenders it. If one keeps these axioms in mind one can generally see the relevant facts in international affairs through the smoke-screen with which the newspapers surround them. At the moment the main facts are:—

2. These games, dating from about the time of World War I, from the illustrations used for early sets (so that Orwell might have played *L'Attaque*, the army game, or *Dover Patrol*, the naval equivalent), were still on sale forty years after Orwell made this comparison with the United Nations Organisation and international negotiations.

(i) The Russians, whatever they may say, will not agree to genuine inspection of their territories by foreign observers.

(ii) The Americans, whatever they may say, will not let slip the technological lead in armaments.

(iii) No country is now in a condition to fight an all-out major war.

These, although they may be superseded later, are at present the real counters in the real game, and one gets nearer the truth by constantly remembering them than by alternately rejoicing and despairing over the day-to-day humbug of conferences.

'As I Please', 66: Overindulging at Christmas

Tribune, 20 DECEMBER 1946

An advertisement in my Sunday paper sets forth in the form of a picture the four things that are needed for a successful Christmas. At the top of the picture is a roast turkey; below that, a Christmas pudding; below that, a dish of mince pies; and below that, a tin of——'s Liver Salt.[1]

It is a simple recipe for happiness. First the meal, then the antidote, then another meal. The ancient Romans were the great masters of this technique. However, having just looked up the word *vomitorium*[2] in the Latin dictionary, I find that after all it does *not* mean a place where you went to be sick after dinner. So perhaps this was not a normal feature of every Roman home, as is commonly believed.

Implied in the above-mentioned advertisement is the notion that a good meal means a meal at which you over-eat yourself. In principle I agree. I only add in passing that when we gorge ourselves this Christmas, if we do get the chance to gorge ourselves, it is worth giving a thought to the thousand million human beings, or thereabouts, who will be doing no such thing. For in the long run our Christmas dinners would be safer if we could make sure that everyone else had a Christmas dinner as well. But I will come back to that presently.

The only reasonable motive for not overeating at Christmas would be that somebody else needs the food more than you do. A deliberately austere Christmas would be an absurdity. The whole point of Christmas is that it is a debauch—as it was probably long before the birth of Christ was arbitrarily fixed at that date. Children know this very well. From their point of view Christmas is not a day of temperate enjoyment, but of fierce pleasures which they are quite willing to pay for with a certain amount of pain. The awakening at about 4 a.m. to inspect your stocking; the quarrels over toys all through the morning, and the exciting whiffs

1. Andrews Liver Salts, a powder making an effervescent drink with purgative properties.
2. A vomitorium was a door or opening giving access to a large building in Roman times enabling large crowds to enter or leave readily. Aldous Huxley had erroneously used it in *Antic Hay,* chap xviii (1923) as meaning a place where Romans at a feast went to be sick. Huxley taught Orwell at Eton and he taught his pupils rare and strange words and a taste for words and their accurate and significant use (Crick, p. 117, quoting Steven Runciman and John Grotrian).

of mincemeat and sage-and-onions escaping from the kitchen door; the battle with enormous platefuls of turkey, and the pulling of the wishbone; the darkening of the windows and the entry of the flaming plum-pudding; the hurry to make sure that everyone has a piece on his plate while the brandy is still alight; the momentary panic when it is rumoured that Baby has swallowed the threepenny bit; the stupor all through the afternoon; the Christmas cake with almond icing an inch thick; the peevishness next morning and the castor oil on December 27th—it is an up and-down business, by no means all pleasant, but well worthwhile for the sake of its more dramatic moments.

Teetotallers and vegetarians are always scandalised by this attitude. As they see it, the only rational objective is to avoid pain and to stay alive as long as possible. If you refrain from drinking alcohol, or eating meat, or whatever it is, you may expect to live an extra five years, while if you over-eat or over-drink you will pay for it in acute physical pain on the following day. Surely it follows that all excesses, even a once-a-year outbreak such as Christmas, should be avoided as a matter of course?

Actually it doesn't follow at all. One may decide, with full knowledge of what one is doing, that an occasional good time is worth the damage it inflicts on one's liver. For health is not the only thing that matters: friendship, hospitality, and the heightened spirits and change of outlook that one gets by eating and drinking in good company are also valuable. I doubt whether, on balance, even outright drunkenness does harm, provided it is infrequent—twice a year, say. The whole experience, including the repentance afterwards, makes a sort of break in one's mental routine, comparable to a weekend in a foreign country, which is probably beneficial.

In all ages men have realised this. There is a wide consensus of opinion stretching back to the days before the alphabet, that whereas habitual soaking is bad, conviviality is good, even if one does sometimes feel sorry for it next morning. How enormous is the literature of eating and drinking, especially drinking, and how little that is worth while has been said on the other side! Offhand I can't remember a single poem in praise of water, i.e. water regarded as a drink.[3] It is hard to imagine what one could say about it. It quenches thirst: that is the end of the story. As for poems in praise of wine, on the other hand, even the surviving ones would fill a

---

3. Orwell had probably forgotten Horace's ode to the Bandusian spring (III, 13), which would have been likely to come his way as a classical specialist at Eton.

shelf of books. The poets started turning them out on the very day when the fermentation of the grape was first discovered. Whisky, brandy and other distilled liquors have been less eloquently praised, partly because they came later in time. But beer has had quite a good press, starting well back in the Middle Ages, long before anyone had learned to put hops in it. Curiously enough, I can't remember a poem in praise of stout, not even draught stout, which is better than the bottled variety, in my opinion. There is an extremely disgusting description in *Ulysses* of the stout-vats in Dublin. But there is a sort of back-handed tribute to stout in the fact that this description, though widely known, has not done much towards putting the Irish off their favourite drink.

The literature of eating is also large, though mostly in prose. But in all the writers who have enjoyed describing food, from Rabelais to Dickens and from Petronius to Mrs. Beeton, I cannot remember a single passage which puts dietetic considerations first. Always food is felt to be an end in itself. No one has written memorable prose about vitamins, or the dangers of an excess of proteins, or the importance of masticating every-thing thirty-two times. All in all, there seems to be a heavy weight of testimony on the side of over-eating and over-drinking, provided always that they take place on recognised occasions, and not too frequently.

But ought we to over-eat and over-drink this Christmas? We ought not to, nor will most of us get the opportunity. I am writing in praise of Christmas, but in praise of Christmas 1947, or perhaps 1948. The world as a whole is not exactly in a condition for festivities this year. Between the Rhine and the Pacific there cannot be very many people who are in need of——'s Liver Salt. In India there are, and always have been, about 100 million people who only get one square meal a day. In China, condi-tions are no doubt much the same. In Germany, Austria, Greece and elsewhere, scores of millions of people are existing on a diet which keeps breath in the body but leaves no strength for work. All over the war-wrecked areas from Brussels to Stalingrad, other uncounted millions are living in the cellars of bombed houses, in hide-outs in the forests, or in squalid huts behind barbed wire. It is not so pleasant to read almost simultaneously that a large proportion of our Christmas turkeys will come from Hungary, and that the Hungarian writers and journalists—presum-ably not the worse-paid section of the community—are in such desperate straits that they would be glad to receive presents of saccharine and cast-off clothing from English sympathisers. In such circumstances we could hardly have a 'proper' Christmas, even if the materials for it existed.

But we will have one sooner or later, in 1947, or 1948, or maybe even in 1949. And when we do, there may be no gloomy voices of vegetarians or teetotallers to lecture us about the things that we are doing to the linings of our stomachs. One celebrates a feast for its own sake, and not for any supposed benefit to the lining of one's stomach. Meanwhile Christmas is here, or nearly. Santa Claus is rounding up his reindeer, the postman staggers from door to door beneath his bulging sack of Christmas cards, the black markets are humming, and Britain has imported over 7,000 crates of mistletoe from France. So I wish everyone an old-fashioned Christmas in 1947, and meanwhile, half a turkey, three tangerines, and a bottle of whisky at not more than double the legal price.

Extracts from 'As I Please', 66: The Gap Between Function and Reward on a Luxury Liner; Persecution of Writers in USSR

Tribune, 3 JANUARY 1947

The Gap Between Function and Reward on a Luxury Liner

Nearly a quarter of a century ago I was travelling on a liner to Burma. Though not a big ship, it was a comfortable and even a luxurious one, and when one was not asleep or playing deck games one usually seemed to be eating. The meals were of that stupendous kind that steamship companies used to vie with one another in producing, and in between times there were snacks such as apples, ices, biscuits and cups of soup, lest anyone should find himself fainting from hunger. Moreover, the bars opened at ten in the morning, and, since we were at sea, alcohol was relatively cheap.

The ships of this line were mostly manned by Indians, but apart from the officers and the stewards they carried four European quartermasters whose job was to take the wheel. One of these quartermasters, though I suppose he was only aged forty or so, was one of those old sailors on whose back you almost expect to see barnacles growing. He was a short, powerful, rather ape-like man, with enormous forearms covered by a mat of golden hair. A blond moustache which might have belonged to Charlemagne completely hid his mouth. I was only twenty years old[1] and very conscious of my parasitic status as a mere passenger, and I looked up to the quartermasters, especially the fair-haired one, as godlike beings on a par with the officers. It would not have occurred to me to speak to one of them without being spoken to first.

One day, for some reason, I came up from lunch early. The deck was empty except for the fair-haired quartermaster, who was scurrying like a rat along the side of the deck-houses, with something partially concealed between his monstrous hands. I had just time to see what it was before he shot past me and vanished into a doorway. It was a pie dish containing a half-eaten baked custard pudding.

At one glance I took in the situation—indeed, the man's air of guilt made it unmistakable. The pudding was a left-over from one of the passengers' tables. It had been illicitly given to him by a steward, and he was carrying it off to the seamen's quarters to devour it at leisure. Across

---

1. He was only nineteen, though his passport showed he was twenty.

more than twenty years I can still faintly feel the shock of astonishment that I felt at that moment. It took me some time to see the incident in all its bearings: but do I seem to exaggerate when I say that this sudden revelation of the gap between function and reward—the revelation that a highly-skilled craftsman, who might literally hold all our lives in his hands, was glad to steal scraps of food from our table—taught me more than I could have learned from half a dozen Socialist pamphlets?

Persecution of Writers in USSR

A news item to the effect that Yugoslavia is now engaged on a purge of writers and artists led me to look once again at the reports of the recent literary purge in the U.S.S.R., when Zoschenko, Akhmatova[2] and others were expelled from the Writers' Union.

In England this kind of thing is not happening to us as yet, so that we can view it with a certain detachment, and, curiously enough, as I look again at the accounts of what happened, I feel somewhat more sorry for the persecutors than for their victims. Chief among the persecutors is Andrei Zhdanov, considered by some to be Stalin's probable successor.[3] Zhdanov, though he has conducted literary purges before, is a full-time politician with—to judge from his speeches—about as much knowledge of literature as I have of aerodynamics. He does not give the impression of being, according to his own lights, a wicked or dishonest man. He is truly shocked by the defection of certain Soviet writers, which appears to him as an incomprehensible piece of treachery, like a military mutiny in the middle of a battle. The purpose of literature is to glorify the Soviet Union; surely that must be obvious to everyone? But instead of carrying out their plain duty, these misguided writers keep straying away from the

2. Anna Akhmatova (1888–1966) was a poet whose works were condemned in 1920 and again in 1946. She was rehabilitated in the 1950s and officially recognised at her death. Mikhail Zoschenko (1895–1957 or 1958), Soviet satirist, particularly in short-story and sketch form, who in the 1930s and 1940s suffered severely from critics of the socialist-realist persuasion. He was vilified for his satirical anecdotes and reminiscences and was criticised for malicious distortions of popular speech. His expulsion from the Union of Soviet Writers in 1946 virtually brought to an end his creative-writing career.
3. Andrei Aleksandrovich Zhdanov (1896–1948), Secretary of the Central Committee in charge of ideology and a close associate of Stalin, was an advocate of socialist realism in the 1930s. He was largely responsible for initiating a Communist Party policy in 1946 directed against Mikhail Zoschenko, Anna Akhmatova, and Boris Pasternak in particular. This oppressive cultural policy was given the name 'Zhdanovshchina'. Zhdanov did not succeed Stalin; Stalin survived him.

paths of propaganda, producing non-political works, and even, in the case of Zoschenko, allowing a satirical note to creep into their writings. It is all very painful and bewildering. It is as though you set a man to work in an excellent, up-to-date, air-conditioned factory, gave him high wages, short hours, good canteens and playing-grounds, a comfortable flat, a nursery-school for his children, all-round social insurance and music while you work—only to find the ungrateful fellow throwing spanners into the machinery on his very first day.

What makes the whole thing somewhat pathetic is the general admission—an honest admission, seeing that Soviet publicists are not in the habit of decrying their own country—that Russian literature as a whole is not what it ought to be. Since the U.S.S.R. represents the highest existing form of civilisation, it is obvious that it ought to lead the world in literature as in everything else. 'Surely,' says Zhdanov, 'our new Socialist system, embodying all that is best in the history of human civilisation and culture, is capable of creating the most advanced literature, which will leave far behind the best creations of olden times.' *Izvestia* (as quoted by the New York paper, *Politics*), goes further: 'Our culture stands on an immeasurably higher level than bourgeois culture. . . . Is it not clear that our culture has the right not to act as pupil and imitator but, on the contrary, to teach others the general human morals?' And yet somehow the expected thing never happens. Directives are issued, resolutions are passed unanimously, recalcitrant writers are silenced: and yet for some reason a vigorous and original literature, unmistakably superior to that of capitalist countries, fails to emerge.

All this has happened before, and more than once. Freedom of expression has had its ups and downs in the U.S.S.R., but the general tendency has been towards tighter censorship. The thing that politicians are seemingly unable to understand is that you cannot produce a vigorous literature by terrorising everyone into conformity. A writer's inventive faculties will not work unless he is allowed to say approximately what he feels. You can destroy spontaneity and produce a literature which is orthodox but feeble, or you can let people say what they choose and take the risk that some of them will utter heresies. There is no way out of that dilemma so long as books have to be written by individuals.

That is why, in a way, I feel sorrier for the persecutors than for the victims. It is probable that Zoschenko and the others at least have the satisfaction of understanding what is happening to them: the politicians who harry them are merely attempting the impossible. For Zhdanov and his kind to say, 'The Soviet Union can exist without literature,' would be reasonable. But that is just what they can't say. They don't know what literature is, but they know that it is important, that it has prestige value, and that it is necessary for propaganda purposes, and they would like to encourage it, if only they knew how. So they continue with their purges and directives, like a fish bashing its nose against the wall of an aquarium again and again, too dim-witted to realise that glass and water are not the same thing.

Extracts from 'As I Please', 72: The Fate of Burmese Minorities; H.G. Wells on Printing Errors

Tribune, 7 FEBRUARY 1947

The Fate of Burmese Minorities

About the time when Sir Stafford Cripps came back from India, I heard it remarked that the Cripps offer had not been extended to Burma because the Burmese would have accepted it. I don't know whether any such calculation really entered into the minds of Churchill and the rest. It is perfectly possible at any rate, I think that responsible Burmese politicians would have accepted such an offer, although at that moment Burma was in process of being over-run by the Japanese. I also believe that an offer of Dominion Status would have been gladly accepted if we had made it in 1944 and had named a definite date. As it is, the suspicions of the Burmese have been well roused, and it will probably end by our simply getting out of Burma on the terms least advantageous to both countries.

If that happens, I should like to think that the position of the racial minorities could be safeguarded by something better than promises. They number ten to twenty per cent. of the population, and they present several different kinds of problem. The biggest group, the Karens, are a racial enclave living largely within Burma proper. The Kachins and other frontier tribes are a good deal more backward and more different from the Burmese in customs and appearance. They have never been under Burmese rule —indeed, their territories were only very sketchily occupied even by the British. In the past they were well able to maintain their independence, but probably would not be able to do so in the face of modern weapons. The other big group, the Shans, who are racially akin to the Siamese, enjoyed some faint traces of autonomy under British rule. The minority who are in the most difficult position of all are the Indians. There were over a million of them in Burma before the war. Two hundred thousand of them fled to India at the time of the Japanese invasion—an act which demonstrated better than any words could have done their real position in the country.

I remember twenty years ago a Karen remarking to me, 'I hope the British will stay in Burma for two hundred years.'—'Why?'—'Because we do not wish to be ruled by Burmese.' Even at the time it struck me that sooner or later this would become a problem. The fact is that the question of minorities is literally insoluble so long as nationalism remains a real force. The desire of some of the peoples of Burma for autonomy is genuine, but it cannot be satisfied in any secure way unless the sovereignty of Burma as a whole is interfered with. The same problem comes up in a hundred other places. Ought the Sudan to be independent of Egypt? Ought Ulster to be independent of Eire? Ought Eire to be independent of Britain? And so on. Whenever A is oppressing B, it is clear to people of good will that B ought to be independent, but then it always turns out that there is another group, C, which is anxious to be independent of B. The question is always *how large* must a minority be before it deserves autonomy. At best, each case can only be treated on its merits in a rough and ready way: in practice, no one is consistent in his thinking on this subject, and the minorities which win the most sympathy are those that have the best means of publicity. Who is there who champions equally the Jews, the Balts, the Indonesians, the expelled Germans, the Sudanese, the Indian Untouchables and the South African Kaffirs? Sympathy for one group almost invariably entails callousness towards another.

H.G. Wells on Printing Errors

When H. G. Wells's *The Island of Doctor Moreau* was reprinted in the Penguin Library, I looked to see whether the slips and misprints which I remembered in earlier editions had been repeated in it. Sure enough, they were still there. One of them is a particularly stupid misprint, of a kind to make most writers squirm. In 1941 I pointed this out to H. G. Wells, and asked him why he did not remove it. It had persisted through edition after edition ever since 1896. Rather to my surprise, he said that he remembered the misprint, but could not be bothered to do anything about it. He no longer took the faintest interest in his early books: they had been written so long ago that he no longer felt them to be part of himself. I have never been quite sure whether to admire this attitude or not. It is magnificent to be so free from literary vanity. And yet, what writer of Wells's gifts, if he had had any power of self-criticism or regard for his own reputation, would have poured out in fifty years a total of ninety-five books, quite two-thirds of which have already ceased to be readable?

Extracts from 'As I Please', 73: Poles in Scotland; Scottish Nationalism

Tribune, 14 FEBRUARY 1947

Poles in Scotland

Here are some excerpts from a letter from a Scottish Nationalist. I have cut out anything likely to reveal the writer's identity. The frequent references to Poland are there because the letter is primarily concerned with the presence of exiled Poles in Scotland:

> The Polish forces have now discovered how untrue it is to say 'An Englishman's word is his bond.' We could have told you so hundreds of years ago. The invasion of Poland was only an excuse for these brigands in bowler hats to beat up their rivals the Germans and the Japs, with the help of Americans, Poles, Scots, Frenchmen, etc., etc. Surely no Pole believes any longer in English promises. Now that the war is over you are to be cast aside and dumped in Scotland. If this leads to friction between the Poles and Scots so much the better. Let them slit each other's throats and two problems would be thereupon 'solved.' Dear, kind little England! It is time for all Poles to shed any ideas they may have about England as a champion of freedom. Look at her record in Scotland, for instance. And please don't refer to us as 'Britons.' There is *no* such race. We are Scots and that's good enough for us. The English changed their name to British: but even if a criminal changes his name he can be known by his fingerprints. . . . Please disregard any anti-Polish statement in the *John O'Groat Journal.*[1] It is a boot-licking pro-English (pro-Moscow you would call it) rag. Scotland experienced her Yalta in 1707 when English gold achieved what English guns could not do. But we will never accept defeat. After more than two hundred years we are still fighting for our country and will never acknowledge defeat whatever the odds.

There is a good deal more in the letter, but this should be enough. It will be noted that the writer is not attacking England from what is called a

---

1. The name of the journal is left as a blank in 'As I Please', but it appears in the original letter, of course. It has been restored here.

'left' standpoint, but on the ground that Scotland and England are enemies *as nations*. I don't know whether it would be fair to read race-theory into this letter, but certainly the writer hates us as bitterly as a devout Nazi would hate a Jew. It is not a hatred of the capitalist class, or anything like that, but *of England*. And though the fact is not sufficiently realised, there is an appreciable amount of this kind of thing knocking about. I have seen almost equally violent statements in print.

Scottish Nationalism

Up to date the Scottish Nationalist movement seems to have gone almost unnoticed in England. To take the nearest example to hand, I don't remember having seen it mentioned in *Tribune*, except occasionally in book reviews. It is true that it is a small movement, but it could grow, because there is a basis for it. In this country I don't think it is enough realised—I myself had no idea of it until a few years ago—that Scotland has a case against England. On economic grounds it may not be a very strong case. In the past, certainly, we have plundered Scotland shamefully, but whether it is *now* true that England as a whole exploits Scotland as a whole, and that Scotland would be better off if fully autonomous, is another question. The point is that many Scottish people, often quite moderate in outlook, are beginning to think about autonomy and to feel that they are pushed into an inferior position. They have a good deal of reason. In some areas, at any rate, Scotland is almost an occupied country. You have an English or Anglicised upper-class, and a Scottish working-class which speaks with a markedly different accent, or even, part of the time, in a different language. This is a more dangerous kind of class division than any now existing in England. Given favourable circumstances it might develop in an ugly way, and the fact that there was a progressive Labour Government in London might not make much difference.

No doubt Scotland's major ills will have to be cured along with those of England. But meanwhile there are things that could be done to ease the cultural situation. One small but not negligible point is the language. In the Gaelic-speaking areas, Gaelic is not taught in the schools. I am speaking from limited experience, but I should say that this is beginning to cause resentment. Also, the B.B.C. only broadcasts two or three half-hour Gaelic programmes a week, and they give the impression of being rather amateurish programmes. Even so they are eagerly listened to. How easy it would be to buy a little goodwill by putting on a Gaelic programme at least once daily.

At one time I would have said that it is absurd to keep alive an archaic language like Gaelic, spoken by only a few hundred thousand people. Now I am not so sure. To begin with, if people feel that they have a special culture which ought to be preserved, and that the language is part of it, difficulties should not be put in their way when they want their children to learn it properly. Secondly, it is probable that the effort of being bi-lingual is a valuable education in itself. The Scottish Gaelic-speaking peasants speak beautiful English, partly, I think, because English is an almost foreign language which they sometimes do not use for days together. Probably they benefit intellectually by having to be aware of dictionaries and grammatical rules, as their English opposite numbers would not be.

At any rate, I think we should pay more attention to the small but violent separatist movements which exist within our own island. They may look very unimportant now, but, after all, the Communist Manifesto was once a very obscure document, and the Nazi Party only had six members when Hitler joined it.

'As I Please', 75B: Handwriting and Creative Writing

Manchester Evening News for *Tribune*, 28 FEBRUARY 1947[1]

A serious fuel crisis at this time led to many national power cuts; Tribune *and a number of other journals had to suspend publication.* The Observer, Manchester Evening News, *and the* Daily Herald *offered* Tribune *the hospitality of its columns during the fuel crisis. As a consequence, short sections of 'As I Please' were printed elsewhere, as here in the* Manchester Evening News.

One thing one notices in these days when typewriters have become so scarce is the astonishing badness of nearly everyone's handwriting.

A handwriting which is both pleasant to look at and easy to read is now a very rare thing. To bring about an improvement we should probably have to evolve a generally accepted 'style' of writing such as we possessed in the past and have now lost.

For several centuries in the Middle Ages the professional scribes wrote an exquisite script, or rather a series of scripts, which no one now living could equal. Then handwriting declined, reviving in the nineteenth century after the invention of the steel pen. The style then favoured was 'copperplate.' It was neat and legible, but it was full of unnecessary lines and did not fit in with the modern tendency to get rid of ornament wherever possible. Then it became the fashion to teach children script, usually with disastrous results. To write script with real neatness one practically has to learn to draw, and it is impossible to write it as rapidly as a cursive hand. Many young or youngish people now make use of an uneasy compromise between script and copperplate, and indeed there are many adult and fully literate people whose handwriting has never properly 'formed.'

It would be interesting to know whether there is any connection between neat handwriting and literary ability. I must say that the modern examples I am able to think of do not seem to prove much. Miss Rebecca West has an exquisite handwriting, and so has Mr. Middleton Murry. Sir

---

1. Another section, numbered in *CW* as 75A, appeared the preceding day in the *Daily Herald*. One of the trade papers to which the *Manchester Evening News* gave hospitality during the crisis was *The Shoe and Leather Record*. In a report from that journal printed immediately below Orwell's column was a statement that the fuel crisis had caused a loss in production of 10,000,000 shoes, giving added point to Orwell's difficulty in finding footwear.

Osbert Sitwell, Mr. Stephen Spender, and Mr. Evelyn Waugh all have handwritings which, to put it as politely as possible, are not good. Professor Laski writes a hand which is attractive to look at but difficult to read. Arnold Bennett wrote a beautiful tiny hand over which he took immense pains. H. G. Wells had an attractive but untidy writing. Carlyle's writing was so bad that one compositor is said to have left Edinburgh in order to get away from the job of setting it up. Mr. Bernard Shaw writes a small, clear but not very elegant hand. And as for the most famous and respected of living English novelists, his writing is such that when I was at the B.B.C. and had the honour of putting him on the air once a month there was only one secretary in the whole department who could decipher his manuscripts.[2]

2. The reference is to E.M. Forster's handwriting.

Extract from 'As I Please', 77: Rationalised Spelling and Imperial Measure

Tribune, 14 MARCH 1947

I have not yet read more than a newspaper paragraph about Nu Speling in connection with which somebody is introducing a Bill in Parliament, but if it is like most other schemes for rationalising our spelling, I am against it in advance, as I imagine most people will be.[1]

Probably the strongest reason for resisting rationalised spelling is laziness. We have all learned to read and write already, and we don't want to have to do it over again. But there are other more respectable objections. To begin with unless the scheme were rigidly enforced, the resulting chaos, with some newspapers and publishing houses accepting it, others refusing it, and others adopting it in patches, would be fearful. Then again, anyone who had learned only the new system would find it very difficult to read books printed in the old one, so that the huge labour of re-spelling the entire literature of the past would have to be undertaken.[2] And again, you can only fully rationalise spelling if you give a fixed value to each letter. But this means standardising pronunciation, which could not be done in this country without an unholy row. What do you do, for instance, about words like 'butter' or 'glass,' which are pronounced in different ways in London and Newcastle? Other words, such as 'were,' are pronounced in two different ways according to individual inclination, or according to context.

However, I do not want to pre-judge the inventors of Nu Speling. Perhaps they have already thought of a way round these difficulties. And certainly our existing spelling system is preposterous and must be a torment to foreign students. This is a pity, because English is well fitted to be the universal second language, if there ever is such a thing. It has a large start over any natural language and an enormous start over any

---

1. 'Nu Speling' was presented to Parliament (as New Spelling) in 1949. It was to be introduced in three stages: 1. for five years in primary schools, after which old spelling would not be taught; 2. for five years in advertising and public announcements; and 3. thereafter in all legal documents and records; new literature would not be copyrighted unless in new spelling. The bill was rejected by 87 votes to 84. (David Crystal, *The Cambridge Encyclopedia of Language* (1987), which calls it Nue Spelling, see pp. 215–6.)
2. Compare the rewriting of earlier texts, for example, Shakespeare, in Newspeak in *Nineteen Eighty-Four;* see CW, IX, 325.

manufactured one, and apart from the spelling it is very easy to learn. Would it not be possible to rationalise it by little and little, a few words every year? Already some of the more ridiculous spellings do tend to get killed off unofficially. For instance, how many people now spell 'hiccup' as 'hiccough?'

Another thing I am against in advance—for it is bound to be suggested sooner or later—is the complete scrapping of our present system of weights and measures.[3]

Obviously you have got to have the metric system for certain purposes. For scientific work it has long been in use, and it is also needed for tools and machinery, especially if you want to export them. But there is a strong case for keeping on the old measurements for use in everyday life. One reason is that the metric system does not possess, or has not succeeded in establishing, a large number of units that can be visualised. There is, for instance, effectively no unit between the metre, which is more than a yard, and the centimetre, which is less than half an inch. In English you can describe someone as being five feet three inches high, or five feet nine inches, or six feet one inch, and your hearer will know fairly accurately what you mean. But I have never heard a Frenchman say, 'He is a hundred and forty-two centimetres high'; it would not convey any visual image. So also with the various other measurements. Rods and acres, pints, quarts and gallons, pounds, stones and hundredweights, are all of them units with which we are intimately familiar, and we should be slightly poorer without them. Actually, in countries where the metric system is in force a few of the old measurements tend to linger on for everyday purposes, although officially discouraged.

There is also the literary consideration, which cannot be left quite out of account. The names of the units in the old system are short homely words which lend themselves to vigorous speech. Putting a quart into a pint pot is a good image, which could hardly be expressed in the metric system. Also, the literature of the past deals only in the old measurements, and many passages would become an irritation if one had to do a sum in arithmetic when one read them, as one does with those tiresome versts[4] in a Russian novel.

3. European Community Directive 89/617 phased out British imperial measures. Parliament's Units of Measurement Regulations, 1995, makes it a criminal offence to sell, for example, fruit or vegetables by the pound.
4. Here versts was set as verses. A verst is about two-thirds of a mile or approximately one kilometre.

> The emmet's inch[5] and eagle's mile
> Make lame philosophy to smile:

Fancy having to turn that into millimetres!

5. An emmet is an ant.

Extracts from 'As I Please', 79: Mass Observation; Seeking Spring

Tribune, 28 MARCH 1947

Mass Observation

I have been reading with interest the February–March bulletin of Mass-Observation, which appears just ten years after this organisation first came into being. It is curious to remember with what hostility it was greeted at the beginning. It was violently attacked in the *New Statesman*, for instance, where Mr. Stonier[1] declared that the typical Mass–Observer would have 'elephant ears, a loping walk and a permanent sore eye from looking through keyholes,' or words to that effect. Another attacker was Mr. Stephen Spender.[2] But on the whole the opposition to this or any other kind of social survey comes from people of Conservative opinions, who often seem to be genuinely indignant at the idea of finding out what the big public is thinking.

If asked why, they generally answer that what is discovered is of no interest, and that in any case any intelligent person always knows already what are the main trends of public opinion. Another argument is that social surveys are an interference with individual liberty and a first step towards totalitarianism. The *Daily Express* ran this line for several years and tried to laugh the small social survey unit instituted by the Ministry of Information out of existence by nicknaming it Cooper's Snoopers.[3] Of course, behind much of this opposition there lies a well-justified fear of finding that mass sentiment on many subjects is not Conservative.

But some people do seem sincerely to feel that it is a bad thing for the Government to know too much about what people are thinking, just as others feel that it is a kind of presumption when the Government

---

1. George Walter Stonier (1903–1985), Australian-born journalist who was assistant literary editor of *The New Statesman and Nation*, 1928–45. In *When I Was* (1989) Desmond Hawkins says Kingsley Martin 'seemed content to let Stonier run the literary section more or less as he pleased. Stonier wrote a number of plays for the BBC.

2. Stephen Spender (1909–1995), poet, dramatist, and critic, he and Orwell first met before the war.

3. Alfred Duff Cooper (1890–1954), politician and author. When Churchill succeeded Chamberlain as prime minister in May 1940, Duff Cooper was made Minister of Information, a post he did not enjoy. It was in this period that the MOI social survey unit, 'Cooper's Snoopers', was set up. He wrote an important autobiography, *Old Men Forget* (1953).

tries to educate public opinion. Actually you can't have democracy unless both processes are at work. Democracy is only possible when the law-makers and administrators know what the masses want, and what they can be counted on to understand. If the present Government paid more attention to this last point, they would word some of their publicity differently. Mass-Observation issued a report last week on the White Paper on the economic situation. They found, as usual, that the abstract words and phrases which are flung to and fro in official announcements mean nothing to countless ordinary citizens. Many people are even flummoxed by the word 'assets,' which is thought to have something to do with 'assist'!

The Mass-Observation bulletin gives some account of the methods its investigators use, but does not touch on a very important point, and that is the manner in which social surveys are financed. Mass-Observation itself appears to keep going in a hand-to-mouth way by publishing books and by undertaking specific jobs for the Government or for commercial organisations. Some of its best surveys, such as that dealing with the birth-rate, were carried out for the Advertising Service Guild. The trouble with this method is that a subject only gets investigated if some large, wealthy organisation happens to be interested in it. An obvious example is anti-semitism, which I believe has never been looked into, or only in a very sketchy way. But anti-semitism is only one variant of the great modern disease of nationalism. We know very little about the real causes of nationalism, and we might conceivably be on the way towards curing it if we knew more. But who is sufficiently interested to put up the thousands of pounds that an exhaustive survey would cost?

Seeking Spring

For the last five minutes I have been gazing out of the window into the square, keeping a sharp look-out for signs of spring. There is a thinnish patch in the clouds with a faint hint of blue behind it, and on a sycamore tree there are some things that look as if they might be buds. Otherwise it is still winter. But don't worry! Two days ago, after a careful search in Hyde Park, I came on a hawthorn bush that was definitely in bud, and some birds, though not actually singing, were making noises like an orchestra tuning up. Spring is coming after all, and recent rumours that this was the beginning of another Ice Age were unfounded. In only three weeks' time we shall be listening to the cuckoo, which usually gives tongue about the fourteenth of April. Another three weeks after that, and we shall be basking under blue skies, eating ices off barrows and neglecting to lay up fuel for next winter.

How appropriate the ancient poems in praise of spring have seemed these last few years! They have a meaning that they did not have in the days when there was no fuel shortage and you could get almost anything at any time of year. Of all passages celebrating spring, I think I like best those two stanzas from the beginning of one of the Robin Hood ballads. I modernise the spelling:

> When shaws be sheen and swards full fair,
> And leaves both large and long,
> It is merry walking in the fair forest
> To hear the small birds' song.
>
> The woodwele sang and would not cease,
> Sitting upon the spray,
> So loud he wakened Robin Hood
> In the greenwood where he lay.

But what exactly was the woodwele? The Oxford Dictionary seems to suggest that it was the woodpecker, which is not a notable songster, and I should be interested to know whether it can be identified with some more probable bird.

'In Defence of Comrade Zilliacus'

unpublished[1], Aug/Sept(?) 1947

Some weeks ago Mr K. Zilliacus addressed a long and, as usual, abusive letter to *Tribune*, in which he accused it of having no definite and viable foreign policy, but of being in effect an anti-Russian paper while keeping up a show of hostility to Ernest Bevin. Bevin, he said, was far more realistic than *Tribune*, since he grasped that to oppose Russia it was necessary to rely on America and 'bolster up Fascism,' while *Tribune* was merely sitting on the fence, uttering contradictory slogans and getting nowhere.

I am not often in agreement with Mr Zilliacus,[2] and it is therefore all the more of a pleasure to record my agreement with him on this occasion. Granting him his own special terminology, I think his accusation is fully justified. One must remember, of course, that in the mouths of Mr Zilliacus and his associates, words like democracy, Fascism or totalitarianism do not bear quite their normal meanings. In general they tend to turn into their opposites, Fascism meaning unfaked elections, democracy meaning minority rule, and so on. But this does not alter the fact that he is dwelling on real issues—issues on which *Tribune* has consistently, over a period of years, failed to make its position clear. He knows that the only big political questions in the world today are: for Russia—against Russia, for America—against America, for democracy—against democracy. And though he may describe his own activities in different words from what most of us would use, at least we can see at a glance where he stands.

But where does *Tribune* stand? I know, or think I know, what foreign policy *Tribune* favours, but I know it by inference and from private contacts. Casual readers can, and to my knowledge do, draw very different impressions. If one had to sum up *Tribune's apparent* policy in a single word, the name one would have to coin for it would be anti-Bevinism.

1. Intended for the *Tribune*.
2. Konni Zilliacus (1894–1967) was at the time a left-wing Labour MP. He was expelled from the Party in 1949 for persistent criticism of its foreign policy and lost his seat in the 1950 General Election when standing as an Independent Labour candidate. He re-entered Parliament in 1955 as a Labour MP.

The first rule of this 'ism' is that when Bevin[3] says or does something, a way must be found of showing that it is wrong, even if it happens to be what *Tribune* was advocating in the previous week. The second rule is that though Russian policy may be criticised, extenuating circumstances must always be found. The third rule is that when the United States can be insulted, it must be insulted. The effect of framing a policy on these principles is that one cannot even find out what solution *Tribune* offers for the specific problems it most discusses. To take some examples. Is *Tribune* in favour of clearing out of Greece unconditionally? Does *Tribune* think the USSR should have the Dardanelles? Is *Tribune* in favour of unrestricted Jewish immigration into Palestine? Does *Tribune* think Egypt should be allowed to annex the Sudan? In some cases I know the answers, but I think it would be very difficult to discover them simply by reading the paper.

Part of the trouble, I believe, is that after building Bevin up into Public Enemy Number One, *Tribune* has found out that it is not genuinely in disagreement with him. Certainly there are real differences over Palestine, Spain and perhaps Greece, but broadly, I think, he and *Tribune* stand for the same kind of policy. There are, it is generally agreed, only three possible foreign policies for Great Britain. One is to do as Mr Zilliacus would have us do, ie., to become part of the Russian system, with a government perhaps less servile than that of Poland or Czechoslovakia, but essentially similar. Another is to move definitely into the orbit of the United States. And another is to become part of a federation of western European Socialist republics, including if possible Africa, and again if possible (though this is less likely) the British dominions. *Tribune*, I infer—for it has never been clearly stated—favours the third policy, and so I believe does Bevin, that is to say, the Government. But *Tribune* is not only involved in its personal feud with Bevin; it is also unwilling to face two facts—very unpopular facts at the moment —which must be faced if one is to discuss a Western union seriously.

3. Ernest Bevin (1881–1951), a self-taught orphan who developed as one of the, if not *the*, most powerful and forceful trade-union leaders in Britain. He won a momentous court case for his union in 1929 against a leading barrister so earning the soubriquet, 'the dockers' KC' [King's Counsel]. From 1921 to 1940 he was General Secretary of the Transport and General Workers' Union. In 1940 he became an MP and Churchill appointed him to the War Cabinet as Minister of Labour and National Service. From 1945–51 he was Foreign Secretary in Attlee's administration. Despite their political differences, he and Churchill shared certain 'bulldog characteristics'.

One is that such a union could hardly succeed without a friendly America behind it, and the other is that however peaceful its intentions might be, it would be bound to incur Russian hostility. It is exactly here that *Tribune* has failed as an organ of opinion. All its other equivocations, I believe, spring from a dread of flouting fashionable opinion on the subject of Russia and America.

One very noticeable thing in *Tribune* is the pretence that Bevin's policy is exclusively his own. Apparently he is a sort of runaway horse dragging an unwilling Cabinet behind him, and our policy would have been quite different—above all, our relations with the USSR would have been better —if only we had had a more enlightened foreign secretary. Now it is obvious that this cannot be so. A minister who is really thwarting the will of the rest of the government does not stay in office for two years. Why then the attempt to put all the blame on one person? Was it not because otherwise it would have been necessary to say a very unpopular thing: namely that a Labour Government, as such, is almost bound to be on bad terms with the government of the USSR? With a government headed by Pritt and Zilliacus we could no doubt have excellent relations, of a kind, with Russia, and with a government headed by Churchill and Beaverbrook we could probably patch up some kind of arrangement: but any government genuinely representative of the Labour movement *must* be regarded with hostility. From the point of view of the Russians and the Communists, Social Democracy is a deadly enemy, and to do them justice they have frequently admitted it. Even such controversial questions as the formation of a Western union are irrelevant here. Even if we had no influence in Europe and made no attempt to interfere there, it would still be to the interest of the Russian government to bring about the failure of the British Labour government, if possible. The reason is clear enough. Social Democracy, unlike capitalism, offers an alternative to Communism, and if somewhere or other it can be made to work on a big scale—if it turns out that after all it *is* possible to introduce Socialism without secret police forces, mass deportations and so forth—then the excuse for dicta-torship vanishes. With a Labour government in office, relations with Russia, bad already, were bound to deteriorate. Various observers pointed this out at the time of the General Election, but I do not remember *Tribune* doing so, then or since. Was it not because it was easier, more popular, to encourage the widespread delusion that 'a government of the Left can get on better with Russia' and that Communism is much the same thing as Socialism, only more so—and then, when things didn't turn out that way, to register pained surprise and look round for a scapegoat?

And what, I wonder, is behind *Tribune's* persistent anti-Americanism? In *Tribune* over the past year I can recall three polite references to America (one of those was a reference to Henry Wallace) and a whole string of petty insults. I have just received a letter from some students at an American university. They ask me if I can explain why *Tribune* thinks it necessary to boo at America. What am I to say to these people? I shall tell them what I believe to be the truth—namely that *Tribune's* anti-Americanism is not sincere but is an attempt to keep in with fashionable opinion. To be anti-American nowadays is to shout with the mob. Of course it is only a minor mob, but it is a vocal one. Although there was probably some growth of ill-feeling as a result of the presence of the American troops, I do not believe the mass of the people in this country are anti-American politically, and certainly they are not so culturally. But politico-literary intellectuals are not usually frightened of mass opinion. What they are frightened of is the prevailing opinion within their own group. At any given moment there is always an orthodoxy, a parrot cry which must be repeated, and in the more active section of the Left the orthodoxy of the moment is anti-Americanism. I believe part of the reason (I am thinking of some remarks in Mr G. D. H. Cole's last 1143-page compilation[4]) is the idea that if we can cut our links with the United States we might succeed in staying neutral in the case of Russia and America going to war. How anyone can believe this, after looking at the map and remembering what happened to neutrals in the late war, I do not know. There is also the rather mean consideration that the Americans are *not* really our enemies, that they are unlikely to start dropping atomic bombs on us or even to let us starve to death, and therefore that we can safely take liberties with them if it pays to do so. But at any rate the orthodoxy is there. To speak favourably of America, to recall that the Americans helped us in 1940 when the Russians were supplying the Germans with oil and setting on their Communist parties to sabotage the war effort, is to be branded as a 'reactionary.' And I suspect that when *Tribune* joins in the chorus it is more from fear of this label than from genuine conviction.

Surely, if one is going to write about foreign policy at all, there is one question that should be answered plainly. It is: 'If you *had* to choose

4. *The Intelligent Man's Guide to the Post-War World* (1947).

between Russia and America, which would you choose?' It will not do to give the usual quibbling answer, 'I refuse to choose.' In the end the choice may be forced upon us. We are no longer strong enough to stand alone, and if we fail to bring a western European union into being, we shall be obliged, in the long run, to subordinate our policy to that of one Great Power or the other. And in spite of all the fashionable chatter of the moment, everyone knows in his heart that we should choose America. The great mass of people in this country would, I believe, make this choice almost instinctively. Certainly there is a small minority that would choose the other way. Mr Zilliacus, for instance, is one of them. I think he is wrong, but at least he makes his position clear. I also know perfectly well what *Tribune's* position is. But has *Tribune* ever made it clear?

How subject we are in this country to the intellectual tyranny of minorities can be seen from the composition of the press. A foreign observer who judged Britain solely by its press would assume that the Conservative party was out and away the strongest party, with the Liberals second, the Communists third and the Labour party nowhere. The one genuine mass party has no daily paper that is undisputedly its own, and among the political weeklies it has no reliable supporter. Suppose *Tribune* came out with a plain statement of the principles that are implicit in some of its individual decisions—in its support of conscription, for instance. Would it be going against the main body of Labour party opinion? I doubt it. But it would be going against the fashionable minority who can make things unpleasant for a political journalist. These people have a regular technique of smears and ridicule—a whole specialised vocabulary designed to show that anyone who will not repeat the accepted catchwords is a rather laughable kind of lunatic. Mr Zilliacus, for instance, accuses *Tribune* of being 'rabidly anti-Russian' (or 'rabidly anti-Communist'—it was one or the other.) The key-word here is rabid. Other words used in this context are insensate, demented, 'sick with hatred' (the *New Republic's* phrase) and maniacal. The upshot is that if from time to time you express a mild distaste for slave-labour camps or one-candidate elections, you are either insane or actuated by the worst motives. In the same way, when Henry Wallace is asked by a newspaper interviewer why he issues falsified versions of his speeches to the press, he replies: 'So you are one of these people who are clamouring for war with Russia?' It doesn't answer the question, but it would frighten most people into silence. Or there is the milder kind of ridicule that consists in pretending that a reasoned opinion is indistin-guishable from an absurd out-of-date prejudice. If you do not like

Communism you are a red-baiter, a believer in Bolshevik atrocities, the nationalisation of women, Moscow Gold, and so on. Similarly, when Catholicism was almost as fashionable among the English intelligentsia as Communism is now, anyone who said that the Catholic Church was a sinister organisation and no friend to democracy, was promptly accused of swallowing the worst follies of the No-Popery organisations, of looking under his bed lest Jesuits should be concealed there, of believing stories about babies' skeletons dug up from the floors of nunneries, and all the rest of it. But a few people stuck to their opinion, and I think it is safe to say that the Catholic Church is less fashionable now than it was then.

After all, what does it matter to be laughed at? The big public, in any case, usually doesn't see the joke, and if you state your principles clearly and stick to them, it is wonderful how people come round to you in the end. There is no doubt about whom *Tribune* is frightened of. It is frightened of the Communists, the fellow-travellers and the fellow-travellers of fellow-travellers. Hence its endless equivocations: a paragraph of protest when this of our friends is shot—silence when that one is shot, denunciation of this one faked election—qualified approval of that one, and so on. The result is that in American papers I have more than once seen the phrase 'the Foot-Zilliacus group' (or words to that effect.) Of course Foot[5] and Zilliacus are not allies, but they can appear so from the outside. Meanwhile, does this kind of thing even conciliate the people it is aimed at? Does it conciliate Mr Zilliacus, for instance? He has been treated with remarkable tenderness by *Tribune*. He has been allowed to infest its correspondence columns like a perennial weed, and when a little while ago *Tribune* reviewed a book of his, I looked in vain in that review[6] for any plain statement of what he is or whose interests he is serving. Instead

5. Michael Foot (1913–2010), left-wing author and intellectual. He was one of the anonymous authors of the powerful indictment of pre-war appeasers, *Guilty Men* (1940). He was a director of *Tribune* and served as a Labour MP, 1945–55 and 1960–92. He was elected Leader of the Labour Party in 1980 and was largely responsible for the manifesto for the 1983 election which Labour lost, that manifesto being described by one of his colleagues (Gerald Kaufman) as 'the longest suicide note in history'. Though he did not achieve the highest political eminence he was widely seen as a man of great integrity.

6. The review was by T. R. Fyvel, of *Mirror of the Present* by Konni Zilliacus, *Tribune*, 6 June 1947. Fyvel had reviewed *Animal Farm* in *Tribune* on 24 August 1945. The review was short and bland, doing little more than recount 'the story'. It seems to avoid being percipient – hardly what might be expected of *Tribune*. *Animal Farm* was described as a 'gentle satire', a 'sad and gentle tale', and 'one of the best and most simply written books for the child of today'.

there was only a mild disagreement, a suggestion that he was perhaps a little over-zealous, a little given to special pleading—all this balanced by praise wherever possible, and headed by the friendly title, 'The Fighting Propagandist.' But is Mr Zilliacus grateful? On the contrary, only a few weeks later he turns round and without any provocation delivers a good hard boot on the shins.

It is hard to blame him, since he knows very well that *Tribune* is not on his side and does not really like him. But whereas he is willing to make this clear, *Tribune*, in spite of occasional side-thrusts, is not. I do not claim for Mr Zilliacus that he is honest, but at least he is sincere. We know where he stands, and he prefers to hit his enemies rather than his friends. Of course it is true that he is saying what is safe and fashionable at this moment, but I imagine he would stick to his opinions if the tide turned.

Review: James Laughlin, ed., *Spearhead: Ten Years' Experimental Writing in America*

Times Literary Supplement, [1] 17 APRIL 1948

Anthony Powell (1905–2000), novelist – famous particularly for the series A Dance to the Music of Time *– and friend of Orwell's, was one of the principal reviewers for the* Times Literary Supplement *at this time. In* George Orwell: A Life, *Bernard Crick states that Powell had steered* Nineteen Eighty-Four *for review 'into comprehending hands' – those of Julian Symons (p. 563), and he probably thought Orwell would enjoy reviewing* Spearhead. *Orwell's review was published anonymously as was then the custom of the* TLS.

The exchange of literary intelligence between country and country is still far from brisk, even where there is no political obstruction. Only the other day a critic in a French weekly review could remark that, so far as he was aware, the United States had not produced any new writers since 1939. We ourselves, not being dependent on translations, are able to be a little better informed, but even so it is a fact that most of the younger American writers are only known to this country because of stray contributions to magazines. Few of them have yet appeared here in book form. *Spearhead,* Mr. James Laughlin's anthology of recent American prose and verse, is therefore useful, although, as he admits himself, it is not fully representative.

An anthology of this kind is not, of course, intended to give a picture of the American literary scene as a whole. Mr. Laughlin has explicitly confined himself to experimental and 'non-commercial' writing, and most of the contents are drawn from such magazines as the *Kenyon Review* and the *Partisan Review,* or from his own annual miscellany, *New Directions.* Even so, the selection is less interesting than it might have been, since it consists almost entirely of 'creative' writing—that is, poems and stories—while much of the best and liveliest American writing of the past ten years has been done by literary critics and political essayists. An anthology based mainly on the 'little reviews' ought not to leave out Lionel Trilling, Dwight

---

1. Orwell's initial notes for this review survive (see *CW,* XIX, 317). Orwell had written to James Laughlin (1914–97) on 16 July 1940 in response to Laughlin's request that he might publish Orwell's essay on Henry Miller, 'Inside the Whale'. Laughlin was a poet and book publisher; he founded New Directions Publishing, and Orwell's essay appeared in *New Directions in Prose and Poetry* (1940). The preparatory notes Orwell made for this review are reproduced in *CW.*

Macdonald, Clement Greenberg and Nicola Chiaramonte: one might also have expected to find Edmund Wilson, Mary McCarthy and Saul Bellow. However, this book does introduce to the English reader a number of young writers who are less known here than they deserve to be—for example, Paul Goodman, Karl Shapiro, Delmore Schwartz and Randall Jarrell. There are also, of course, contributions from various 'established' writers (William Carlos Williams, E. E. Cummings, Henry Miller and others), and even from such veterans as Ezra Pound and Gertrude Stein.

One fact this book brings out is that American literary intellectuals are still very much on the defensive. There is evidently much more feeling that the writer is a hunted heretic and that 'avant garde' literature, as it is rather solemnly called, is totally different from popular literature, than exists in England. But one cannot help noticing, while reading Mr. Laughlin's introduction and then the items that follow it, that this feeling of isolation is largely unjustified. To begin with, the 'avant garde' and the 'commercial' obviously overlap, and are even difficult to distinguish from one another. A number of the stories in this book, notably those of Jack Jones, Robert Lowry and Tennessee Williams, would fit easily into dozens of big-circulation magazines. But in addition, it is doubtful whether American literature during the past ten or fifteen years has the 'experimental' character that Mr Laughlin claims for it. During that period literature has extended its subject matter, no doubt, but there has been little or no technical innovation. There has also been surprisingly little interest in prose as such, and an all-round tolerance of ugly and slovenly writing. Even in verse it could probably be shown that there has been no real innovator since Auden, or even since Eliot, to whom Auden and his associates admittedly owed a great deal.

No English prose-writer in the immediate past has played with words as Joyce did, nor on the other hand has anyone made a deliberate attempt to simplify language as Hemingway did. As for the sort of cadenced 'poetic' prose that used to be written by, for instance, Conrad, Lawrence or Forster, no one nowadays attempts anything of the kind. The most recent writer of intentionally rhythmical prose is Henry Miller, whose first book was published in 1935, when he was already not a young man. A striking thing about the prose-writers in Mr. Laughlin's collection is how like one another they all are in manner, except when they drop into dialect. The Anarchist Paul Goodman, for instance, certainly has unusual subject-matter for his stories, but his manner of approach is conservative enough. So also with the stories—again, unusual in theme—by H. J. Kaplan and John Berryman. No one to-day could produce a book of parodies corresponding to Max

Beerbohm's *A Christmas Garland*: the differences between one writer and another, at any rate the surface differences, are not great enough. It is true, however, that the contemporary lack of interest in the technique of prose has its good side, in that a writer who is not expected to have a 'style' is not tempted to practise affectations. This reflection is forced on one by the most noticeably mannered writer in the collection, Djuna Barnes, who seems to have been disastrously influenced by Rabelais, or possibly by Joyce.

The verse in this anthology is very uneven, and a better selection would have been possible. Randall Jarrell, for instance, is represented by five poems, including the excellent 'Camp in the Prussian Forest'; but his tiny masterpiece, 'The Ball Turret Gunner,' which ends with the memorable line, 'When I died they washed me out of the turret with a hose,' is not there. Perhaps the best poem in the book is by E. E. Cummings. He is an irritating writer, partly because of his largely meaningless typographical tricks, partly because his restless bad temper soon provokes a counter-reaction in the reader, but he has a gift for telling phrases (for instance, his often-quoted description of Soviet Russia—'Vicariously childlike kingdom of slogan'), and, at his best, for neat, rapidly moving verse. In this collection he is at the top of his form in a short poem in praise of Olaf, a conscientious objector, which has slightly the air of being a pastiche of *Struwwelpeter*. Olaf's barely printable punishments at the hands of the military are first described, and then:—

> Our president, being of which
> assertions duly notified
> threw the yellowsonofabitch
> into a dungeon, where he died
>
> Christ (of His mercy infinite)
> i pray to see; and Olaf, too
> preponderatingly because
> unless statistics lie he was
> more brave than me; more blond than you.[2]

2. Cummings's lines (*Poems 1923–1954*) should read (closed up as shown):
   line 1: our president,being of which
   l. 4: into a dungeon,where he died
   l. 5: Christ(of His mercy infinite)
   l. 6: i pray to see;and Olaf, too
   l. 9: more brave than me:more blond than you.

Throughout this anthology the best poems, almost without exception, are the ones that rhyme and scan in a more or less regular manner. Much of the 'free' verse is simply prose arranged in lines of arbitrary length, or sometimes in highly elaborate patterns, with the initial word moving this way and that across the page, apparently on the theory that a visual effect is the same thing as a musical rhythm. If one takes passages of this so-called verse and rearranges them as prose, it becomes actually indistinguishable from prose, except, in some cases, by its subject-matter. A couple of examples will be enough:

It was an icy day. We buried the cat, then took her box and set match to it in the back yard. Those fleas that escaped earth and fire died by the cold. (William Carlos Williams.)

The old guy put down his beer. Son, he said (and a girl came over to the table where we were: asked us by Jack Christ to buy her a drink). Son, I am going to tell you something the like of which nobody ever was told. (Kenneth Patchen.)

Kenneth Rexroth's long poem, 'The Phoenix and the Tortoise,' which again looks like prose if rearranged as prose, is perhaps in a different category. Such a passage as this, for instance:—

> The institution is a device
> For providing molecular
> Process with delusive credentials.
> 'Value is the reflection
> Of satisfied appetite,
> The formal aspect of the tension
> Generated by resolution
> Of fact.' Over-specialization,
> Proliferation, gigantism.

is not verse in the ordinary sense, but this is probably due not to sheer slovenliness but to the notion, perhaps derived from Ezra Pound or from translations of Chinese poems, that poetry can consist of lapidary statements without any rhythmical quality. The weakness of this method of writing is that it sacrifices not only the musical appeal of verse but also its mnemonic function. It is precisely the fact of having recognizable rhythms, and usually rhyme as well, that makes it possible for verse, unlike prose, to exist apart from the printed page. An enormous amount of 'free' verse has been produced during the past thirty or forty years, but only so much of it has survived, in the sense of being remembered by heart, as contained cadences of a kind impossible in prose. The chief reason, at any rate in England and America, for breaking away from conventional verse-forms was that the English language is exceptionally poor in rhymes; a deficiency already obvious to the poet of the nineties who wrote:—

> From Austin back to Chaucer,
> My wearied eyes I shove,
> But never came across a
> New word to rhyme with love.

This shortcoming naturally had a cumulative effect, and by the Georgian period it had led to an unbearable staleness and artificiality. The way out was through the total or partial abandonment of rhyme, or through double rhymes and the use of colloquial words which would previously have been considered undignified, but which allowed the stock of available rhymes to be extended. This, however, did not do away with the need for rhythm but, if anything, increased it. Indeed, successful rhymeless poems—for example, Auden's *Spain*, or many passages in Eliot's work—tend to be written in strongly accented, non-iambic metres. Recently, as one can see even in this anthology, there has been a tendency to return to traditional stanza forms, usually with a touch of raggedness that is a legacy from 'free' verse. Karl Shapiro, for instance, is very successful in handling what is really an adaptation of the popular ballad, as in his poem 'Fireworks':—

> In the garden of pleistoscene flowers we wander like Alice
> Where seed sends a stalk in the heavens and pops from a pod
> A Blue blossom that hangs in the distance and opens its chalice
> And falls in the dust of itself and goes out with a nod.
> How the hairy tarantulas crawl in the soft of the ether
> Where showers of lilies explode in the jungle of creepers;
> How the rockets of sperm hurtle up to the moon and beneath her
> Deploy for the eggs of the astral and sorrowful sleepers!

Of the short stories in this anthology perhaps the best is John Berryman's 'The Imaginary Jew'; it describes a young man who goes to a political meeting, full of generous sentiments and disgusted by anti-semitism, and then suddenly gains a much deeper insight into the Jewish problem through the accident of being mistaken for a Jew himself. Paul Goodman's story, 'A Ceremonial,' which supposedly takes place 'not long after the establishment among us of reasonable institutions'—that is, after the Anarchist revolution—is a spirited attempt to describe happiness, a feat which no writer has ever quite accomplished. H. J. Kaplan's longish story, 'The Mohammedans,' is the kind of which one feels inclined to say that it shows great talent but one is not certain what it is about. Georg Mann's satire on Communism, 'Azef Wischmeier, the Bolshevik Bureaucrat,' would have been funny if it had been a dozen pages long instead of nearly fifty. There is a long extract from Henry Miller's *Tropic of Capricorn*. Like all of its author's earlier writings, it contains some fine passages, but it would have been better to pick a chapter from the less *exagéré Tropic of Cancer*, which remains Miller's masterpiece, and which is still a very rare book, so successfully has it been hunted down by the police of all countries.

Apart from the written pieces, the anthology includes two sets of fairly good but not outstanding photographs. One set, taken by Walker Evans, accompanies a piece of 'reportage' on the southern cotton farmers by James Agee.[3] The other set, by Wright Morris, consists of photographs of buildings, mostly ruinous, each accompanied by a long caption in the form of a sort of prose poem. These captions are nothing very much in themselves, but the idea is a good one and might be profitably followed up. The other chief curiosity of the book is a collection, compiled by Mr. Laughlin, of the poems of Samuel Greenberg, a Jewish youth, son of very poor parents, who died about 1918, aged less than twenty. They are queer poems, full of misspellings and neologisms, and sometimes more like growing embryos than completed writings, but they show considerable power. Mr. Laughlin demonstrates by parallel quotations that Hart Crane lifted numerous lines from Greenberg without acknowledgment.

All in all, this book is useful, in that it introduces about forty American writers, of whom more than half are unknown or barely known in England; but it would have been a good deal better if it had been compiled expressly for an English audience. Actually it is a book designed for America, evidently imported into this country in sheets (Henry Miller's favourite verb has been laboriously blacked out by hand, over a stretch

---

3. From *Let Us Now Praise Famous Men* (Boston, MA, 1941).

of fifty pages), and it is likely to give English readers a somewhat lopsided impression. It should be repeated that where American writing particularly excels at this moment is in literary criticism and in political and sociological essays. This, no doubt, is largely because in the United States there is more money, more paper and more spare time. The magazines are fatter, the 'angels' are richer, and, above all, the intelligentsia, in spite of its sense of grievance, is numerous enough to constitute a public in itself. Long, serious controversies, of a kind extinct in England, can still happen; and, for instance, the battles that raged round the question of 'supporting' the late war, or round the ideas of James Burnham or Van Wyck Brooks, produced material that would have been better worth reprinting, and more representative, than much of the contents of *Spearhead*. Moreover, the book suffers from the fact that it is neither uncompromisingly 'high-brow,' nor, on the other hand, is it a cross-section of current American literature. It leaves out several of the best living American writers on the ground that they are not *avant garde*, while at the same time it includes Kay Boyle and William Saroyan. It also—but perhaps this is unavoidable in any bulky anthology compiled from contemporary work—includes one or two pieces of sheer rubbish. The editors of the Falcon Press are to be congratulated for their enterprise, but another time they would do better to choose their material for themselves and to cast the net more widely.

Review: Graham Greene, *The Heart of the Matter*

New Yorker, 17 JULY 1948

On 26 August 1946 the New Yorker *approached Orwell suggesting he might review for them. This seems to have been arranged through Elizabeth R. Otis of the New York agents, McIntosh & Otis. On 15 October he told Dwight Macdonald he hoped to write reviews for the* New Yorker, *but it was not until 19 April 1947 that his first review (of* Lady Gregory's Journal) *was published. This review was his second and final contribution which the* New Yorker *published.*

A fairly large proportion of the distinguished novels of the last few decades have been written by Catholics and have even been describable as Catholic novels. One reason for this is that the conflict not only between this world and the next world but between sanctity and goodness is a fruitful theme of which the ordinary, unbelieving writer cannot make use. Graham Greene used it once successfully, in *The Power and the Glory*, and once, with very much more doubtful success, in *Brighton Rock*. His latest book, *The Heart of the Matter* (Viking), is, to put it as politely as possible, not one of his best, and gives the impression of having been mechanically constructed, the familiar conflict being set out like an algebraic equation, with no attempt at psychological probability.

Here is the outline of the story: The time is 1942 and the place is a West African British colony, unnamed but probably the Gold Coast. A certain Major Scobie, Deputy Commissioner of Police and a Catholic convert, finds a letter bearing a German address hidden in the cabin of the captain of a Portuguese ship. The letter turns out to be a private one and completely harmless, but it is, of course, Scobie's duty to hand it over to higher authority. However, the pity he feels for the Portuguese captain is too much for him, and he destroys the letter and says nothing about it. Scobie, it is explained to us, is a man of almost excessive conscientiousness. He does not drink, take bribes, keep Negro mistresses, or indulge in bureaucratic intrigue, and he is, in fact, disliked on all sides because of his uprightness, like Aristides the Just. His leniency toward the Portuguese captain is his first lapse. After it, his life becomes a sort of fable on the theme of 'Oh, what a tangled web we weave,'[1] and in

---

1. From Sir Walter Scott's *Marmion*, VI, xvii. It continues: 'When first we practise to deceive!'

every single instance it is the goodness of his heart that leads him astray. Actuated at the start by pity, he has a love affair with a girl who has been rescued from a torpedoed ship. He continues with the affair largely out of a sense of duty, since the girl will go to pieces morally if abandoned; he also lies about her to his wife, so as to spare her the pangs of jealousy. Since he intends to persist in his adultery, he does not go to confession, and in order to lull his wife's suspicions he tells her that he has gone. This involves him in the truly fearful act of taking the Sacrament while in a state of mortal sin. By this time, there are other complications, all caused in the same manner, and Scobie finally decides that the only way out is through the unforgivable sin of suicide. Nobody else must be allowed to suffer through his death; it will be so arranged as to look like an accident. As it happens, he bungles one detail, and the fact that he has committed suicide becomes known. The book ends with a Catholic priest's hinting, with doubtful orthodoxy, that Scobie is perhaps not damned. Scobie, however, had not entertained any such hope. White all through, with a stiff upper lip, he had gone to what he believed to be certain damnation out of pure gentlemanliness.

I have not parodied the plot of the book. Even when dressed up in realistic details, it is just as ridiculous as I have indicated. The thing most obviously wrong with it is that Scobie's motives, assuming one could believe in them, do not adequately explain his actions. Another question that comes up is: Why should this novel have its setting in West Africa? Except that one of the characters is a Syrian trader, the whole thing might as well be happening in a London suburb. The Africans exist only as an occasionally mentioned background, and the thing that would actually be in Scobie's mind the whole time—the hostility between black and white, and the struggle against the local nationalist movement—is not mentioned at all. Indeed, although we are shown his thoughts in considerable detail, he seldom appears to think about his work, and then only of trivial aspects of it, and never about the war, although the date is 1942. All he is interested in is his own progress toward damnation. The improbability of this shows up against the colonial setting, but it is an improbability that is present in 'Brighton Rock' as well, and that is bound to result from foisting theological preoccupations upon simple people anywhere.

The central idea of the book is that it is better, spiritually higher, to be an erring Catholic than a virtuous pagan. Graham Greene would probably subscribe to the statement of Maritain, made apropos of Léon Bloy, that 'there is but one sadness—not to be a saint,'[2] A saying of Péguy's is quoted on the title page of the book to the effect that the sinner is 'at the very heart of Christianity' and knows more of Christianity than anyone else does, except the saint. All such sayings contain or can be made to contain, the fairly sinister suggestion that ordinary human decency is of no value and that any one sin is no worse than any other sin. In addition, it is impossible not to feel a sort of snobbishness in Mr. Greene's attitude, both here and in his other books written from an explicitly Catholic standpoint. He appears to share the idea, which has been floating around ever since Baudelaire, that there is something rather distingué in being damned; Hell is a sort of high-class night club, entry to which is reserved for Catholics only, since the others, the non-Catholics, are too ignorant to be held guilty, like the beasts that perish. We are carefully informed that Catholics are no better than anybody else; they even, perhaps, have a tendency to be worse, since their temptations are greater. In modern Catholic novels, in both France and England, it is, indeed, the fashion to include bad priests, or at least inadequate priests, as a change from Father Brown. (I imagine that one major objective of young English Catholic writers is not to resemble Chesterton.) But all the while—drunken, lecherous, criminal, or damned outright—the Catholics retain their superiority, since they alone know the meaning of good and evil. Incidentally, it is assumed in *The Heart of the Matter*, and in most of Mr. Greene's other books, that no one outside the Catholic Church has the most elementary knowledge of Christian doctrine.

This cult of the sanctified sinner seems to me to be frivolous, and underneath it there probably lies a weakening of belief, for when people really believed in Hell, they were not so fond of striking graceful attitudes on its brink. More to the point, by trying to clothe theological speculations in flesh and blood, it produces psychological absurdities. In *The Power and the Glory*, the struggle between this-worldly and other-worldly values is convincing because it is not occurring inside one person. On the one side, there is the priest, a poor creature in some ways but made heroic by his belief in his own thaumaturgic powers; on the other side, there is the lieutenant, representing human justice and material progress, and also a heroic figure after his fashion. They can respect each other, perhaps,

---

2. Orwell had recently been reading Bloy and Péguy, Bloy in an edition with an introduction by Maritain; see letter to Julian Symons, 10 July 1948 (*A Life in Letters*, p. 413).

but not understand each other. The priest, at any rate, is not credited with any very complex thoughts. In *Brighton Rock*, on the other hand, the central situation is incredible, since it presupposes that the most brutishly stupid person can, merely by having been brought up a Catholic, be capable of great intellectual subtlety. Pinkie, the racecourse gangster, is a species of satanist, while his still more limited girlfriend understands and even states the difference between the categories 'right and wrong' and 'good and evil.' In, for example, Mauriac's *Thérèse* sequence,[3] the spiritual conflict does not outrage probability, because it is not pretended that Thérèse is a normal person. She is a chosen spirit, pursuing her salvation over a long period and by a difficult route, like a patient stretched out on the psychiatrist's sofa. To take an opposite instance, Evelyn Waugh's *Brideshead Revisited*, in spite of improbabilities, which are traceable partly to the book's being written in the first person, succeeds because the situation is itself a normal one. The Catholic characters bump up against problems they would meet with in real life; they do not suddenly move onto a different intellectual plane as soon as their religious beliefs are involved. Scobie is incredible because the two halves of him do not fit together. If he were capable of getting into the kind of mess that is described, he would have got into it years earlier. If he really felt that adultery is mortal sin, he would stop committing it; if he persisted in it, his sense of sin would weaken. If he believed in Hell, he would not risk going there merely to spare the feelings of a couple of neurotic women. And one might add that if he were the kind of man we are told he is—that is, a man whose chief characteristic is a horror of causing pain—he would not be an officer in a colonial police force.

There are other improbabilities, some of which arise out of Mr. Greene's method of handling a love affair. Every novelist has his own conventions, and, just as in an E.M. Forster novel there is a strong tendency for the characters to die suddenly without sufficient cause, so in a Graham Greene novel there is a tendency for people to go to bed together almost at sight and with no apparent pleasure to either party. Often this is credible enough, but in *The Heart of the Matter* its effect is to weaken a motive that, for the purposes of the story, ought to be a very strong one. Again, there is the usual, perhaps unavoidable, mistake of making everyone too highbrow. It is not only that Major Scobie is a theologian. His wife, who

---

3. In his letter to Julian Symons, 21 March 1948, Orwell said he had just read *Thérèse* and 'it started me thinking about Catholic novelists'.

is represented as an almost complete fool, reads poetry, while the detective who is sent by the Field Security Corps to spy on Scobie even writes poetry. Here one is up against the fact that it is not easy for most modern writers to imagine the mental processes of anyone who is not a writer.

It seems a pity, when one remembers how admirably he has written of Africa elsewhere, that Mr. Greene should have made just this book out of his wartime African experiences. The fact that the book is set in Africa while the action takes place almost entirely inside a tiny white community gives it an air of triviality. However, one must not carp too much. It is pleasant to see Mr. Greene starting up again after so long a silence, and in postwar England it is a remarkable feat for a novelist to write a novel at all. At any rate, Mr. Greene has not been permanently demoralized by the habits acquired during the war, like so many others. But one may hope that his next book will have a different theme,[4] or, if not, that he will at least remember that a perception of the vanity of earthly things, though it may be enough to get one into Heaven, is not sufficient equipment for the writing of a novel.[5]

4. Greene's next book was one of his 'entertainments', *The Third Man* (1950); that was followed by *The End of the Affair* (1951).
5. In his letter to Orwell of 22 July 1948 (see *CW*, 3424, n. 4), Fredric Warburg said Orwell's review of *The Heart of the Matter* was 'fluttering the dovecots'. Warburg's copy of *The New Yorker* had not yet arrived, so he had not read the review but he had just seen a director of Viking Press, Greene's New York publisher, who had shown the review to Graham Greene. On 11 August 1948, D. F. Boyd, Chief Producer, Talks Department, BBC, wrote to Orwell to say that he had read his review of *The Heart of the Matter* and was reminded that the BBC wanted to find out whether he could undertake some broadcasting for them. No answer has been traced, but Orwell did not broadcast again.

Review: Jean-Paul Sartre, *Portrait of the Anti-Semite*; tr. Erik de Mauny

The Observer, 7 NOVEMBER 1948

Anti-Semitism is obviously a subject that needs serious study, but it seems unlikely that it will get it in the near future. The trouble is that so long as anti-Semitism is regarded simply as a disgraceful aberration, almost a crime, anyone literate enough to have heard the word will naturally claim to be immune from it; with the result that books on anti-Semitism tend to be mere exercises in casting motes out of other people's eyes. M. Sartre's book is no exception, and it is probably no better for having been written in 1944, in the uneasy, self-justifying, quisling-hunting period that followed on the Liberation.[1]

At the beginning, M. Sartre informs us that anti-Semitism has no rational basis: at the end, that it will not exist in a classless society, and that in the meantime it can perhaps be combated to some extent by education and propaganda. These conclusions would hardly be worth stating for their own sake, and in between them there is, in spite of much cerebration, little real discussion of the subject, and no factual evidence worth mentioning.

We are solemnly informed that anti-Semitism is almost unknown among the working class. It is a malady of the bourgeoisie, and, above all, of that goat upon whom all our sins are laid, the 'petty bourgeois.' Within the bourgeoisie it is seldom found among scientists and engineers. It is a peculiarity of people who think of nationality in terms of inherited culture and of property in terms of land.

Why these people should pick on Jews rather than some other victim M. Sartre does not discuss, except, in one place, by putting forward the ancient and very dubious theory that the Jews are hated because they are supposed to have been responsible for the Crucifixion. He makes no

---

1. The taking of revenge by French men and women on their own people after World War II was particularly savage. David Pryce-Jones in his *Paris in the Third Reich* (1981) quotes Robert Aron's conservative estimate that there were between 30,000 and 40,000 summary executions. Adrien Tixier, the post-war Minister of Justice, gave a figure of 105,000 executions between June 1944 and February 1945. Although fiction, Allan Massie's fine novel, *A Question of Loyalties* (2002), gives a moving account of the conflicting emotions of those of all persuasions following France's defeat by Germany in 1940.

attempt to relate anti-Semitism to such obviously allied phenomena as, for instance, colour prejudice.

Part of what is wrong with M. Sartre's approach is indicated by his title. 'The' anti-Semite, he seems to imply all through the book, is always the same kind of person, recognisable at a glance and, so to speak, in action the whole time. Actually one has only to use a little observation to see that anti-Semitism is extremely widespread, is not confined to any one class, and, above all, in any but the worst cases, is intermittent.

But these facts would not square with M. Sartre's atomised vision of society. There is, he comes near to saying, no such thing as a human being, there are only different categories of men, such as 'the' worker and 'the' bourgeois, all classifiable in much the same way as insects. Another of these insectlike creatures is 'the' Jew, who, it seems, can usually be distinguished by his physical appearance. It is true that there are two kinds of Jew, the 'Authentic Jew,' who wants to remain Jewish, and the 'Inauthentic Jew,' who would like to be assimilated; but a Jew, of whichever variety, is not just another human being. He is wrong, at this stage of history, if he tries to assimilate himself, and we are wrong if we try to ignore his racial origin. He should be accepted into the national community, not as an ordinary Englishman, Frenchman, or whatever it may be, but as a Jew.

It will be seen that this position is itself dangerously close to anti-Semitism. Race-prejudice of any kind is a neurosis, and it is doubtful whether argument can either increase or diminish it, but the net effect of books of this kind, if they have an effect, is probably to make anti-Semitism slightly more prevalent than it was before. The first step towards serious study of anti-Semitism is to stop regarding it as a crime. Meanwhile, the less talk there is about 'the' Jew or 'the' anti-Semite, as a species of animal different from ourselves, the better.

Review: T.S. Eliot, *Notes Towards the Definition of Culture*

The Observer, 28 NOVEMBER 1948

In his new book, *Notes towards the Definition of Culture*, Mr. T. S. Eliot argues that a truly civilised society needs a class system as part of its basis. He is, of course, only speaking negatively. He does not claim that there is any method by which a high civilisation can be created. He maintains merely that such a civilisation is not likely to flourish in the absence of certain conditions, of which class distinctions are one.

This opens up a gloomy prospect, for on the one hand it is almost certain that class distinctions of the old kind are moribund, and on the other hand Mr. Eliot has at the least a strong *prima facie* case.

The essence of his argument is that the highest levels of culture have been attained only by small groups of people—either social groups or regional groups—who have been able to perfect their traditions over long periods of time. The most important of all cultural influences is the family, and family loyalty is strongest when the majority of people take it for granted to go through life at the social level at which they were born. Moreover, not having any precedents to go upon, we do not know what a classless society would be like. We know only that, since functions would still have to be diversified, classes would have to be replaced by 'élites,' a term Mr. Eliot borrows with evident distaste from the late Karl Mannheim.[1] The élites will plan, organise and administer: whether they can become the guardians and transmitters of culture, as certain social classes have been in the past, Mr. Eliot doubts, perhaps justifiably.

As always, Mr. Eliot insists that tradition does not mean worship of the past; on the contrary, a tradition is alive only while it is growing. A class can preserve a culture because it is itself an organic and changing thing. But here, curiously enough, Mr. Eliot misses what might have been the strongest argument in his case. This is, that a classless society directed by élites may ossify very rapidly, simply because its rulers are able to choose their successors, and will always tend to choose people resembling themselves.

---

1. Karl Mannheim (1883–1947), Austro-Hungarian sociologist who, after teaching in Germany, went to England and taught at the University of London. Orwell might have had in mind his *Ideology and Utopia* (1929), but the concept of the élite owes more in its origination to Vilfredo Pareto (1848–1923), Italian sociologist and economist.

Hereditary institutions—as Mr. Eliot might have argued—have the virtue of being unstable. They must be so, because power is constantly devolving on people who are either incapable of holding it, or use it for purposes not intended by their forefathers. It is impossible to imagine any hereditary body lasting so long, and with so little change, as an adoptive organisation like the Catholic Church. And it is at least thinkable that another adoptive and authoritarian organisation, the Russian Communist Party, will have a similar history. If it hardens into a class, as some observers believe it is already doing, then it will change and develop as classes always do. But if it continues to co-opt its members from all strata of society, and then train them into the desired mentality, it might keep its shape almost unaltered from generation to generation. In aristocratic societies the eccentric aristocrat is a familiar figure, but the eccentric commissar is almost a contradiction in terms.

Although Mr. Eliot does not make use of this argument, he does argue that even the antagonism between classes can have fruitful results for society as a whole. This again is probably true. Yet one continues to have, throughout his book, the feeling that there is something wrong, and that he himself is aware of it. The fact is that class privilege, like slavery, has somehow ceased to be defensible. It conflicts with certain moral assumptions which Mr Eliot appears to share, although intellectually he may be in disagreement with them.

All through the book his attitude is noticeably defensive. When class distinctions were vigorously believed in, it was not thought necessary to reconcile them either with social justice or with efficiency. The superiority of the ruling classes was held to be self-evident, and in any case the existing order was what God had ordained. The mute inglorious Milton[2] was a sad case, but not remediable on this side of the grave.

This, however, is by no means what Mr. Eliot is saying. He would like, he says, to see in existence both classes *and* élites. It should be normal for the average human being to go through life at his predestined social level, but on the other hand the right man must be able to find his way into the right job. In saying this he seems almost to give away his whole case. For if class distinctions are desirable in themselves, then wastage of talent, or inefficiency in high places, are comparatively unimportant. The social misfit, instead of being directed upwards or downwards, should learn to be contented in his own station.

---

2. In Thomas Gray's 'Elegy Written in a Country Churchyard', st. 15: 'Some mute inglorious Milton here may rest.'

Mr. Eliot does not say this: indeed, very few people in our time would say it. It would seem morally offensive. Probably, therefore, Mr. Eliot does not believe in class distinctions as our grandfathers believed in them. His approval of them is only negative. That is to say, he cannot see how any civilisation worth having can survive in a society where the differences arising from social background or geographical origin have been ironed out.

It is difficult to make any positive answer to this. To all appearances the old social distinctions are everywhere disappearing, because their economic basis is being destroyed. Possibly new classes are appearing, or possibly we are within sight of a genuinely classless society, which Mr. Eliot assumes would be a cultureless society. He may be right, but at some points his pessimism seems to be exaggerated. 'We can assert with some confidence,' he says, 'that our own period is one of decline; that the standards of culture are lower than they were 50 years ago; and that the evidence of this decline is visible in every department of human activity.'

This seems true when one thinks of Hollywood films or the atomic bomb, but less true if one thinks of the clothes and architecture of 1898, or what life was like at that date for an unemployed labourer in the East End of London. In any case, as Mr. Eliot himself admits at the start, we cannot reverse the present trend by conscious action. Cultures are not manufactured, they grow of their own accord. Is it too much to hope that the classless society will secrete a culture of its own? And before writing off our own age as irrevocably damned, is it not worth remembering that Matthew Arnold and Swift and Shakespeare—to carry the story back only three centuries—were all equally certain that they lived in a period of decline?

'Evelyn Waugh', unfinished essay

APRIL(?) 1949

Evelyn Waugh visited Orwell in the sanatorium at Cranham. Crick records: 'Many people came to visit [Orwell], some fearing that he was dying, others simply to entertain him in his isolation. [Anthony] Powell and [Malcolm] Muggeridge, who did their share of visiting persuaded Evelyn Waugh, who neither knew Orwell nor particularly cared for his writing, to visit him; simply because he lived nearby [about eighteen miles away]. As one worthy in the world of English letters to another, he did this kindness several times. "I should have loved to see them together," wrote Muggeridge, "his country gentleman's outfit and Orwell's proletarian one both straight out of back numbers of Punch" (Crick, 556). In the entry to his diary for 31 August 1945, Waugh says that his 'Communist cousin Claud [Cockburn]' warned him against Trotskyist literature, 'so that I read and greatly enjoyed Orwell's Animal Farm' *(Diaries 1911–1965, edited by Michael Davie). Unfortunately, Orwell seems not to have kept a diary in 1949.*

Within the last few decades, in countries like Britain or the United States, the literary intelligentsia has grown large enough to constitute a world in itself. One important result of this is that the opinions which a writer feels frightened of expressing are not those which are disapproved of by society as a whole. To a great extent, what is still loosely thought of as heterodoxy has become orthodoxy. It is nonsense to pretend, for instance, that at this date there is something daring and original in proclaiming yourself an anarchist, an atheist, a pacifist, etc. The daring thing, or at any rate the unfashionable thing, is to believe in God or to approve of the capitalist system. In 1895, when Oscar Wilde was jailed, it must have needed very considerable moral courage to defend homosexuality. Today it would need no courage at all: today the equivalent action would be, perhaps, to defend antisemitism. But this example that I have chosen immediately reminds one of something else—namely, that one cannot judge the value of an opinion simply by the amount of courage that is required in holding it. There is still such a thing as truth and falsehood, it is possible to hold true beliefs for the wrong reasons, and—though there may be no advance in human intelligence—the prevailing ideas of one age are sometimes demonstrably less silly than those of another.

In our own day, the English novelist who has most conspicuously defied his contemporaries is Evelyn Waugh. Waugh's outlook on life is, I should say, false and to some extent perverse, but at least it must be said for him that he adopted it at a time when it did not pay to do so, and his literary reputation has suffered accordingly. It is true, of course, that he has had immense *popular* success (a thing that does not seem to have any connection, positive or negative, with critical acclaim), and also that he has been underrated partly because he is a 'light' writer whose special gift is for something not far removed from low farce. But his main offence in the eyes of his fellow-writers has always been the reactionary political tendency which was already clearly apparent even in such light-hearted books as *Decline and Fall* and *Vile Bodies*. Chronologically Waugh belongs to the generation of Auden and Spender, though he would be about five years older than most of the leading members of the group. This generation, almost en bloc, was politically 'left,' in a Popular-Front style, with Communist leanings. There were, of course, a few writers of about the same age who did not fit into the pattern—for instance, there were William Empson, William Plomer, V. S. Pritchett and Graham Greene. But of these, the first three were merely lacking in political zeal and not in any way hostile to the Popular-Front orthodoxy, while Graham Greene— the fact has passed almost unnoticed, no doubt because of the unjustified assumption that a Catholic is the same thing as a Conservative—was himself politically 'left,' in an ill-defined, unobtrusive way. In the whole of this age-group, the only loudly discordant voice was Waugh's. Even his first book, the life of Rossetti, published in 1927, displays a sort of defiant Conservatism, which expresses itself, as was natural at that date, in aesthetic rather than political terms.

Waugh is the latest, perhaps the last, of a long line of English writers whose real driving force is a romantic belief in aristocracy. At a casual glance, *Decline and Fall, Vile Bodies*, and considerable passages, at least, in nearly all the subsequent books, appear to consist of nothing but a sort of high-spirited foolery, owing something to Norman Douglas and perhaps a little to 'Saki,' and tinged by the kind of innocent snobbishness that causes people to wait twenty-four hours on the pavement to get a good view of a royal wedding. If one looks only a little way below the surface, however, one sees that though the approach is at the level of farce, the essential theme is serious. What Waugh is trying to do is to use the feverish, cultureless modern world as a set-off for his own conception of a good and stable way of life. The seeming imoralism of these books (the jokes turn not merely upon adultery but upon prostitution, homosexuality, suicide, lunacy and cannibalism) is merely a reversion to the older tradition of English humour, according to which any event can be funny provided that it either didn't happen or happened a long time ago. In *Decline and Fall*, for instance, the funniest episode is the sawing-off of a clergyman's head. If one were asked to believe this it would be merely disgusting, but being impossible it is acceptable, like the events in, for instance, the *Miller's Tale*, which would seem by no means funny if they happened in real life. Waugh's books certainly owe some of their popularity to their air of naughtiness, but none of them (except, perhaps, to some small extent, *Decline and Fall*) is intended to be morally subversive. They are really sermons in farcical shape, and kept in farcical shape by avoidance of comment. In *Decline and Fall, Vile Bodies, Scoop* and, to a less extent, *A Handful of Dust* the central character is a passive figure who simply lets things happen to him and hardly appears to notice the difference between good and evil, or even between pain and pleasure: in *Black Mischief* and *The Loved One* he is not passive, but his motives are unexplained. The general outline of these books resembles that of *Candide*, and in very broad terms the 'moral' is also the same: 'Look, this is what the world is like. Is it really necessary to behave quite so foolishly?' But, of course, Waugh's notion of reasonable conduct is very different from Voltaire's.

In all Waugh's books up to *Brideshead Revisited*, which perhaps indicates a new departure, the idea of sanity and moral integrity is mixed up with the idea of country life—upper-class country life—as it was lived a couple of generations ago. Already in *Vile Bodies* there is an irrelevant outburst in favour of the older kind of minor aristocracy, the people who still have, or used to have, a sense of obligation and a fixed code of behaviour, as against the mob of newspaper peers, financiers, politicians and playboys with whom the book deals:

> . . . a great concourse of pious and honourable people (many of whom made the Anchorage House reception the one outing of the year), their women-folk well gowned in rich and durable stuffs, their men-folk ablaze with orders; people who had represented their country in foreign places and sent their sons to die for her in battle, people of decent and temperate life, uncultured, unaffected, unembarrassed, unassuming, unambitious people, of independent judgement and marked eccentricities, kind people who cared for animals and the deserving poor, brave and rather unreasonable people, that fine phalanx of the passing order, approaching, as one day at the

Last Trump they hoped to meet their Maker, with decorous and frank cordiality to shake Lady Anchorage by the hand at the top of her staircase . . .

Here 'animals and the deserving poor' may perhaps be meant ironically, but the note of affection and esteem, out of tune with most of the rest of the book, is unmistakeable. In *A Handful of Dust* the theme is made more explicit. On the one side the foolish, glittering life of fashionable London: on the other the country house, the succession that must be maintained, the fields and woods that must not be allowed to decay. As an earlier writer in the *Partisan Review* has pointed out, whenever the action of Waugh's books takes place in England, a house, an old house, always plays an important part in it. In *Decline and Fall* the house, in process of being ravaged, is already there. In *A Handful of Dust*—this time a somewhat ridiculous house but beautiful in its owner's eyes—it is the pivot of the story. In *Brideshead Revisited* it appears in more magnificent form. But it is probably as it appears in *Scoop* and *Vile Bodies* that it corresponds most closely with Waugh's private ideal. Everyone knows, at least traditionally, the kind of house that is there described—the middle-sized country house which required, in the days of its glory, about ten servants, and which has now, if it is not merely derelict, been turned into a hotel, a boarding school or a lunatic asylum. All the familiar scenery is there, whether or not Waugh mentions it in detail: the 'wet, bird-haunted lawns' and the walled garden with its crucified pear-trees; the large untidy porch with its litter of raincoats, waders, landing-nets and croquet mallets; the plastery smell of the flagged passage leading to the gunroom; the estate map on the library wall; the case of stuffed birds over the staircase. To Waugh, this is magic, or used to be magic, and it would be [a] waste of time to try to exorcise it from his mind merely by pointing out that

The typescript breaks off at this point.

Last of Orwell's Statements on 1984

22 JULY 1949

There are different versions of this statement, the first being a much longer expla-nation written by his publisher, Fred Warburg, on Orwell's behalf. This was prompted by misunderstandings of what Orwell was concerned with in the novel, especially in the New York Daily News. *Orwell was also asked for a statement by the United Automobile Workers Union. Life had had a statement expressing Orwell's views telephoned to it but it did not use that, instead it published the letter Orwell had sent to Francis A Henson of the UAW, having telephoned Orwell in Cranham Hospital seeking his permission. The* Socialist Call *said it had asked Orwell for a statement and it published this in full on its front page under the heading 'Orwell Tells CALL "1984" Does NOT Attack Socialism'. This was published on 22 July 1949. This is the shortest and clearest version and makes plain he still supported the British Labour Party.*

My recent novel '1984' is NOT intended as an attack on socialism, or on the British Labour Party (of which I am a supporter) but as a show-up of the perversions to which a centralized economy is liable and which have already been partly realized in Communism and Fascism.

I do not believe that the kind of society which I described necessarily will arrive, but I believe (allowing of course for the fact that the book is a satire) that something resembling it could arrive. I believe also that totalitarian ideas have taken root in the minds of intellectuals everywhere, and I have tried to draw these ideas out to their logical consequences.

The scene of the book is laid in Britain in order to emphasize that the English speaking races are not innately better than anyone else and that totalitarianism, **if not fought against,** could triumph anywhere.

Orwell's Death

George Orwell spent the last weeks of his life in Room 65 of the private wing of University College Hospital, London. It is illustrated on p. 101 of John Thompson's *Orwell's London* (1984). The room was later converted to an office. Although he was very ill, arrangements were being made for him to fly to Switzerland for treatment, although that must have been a forlorn hope. Nevertheless, he had evidently not despaired for he had ensured that he had his fishing rod in his room ready to take with him. Sonia spent much of Friday the 20th with him but in the event he died alone, of a massive haemorrhage of the lung, in the early hours of Saturday 21 January 1950.

On 18 January 1950 he had written a will in which he stipulated:

> *I direct that my body shall be buried (not cremated) according to the rites of the Church of England in the nearest convenient cemetery, and that there shall be placed over my grave a plain brown stone bearing the inscription 'Here lies Eric Arthur Blair born June 25th 1903, died----'; in case any suggestion should arise I request that no memorial service be held for me after my death and that no biography of me shall be written.*

As a memorial to the writer who had done so much to grace *Tribune's* pages, the journal reprinted 'As I Please', 66, of 3 January 1947. This appropriately dealt with two of Orwell's concerns, the inequity of financial rewards and the persecution of writers in the USSR (see page 404).

A funeral service was arranged by Malcolm Muggeridge and this took place on 26 January at Christ Church, Albany Street, London, NW1. It was conducted by the Revd W.V.C. Rose. Later that day Orwell was buried in the churchyard of All Saints, Sutton Courtney, Berkshire, the arrangements for that having been negotiated by David Astor.

On that day Fredric Warburg wrote to Robert Giroux (of Harcourt Brace): 'This morning I attended the funeral service for George Orwell, one of the most melancholy occasions of my life, and feel not only that a good author and a good friend has passed from this list but that English literature has suffered an irreparable loss.'

Anthony Powell read a lesson from *Ecclesiastes*, xii, containing the verse: 'Or ever the silver cord be loosed, or the golden bowl be broken, or the pitcher broken at the fountain, or the wheel broken at the cistern.' Later he would write in his memoirs, 'For some reason George Orwell's funeral was one of the most harrowing I have ever attended.'

In his biography of Orwell, D.J. Taylor concludes his account of Orwell's death with this:

One of Orwell's peripheral worries about Switzerland – he had been similarly anxious about Spain – was the quality of the tea. How would he get the 'proper' brands he liked? Paul Potts, who turned up later in the evening [of the 20th] had brought a packet with him. Looking through the glass window of the door of Room 65 he saw that his friend was asleep, and decided to leave the gift propped against the jamb. With the possible exception of a passing nurse, he was the last person to see Orwell alive.

APPENDIX I

This passage is included in Orwell's manuscript draft of Nineteen Eighty-Four. *It was omitted by Orwell from his finalised text. It is reproduced here, as Orwell amended it, from the Facsimile edition (pp. 178–79). Winston has just left O'Brien's flat, Julia having gone on ahead of him (Part II, end of section VIII, p. 186):*

As Winston passed down the passage he saw that O'Brien was already standing beside the switch that controlled the telescreen. The incident was closed. Another half-minute, & O'Brien would be back at his interrupted work on behalf of the Party.

It was almost dark outside. He walked rather dreamily in the direction of the Tube station, with O'Brien's hand-clasp still tingling in his fingers. What a man, he kept thinking, what a man! He did not think of Goldstein, or the Book, or the Brotherhood, or the razor-blade, but only of O'Brien, whose powerful body & hard masculine mind seemed equal to beating the Party single-handed, & who nevertheless knew the last line of 'Oranges & lemons' & did not think such things foolish or unimportant. He had gone perhaps two hundred metres, & was in the dark patch midway between two street lamps, when he was startled by something soft bumping against him. The next moment Julia's arms were clinging tightly round him.

'You see I've broken my first order,' she whispered with her lips close against his ear. 'But I couldn't help it. We hadn't fixed up abt tomorrow. Listen.' In the usual manner she gave him instructions abt their next meeting. 'And now, good-night, my love, good-night!'

She kissed his cheek almost violently a number of times, then slipped away into the shadow of the wall & promptly disappeared. Her lips had been cold, & in the darkness it had seemed to him that her face was pale. He had a curious feeling that although the purpose for which she had waited was to arrange another meeting, this embrace she had given him was intended as some kind of good-bye.

APPENDIX II: ESTIMATES OF ORWELL'S EARNINGS, 1922–45

Table 1: Estimated Earnings, 1922–35

	1922–27	1928–29	1930	1931	1932	1933	1934	1935
Regular	£3,000				Apr←Jly	Sep→Dec		
Employment	+ bonuses			,	H'thrns	Frays		
	over 5 years				@£2?	@£4?		
					£60?	£50+£48?		
Occasional		Tutor £15?	Tutor	Tutor			Oct: Booklvrs Cr	
Employment		Plongeur	Sch Hol	Sch Hol			@15/-pw	
		£15	£20?	£25?			£10	£40
			£10←odd jobs→£10					

BOOKS

	1922–27	1928–29	1930	1931	1932	1933	1934	1935
[Advances]						D&O £140	BD(US)	BD £119
Calculated						[£40]	£166	
as 1937							[£50]	CD £74
Contact						US D&O		D&O Fr
less 12⅛%						£95		£5 .....
Sub-Total (Books)						£235	£166	£198

ARTICLES

	1922–27	1928–29	1930	1931	1932	1933	1934	1935
e.g. @:		Monde 2		Adph 2				
Adph £2		PrCiv 4		NS&N 1	NS&N 1			
Trb to £5								
NEW nil		GK's 1						

REVIEWS

	1922–27	1928–29	1930	1931	1932	1933	1934	1935
e.g. @			Adph 4	Adph 3	Adph 4	Adp 3	Adph 6	Adph 3
Adph £2					NEW 1			NEW 3
Trb 10s–£2								
Hor £2								
NS&N £2								
NEW nil								

OTHER

	1922–27	1928–29	1930	1931	1932	1933	1934	1935
p = poem £2						Adph 3p	Adph 1p	Adph 1p
Th/Flm £1								

	1922–27	1928–29	1930	1931	1932	1933	1934	1935
Sub-Total (Jnls)		£14	£8	£12	£10	£12	£14	£8
total (est)	over 5 yrs	over 2 yrs						
	£3,000	£44	£38	£47	£70	£345	£190	£246
	+ bonuses							

For a full explanation of these estimates see 'Orwell; Balancing the Books', *The Library*, Vɪ, 16 (1994), pp. 77–100.

TABLE 2: Estimated Earnings, 1936–45

1936	1937	1938	1939	1940	1941	1942	1943	1944	1945
	Jan–Jun	Sep←→Mar			Aug←BBC→Nov		Dec←LitEd Trb→Feb		
	Spain	Marrakesh			£267	£640	£580	[cf Connolly Hor=£400]	
		£300 loan					£33	£400?	£66
–Jan Wgn								Feb–May (Jn)	
£50?								Obs £500	
£3	£15	— £12 (Shop)						+ MEN £42?	
CD(US)	RWP	HtC	CUFA	D&O (Pgn)	Lion&Uni	KTAF		BD	AF
£33	£594	Adv £150	£100?	£91	say £150	(chp iss)		(Pgn)	£88
KTAF£65	[£100]	[Ear'd]	[stock	I. Whale	? B'tyl of	£6.49		£148	
[£75]		c £130]	bombed]	£30?	Left nil?			AF (Adv)	Eng Ppl
.....£5	.....£5	.....£5	.....£5	[£20]				£90	£20
				[stk b'd]					Tlk/India
									£16
£103	£599	£155	£105	£121	£150+?	£6.49		£238	£124
NEW 2	NEW 2	Adph 1	H'way 1	FNWtg 1	PartR 3	PartR 4	PartR 1		
NWtg 1	C'try 1	NLdr 1	NWtg 1	+ Rpt	(@£2.50)	Trb 2	Trb 3		
Ftny 1			LftF 1	T&T 2	LftNs 3	Hor 1	Obs 1	LISTED IN	
				Hor 2	DExpr 1	Obs 3	NRoad 1	PAYMENTS BOOK	
				Trb 1	Hor 2	FabS 1		(totals below)	
				NS&N 1	E.Std 1				
					PixPt 1				
					NRep 1				
					NDir 1				
Adph 2		Adph 1	Adph 5	Adph 3	Adph 1				
NEW 9	NEW 2	NEW 7	NEW 3	NEW 2					
T&T 7	T&T 7	T&T 2	T&T 3	T&T 10	T&T 1		T&T 1		
List 2		List 2	List 1	List 4	List 1	List 1	List 1		
(1–1½gn)		NLdr 1	PceN 1	(1–2½gn)	(1gn)	Obs 3			
	NS&N 1	NS&N 1		NS&N 9	NS&N 6	NS&N 1	NS&N 1		
				Hor 5	Hor 2	Hor 1	Hor 1		
				Trb 10		Trb 1	Trb 2		
				L&L 2					
				LabS 1					
Adph 1p				⎰ ThR 14	ThR 11		+		
			T&T ⎱	FlmR 7	FlmR 20		Payt Bk		
				B'ct 1	B'ct 4		£154.....	£541.....	£782
				BkFwd 2					
£35	£20	£20	£25	£159	£156	£60	£40		
£206	£631	£175+loan+£130		£280	£573	£706	£807	£1179	£1514
(inc exp)									

1939←Eileen employed as Civil Servant→1944

ACKNOWLEDGEMENTS

I am grateful to all those who have facilitated the production of this volume, especially to Bill Hamilton representing the Orwell Estate, Ellie Steel who supervised the production on behalf of Random House and to Palimpsest for so efficiently scanning the original typesetting to produce a computer-editable text for me. When I was putting the *Complete Works* together, my wife, Sheila, proved not only an excellent and patient proofreader but adept at asking me pertinent questions especially about my notes. Alas, her sight is no longer such as to enable her to read proofs. I am therefore particularly grateful to Briony Everroad and Myra Jones for their copy-editing and proofreading. Without their assiduous efforts far too many literals would have shamed this text. Thanks also to Vicki Robinson for the index. And, of course, I continue to be grateful to Ian Angus for his wise advice and practical help in the production of the twenty-volume edition.

Richard Young very generously let me have a copy of Daniel George's BBC talk on Orwell which he had discovered. This shows how Orwell was beginning to be appreciated as a journalist just after the War and I am delighted to include it in this volume.

I am once again grateful to Jacquie Kavanagh. Although she has now retired from presiding over the BBC Written Archives at Caversham Park she went out of her way once again to facilitate the reproduction of Daniel George's talk. I am also grateful to Jessica Hogg who checked the Archive to confirm that its text was the same as that reproduced in this volume. I am grateful to the BBC for allowing this talk to be reproduced.

It was originally my intention to include a long section from *England Your England* but eventually I decided it would unbalance the selection. A little later, Mr Billy Hayes, General Secretary of the Communication Workers Union, found a passage from Orwell that I had been unable to pinpoint for him. He discovered the source in Penguin's 'Great Ideas' series devoted to Orwell (2004), a copy of which he was good enough to send me. That prompted me to include from *England Your England* Orwell's 'Proposed War Aims'.

And, as so often, I am immensely grateful to my grandson, Tom, whose skill in computer technology has come to my aid time and again. Without that skill and his seemingly unending patience I should not have been able to edit this volume on a word-processor.

There are two people to whom I owe a debt of gratitude for my starting out on the long trail editing Orwell some thirty-two years ago: Ian Willison and the late, and much missed, Barry Bloomfield. I had contributed the sections on Book Production and Distribution (cols. 33–130) and on Newspapers and Magazines (cols. 1329–1408) under Ian's editorship to *The New Cambridge Bibliography of English Literature*, volume 4, 1900–1950 (1972) and Barry knew me through my editing of the Bibliographical Society's journal, *The Library*, 1971–1982. It was they who, when Tom Rosenthal turned to them for suggestions as to who might prepare corrected editions of Orwell's nine books, put my name forward. I am profoundly grateful to them for the trust they then placed in me and the opportunity this has given me to do something I believe to be very worthwhile.

SELECTIVE CHRONOLOGY

25 June 1903:	Eric Arthur Blair born in Motihari, Bengal, India
1904:	With his mother and sister Marjorie settles in England at Henley-on-Thames
1908–11:	Attends day-school, run by Anglican nuns, Henley-on-Thames
Sept 1911–Dec 1916:	Boarder at St Cyprian's preparatory school, Eastbourne, Sussex
2 October 1914:	First publication: the poem, 'Awake! Young Men of England'
Jan–March 1917 (Lent Term):	Scholar at Wellington College
May 1917–Dec 1921:	King's Scholar, Eton College
Oct 1922–Dec 1927:	Serves in Indian Imperial Police, Burma
Autumn 1927:	First expedition to examine conditions of the poor, East End of London
Spring 1928–1929:	Lives in Paris working at becoming a writer
7 March 1929:	Admitted to Hôpital Cochin, Paris, with pneumonia
1930–31:	Uses his parents' home in Southwold as base for tramping and writing
Apr 1932–Jul 1933:	Teaches at The Hawthornes, a private school for boys aged 10–16
19 Nov 1932:	Suggests several pen-names to his publisher; selects 'George Orwell'
9 Jan 1933:	*Down and Out in Paris and London* published
Autumn 1933:	Teaches at Fray's College, Uxbridge, Middlesex; develops pneumonia
25 Oct 1934:	*Burmese Days* published by Harper & Brothers, New York
Oct 1934–Jan 1936:	Part-time assistant at Booklovers' Corner, Hampstead
11 March 1935:	*A Clergyman's Daughter* published

24 June 1935: Gollancz publishes 'censored' edition of *Burmese Days*

31 Jan–30 Mar 1936: In North of England studying the economically depressed areas

2 April 1936: Moves to The Stores, Wallington, Hertfordshire

20 April 1936: *Keep the Aspidistra Flying* published

9 June 1936: Marries Eileen O'Shaughnessy

Christmas 1936: Leaves to fight for Republicans in Spanish Civil War

8 March 1937: *The Road to Wigan Pier* published

20 May 1937: Wounded in throat by Fascist sniper at Huesca

23 June 1937: Escapes from Spain with Eileen

15 Mar–1 Sept 1938: Patient at Preston Hall Sanatorium, Aylesford, Kent, with tuberculosis

25 April 1938: *Homage to Catalonia* published by Secker & Warburg having been rejected by Victor Gollancz

2 Sept 1938–26 Mar 1939: In French Morocco – mainly at Marrakech

12 June 1939: Gollancz publishes *Coming Up for Air*

28 June 1939: Orwell's father, Richard Blair, dies at Southwold with Orwell at his side

11 March 1940: *Inside the Whale and Other Essays* published by Gollancz

29 March 1940: First contribution to *Tribune* published

May 1940–Nov 1943: Serves as sergeant in the Home Guard

19 Feb 1941: *The Lion and the Unicorn* published by Secker & Warburg

3 Mar 1941: Gollancz publishes *Betrayal of the Left* with two chapters by Orwell

18 Aug–23 Nov 1943: Talks Assistant, later Talks Producer, BBC India section

21 Nov 1941: Writes first of some 220 newsletters for India, Malaysia and Indonesia

19 Mar 1943: Orwell's mother, Ida Blair, dies

18 Nov 1943: *Talking to India,* ed. by Orwell, published by Allen & Unwin

23 Nov 1943: Leaves BBC and joins *Tribune as* Literary Editor

3 Dec 1943: First of his eighty personal columns, *As I Please*, published in *Tribune*

9 Dec 1943: Starts reviewing for *Manchester Evening News*

14 May 1944: Richard Horatio Blair, born; adopted by the Orwells, June 1944

28 June 1944: The Orwells' flat bombed; they move into Inez Holden's flat, near Baker Street, London

Summer 1944: Visits Jura for the first time

Early Oct 1944: Moves to Canonbury Square, Islington, London

15 Feb–24 May 1945: War correspondent in France, Germany and Austria for *The Observer* and *Manchester Evening News*

29 March 1945: Eileen Blair dies whilst under anaesthetic

Aug 1945: Elected Vice-Chairman, Freedom Defence Committee

17 Aug 1945: After many rejections *Animal Farm* published by Secker & Warburg

10–22 Sept 1945: Stays in fisherman's cottage, Jura

14 Feb 1946: *Critical Essays* published by Secker & Warburg

29 Apr 1946: *Critical Essays* (as *Dickens, Dali & Others*) published by Reynal & Hitchcock, New York

3 May 1946: Orwell's sister, Marjorie Dakin, dies

23 May–13 Oct 1946: Rents Barnhill on Jura

July 1946: *James Burnham and the Managerial Revolution* published by the Socialist Book Centre, London

Nov 1946: 'How the Poor Die' published in *Now*

14 Jan 1947: Orwell's adaptation of *Animal Farm* broadcast by BBC Third Programme

4 Apr 1947: Eightieth and final 'As I Please' published

31 May 1947: Sends Warburg version of 'Such, Such Were the Joys'

Aug 1947:	*The English People* published by Collins
Sept 1947:	Gives up lease of The Stores, Wallington
31 Oct 1947:	Very ill and reduced to working in bed
20 Dec 1947–28 Jul 1948:	Patient in Hairmyres Hospital, East Kilbride with tuberculosis of the left lung
28 Jul 1948–Jan 1949:	At Barnhill, Jura
4 Dec 1948:	Completes typing *Nineteen Eighty-Four*; has serious relapse
Dec 1948:	Surrenders lease of Canonbury Square flat
6 Jan–3 Sept 1949:	Patient at Cotswold Sanatorium, Cranham, with tuberculosis
Mar 1949:	Corrects proofs of *Nineteen Eighty-Four*
9 Apr 1949:	Despatches his final review (Winston Churchill's *Their Finest Hour*)
8 Jun 1949:	*Nineteen Eighty-Four* published by Secker & Warburg
13 June 1949:	*Nineteen Eighty-Four* published in New York by Harcourt, Brace
27 Aug 1949:	NBC broadcasts adaptation of *Nineteen Eighty-Four* starring David Niven
3 Sept 1949:	Transferred to University College Hospital, London
13 Oct 1949:	Marries Sonia Brownell
18 Jan 1950:	Signs his will on eve of proposed journey to recuperate in Switzerland
21 Jan 1950:	Dies of pulmonary tuberculosis, aged 46
26 Jan 1950:	Buried, as Eric Arthur Blair, All Saints, Sutton Courtenay, Berks.

A SHORT LIST OF FURTHER READING

All Orwell's writings – and, with their accompanying notes, they run to some 9,000 pages – are to be found in *The Complete Works of George Orwell*, ed. Peter Davison, assisted by Ian Angus and Sheila Davison, 1998; second paperback edition, 2000–2 (Orwell's books take up the first nine volumes and are also published by Penguin with the same pagination); *The Facsimile of the Manuscript of 'Nineteen Eighty-Four'*, published in 1984; and the volume supplementary to *The Complete Works* published in 2006: *The Lost Orwell*, ed. Peter Davison. The texts reproduced in this selection are drawn from the above volumes but I have regularised Orwell's idiosyncratic spellings (marked by ° in those volumes) and Anglicized most American spellings. Often only sections of the *Tribune* 'As I Please' columns and the 'London Letters' to *Partisan Review* have been selected; in the main the ensuing correspondence (often voluminous to *Tribune*) is not reprinted. The complete texts and the correspondence that arose will be found in *Complete Works*. Titles for extracts from 'As I Please' columns and from the 'London Letters' have been provided by the editor unless stated otherwise.

Penguin Books have published four collections of essays which I also edited; these have notes additional to those in *Complete Works* and each volume includes one of Orwell's books. They are:

Orwell in Spain (with *Homage to Catalonia*), 393 pages

Orwell's England (with *The Road to Wigan Pier*), 432 pages with 32 pages of plates

Orwell and the Dispossessed (with *Down and Out in Paris and London*), 424 pages

Orwell and Politics (with *Animal Farm*), 537 pages

Reference might also be made to the companion volumes to this collection, *Orwell: Diaries*, 2009, and *Orwell: A Life in Letters*, 2010.

The Collected Essays, Journalism and Letters of George Orwell, ed. Sonia Orwell and Ian Angus, 4 volumes, 1968, are now out of print. Two volumes of essays drawn from my edition were published by Harcourt Inc. in New York, ed. George Packer, in 2008: *Facing Unpleasant Facts* and *All Art is Propaganda*.

FOOTNOTE REFERENCES

References to the *Complete Works* are by volume number + page(s); e.g. XX, 100–2. References to books listed below are by the author's name + page number. There is a vast number of studies of Orwell and many are out of print and difficult to find locally. I have in the main restricted those listed to books recently published.

BIOGRAPHIES

Gordon Bowker, *George Orwell*, Little Brown, 2000.

Jacintha Buddicom, *Eric & Us* (1974), second edition with an important Postscript by Dione Venables, Finlay Publishing, Chichester, 2006.

Audrey Coppard and Bernard Crick, *Orwell Remembered*, Ariel (BBC), 1984.

Robert Colls, *George Orwell: English Rebel*, OUP, 2013.

Bernard Crick, *George Orwell: A Life*, Secker & Warburg, 1980; Penguin, 1992 (with important new appendix). As *Crick*.

Scott Lucas, *Orwell*, Haus Publishing, 2003.

Jeffrey Meyers, *Orwell: Wintry Conscience of a Generation*, Norton, NY, 2000.

Michael Shelden, *Orwell: The Authorised Biography*, Harper Collins, NY, 1991; William Heinemann, London, 1991.

Hilary Spurling, *The Girl from the Fiction Department: A Portrait of Sonia Orwell*, Hamish Hamilton, 2002.

D.J. Taylor, *Orwell: The Life*, Chatto & Windus, 2003.

John Thompson, *Orwell's London* (with many photographs by Philippa Scoones), Fourth Estate, 1984 (as *Thompson*).

Stephen Wadhams, *Remembering Orwell*, Penguin Canada, 1984.

CRITICAL STUDIES

Philip Bounds, *Orwell & Marxism: The Political and Cultural Thinking of George Orwell*, I.B. Taurus, 2009.

Thomas Cushman and John Rodden, *George Orwell: Into the Twenty-first Century*, Paradigm Publishers, Boulder, Colorado, 2004.

Christopher Hitchens, *Orwell's Victory*, Allen Lane (as *Why Orwell Matters* in USA), 2002.

Douglas Kerr, *George Orwell*, Northcote House: Writers and their Work, 2003.

Emma Larkin, *Secret Histories: Finding George Orwell in a Burmese Teashop*, John Murray, 2004.

Daniel J. Leab, *Orwell Subverted: The CIA and the Filming of 'Animal Farm'*, Pennsylvania State University Press, 2007.

The Cambridge Companion to George Orwell, ed. John Rodden, CUP, 2007.

John Rodden, *Every Intellectual's Big Brother: George Orwell's Literary Siblings*, University of Texas, Austin, 2006.

John Rodden, *The Politics of Literary Reputation: The Making and Claiming of 'St. George' Orwell*, OUP, 1989.

Loraine Saunders, *The Unsung Artistry of George Orwell: The Novels from 'Burmese Days' to 'Nineteen Eighty-Four'*, Ashgate, Aldershot and Burlington VT, 2008.

Hugh Thomas, *The Spanish Civil War*, 1961; third Penguin edn., 1997.

WEBSITES

Orwell Society: www.orwellsociety.com – site of the Orwell Society which issues a Newsletter. The site has an index of articles it has published and events.

Orwell Prize website: www.theorwellprize.co.uk

INDEX

All works are by Orwell unless otherwise stated.

'Censure en Angleterre, La' 1

Chamberlain, Neville 66, 97, 123, 125, 135, 137, 158, 328

Chesterton, G. K. 12, 107, 202, 240, 262, 437
  Criticisms and Opinions of the Works of Charles Dickens 31–2

Chevalier, Maurice 343*n*2

Chiaramonte, Nicola 429

Childe, Gordon 6

children
  books read 106–7, 384–5
  in wartime London 291–2

China/Chinese 175, 222, 251

Chitale, Venu 172

Chleuh, the 199

Christianity 38, 96, 142, 150, 184–5, 206, 437
  'Decay in Christian Belief' 265–6
  see also Anglo-Catholic movement; Catholic Church

Christian Peace Movement 161

Christie, Agatha 237, 241

Christmas overindulgence 400–3

Christy & Moore 269, *see also* Moore, Leonard

Churchill, Winston 66, 142*n*, 293, 408
  and Beaverbrook 170–71, 423
  and 'Branch Street' children 292
  closes Crown Film Unit 141*n*3
  and Communist support 155–6
  German attitude to 161, 168
  government 124*n*3, 418*n*3, 422*n*, 423
  and Roosevelt 198*n*, 293
  his shaky position 166–7, 301
  speeches 85*n*1, 167, 169

cigarettes and tobacco 100, 163, 201, 250, 258, 276*n*, 289, 332, 333, 372, 397
  'Books v. Cigarettes' 358–62

class(es) 124–8, 146, 152, 165–6, 243, 302, 303, 374, 343

and anti-American feeling 156–7, 161

and anti-Semitism (Sartre) 440

Matthew Arnold on 118

in Bramah 110–11

and the British army 77–80

in Dickens 31

Eliot on 442–4

in Gissing 224–5

and Government 81, 82, 110, 130–31, 134, 166, 344

and the Home Guard 230

in Jack London 108, 109, 215

and public schools 117, 118–19

in Scotland 411

and the war 8, 128, 129, 130–31, 134, 135, 154, 164–5, 304, 305, 329–30, 336

in Waugh 447–8

in Wodehouse 325–6, 327

see also working classes, the

Clergyman's Daughter, A 36

clothes rationing 263–4

Cockburn, Claud 445

Cole, G. D. H. 241
  The Common People (with Postgate) 102
  The Intelligent Man's Guide to the Post-War World 424

Cole, Hubert 320*n*

Cole, Margaret 241

'colour bars' 289–90

Comfort, Alexander 160 *and n*6, 372*n*3
  The Joy of Sex 160*n*6

Coming Up for Air 4

Commentary see Contemporary Jewish Record

'Common Lodging Houses' 2, 25–8

Communards, the 132

Communism/Communists 43, 57, 234, 423, 433, 449
  in France 14, 200*n*2, 335